Prentice Hall Brief Review

The Living Environment

John Bartsch / Mary P. Colvard

LEARNING COMPANY

About the Authors

John Bartsch and **Mary Colvard** each have taught high school biology for over 30 years. Their many professional activities include working for the New York State Education Department as Education Specialists and serving the Science Teachers Association of New York State (STANYS) as officers, on the Board of Directors, and on various committees. They were also coordinating biology mentors for the Biology and Chemistry Mentor Network.

Mr. Bartsch has written a chemical safety manual, worked on several writing projects for Pearson, attended and worked as a consultant/instructor for the Cornell Institute for Biology Teachers (CIBT) program, and is a long-time member of both the National Association of Biology Teachers (NABT) and the National Science Teachers Association (NSTA).

Ms. Colvard has developed activities for CIBT, the Howard Hughes Medical Institute Holiday Lectures, and the Cold Spring Harbor Dolan DNA Learning Center. She has also served on the Board of Directors for NABT and on several National Research Council Committees.

Teacher Reviewers and Contributors

Anthony (Bud) Bertino
Canandaigua Academy
Canandaigua, New York

Patricia L. Nolan
Scotia-Glenville High School
Scotia, New York

Elise Russo, Ed.D.
Administrator for Secondary Curriculum
Amityville Union Free School District
Amityville, New York

Content Reviewer

Jerry Sanders

ISBN-13: 978-1-4188-3596-5
ISBN-10:   1-4188-3596-X

3   22

Brief Review in
The Living Environment

New York Standards

Standard Key Idea

4.2.1

Performance Indicator

4.1 Intro	4.1.2d	4.1.2h
4.1.2a	4.1.2e	4.1.2i
4.1.2b	4.1.2f	4.1.2j
4.1.2c	4.1.2g	4.1.3a

4.1.2c	4.5.1f	4.5.2g
4.1.2d	4.5.1g	4.5.2h
4.5 Intro	4.5.2a	4.5.2i
4.5.1a	4.5.2b	4.5.2j
4.5.1b	4.5.2c	4.5.3a
4.5.1c	4.5.2d	4.5.3b
4.5.1d	4.5.2e	
4.5.1e	4.5.2f	

4.2 Intro	4.2.1g	4.2.2c
4.2.1a	4.2.1h	4.2.2d
4.2.1b	4.2.1i	4.2.2e
4.2.1c	4.2.1j	4.3.1c
4.2.1d	4.2.1k	4.3.1d
4.2.1e	4.2.2a	
4.2.1f	4.2.2b	

4.4 Intro	4.4.1e	
4.4.1a	4.4.1f	
4.4.1b	4.4.1g	
4.4.1c	4.4.1h	
4.4.1d		

4.3 Intro	4.3.1f	4.3.1l
4.3.1a	4.3.1g	
4.3.1b	4.3.1h	
4.3.1c	4.3.1i	
4.3.1d	4.3.1j	
4.3.1e	4.3.1k	

4.1 Intro	4.6 Intro	4.6.1g
4.1.1a	4.6.1a	4.6.2a
4.1.1b	4.6.1b	4.6.2b
4.1.1c	4.6.1c	4.6.3a
4.1.1d	4.6.1d	4.6.3b
4.1.1e	4.6.1e	4.6.3c
4.1.1f	4.6.1f	

iii

New York Standards

4.7 Intro	4.7.2b
4.7.1a	4.7.2c
4.7.1b	4.7.3a
4.7.1c	4.7.3b
4.7.2a	

1.1.1a	1.2.1	1.3.2
1.1.1b	1.2.2a	1.3.3
1.1.1c	1.2.3a	1.3.4a
1.1.2a	1.2.3b	1.3.4b
1.1.2b	1.2.3c	1.3.4c
1.1.3a	1.2.4	1.3.5a
1.1.3b	1.3.1a	1.3.5b
1.1.4a		

Appendix A: Bullets 5, 9–17

Appendix A: Bullets 1–8

Separate Teacher Answer Key Contents:

Teacher Strategies/Explanations of Topic Openers

Diagnostic Tests with Answers

Topic Quizzes with Answers

Answers to Review Questions

Answers to Regents Exam Practice Questions

About This Book

This book is designed to enhance review of the concepts, skills, and applications of The Living Environment Core Curriculum that may be tested on the Living Environment Regents Examination. For nearly all students, passing this examination will be a requirement for graduation from high school.

Features

Content Review

The Regents Examination will be based entirely on the content and understandings specifically addressed by The Living Environment Core Curriculum. **For the most part, any material *not* addressed in the core curriculum is not included in this book.**

Vocabulary Many exam questions require an understanding of the language of biology.

Bold Words Bold-type terms listed at the beginning of a topic are defined within. These terms are likely to appear on the exam.

Underlined Words Underlined terms are either words that appear as bold in other topics or that describe basic biological concepts, or are words commonly used in discussions of science concepts.

Real-world Examples Many real-world examples are included to reinforce content understandings. Use these examples or others of your choosing to answer questions on the exam. The examples you choose demonstrate your understanding of the content as well as your ability to apply these understandings to the real world.

Sidebars

Memory Jogger Recalls relevant information covered elsewhere in this book or previous science courses.

Digging Deeper Goes beyond what you need to know to help you better understand the required material.

Review Questions Questions similar to those on the exam, totaling more than 400, appear throughout each topic to clarify and reinforce understanding.

Practice Questions for the New York Regents Exam

A total of more than 300 practice questions are written and organized for each topic in the format of the exam.

Part A Multiple-choice questions test knowledge of concepts.

Part B Both multiple-choice and constructed-response questions test understandings and skills.

Part C These questions often require extended constructed responses with more detailed answers supported by applications or examples. Each question is worth one point as indicated by the [1] at the end of each item or bullet.

Reference and Support

Strategies for Answering Test Questions Support to help you interpret and answer the range of exam questions.

Appendix *NY State Required Laboratory Activities* Information regarding the skills, content, and types of questions you can expect to find on Part D of the Regents Examination.

Glossary Defines all bold vocabulary words and underlined words appearing in the topics.

Index Cross-references concepts in the topics.

Regents Examinations

The most recent released Regents Examinations are reproduced at the end of this book to provide practice in taking actual Regents Examinations.

Answer Key with Diagnostic Tests A separate Answer Key includes all answers to the Review and Practice Questions plus topic-by-topic Diagnostic Tests to help determine which concepts require more intense review and Topic Quizzes for quick assessment with different questions.

Strategies for Answering Test Questions

This section provides strategies to help you answer various types of questions on The Living Environment Regents Examination. Strategies are provided for answering multiple-choice and constructed-response questions as well as for questions based on diagrams, data tables, and graphs. For each type of question, practice questions are provided to show you how to apply the strategies to answer specific questions.

Strategies for Multiple-Choice Questions

Multiple-choice questions account for more than 50 percent of The Living Environment Regents Examination. Part A is totally made up of multiple-choice questions, and Parts B and D include some. Therefore, it is important to be good at deciphering multiple-choice questions. Here are a few helpful strategies. For any one question, not all strategies will need to be used. The numbers are provided for reference, not to specify an order (except for Strategies 1 and 2).

1. Always read the entire question, but wait to read the choices. (See Strategy 4.)

2. Carefully examine any data tables, diagrams, or photographs associated with the question.

3. Underline key words and phrases in the question that signal what you should be looking for in the answer. This will make you read the question more carefully. This strategy applies mostly to questions with a long introduction.

4. Try to think of an answer to the question before looking at the choices given. If you think you know the answer, write it on a separate piece of paper before reading the choices. Next, read all of the choices and compare them to your answer before making a decision. Do not select the first answer that seems correct. If your answer matches one of the choices, and you are quite sure of your response, you are probably correct. Even if your answer matches one of the choices, carefully consider all of the answers, because the

obvious choice is not always the correct one. If there are no exact matches, re-read the question and look for the choice that is most similar to your answer.

5. Eliminate any choices that you know are incorrect. Lightly cross out the numbers for those choices on the exam paper. Each choice you can eliminate increases your chances of selecting the correct answer.

6. If the question makes no sense after reading through it several times, leave it for later. After completing the rest of the exam, return to the question. Something you read on the other parts of the exam may give you some ideas about how to answer this question. If you are still unsure, go with your best guess. There is no penalty for guessing, but answers left blank will be counted as wrong. If you employ your best test-taking strategies, you just may select the correct answer.

Practice Questions

1. Most of the oxygen that enters the atmosphere results from the process of
   (1) respiration   (3) excretion
   (2) photosynthesis   (4) digestion

Explanation of Answer Use strategy 5. Eliminating choices 3 and 4 may be easy, but think about the other two choices carefully before choosing your final answer. Be sure that you are not confusing respiration with photosynthesis. The correct answer is choice (2), photosynthesis.

2. Cellular respiration in humans occurs in
   (1) red blood cells, only
   (2) the cells of the lungs, only
   (3) the cells of the digestive system, only
   (4) all the cells of the body

Explanation of Answer Use strategy 4. Note that the question is asking where cell respiration occurs in humans. Your answer before reading the choices should say that respiration occurs in all of the cells of the body or that respiration occurs in the mitochondria. All of the choices are different types of cells. Think about what cell respiration is, and why cells respire. Lung cells and red blood cells help obtain and carry oxygen, but cell respiration is a process that releases energy in *all* cells. Therefore, the correct answer is choice (4), all the cells of the body.

---

3. A number of white potato plants are grown by placing pieces of one potato in the ground. This method of reproduction is most similar to

   (1) sexual reproduction
   (2) cloning
   (3) genetic engineering
   (4) zygote formation

Explanation of Answer Use strategy 5. You should be able to eliminate choices 1 and 4, since both are related to the same form of reproduction. The fusion of sex cells (during sexual reproduction) results in the formation of a zygote. Since there can be only one correct answer, these will not work. Genetic engineering refers to the manipulation of genes leading to the development of new combinations of traits and new varieties of organisms. Since only one parent (potato) is involved, the genetic makeup of the new potato plants will be the same as the original plant. Therefore, cutting up a potato and planting the pieces is most like choice (2), cloning. This is a form of asexual reproduction in which all offspring are genetic copies.

---

4. Overexposure of animals to X-rays is dangerous, because X-rays are known to damage DNA. A direct result of this damage is cells with

   (1) unusually thick cell membranes
   (2) no organelles located in the cytoplasm
   (3) abnormally large chloroplasts
   (4) changes in chromosome structure

Explanation of Answer Use strategy 3. As you read this question, underline key words: Overexposure of <u>animals</u> to <u>X-rays</u> is dangerous, because X-rays are known to <u>damage</u> <u>DNA</u>. A <u>direct</u> <u>result</u> of this damage is cells with (4) changes in chromosome structure. You should know that chromosomes are composed of DNA molecules and that X-rays can cause mutations, which are changes in DNA and/or chromosome

structure. Choices 1, 2, and 3 can be eliminated, since even if they could occur, it would not be a *direct* *result* of the <u>DNA</u> being <u>damaged</u>.

Strategies for Constructed–Response Questions

Some questions in Parts B and D, and all questions in Part C of The Living Environment Regents Examination require a constructed response. Some of these questions require you to write one or two words, while others require much more. Students who use complete sentences when appropriate tend to have more organized answers. As a result, they usually get higher scores. Remember, someone other than your teacher will be reading your answers and scoring your paper. Make your answers clear!

No matter which type of answer is requested, the following strategies will help you write constructed responses.

1. Always read through the entire question.

2. Underline key words and phrases in the question that signal what you should be looking for in the answer. This will make you read the question more carefully.

3. Write a few notes to yourself, about what should be included in the answer.

4. Pay attention to key words that indicate how to answer the question and what you need to say in your answer. Several of these words are very common. For example, you might be asked to identify, describe, explain, state, compare, contrast, or design. The table on the next page lists key words and directions for your answers.

5. When you write your answer, don't be so general that you are not really saying anything. Be very specific. You should use the correct terms and clearly explain the processes and relationships. Be sure to provide details, such as the names of processes, names of structures, and, if it is appropriate, how they are related. If only one example or term is required, do not give two or more. If one is correct and the other is wrong, your answer will be marked wrong.

Using Key Words to Direct Your Answers	
Key Word	What Direction Your Answers Should Take
Analyze	• Break the idea, concept, or situation into parts, and explain how they relate. • Carefully explain relationships, such as cause and effect.
Compare	• Relate two or more topics with an emphasis on how they are alike. • State the similarities between two or more examples.
Contrast	• Relate two or more topics with an emphasis on how they are different. • State the differences between two or more examples.
Define	• State the exact meaning of a topic or word. • Explain what something is or what it means.
Describe	• Illustrate the subject using words. • Provide a thorough account of the topic. • Give complete answers.
Discuss	• Make observations about the topic or situation using facts. • Thoroughly write about various aspects of the topic or situation.
Design	• Plan an experiment or component of an experiment. Map out your proposal, being sure to provide information about all of the required parts.
Explain	• Clarify the topic of the question by spelling it out completely. • Make the topic understandable. • Provide reasons for the outcome.
State	• Express in words. • Explain or describe using at least one fact, term, or relationship.

6. If a question has two or three parts, answer each part in a separate paragraph or bullet. This will help the person scoring your paper find all of the information. Don't risk losing credit for one part of the question by spending too much time on another part. Check to be sure you have an answer for *each* of the questions!

7. Whenever it is appropriate, answer in complete sentences. A sentence should always have a subject and a verb, and not start with the word *because*. Note that you will not lose points for incorrect grammar, spelling, punctuation, or poor penmanship. However, such errors and poor penmanship could impair your ability to make your answer clear to the person scoring your paper. If that person cannot understand what you are trying to say, you will not receive credit for the question.

Practice Questions

5. State one safety precaution that a student should use when heating liquid in a test tube. [1]

Sample Answer When heating liquid in a test tube, the student should wear safety goggles.

6. The diagram below shows the setup of an experiment.

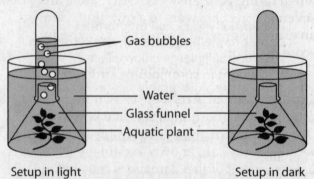

Setup in light　　　　　Setup in dark

State a problem that could be investigated using this experimental setup. [1]

Sample Answer Is light needed for photosynthesis?

Tip Note that "State a problem" here really means to state a question. You are not expected to describe a problem (fault) with this setup.

7. The diagram below shows two ways in which grains, such as wheat or corn, can provide food for humans.

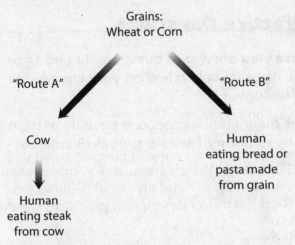

Grains:
Wheat or Corn

"Route A"

"Route B"

Cow

Human eating steak from cow

Human eating bread or pasta made from grain

Select which "Route," A or B, involves the least energy loss and explain why this is true. [1]

Hint You should have underlined the words "Select which Route" and "explain why", to be clear on what your answer must include. If you do not identify the route, you could lose credit for the question, even though you correctly explained why.

Scoring Guide Teachers are provided with Scoring Guides and Sample Answers to use when rating your answers. Often there are several correct answers to a question. Here is an example of what teachers would use to score question 7:
[1] Allow 1 credit for Route B and explaining why this is true. Acceptable responses include, but are not limited to:
- Route B involves the least energy loss because some energy is lost at each step on a food chain.
- Route B because the energy goes directly from the corn to the human, so less is lost. That is not the case with Route A.

8. Provide two reasons why it is important to preserve biodiversity. [1]

Scoring Guide and Sample Answers Allow 1 credit for *two* correct reasons. Acceptable responses include, but are not limited to:
- Biodiversity ensures the availability of a variety of genetic material.
- Biodiversity may allow us to find plants or animals that could be used as new medicines.
- Biodiversity helps an ecosystem remain stable.
- A lot of tropical plants may contain chemicals people can use to cure cancer or HIV.
- Loss of species from an ecosystem could disrupt the food web.

Hint Very few questions will ask for a two part answer like this one, but if you get one, be sure to give two reasons, or you will not receive credit.

Base your answers to questions 9 through 12 on the information and paragraph below and on your knowledge of biology.

It is possible to collect human sperm and to use this sperm later to fertilize eggs in a process called *artificial insemination*. The collected sperm samples are frozen and stored in a sperm bank until needed. When a woman makes use of a sperm bank, she requests sperm from a donor with the physical features she wants for her baby. The name of the donor is not revealed. The artificial insemination process involves placing the sperm in the woman's body and allowing fertilization to occur in the normal manner.

9. A woman whose husband cannot produce sperm becomes pregnant through artificial insemination. Explain how the baby's DNA will compare to the DNA of the woman and her husband. [1]

10. If a woman were given sperm from the same donor for three different pregnancies, and she had three daughters, would the three girls look alike, or would they be different? Support your answer. [1]

11. A developing embryo must be protected from harmful environmental factors. Identify one way a pregnant woman could avoid exposing the developing embryo to environmental risks. [1]

12. Artificial insemination is also used on animals. State one benefit farmers or animal breeders gain from using artificial insemination. [1]

Scoring Guide For questions 9 through 12:

9. Allow one credit. Acceptable responses include, but are not limited to:

   - The baby received DNA from the mother, but none from the mother's husband.

   - The baby's DNA sequence would have much (one half) in common with the mother's DNA sequence, but it would have no specific resemblance to the DNA of the woman's husband.

10. Allow 1 credit for stating that the girls would not look alike and explaining why they would not look alike. Acceptable responses include, but are not limited to:

   - The girls would look different from each other, since they came from different eggs and sperm, each containing unique DNA information.

11. Allow 1 credit. Acceptable responses include, but are not limited to:

   - Do not drink alcohol/do drugs.

   - Do not smoke.

   - Do not eat an unhealthy diet.

12. Allow one credit. Acceptable responses include, but are not limited to:

   - They could breed animals that live far apart without transporting them to the same location.

   - It would be cheaper than buying an animal to breed with other animals on the farm.

   - One animal could produce hundreds of offspring with desired traits in many different locations in a short period of time.

Strategies for Questions Based on Diagrams

Both multiple-choice and constructed-response questions frequently include diagrams or pictures. Usually the diagrams provide information needed to answer the question. The diagrams may be realistic, or they may be a representation of how parts interact or show a sequence of events that occurs in a system.

Practice Questions

Base your answer to questions 13 and 14 on the diagram below and on your knowledge of biology.

The diagram illustrates one possible pattern in the evolution of several groups of animals.

- **First, study the diagram.** Ask yourself what the diagram is about and what it shows you. Read the title or description provided, if there is one.

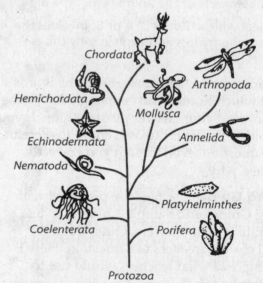

You are told that the diagram represents a possible sequence of events in the evolution of a number of organisms. Based on the illustration, you see that *Protozoa* are the common ancestor of all the other animals shown. It also indicates that *Porifera, Platyhelminthes, Nematoda,* and *Coelenterata* existed before *Echinodermata, Hemichordata, Chordata, Arthropoda, Annelida,* and *Mollusca*. The diagram also shows that *Platyhelminthes* and *Nematoda* are very closely related, as are *Arthropoda, Annelida,* and *Mollusca*.

You need to know that the closer the point of branching, the more closely related the organisms. The farther apart the point of branching, the more distant the relationship.

- **Second, read the question.**

13. Which inference does the diagram best support?

(For this type of question, it is difficult to try to anticipate what the correct answer might be. Carefully read each of the choices, one at a time, and see if they make sense by looking back at the diagram. As you do this, eliminate any choices you can.)

(1) Members of the animal kingdom are more complex than members of the plant kingdom.
(2) Members of the animal kingdom and members of the plant kingdom share common ancestry.
(3) Chordates are more closely related to arthropods than to echinoderms.
(4) Members of the group *Echinodermata* and the group *Annelida* share a common ancestor.

Explanation of Answer There is no information provided about plants by the diagram; you can eliminate choices 1 and 2 based on what you see here or even on what you have learned during the year.

According to the diagram, chordates are more closely related to *Echinodermata* than they are to *Arthropoda*—the opposite of what choice (3) states—because *Echinodermata* branches off the same line that chordates are on. Arthropod ancestors branched before that.

The correct answer is (4), Members of the group *Echinodermata* and the group *Annelida* share a common ancestor. All of the animals on this evolutionary diagram share a common ancestor—*Protozoa*.

14. Which two groups of organisms in the diagram are shown to be the most closely related?

(Before reading the choices provided, think about how you could tell which organisms are most closely related (by two organisms being close together on one branch). Then apply this to eliminate obviously wrong choices. Do not select the first answer that seems correct.)

(1) Porifera and Echinodermata
(2) Chordata and Platyhelminthes
(3) Mollusca and Annelida
(4) Arthropoda and Coelenterata

Explanation of Answer Choices 1, 2, and 4 have separate branches and are widely separated. Therefore, these choices can be eliminated. *Mollusca* and *Annelida* are the only two groups that share a common side branch on the diagram. Therefore, the correct answer is (3), *Mollusca* and *Annelida*.

- **First, study the diagram for Question 15.**
  This illustration shows a rabbit and a plant giving off CO_2 and taking in O_2 from the environment. This analysis of the illustration indicates that materials are being cycled through the environment.

- **Second, read the question.**

15. Which ecological principle is best illustrated by the following diagram?

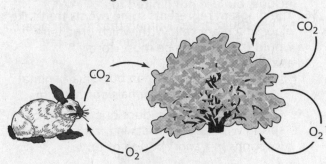

(Before reading the choices provided, think about the diagram and what the question is asking. It seems that the ecological principle illustrated here has something to do with cycles in the environment. As you read the choices, eliminate any choices that you can.)

(1) In an ecosystem, material is cycled among the organisms and their environment
(2) In ecosystems the number of producers and consumers is always equal.
(3) Competition within a species results in natural selection.
(4) An ecosystem requires a constant source of energy.

Explanation of Answer Ecosystems normally contain more producers than consumers but this varies. The number of each is not "always" equal so choice 2 is incorrect. Choices 3 and 4 are not addressed by the illustration. It does not show competition within the rabbit species. There is no energy source shown in the diagram, nor is the ecosystem requirement for a constant energy source illustrated. Therefore, you would probably select the correct answer as being choice (1), In an ecosystem, material is cycled among the organisms and their environment.

- **First, study the diagram for Question 16.** Ask yourself what the diagram is about and what it shows you. It shows CO_2 and H_2O entering, and sugar and O_2 leaving. The illustration seems to have something to do with photosynthesis, since CO_2 and H_2O are raw materials and sugar and O_2 are products.
- **Second, read the question.**

16. The diagram represents some events that take place in a plant cell. With which organelle would these events be most closely associated?

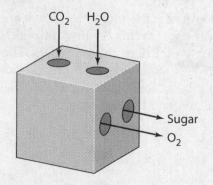

(Before reading the choices provided, write what you think the answer should be on a separate piece of paper. Then compare your answer to the choices provided.)

(1) mitochondrion   (3) ribosome
(2) chloroplast   (4) vacuole

Explanation of Answer Mitochondria are associated with cellular respiration, ribosomes with protein synthesis, and vacuoles with storage. Since this diagram illustrates photosynthesis, which occurs in chloroplasts in plant cells, the correct answer is choice (2).

Note: If you realized that the process was either photosynthesis or respiration but weren't sure which one, you at least could narrow your choices to 1 and 2 and improve your chances of guessing the right one.

Base your answers to questions 17 and 18 on the information below, and on your knowledge of biology.

The map was drawn by an ecologist. It represents the vegetation around a small pond in a forest located in New York State.

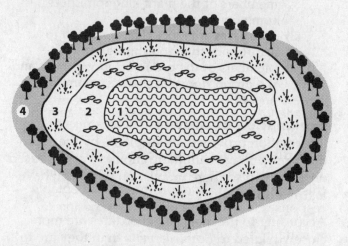

KEY
Open water   Forest
Shallow water containing pond plants   Wet area with grass and cattails

- **First, study the diagram.** Think about what the diagram shows you. Did you read the information at the top of the illustration?

If you were approaching the pond from the forest, you would walk through trees, then wet areas with tall plants, such as cattails and grasses. The ground would be wet and squishy. Next, you would enter shallow water in which many rooted plants grow. From this point, open water would be visible. The water would be much deeper, and you would probably not be able to walk but would need to swim or use a boat. There are many different questions you could be asked about this diagram.

- **Second, read the questions.**

17. Describe one specific way this environment would be likely to change if it were left undisturbed by humans for 100 years. [1]

Sample Answers The pond environment will probably fill in, leaving mostly forest.

OR

The species present in the nonforest communities will disappear, and forest plants and animals will replace them.

Explanation of Answers Both answers relate to the idea of ecological succession. All ecosystems progress through a series of changes during which one community modifies the environment, making it more suitable for another community. The organic matter from decaying vegetation will gradually fill the pond.

---

18. Identify two organisms in this ecosystem that are producers. [1]

Sample Answers and Scoring Guide Allow 1 credit for correctly identifying *two* organisms in this ecosystem that are producers. Acceptable responses include, but are not limited to:

- cattails and grass
- trees and pond plants

Explanation of Answer Producers are organisms that are capable of taking inorganic raw materials from the environment and synthesizing their own food. Plants are producers. *Be sure you only identify plants from this ecosystem, not just any producer organism.*

Strategies for Questions Based on Data Tables

Most data tables contain information that summarizes a topic. A table uses rows and columns to condense information and to present it in an organized way. Rows are the horizontal divisions going from left to right across the table, while columns are vertical divisions going from top to bottom. Column headings name the type of information included in a table. Sometimes different categories of information are listed down the left-hand column of the table.

Examine the sample data table below. It provides information collected during an old study of the death rates of policy holders of a large life insurance company.

Before attempting to answer any questions based on the data, go through the following steps:

Deaths as a Result of Disease		
Cause of Death	Deaths per 100,000 People	
	1911	1957
Tuberculosis	224.6	6.7
Communicable disease	58.9	0.1
Cancer	69.3	136.2
Heart disease	156.4	256.2

1. Find the title of the table. It is usually located across the top. What is the title of the sample table? (Answer: Deaths as a Result of Disease)

2. Determine the number of columns in the table and their purpose. Do this for the sample table. (Answer: There are three columns. They show the causes of death and deaths per 100,000 people during the years of 1911 and 1957.)

3. Determine the number of rows and their purpose. Do this for the sample table. (Answer: There are four rows. The rows provide you with the number of deaths due to tuberculosis, communicable diseases, cancer, and heart disease.)

4. Read across the rows and down the columns to determine what the relationships are. Do this for the table shown. Notice how the numbers of deaths changed for each disease between 1911 and 1957. Some decreased and some increased.

Now you are ready to read the question with the sample data table and answer it.

19. The study most clearly indicated that during the time period examined

(1) cancer of the lungs was increasing
(2) people were living longer
(3) children were safer from communicable diseases
(4) better housing reduced deaths from tuberculosis

Explanation of Answer Choice 1 doesn't work because even though cancer death rates increased from 69.3 to 136.2 per 100,000, there is no way to tell what type or types of cancer caused the difference. Choice 2 is not correct because you have no information about how long people were living in either 1911 or 1957. Choice 4 is not correct because no information is provided about what caused the decrease in deaths due to tuberculosis. You only know that the death rate decreased from 224.6 in 1911 to 6.7 per 100,000 in 1957. The correct answer is choice (3), children were safer from communicable diseases. The number of those deaths decreased from 58.9 per 100,000 in 1911 to 0.1 per 100,000 in 1957.

Practice Questions

Base your answers to questions 20 and 21 on the information below and on your knowledge of biology.

A dog was placed in a special room free of unrelated stimuli. On repeated trials, a tone was sounded for 5 seconds; approximately 2 seconds later, the dog was given food. Trials 1, 10, 20, 30, 40, and 50 were test trials; that is, the tone was sounded for 30 seconds and no food was given. The following data were collected:

Data Table		
Test Trial Number	Drops of Saliva Secreted	Number of Seconds Between Onset of the Tone and Salivation
1	0	—
10	6	18
20	20	9
30	60	2
40	62	1
50	59	2

20. The greatest increase in the number of drops of saliva secreted occurred between test trials

(1) 1 and 10   (3) 20 and 30
(2) 10 and 20   (4) 30 and 40

Explanation of Answer The increase for choice 1 amounted to 6 drops, since it increased from 0 drops to 6 drops between Test Trial Numbers 1 to 10. Choice 2 resulted in an increase of 14 drops, since Test Trial Number 10 resulted in 6 drops, while Test Trial Number 20 resulted in 20 drops. The difference is 14 drops. Choice (4) only resulted in an increase of 2 drops. The correct answer is choice (3), 20 to 30. The number of drops of saliva secreted increased from 20 in Test Trial 20 to 60 in Test Trial 30, for an increase of 40 drops of saliva.

21. At test trial 60, the number of drops of saliva secreted would probably be closest to

(1) 75   (2) 55   (3) 35   (4) 25

Explanation of Answer Choice 1 is wrong, since it shows a large increase. Choices 3 and 4 are incorrect, because the decrease in number of drops is very large. These numbers do not fit the trend shown in the data table. The correct answer is choice 2, because the number of drops of saliva secreted between trials 30 and 50 has been changing slowly and at trial 50 has started to go down.

Strategies for Questions Based on Graphs

Graphs represent relationships in a visual form that is easy to read. Three different types of graphs commonly used on science Regents examinations are line graphs, bar graphs, and circle graphs. Line graphs are the most common, and they show the relationship between two changing quantities, or variables. When a question is based on any of the three types of graphs, the information you need to correctly answer the question can usually be found on the graph.

When answering a question that includes a graph, first ask yourself these questions:

- What information does the graph provide?
- What are the variables?
- What seems to happen to one variable as the other changes?

After a careful analysis of the graph, use these strategies along with the other strategies you have learned:

- Read the question.
- Read each of the possible answers and consider which is the correct choice by referring to the graph.

Practice Questions

Use the graph below to answer questions 22 and 23.

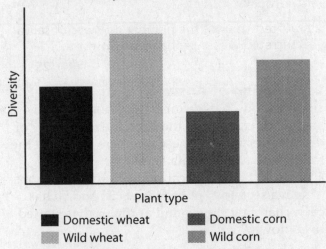

Genetic Diversity in Corn and Wheat Varieties

22. Which types of plants represented on the graph have the greatest diversity?

   (1) wild wheat and wild corn
   (2) wild wheat and domestic corn
   (3) domestic wheat and wild corn
   (4) domestic wheat and domestic corn

Explanation of Answer Choices 2, 3, and 4 do not work, because they each contain one or more of the domestic plant types that do not extend as high on the diversity scale. The correct choice is (1), wild wheat and wild corn. The bars for wild wheat and corn extend higher on the diversity scale than the others.

23. If the environment were to change dramatically or a new plant disease affecting both corn and wheat were to strike, which of the plant types would be most likely to survive?

   (1) wild wheat   (3) wild corn
   (2) domestic wheat   (4) domestic corn

Explanation of Answer To be able to answer this question correctly, you need to know two things. First, biodiversity increases the stability of an ecosystem. Second, the diversity of species increases the chance that some will survive in the face of environmental changes. Therefore, the bar representing the plant with the greatest diversity would be the best choice for an answer. For that reason, the correct answer is choice (1), wild wheat.

24. Which statement best describes the relationship between enzyme action and temperature shown in the graph below?

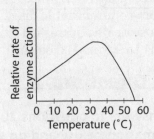

(Remember to first study the graph in order to determine what it is about and what information it gives you about the variables. Then read the question and analyze the choices by referring to the graph.)

   (1) Enzyme synthesis begins at 30°C.
   (2) Enzyme activity constantly increases with increasing temperature.
   (3) The pH has a greater effect on this enzyme than temperature does.
   (4) Enzyme activity increases as the temperature increases from 22°C to 34°C.

Explanation of Answer Choice 1 is not correct since the graph tells you nothing about enzyme synthesis. The graph starts to show data at 30°C, but shows nothing about synthesis. Choice 2 is wrong, because enzyme activity does not continue to increase. It starts to decrease rapidly at about 37°C. Choice 3 is incorrect, since there is no mention of pH anywhere on the graph. The correct answer is choice 4. If you follow the graph line, it does show an increase in relative rate of enzyme activity as the temperature increases from 22°C to 34°C.

Similarities and Differences Among Living Organisms

Body Systems at Work

What do YOU Think?

Blood vessels in organs of the digestive system pick up nutrients such as glucose, starch, and protein and transport them to cells.

Blood vessels in the respiratory system pick up oxygen and drop off carbon dioxide and water.

Blood vessels in organs of the excretory system drop off wastes from cells and food that was not digested.

Similarities and Differences Among Living Organisms

Vocabulary

active transport	excretion	organelle
amino acids	homeostasis	organic
cell	hormone	receptor molecule
cell membrane	immunity	reproduction
cell respiration	inorganic	respiration
chloroplast	metabolism	ribosome
circulation	mitochondria	simple sugars
cytoplasm	nucleus	synthesis
diffusion	organ	tissue
digestion	organ system	vacuole
enzymes		

Topic Overview

Earth's living environment is made up of millions of diverse organisms, from towering redwood trees, sleek antelope, and mushrooms that grow in huge circles, to microscopic bacteria, one-celled organisms that turn the tides red, and the students in your class.

These living organisms are both similar to and different from each other. They also differ from the nonliving parts of the environment. Although that difference may seem obvious, scientists have not been able to agree upon a simple definition of life.

The Characteristics of Life

Although there is no simple definition of life, most scientists agree that living things share certain characteristics that distinguish them from nonliving things.

- Living things are organized structures. All are made of one or more **cells,** which are the basic units of structure and function. They maintain their cellular organization throughout life.

- Living things use energy to maintain life and to grow and develop. These activities require that the cells carry out various chemical reactions. The combination of all the chemical reactions that occur in an organism is called **metabolism.**

- Living things maintain a fairly stable internal environment even when their external environment changes dramatically. The maintenance of this internal stability is known as **homeostasis.** To maintain homeostasis, organisms must respond and adapt to both their internal and external environments.

- Living things pass hereditary information to new organisms of the same type in the process of **reproduction.**

Only living things share the characteristics of life. Nonliving things have no functioning cells and no metabolic activity; they do not maintain homeostasis, nor do they reproduce.

Diversity Among Living Things

Although living things share the characteristics of life, there are differences among the many kinds of organisms. Throughout history, people have tried to bring order to all the varieties of life on Earth by grouping, or classifying, them. Several classification systems have been popular at different times. As we learn more about the similarities among organisms and how they carry out their life processes, classification systems change. Currently, biologists classify organisms into kingdoms, which are large groups of related organisms.

Similarities Among Living Things

Although living things have many differences, they are also alike in important ways. The first similarity is that they share the characteristics of life. They are made of cells, reproduce, maintain homeostasis, and carry out metabolic activities. They also share similar life processes, chemical composition, and organization.

Life Processes Living things are similar in that they rely on a variety of specific processes to maintain life. Organisms may differ in the way they carry out these processes, however. Some of these life processes include

- obtaining nutrients from the environment and breaking them down for transport
- transporting materials throughout the organism
- breaking nutrients into smaller units to release the chemical energy stored in them through the process known as **cell respiration**
- combining simple substances into complex substances during the process known as **synthesis**
- increasing the size or number of cells through the process of growth
- removing waste products from the organism through the process known as **excretion**
- responding to internal and external stimuli
- reproducing more of their own species

Chemical Composition All living things are made of four main elements—carbon, hydrogen, oxygen, and nitrogen—as well as many other elements in smaller amounts. The elements combine to form molecules.

Organic molecules contain BOTH carbon and hydrogen. Organic molecules include all of the major molecules of life: structural molecules, such as those in cell walls and membranes, as well as biologically active molecules, such as the enzymes that help carry out the chemical reactions of life. DNA, protein, fats, and carbohydrates—such as glucose ($C_6H_{12}O_6$) and starch—are **organic** molecules.

Digging Deeper

Many scientists do not include viruses with living things. The reason is that viruses are not cells. Instead they are made only of protein and genetic material. As a result, viruses do not independently carry out all processes of life. To reproduce, they must invade the cell of a living organism.

Inorganic molecules do *not* contain *both* carbon and hydrogen, but can contain any other combination of elements. Inorganic molecules include salts and minerals, most acids and bases, oxygen (O_2), carbon dioxide (CO_2), and water (H_2O), the most abundant substance in any organism.

Organization The shared organization of specialized structures that work together to accomplish a specific task is another similarity of living things. In other words, organisms share a similar "building plan." The basic structural and functional unit of living things is the cell.

Simple organisms may consist of just one cell; complex organisms may consist of billions of cells. Most cells contain specialized structures called **organelles,** which have specific life maintenance functions.

This organization of cells into increasingly specialized structures is the basis for much of the complex life on Earth. Complex organisms have several advantages over simpler organisms. For example, many complex organisms can explore their environment or gain energy in ways that simpler organisms cannot. In Figure 1-1, notice that the organizational structure of organisms resembles a pyramid with a base of cells.

In multicellular organisms, groups of specialized cells may be grouped into **tissues** to expand how they function. For example, a single muscle cell would not be strong enough to move any organism—not even one as light as a hummingbird. Grouped with other muscle cells, however, muscle tissue can move an elephant.

Different kinds of tissues may be combined to form an **organ** that performs one of the life processes. Several organs may work together as an **organ system** that also performs one of the life processes. For example, the heart is an organ with the function of pumping blood. The organ may be a simple "arch" like the heart of the earthworm, or it may be a complex four-chambered structure like the heart of a monkey. In either case, the organ's function is to pump blood. Each heart is part of an organ system that transports materials throughout the body.

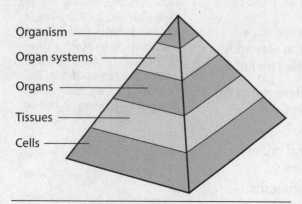

Organism
Organ systems
Organs
Tissues
Cells

Figure 1-1. The structural organization of organisms

Review Questions
Set 1.1

1. State two ways in which a single-celled organism, such as an amoeba, and a human body cell are alike.

2. One characteristic of all living organisms is that they
   (1) make food
   (2) live on land
   (3) maintain homeostasis
   (4) move from place to place

3. Which sequence is listed in order from simplest to most complex?
   (1) tissue → cell → organ system → organ
   (2) cell → tissue → organ → organ system
   (3) cell → tissue → organism → organ
   (4) organism → tissue → organ → organ system

4. A student brings a specimen and claims it is a living organism. Explain how a microscope could be used to determine if the specimen is a living thing.

5. A biologist would most likely study all of the chemical activities of an organism to obtain information about the organism's
   (1) number of mutations
   (2) reproductive cycle
   (3) development
   (4) metabolism

6. Cells are to tissues as organs are to
   (1) organ systems   (3) genes
   (2) cells   (4) organelles

7. The ability of an organism to maintain internal stability is known as
   (1) metabolism   (3) circulation
   (2) homeostasis   (4) excretion

8. State two ways living and nonliving things differ.

9. Which statement about cells is *not* true?
   (1) One or more cells make up all living organisms.
   (2) Cells carry on the basic life functions of living organisms.
   (3) Cells contain structures that carry on life functions.
   (4) Most cells cannot reproduce.

10. Living things are made mostly of these four main elements:
   (1) hydrogen, oxygen, nitrogen, and protein
   (2) water, protein, carbohydrate, and fat
   (3) carbon, hydrogen, oxygen, and nitrogen
   (4) glucose, salt, mineral, and base

Cells: The Basic Structure of Life

Many of the world's organisms are made of only one cell, but all organisms—no matter how simple or complex—are made of cells. Each cell contains a jellylike substance surrounded by a thin membrane. Most cells also contain organelles that perform specific tasks for the cell. Despite their seemingly "simple" structure, cells carry out the processes of life and function together in a coordinated manner.

Inside the Cell

The jellylike substance inside the cell is known as the **cytoplasm.** The cytoplasm contains specialized structures, transports materials through the cell, and is the site of many chemical reactions associated with the cell's metabolism.

Organelles Organelles are formed of many different molecules and vary in size, shape, and function. They interact to transport materials, extract energy from nutrients, build proteins, dispose of waste, and store information. Figure 1-2 shows several vital organelles.

Nucleus The **nucleus** is a large structure that controls the cell's metabolism and stores genetic information (DNA in chromosomes). Many people think of the nucleus as the cell's "control center" because it directs the cell's activities.

Vacuoles The storage sacs within the cytoplasm are **vacuoles.** They may contain either wastes or useful materials such as water or food. Some vacuoles are specialized to digest food; others pump excess water out of the cell. Vacuoles in plant cells are usually a lot larger than the vacuoles in animal cells, as shown in Figure 1-2.

Ribosomes The cell contains many tiny structures, called **ribosomes,** that are important to the process of making protein. Some ribosomes are attached to membranes in the cell. Others float in the cytoplasm.

(A) A typical plant cell

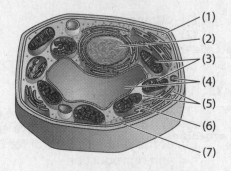

(B) A typical animal cell

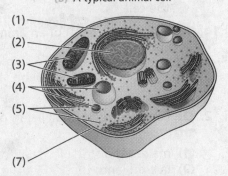

Figure 1-2. Some parts of plant and animal cells: (1) cytoplasm, (2) nucleus, (3) mitochondria, (4) vacuoles, (5) ribosomes, (6) chloroplast, (7) cell membrane.

Mitochondria Mitochondria are pod-shaped structures that contain special proteins, known as **enzymes,** used to extract energy from nutrients. Mitochondria are sometimes called the cell's powerhouses because they release most of the cell's energy.

Chloroplasts The green structures found in plants and some one-celled organisms are **chloroplasts.** They contain the green pigment chlorophyll and capture light energy, which is then used to produce food for the plant. Animal cells do not contain chloroplasts.

Bacteria cells contain no nucleus; their genetic material simply floats in the cytoplasm as a large chromosome. Some bacteria have smaller loops of DNA as well.

Review Questions   Set 1.2

11. Which structure is the boundary between a living cell and its environment?

(1) cell membrane
(2) cytoplasm
(3) vacuole
(4) ribosome

12. The structures labeled A, B, C, and D in the diagram below represent

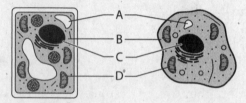

(1) organelles
(2) organs
(3) nuclei
(4) mitochondria

13. The cell nucleus functions

(1) in obtaining energy for the cell
(2) in the storage of digestive enzymes
(3) as the center of control for cell metabolism and reproduction
(4) in the transport of materials throughout the cell

14. The genetic material of an animal cell is found in the

(1) nucleus
(2) cytoplasm
(3) ribosomes
(4) vacuole

15. In the diagram below, structure A is most probably a

(1) mitochondrion   (3) vacuole
(2) ribosome   (4) nucleus

16. Current evidence indicates that ribosomes are most closely associated with

(1) contraction of the cytoplasm
(2) production of DNA
(3) synthesis of protein
(4) regulation of mitosis

17. Mitochondria are organelles that

(1) store digestive enzymes
(2) package cell products
(3) release energy from nutrients
(4) manufacture cell protein

18. Which cell organelles are most closely associated with energy changes in a plant?

(1) mitochondria and chromosomes
(2) chloroplasts and mitochondria
(3) chromosomes and nucleus
(4) chloroplasts and nucleus

19. Which is the most accurate statement concerning protein synthesis in cells?

(1) Proteins are synthesized by mitochondria in all living cells.
(2) Proteins are synthesized at the ribosomes in all living cells.
(3) Proteins are synthesized at the ribosomes in plant cells only.
(4) Proteins are synthesized by nuclei in animal cells only.

The Cell Membrane

The **cell membrane** is a thin structure that surrounds the cell. It is made mainly of fats (lipids), with some proteins embedded throughout. Some of the functions of the cell membrane include

- separating the contents of the cell from the outside environment
- controlling the transport of materials—including waste products—into and out of the cell
- recognizing and responding to chemical signals

Maintaining Separation Cells are organized internally. Without the cell membrane, this organization would be lost.

Unlike animals, plants and most bacteria and fungi have a cell wall outside the cell membrane. This wall of plant cells is made of nonliving material (a carbohydrate called cellulose) that surrounds the cell and gives it strength and rigidity. If the plant gains too much water, its membranes could burst. The cell wall helps prevent this.

Controlling Transport In and Out of the Cell If the cell is to survive, the membrane cannot totally separate the cell from its environment. Some materials, such as water, oxygen, and nutrients, must pass through the membrane and into the cell. Other materials, such as waste products, must pass out of the cell. Molecules can enter or leave a cell through either diffusion or active transport.

Diffusion Molecules are constantly in motion. As they jiggle, they bump into one another, then bounce away like bumper cars at an amusement park. In time, the molecules will have bumped and bounced until they are evenly distributed. The result is that the concentration of molecules in any container remains approximately the same everywhere in the container.

However, when the concentration of molecules is greater in one part of a substance, molecules will spread into areas where their concentration is lower. This movement of molecules from areas of high concentration to areas of low concentration is called **diffusion.** (See Figure 1-4.) Because diffusion results from the normal jiggling of molecules, it requires no outside energy. It is like sledding downhill.

Many molecules diffuse into and out of cells. One of the most important of these molecules is water. The diffusion of water into and out of cells is important to the maintenance of homeostasis. For example, plant cells maintain a stable balance of water and dissolved minerals. This is typically about 98% water and 2% dissolved materials. When salt is spread on roads and walkways, that balance changes. The runoff water from these salted roads may reach concentrations of 5% salt (which means only 95% water). Damage can occur when water in the plant cells diffuses from the higher (98%) concentration in the cell to the lower (95%) concentration outside the cell. Under these conditions, the loss of water places serious stress on the plant. In some cases the plant may die.

Active Transport Moving a molecule from an area of low concentration to an area of high concentration is like pulling a sled uphill. (See Figure 1-5.) It requires energy. Cells must use energy from ATP to transport molecules

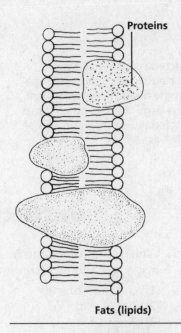

Figure 1-3. **The cell membrane**

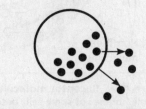

Figure 1-4. Diffusion: These molecules are moving from an area of high concentration to an area of low concentration.

Figure 1-5. Active transport: These molecules are moving from an area of low concentration to an area of high concentration.

from areas of low concentration through the cell membrane to areas of high concentration. The process is called **active transport.**

Many desert plants use active transport to bring water (which is at low concentrations in the soil) into root cells where the water concentration is higher. Some pond organisms use active transport to "collect" calcium or other minerals that are in very low concentrations in the pond water.

Molecules in Cells Both organic and inorganic substances are dissolved in cells and are involved in the chemical reactions that maintain life. Some organic molecules, such as proteins and starches, are too large and complex to enter the cell. Large molecules must first be broken down into simpler molecules in the process known as **digestion.**

The digestion of proteins results in smaller molecules of **amino acids;** the digestion of starches results in **simple sugars.** Digestion is vital because only small molecules, such as amino acids and simple sugars, can enter blood vessels or cells.

When some nutrients from our food enter a cell, they become the building blocks of compounds necessary for life. This process, called cell synthesis, is like manufacturing. Simple molecules (such as amino acids and sugars) are assembled or reassembled into more complex molecules of proteins, starches, DNA, or other substances necessary for life.

Not all nutrients are used as building blocks. Some nutrients that enter a cell are broken down even more to release the energy stored in their chemical bonds. This is the process of cell respiration. All of these processes will be reviewed in detail in later topics.

Recognizing Signals Scientists have learned that certain protein molecules in the cell membrane can receive chemical messages from other cells. These molecules are called **receptor molecules.**

When cells are part of a larger organism, receptor molecules play an important role in the interactions between cells. As shown in Figures 1–6 and 1–7, chemicals produced in the endocrine glands—**hormones**—and chemicals produced by nerve cells are primarily responsible for communication between cells. If nerve or hormone signals are blocked, cellular communication is interrupted, and the organism's homeostasis may be affected.

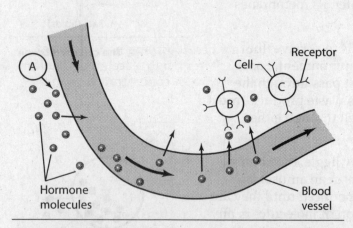

Figure 1-6. **Receptor molecules:** Specific receptor molecules on the membranes of some cells detect hormones that stimulate the cell to respond. In this case, only cell B (not cell C) will respond to the hormone from cell A.

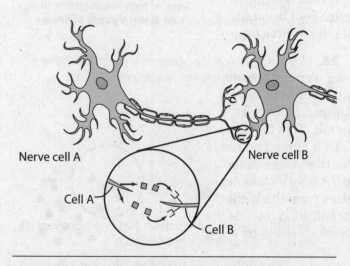

Figure 1-7. **Receptor molecules:** Nerve cells secrete chemicals that signal adjacent nerve, muscle, or gland cells. These secretions are detected by specific receptor molecules on cell membranes.

20. Defective receptor proteins on a cell membrane have the *least* effect on

(1) homeostasis
(2) muscle activity
(3) nerve signals
(4) diffusion

21. In the following diagram, nerve cell A is communicating with nerve cell B. Identify the structures present on the membranes of nerve cell B that enable it to detect a message from nerve cell A.

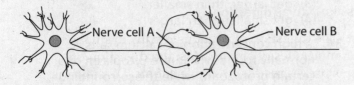

Nerve cell A   Nerve cell B

22. Which process accomplishes the movement of gases illustrated by the arrows in the diagram?

(1) excretion
(2) diffusion
(3) active transport
(4) chemical digestion

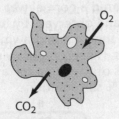

O₂

CO₂

23. In both plant and animal cells, the cell membrane

(1) produces enzymes
(2) controls reproduction
(3) is composed of sugars
(4) regulates diffusion

24. Since the relative concentration of water in the pond in which a paramecium (a single-celled organism) lives is greater than the concentration of water in its cytoplasm, water molecules constantly move from the pond into the paramecium. The best long-term solution to the problem of maintaining a stable internal environment is for the paramecium to

(1) change the water into carbon dioxide and excrete it
(2) store water molecules
(3) incorporate water molecules into its structure
(4) actively transport water molecules out of its cell

25. A biologist diluted a blood sample with distilled water. While observing the sample with a microscope, she noted that the red blood cells had burst. This bursting is most likely the result of which process?

(1) staining
(2) diffusion
(3) digestion
(4) active transport

26. A student using a compound light microscope to study plant cells observed that most of the cells resembled the one shown in the following diagram.

Which diagram best illustrates how the plant cell will appear after being placed in a solution that has a lower water concentration than the cell?

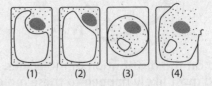

(1)   (2)   (3)   (4)

27. Amino acids tend to diffuse from a blood capillary to the adjacent cell because

(1) this is the only direction they can move
(2) the brain directs the movement into cells
(3) the cell needs the amino acids to make protein
(4) the concentration of amino acids is lower in the cell

28. In the following diagram of a plant cell, the small circles represent water molecules.

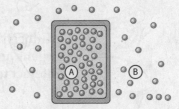

Which statement *best* describes the behavior of most of these water molecules?

(1) They move from region A to region B.
(2) They move from region B to region A.
(3) They do not move in either direction.
(4) Their overall movement is equal in both directions.

29. Nutrients that are not used as building blocks for the cell may be broken down to release the energy stored in their chemical bonds. This process, which provides cells with energy, is called

(1) chemical synthesis   (3) digestion
(2) cell respiration   (4) homeostasis

30. Cytoplasm in a plant cell will shrink if the cell is

(1) placed in a concentrated salt solution
(2) kept warm and moist and in medium light
(3) placed in distilled water
(4) exposed to a different concentration of nitrogen gas

31. The diagram below represents a cell in water. Formulas of molecules that can move freely across the membrane are shown. Some molecules are located inside the cell and others are in the water outside the cell.

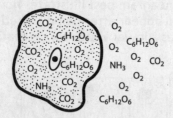

Based on the distribution of molecules, what would most likely happen to these molecules after a few hours?

(1) The concentration of $C_6H_{12}O_6$ will increase inside the cell.
(2) The concentration of CO_2 will increase outside the cell.
(3) The concentration of NH_3 will increase inside the cell.
(4) The concentration of O_2 will increase outside the cell.

32. A cell containing 98% water in its cytoplasm is placed in a 2% salt solution. It should

(1) lose water
(2) gain water
(3) neither lose nor gain water
(4) gain salt because of the high rate of diffusion

33. A cell is placed in distilled water and then transferred to a 5% salt solution. As a result of this procedure, the cell would be likely to

(1) get larger
(2) get smaller
(3) get larger, then smaller
(4) get smaller, then larger

34. A high concentration of calcium salts is normally found within the cytoplasm of a certain protozoan, while the surrounding environment contains a lower concentration of the calcium salts. The higher concentration in the protozoan is most probably the result of

(1) diffusion   (3) active transport
(2) excretion   (4) cellular dehydration

35. A student prepared a normal wet mount slide of an *Elodea* leaf and observed it with a compound microscope. He then made drawing A from his observations. His second drawing, B, shows his observations of the same cell after it was mounted in a 5% salt solution.

A   B

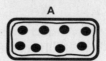 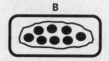

The results are most fully explained by

(1) loss of water from the cell
(2) entrance of water into the cell
(3) shrinkage of the cell wall
(4) entrance of salt into the cell

Multicellular Organisms

Multicellular organisms can be highly complex. They require multiple organs and systems to complete their life processes. These systems must interact to maintain the life of the organism.

Human Body Systems

Humans are complex organisms. Their specialized cells must interact to maintain life. Humans require a variety of organs and organ systems to complete the life processes of digestion, respiration, circulation, excretion, movement, coordination, immunity, and reproduction.

Digestion The human digestive system, shown in Figure 1-8, is a one-way passage through the body. This passageway includes the mouth, stomach, and intestines as well as other organs.

Food enters the body through the mouth and is moved slowly through the system by muscular contractions. The food never actually enters the body tissue. Instead, it is broken down both mechanically (by chewing) and chemically. This produces molecules that are small enough to pass through cell membranes and that can be transported to wherever nutrients can be used by the body. Undigested food is eliminated from the body as solid waste.

Respiration The process of **respiration** uses oxygen to break down food molecules to release energy. The function of the respiratory system is the exchange of gases between the blood of the circulatory system and the environment. The system takes in oxygen for cell respiration and transfers it to the blood. It also removes carbon dioxide—a waste of cell respiration—from the bloodstream and releases it from the body. As shown in Figure 1-9, the lungs and nose are parts of the respiratory system.

Circulation **Circulation** involves the movement of materials inside the cell as well as the movement between parts of a multicellular organism. The function of the human circulatory system, shown in Figure 1-10, is to transport materials throughout the body.

The system carries digested food and oxygen to cells. It also carries wastes from the cells to the lungs, kidneys, and the skin for excretion. The blood vessels of the system also carry chemical messengers (hormones) and the proteins that attack foreign substances to give the body immunity (antibodies). The human circulatory system includes the heart, blood vessels, and blood.

Excretion Many people confuse the process of excretion with the removal of the waste products of digestion. **Excretion,** however, is actually the removal of all the waste produced by the cells of the body. The human excretory system, shown in Figure 1-11, includes the lungs and kidneys as well as the sweat glands in the skin.

Movement Movement of the body involves the interaction of muscles and bones. The <u>muscular</u> and <u>skeletal</u> systems, shown in Figure 1-12, work together to provide movement and support for the body. These body systems make it possible for the organism to avoid danger and to find food, mates, and shelter.

Coordination The nervous system and endocrine system, shown in Figure 1-13, control the coordination of many of the body's activities. Together these systems respond to and send messages to cells throughout the body.

The nervous system sends signals along nerves. The glands of the endocrine system produce chemical messengers (hormones) that travel in the bloodstream. The brain and nerves are part of the nervous system. The endocrine system includes several glands—such as the pancreas and ovaries or testes.

Immunity The immune system increases the body's **immunity**—its ability to resist disease. Some white blood cells of the immune system engulf and

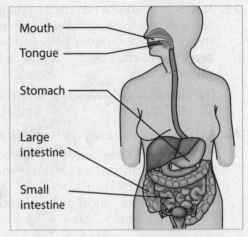

Figure 1-8. **The human digestive system**

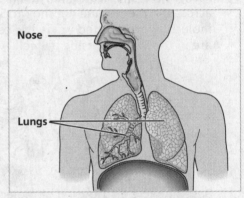

Figure 1-9. **The human respiratory system**

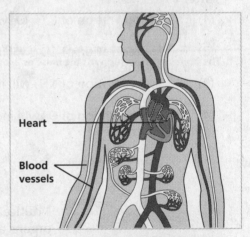

Figure 1-10. **The human circulatory system**

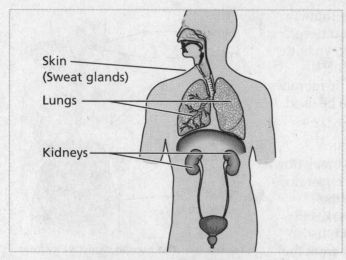

Figure 1-11. **The human excretory system**

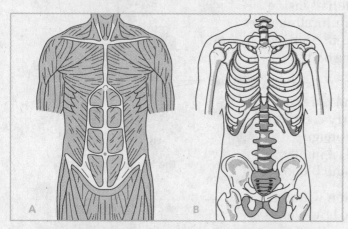

Figure 1-12. **The human muscular** (A) **and skeletal systems** (B): **The bones provide support; the muscles allow movement.**

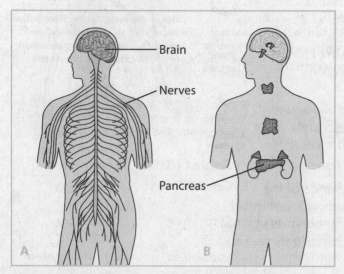

Figure 1-13. **The human nervous** (A) **and endocrine** (B) **systems**

destroy invading bacteria and viruses by digesting them. Others protect the body against specific foreign invaders.

Reproduction The process by which organisms produce new organisms of the same kind is called **reproduction.** The reproductive system releases sex cells and hormones that are critical to the creation of offspring and the regulation of their development. The human reproductive system allows for sexual rather than asexual reproduction. Sexual reproduction makes it possible for two individuals to produce offspring that are of the same species but not exactly like either parent.

Interactions for Life Processes and Regulation

Like all organisms, the human body's systems continually interact to perform life processes. Examples of these interactions may involve several systems.

- Nutrients from the digestive system are transported to cells by the circulatory system.
- The functioning of the reproductive system is regulated by hormones from the endocrine system.
- Body systems also continuously interact to maintain a balanced internal environment (homeostasis). To successfully accomplish this, humans and other complex organisms have a variety of control mechanisms that constantly monitor and correct deviations that could throw the body's internal environment off balance. Examples of these control systems include the regulation of body temperature and blood sugar level.
- When body temperature drops, nerve impulses from the brain signal the muscles to shiver, which generates heat and warms the body.
- Blood sugar level is constantly monitored, and hormones are released as needed to keep it at acceptable levels.

If any organ or organ system does not function properly, the entire organism may fail to maintain homeostasis. The result may be disease or even death. For example, if the heart fails to beat regularly, the circulation of blood will be affected. This may result in a failure of certain materials (oxygen, for example) to flow throughout the body. Without oxygen, cells may stop functioning and death may result.

Comparing Single-celled and Multicellular Organisms

The organelles of single-celled organisms are far less complex than organ systems of multicellular organisms. However, organelles and organ systems are equally capable of completing metabolic activities. For example, the paramecium in Figure 1-15 has a specialized organelle—the food vacuole—that digests food. The human digestive system is more complex and also digests food. The organelle and organ system accomplish the same function: breaking down nutrients so that they can be used by the organism.

Table 1-1 shows examples of life functions that are handled by organelles in single cells and by organ systems in multicellular organisms.

Comparing Humans and Other Organisms

In most biological respects, humans are like other organisms.

- Humans have much the same chemical composition as other organisms. All organisms—from bacteria to tulips to humans—are made of mainly carbon, hydrogen, oxygen, and nitrogen. These elements combine in different ways and amounts to form carbohydrates, proteins, and other essential organic molecules.

- Humans are made up of different kinds of cells that are similar to those found in other animals. For example, human muscles, nerves, and blood cells are similar in structure and function to the muscles, nerves, and blood cells of other complex animals—from geese to gorillas.

- Humans have organ systems and physical characteristics similar to many other complex animals. For example, worms, frogs, and pigs have digestive systems that break down large food molecules. They also have systems that circulate blood. Pig hearts, in fact, are so similar to human hearts that they can be used for transplants.

- Humans reproduce in the same way as many other organisms. For example, fish, amphibians, reptiles, birds, and mammals reproduce sexually; the sperm and egg cell combine, each contributing half of the genetic information to the offspring.

- Humans use the same kind of genetic information as other organisms. Like nearly every living organism—from *E. coli* bacteria and fruit flies to roses and dogs—humans use DNA as their genetic material.

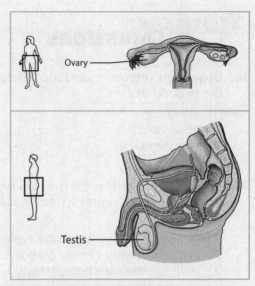

Figure 1-14. **The reproductive systems of the human male and female**

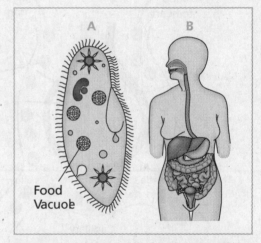

Figure 1-15. **Single-celled and multicellular function:** The food vacuoles in a one-celled organism (A) are much simpler than the human digestive system (B), but they still digest the organism's food.

Table 1-1. The Function of Organelles in Single Cells and Organ Systems in Multicellular Organisms		
Function	**Single Cell**	**Multicellular Organism**
Gas exchange	Cell membrane	Respiratory system
Transport of substances	Cytoplasm	Circulatory system
Nutrition	Specialized vacuoles	Digestive system
Excretion	Cell membrane	Excretory system

36. Organisms remove metabolic cellular wastes by the process of

(1) excretion
(2) absorption
(3) coordination
(4) digestion

37. A similarity between the nervous system and the hormone-secreting system in humans is that they both

(1) are composed of the same type of cells
(2) are composed of many glands
(3) help to maintain homeostasis
(4) secrete chemicals directly into the blood

38. The diagram below shows an air sac surrounded by the thin-walled blood vessels of a human lung.

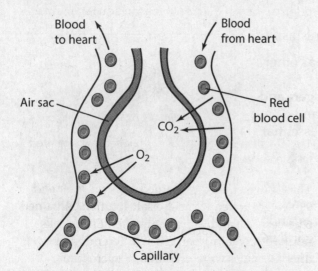

Which two body systems are interacting in the diagram?

(1) respiratory and coordination
(2) respiratory and circulatory
(3) digestive and circulatory
(4) reproductive and coordination

39. Finding shelter, avoiding predators, and obtaining food are most closely related to the ability of an animal to

(1) use structures adapted for movement
(2) increase the rate of mitosis
(3) transport carbon dioxide to cells
(4) excrete waste products of metabolism

40. Which letter in the diagram below indicates a cell structure that functions primarily in the synthesis of protein?

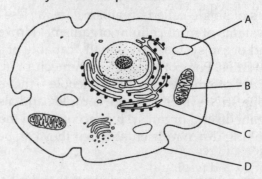

(1) A   (2) B   (3) C   (4) D

41. Inhaling carbon monoxide reduces the ability of red blood cells to carry oxygen. This can lead to brain damage. Which three systems of the body interact in this situation?

(1) digestive, respiratory, and circulatory
(2) immune, circulatory, and digestive
(3) respiratory, circulatory, and nervous
(4) excretory, nervous, and respiratory

42. The activity of all human body systems is coordinated by

(1) the secretion of hormones and the nervous system
(2) the interaction of nerve impulses with the excretory system
(3) the movement of digested food by the circulatory system
(4) the secretion of hormones and the circulatory system

43. Which two systems are most directly involved in providing molecules needed for the synthesis of fats in human cells?

(1) digestive and circulatory
(2) excretory and digestive
(3) immune and muscular
(4) reproductive and circulatory

44. Organ systems of the human body interact to maintain a balanced internal environment. As blood flows through certain organs of the body, the composition of the blood changes because of interactions with those organs. State one change in the composition of the blood as it flows through the respiratory system. [1]

Directions

Review the Test-Taking Strategies section of this book. Then answer the following questions. Read each question carefully and answer with a correct choice or response.

Part A

1 A few bacteria are placed in a nutrient solution. After several hours, thousands of bacteria are present. Which life activities are primarily responsible for this?
   (1) digestion and movement
   (2) digestion and reproduction
   (3) circulation and respiration
   (4) excretion and coordination

2 Mitochondria are organelles that
   (1) are necessary for the process of diffusion to take place
   (2) are found in the nucleus of some cells
   (3) initiate cell division in living cells
   (4) contain respiratory enzymes

3 Most of the enzymes found in the mitochondria are involved in the reactions associated with
   (1) extracting energy from nutrients
   (2) storing energy in nutrients
   (3) DNA production
   (4) protein synthesis

4 Which statement best describes a cell membrane?
   (1) It is found only in animal cells.
   (2) It is a nonliving structure.
   (3) It controls reproduction in a cell.
   (4) It controls the passage of materials into the cell.

5 The transfer of specific molecules through cell membranes is an important factor in the process of
   (1) cytoplasmic flow   (3) homeostasis
   (2) mitotic division   (4) nuclear transfer

6 After a cookie has been eaten and digested, sugar molecules enter the bloodstream by the process of
   (1) active transport   (3) excretion
   (2) diffusion   (4) cellular respiration

7 The concentration of nitrates is often higher in plant roots than it is in the soil around them. Plants maintain this difference in concentration through
   (1) active transport   (3) excretion
   (2) diffusion   (4) coordination

8 In the diagram of root cells below, in which direction would the net flow of water be the greatest as a result of diffusion?
   (1) A to C
   (2) A to B
   (3) B to C
   (4) C to B

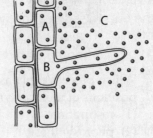

Key
• = Water molecule

9 Diagrams A and B represent two slide preparations of *Elodea* leaves (an aquatic plant).

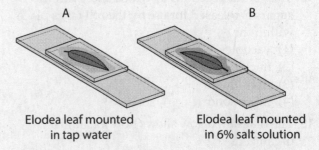

Elodea leaf mounted   Elodea leaf mounted
   in tap water   in 6% salt solution

The tap water used contained 1 percent salt and 99 percent water, while the salt solution contained 6 percent salt and 94 percent water. *Elodea* cells normally contain 1 percent salt. Ten minutes after the slides were prepared, a microscopic examination of cells in leaves A and B would most likely show evidence that
   (1) water had moved out of the cells of leaf B
   (2) salt had moved out of the cells of leaf B
   (3) water had moved into the cells of leaf A
   (4) salt had moved into the cells of leaf A

10 One reason a fish that lives in the ocean may have trouble living in a freshwater lake is that
   (1) there are more carnivores in freshwater habitats
   (2) salt water holds more dissolved nitrogen than fresh water
   (3) more photosynthesis occurs in fresh water than in salt water
   (4) water concentration in the fish is affected by salt levels in its environment

11 Refer to the diagram below of a beaker with a membrane dividing it into two halves containing two kinds of molecules.

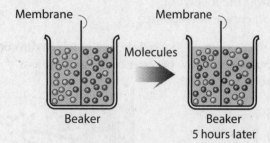

Membrane   Membrane

Molecules

Beaker   Beaker
5 hours later

Which process explains the change in the positions of molecules after five hours?
(1) respiration
(2) photosynthesis
(3) diffusion
(4) excretion

12 Most of the reactions by which energy from sugars is released for use by the cell takes place within the
(1) vacuoles
(2) nuclei
(3) ribosomes
(4) mitochondria

13 The diagram below shows how an animal is organized.

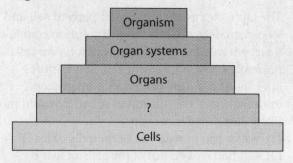

Organism

Organ systems

Organs

?

Cells

Which label is needed to complete the diagram?
(1) atoms   (3) organelles
(2) molecules   (4) tissues

14 Two organs are considered to be a part of the same body system if the organs
(1) are located next to each other
(2) work independently of each other
(3) work together to carry out a life function
(4) are made up of cells with organelles

15 During exercise, the heart beats faster to
(1) carry digestive juices to the small intestine
(2) provide muscles with additional oxygen
(3) lower the blood pressure
(4) digest more food

16 The ability to avoid danger is possible because of the life process of
(1) excretion
(2) reproduction
(3) nutrition
(4) movement

17 The diagram below shows several organs of the human body.

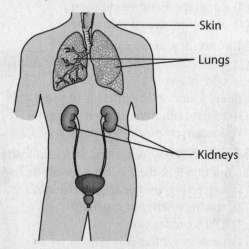

Skin

Lungs

Kidneys

All of these organs interact to help carry out the
(1) removal of waste products
(2) digestion of food
(3) production of hormones
(4) coordination of body movements

18 The circulatory system helps to maintain homeostasis by interacting with the
(1) nervous system and transporting chemicals produced by nerve cells from one cell to another
(2) respiratory system and producing oxygen for gas exchange
(3) digestive system by removing undigested food from the stomach
(4) excretory system in helping to regulate body temperature through sweating

19 In the diagram of the ameba (a single-celled organism), the arrows show the direction of movement of various substances.

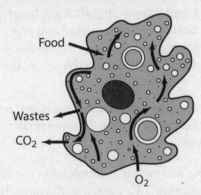

Which of the cell's life activities are represented by the arrows?
(1) digestion, reproduction, and respiration
(2) excretion, transport, and respiration
(3) immunity, digestion, and movement
(4) digestion, coordination, and reproduction

20 All cells are able to continue living because of their ability to
(1) produce food
(2) excrete wastes
(3) produce offspring
(4) produce hormones

21 Which structure in a cell corresponds with the function of the human lungs?
(1) nucleus
(2) vacuole
(3) cell membrane
(4) mitochondria

Part B

22 A scientist wanted to know whether the cells of a particular single-celled green algae could survive without any mitochondria. The scientist removed all of the mitochondria from hundreds of these cells. All of the cells died.

Explain the most likely reason the green algae could not survive without mitochondria. [1]

Base your answers to questions 23 and 24 on the information below and on your knowledge of biology.

Cell communication involves a cell detecting and responding to signals from other cells. Receptor molecules play an important role in these reactions. Human cells have insulin receptors that are needed for the movement of glucose out of the blood.

23 State one way that the shape of the insulin receptor is related to its role in cell communication. [1]

24 A typical human liver cell can have over 90,000 insulin receptors. If a genetic error occurred, resulting in each liver cell in a person having only 1,000 insulin receptors, what specific effect would this have on the liver cells? [1]

25 If vegetables become wilted, they can often be made crisp again by soaking them in water. However, they may lose a few nutrients during this process.

Using the concept of diffusion and concentration, state why some nutrients would leave the plant cell. [1]

26 Describe *one* specific example of diffusion in the human body. In your description be sure to:
- identify the place where your example of diffusion occurs [1]
- identify a substance that diffuses in your example [1]
- state where that substance diffuses from and where it diffuses to, at the place you identified above [1]

Part C

27 A student claims that a dead cell can still carry out diffusion and active transport.

Explain why this claim is not entirely correct. In your answer be sure to explain why a dead cell can or cannot carry on
- diffusion [1]
- active transport [1]

28 Skin cells from a pond animal and skin cells from a land animal were placed in a solution with a 0.85% concentration of salt. When examined later, the cells of the pond animal had swollen and burst, while the cells of the land animal had shrunk.

Explain why the cells responded as they did. In your answer be sure to explain why

- the pond animal cells swelled and burst [1]
- the land animal cells got smaller [1]

29 People sometimes use large quantities of salt to preserve food. The salt kills bacteria that would otherwise cause the food to spoil. Based on your knowledge of diffusion, explain how the salt kills the bacteria. [1]

Base your answers to questions 30 through 33 on the information below and on your knowledge of biology.

The heart of an older person or of someone recovering from a heart attack may become severely weakened or damaged. This sometimes leads to a serious condition called congestive heart failure in which the heart muscle is too weak to pump enough blood throughout the body. As a result, the heart may become exhausted. Sometimes it completely stops.

In a recent study, 2647 patients were given medication called beta-blockers that lowered their risk of death by 34 percent over 15 months (compared to patients who did not take the drugs). Another study reached a similar conclusion.

Although beta-blockers have long been used for treating heart attacks and other medical problems, doctors thought them too dangerous for patients with congestive heart failure. Their reason was that beta-blockers counteract the body's response to adrenaline, a hormone that prepares the body for emergencies by attaching to receptors on heart muscle cells, stimulating the heart to beat faster. Since beta-blockers attach to these adrenaline receptors too, they keep the adrenaline molecules from making contact. This leads to a slowing of the heart, which would appear to cause a problem for a person whose heart is not pumping blood effectively anyway.

The opposite turns out to be the case. When the heart of a person with congestive heart failure is not pumping enough blood, the body responds by releasing more adrenaline to stimulate the heart. As a result, the heart is overstimulated and works even harder—making it more likely to fail. Since beta-blockers interrupt this destructive cycle, the heart stabilizes.

Doctors hope that once more studies are done, proper use of beta-blockers may eventually save many thousands of lives.

30 Describe how adrenaline is involved in the cell-to-cell communication of a person with congestive heart failure. [1]

31 Label the following parts of the illustration of the heart muscle cell below:
1—beta-blocker molecule [1]
2—adrenaline molecule [1]
3—heart cell receptor [1]

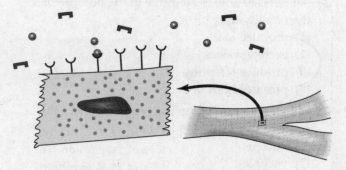

32 Explain how you could tell which objects represent the adrenaline and which represent the beta-blocker in the illustration in question 31. [1]

33 Many drugs have side effects that make them dangerous to some people. For this reason, individuals who take prescription medicine must watch for any unexpected changes in their health.

Based on the information provided in the passage and on your knowledge of biology, describe one possible side effect that might result when people *without* congestive heart failure use beta-blockers. [1]

Homeostasis in Organisms

What do **YOU** *Think?*

Respiration and Photosynthesis

Plants don't carry out respiration. They use photosynthesis instead.

At night, plants use oxygen for respiration just like animals, but not during the day.

I think that animals use oxygen and plants use carbon dioxide for the process of respiration.

I think both plants and animals use oxygen for respiration, and they do this day and night.

Homeostasis in Organisms

Vocabulary

AIDS	dynamic equilibrium	mitochondria
allergy	enzyme	pancreas
antibiotics	feedback mechanism	parasite
antibodies	fungi	pathogen
antigen	gas exchange	pH
ATP	glucose	photosynthesis
bacteria	guard cells	respiration
biochemical processes	homeostasis	stimuli
catalyst	immune system	synthesis
cellular respiration	insulin	vaccine
chloroplast	microbe	virus
disease		

Topic Overview

All living things—from the simplest single-celled bacteria to the most complex multicellular animals—are organized biological systems. To stay alive, all organisms must keep their biological systems stable even though they live in a changing, and sometimes life-threatening, environment. To maintain this stability, organisms continually monitor and respond to changes in the environment. The internal stability that organisms maintain is known as **homeostasis.**

Homeostasis is the maintenance of internal conditions within a narrow range that varies only slightly over time. For example, your body temperature must stay within a specific temperature range (approximately 98.6°F, or 37°C) for you to survive. If you become too hot or too cold, the biochemical processes that keep you alive will begin to fail.

Digging Deeper

Homeostasis sometimes appears with the words *dynamic equilibrium* or *steady state*. These terms all involve the idea of "a constant balance." To picture this concept, it may help to think of a child learning to balance a bicycle. There may be some wobbling back and forth, but generally the rider remains upright.

Basic Biochemical Processes of Living Organisms

Biochemical processes are the chemical processes that occur in living things. All organisms need both energy and raw materials (atoms and molecules) to carry on the internal biochemical processes that are essential for their survival. Two of these enzyme-controlled biochemical processes are photosynthesis and respiration. **Photosynthesis** is the process by which energy is stored in chemical bonds of organic molecules such as carbohydrates. Plants, algae, and many single-celled organisms carry out photosynthesis. Recall that **respiration** is the process by which chemical energy stored in nutrients is released for use in cells. All living organisms carry out respiration.

Storing Energy: Photosynthesis

The energy for life comes primarily from the sun. In Figure 2-1, notice that photosynthesis is the connection between the energy released by the sun and the energy available to living systems.

The cells of organisms that carry out photosynthesis contain light-capturing molecules. In plant cells, these molecules are located in the **chloroplasts,** which are green-colored organelles where photosynthesis occurs. In Figure 2-2, the chloroplasts are the oval structures. You may have seen these green structures on microscope slides of cells prepared from plant leaves.

All plants, algae, and many one-celled organisms use solar energy to convert inorganic molecules (carbon dioxide and water) into any one of several energy-rich organic compounds. One such organic compound is the sugar **glucose**—a simple carbohydrate.

In the chemical reaction shown in Figure 2-3, notice that water and carbon dioxide from the environment are combined to make glucose. Oxygen gas, which is also formed in the process, is released into the environment.

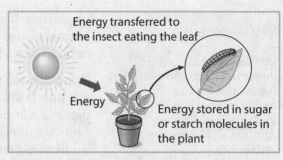

Figure 2-1. Energy transfer: The sun provides energy for most of the life on Earth.

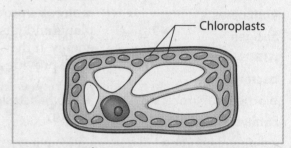

Figure 2-2. Chloroplasts in a typical plant cell: The chloroplasts capture light energy.

$$\text{light energy} + \text{water} + \text{carbon dioxide} \longrightarrow \text{glucose} + \text{oxygen}$$

$$\text{light energy} + 6\ H_2O + 6\ CO_2 \longrightarrow C_6H_{12}O_6 + 6\ O_2$$

Figure 2-3. Photosynthesis

What Happens to the Sugar Produced by Photosynthesis? Plant cells use the organic compounds (such as glucose) from photosynthesis in two ways. Their primary use is to generate ATP molecules during **cellular respiration,** which is the process of releasing the energy in chemical bonds. Glucose is also used as a raw material for building more complex molecules, such as those listed in Table 2-1.

Using Glucose to Produce ATP Molecules One way plants (and animals) use glucose is to generate high energy molecules known as **ATP.** This process occurs during cellular respiration. Energy stored in the chemical bonds of ATP molecules is the energy source for almost all life processes from obtaining, transforming, and transporting materials to eliminating wastes. Because cell processes actually "run" on ATP (rather than glucose), the transfer of energy from glucose to ATP is essential to both plants and the

Table 2-1. Complex Molecules and Their Functions

Molecule	Function
ATP	Supplies energy for cells to run on
DNA	Carries hereditary information
Carbohydrates	Acts as a food reserve molecule
Lipids (fats and oils)	Acts as a food reserve molecule
Protein	Makes up enzymes and many cell parts

organisms that consume them. All organisms—not just plants and animals—use organic food compounds to supply the ATP energy they need to live.

Using Glucose to Build Complex Molecules Cells also use glucose as the starting point for **synthesis** (chemical combining) that forms complex organic compounds. For example, plants store much of the glucose from photosynthesis as starch. Table 2-1 provides some examples of complex molecules and how they are used.

When animals eat plants or other animals, they digest the complex molecules into simpler molecules for their own cells to use. Some of these molecules provide energy for the organism. For example, starches from plants and fats from animals can both be digested and used right away for energy. If they are not all needed for energy, the molecules can be stored as fat to provide a food reserve for the animal.

Table 2-2. Summary of Photosynthesis	
Energy	The energy comes from sunlight as solar energy and ends up in glucose molecules as chemical bond energy.
Materials used	Carbon dioxide gas and water are used; both molecules come from the environment.
Materials produced	Molecules made from the carbon dioxide and water include molecules of the sugar glucose (a simple carbohydrate) and oxygen gas. Oxygen is actually released as a byproduct of photosynthesis.
Time frame	Photosynthesis occurs in plant cells when light is available, which is generally during the daytime.
Location	Photosynthesis occurs in the chloroplasts of plant cells, algae, and some one-celled organisms when they are exposed to light.
Importance of photosynthesis	Organisms either (1) use glucose to synthesize other molecules they need or (2) break down the glucose to release its stored energy.
Relationship to respiration	The energy originally stored in glucose during photosynthesis is transferred to the chemical bonds of ATP. All cells "run" on the energy released from ATP.

Review Questions   Set 2.1

1. In a plant cell, the synthesis of sugar compounds from inorganic raw materials occurs in the

   (1) cell membrane
   (2) mitochondria
   (3) nucleus
   (4) chloroplasts

2. Which word equation represents the process of photosynthesis?

   (1) glucose → alcohol + carbon dioxide
   (2) carbon dioxide + water → glucose + oxygen
   (3) chlorophyll + water → glucose + alcohol
   (4) glucose + oxygen → carbon dioxide + water

3. Which factor *least* influences the rate of photosynthesis?

   (1) atmospheric concentration of carbon dioxide
   (2) time of day
   (3) number of chloroplasts
   (4) concentration of nitrogen in the air

4. The basic raw materials of photosynthesis are

   (1) sugar and carbon dioxide
   (2) oxygen and water
   (3) water and carbon dioxide
   (4) oxygen and sugar

5. Which compound is formed as a common product of the process of photosynthesis?

(1) DNA   (3) chlorophyll
(2) sugar   (4) carbon dioxide

6. In the test tube shown, what is produced by the snail that is used by the plant?

(1) oxygen
(2) carbon dioxide
(3) food
(4) egg cells

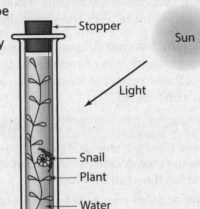

Stopper

Sun

Light

Snail

Plant

Water

7. Which activity occurs during the process of photosynthesis?

(1) Chemical energy from organic molecules is converted into light energy
(2) Organic molecules are absorbed from the environment.
(3) Organic molecules are converted into inorganic food molecules.
(4) Light energy is stored as chemical energy in organic molecules.

8. Photosynthesis in plants requires chloroplasts and light energy.

• Identify two raw materials plants also use in this process [1]
• Explain why these two substances are needed [1]

Releasing Energy: Cell Respiration

All living things need energy to stay alive. Before the energy in the bonds of complex carbohydrates, such as starch, can be used, the molecules must be broken down (digested) into simpler ones, such as glucose.

Then, the glucose (or other simple molecules) must be broken down further. This process involves a series of chemical reactions controlled by **enzymes,** which are special proteins that affect the rate of chemical reactions.

In the final step, the chemical bonds of the glucose molecule are broken, and the energy in those bonds is released. This process of releasing the energy in chemical bonds is called cellular respiration.

In many organisms, cellular respiration requires oxygen, which must be brought into the organism from the environment. Obtaining oxygen from the environment and releasing carbon dioxide is called **gas exchange.**

During cellular respiration, cells capture much of the energy that is released from the glucose bonds. The captured energy is then used to form new bonds in high-energy molecules known as ATP. Figure 2-4 shows how ATP temporarily stores energy. Most of the energy that the cell fails to capture to make ATP is lost to the environment as heat.

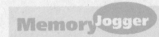

Sometimes people use the term *respiration* when they really mean *breathing. Respiration* is the process that involves oxygen and breaks down food molecules to release energy. *Cellular respiration* refers specifically to the transfer of energy from simple organic molecules like glucose to ATP molecules within cells.

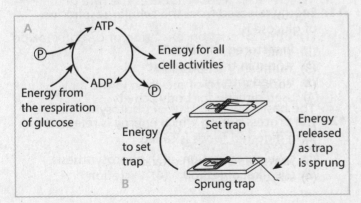

A

ATP

Ⓟ

ADP

Ⓟ

Energy for all cell activities

Energy from the respiration of glucose

Energy to set trap

Set trap

Sprung trap

Energy released as trap is sprung

B

Figure 2-4. Energy storage in ATP molecules: (A) Chemical energy from the breakdown of glucose molecules is used to attach a phosphate (P) to a molecule of ADP. The result is called ATP. When the cell needs energy, the ATP is broken down into ADP. During that process, the phosphate (P), along with the energy that was stored in its chemical bond, is released. (B) A similar form of temporary energy storage occurs when a mousetrap is set. The mechanical energy that is put into the act of setting the trap is stored in the spring. When the trap is sprung, that energy is released.

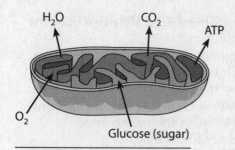

H₂O   CO₂
              ATP

O₂

Glucose (sugar)

Figure 2-5. Cellular respiration in a mitochondrion: Partially broken down glucose molecules and oxygen (O_2) enter the organelle and are rearranged, with the help of enzymes. Water (H_2O) and carbon dioxide (CO_2) are released as waste products. The energy that was stored in the glucose is transferred to ATP molecules.

Cellular respiration in many organisms is completed in organelles called **mitochondria**. (See Figure 2-5.) Mitochondria are common in animal cells. Cells that require more energy contain more mitochondria. For example, muscles require more energy to complete their functions than skin cells do. Muscle cells usually contain mitochondria, which corresponds with their increased energy needs.

As they generate ATP, mitochondria release carbon dioxide and water molecules that come from fragments of molecules that were involved in the reactions. Most cellular processes use ATP as a direct source of energy. Basically, cells "run" on ATP.

Table 2-3. Summary of Cellular Respiration	
Energy	Comes from the chemical bond energy of glucose molecules; ends up in the bonds of ATP where it can be utilized for cell activities
Materials used	Sugar or other energy-rich organic food compounds and oxygen gas from the environment • Food is obtained through photosynthesis in producers and by feeding in consumers. • Oxygen is obtained through gas exchange.
Materials produced	ATP molecules and two waste products— carbon dioxide gas and water. The release of carbon dioxide into the environment is part of the process of gas exchange.
Time frame	Cellular respiration occurs in all cells (including plant cells) 24 hours a day.
Location	Respiration occurs in the cells of all living things. In most organisms, cellular respiration is concluded in mitochondria.
Importance of respiration	All cells "run" on the energy released from ATP. Organisms can use the ATP they make as the source of energy to help them obtain raw materials and nutrients, to transform materials in chemical reactions, to transport materials (for example, active transport), and to eliminate wastes. ATP is essential for metabolic processes. The energy is also used to allow the organism to grow and to move from one place to another.

Digging Deeper

The D in ADP is for **Di**phosphate, or two phosphates. The T in ATP is for **Tri**phosphate, or three phosphates. ADP and ATP are converted back and forth as a phosphate is added or removed.

ADP + P = ATP
ATP − P = ADP

Review Questions

Set 2.2

9. Energy for use in cells is stored in the form of
   (1) chemical bond energy
   (2) physical energy
   (3) heat energy
   (4) mechanical energy

10. In which process do organisms transfer the chemical bond energy in organic molecules to ATP molecules?
    (1) excretion   (3) autotrophic nutrition
    (2) cellular respiration (4) photosynthesis

11. Energy released from the cellular respiration of glucose is
    (1) first stored within ATP
    (2) stored in the liver as fat
    (3) turned into fat
    (4) used directly for body activity

12. The process during which energy is released from digested foods is called
    (1) cellular respiration (3) photosynthesis
    (2) chemical digestion   (4) excretion

13. As a direct result of the life process called cellular respiration in humans,

(1) liquid wastes are eliminated from the body
(2) food is digested and absorbed into the blood
(3) energy is released from digested food within the cells
(4) nutrients are transported within the cells

14. Which process involves the transfer of energy from carbohydrates to ATP molecules?

(1) photosynthesis   (3) digestion
(2) respiration   (4) circulation

15. During respiration, the energy within the bonds of a glucose molecule is released in small amounts in a step-by-step, enzyme-controlled reaction. In this process, the energy released is used to

(1) synthesize ATP
(2) control the process of diffusion
(3) synthesize more glucose
(4) produce oxygen molecules

16. Which statement best describes one of the events taking place in the chemical reaction represented below?

enzymes

$$H_2O + ATP \longrightarrow ADP + P + energy$$

(1) Energy is being stored as a result of cellular respiration.
(2) Energy is being released for metabolic processes.
(3) Decomposition is taking place, resulting in the synthesis of ATP.
(4) Photosynthesis is taking place, resulting in the storage of energy.

17. Compare photosynthesis and respiration with regard to each of the following:

• source of energy [1]
• materials used by each process [1]
• location of each process in the cell [1]
• when each process occurs in plants and animals [1]

18. Which statement most accurately describes the process of respiration?

(1) It occurs only in plants during the daylight hours and usually involves the exchange of gases.
(2) It occurs only in plants during the daylight hours and involves the taking in of preformed organic molecules.
(3) It occurs continuously in the cells of all organisms and involves the synthesis of carbohydrate molecules.
(4) It occurs continuously in the cells of all organisms and often involves an exchange of gases.

19. During daylight hours green plants carry out photosynthesis. Do they also carry out respiration at this time? Support your answer. [1]

Base your answers to questions 20 through 22 on the diagram of a mitochondrion below and on your knowledge of biology.

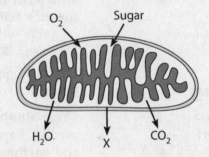

20. The process represented in this diagram is

(1) respiration   (3) photosynthesis
(2) coordination   (4) immunity

21. What term would most appropriately be represented by the "X"?

(1) ATP   (3) antibodies
(2) chlorophyll   (4) glucose

22. What is present within the mitochondrion that allows the reaction to occur?

(1) enzymes   (3) bacteria
(2) chlorophyll   (4) carbon dioxide

Enzymes

A **catalyst** is any substance that can affect the rate of a chemical reaction without itself being changed or used up during the reaction. Because it is neither changed nor used up, the catalyst is capable of carrying out the same function again and again. Protein catalysts known as enzymes affect the chemical reactions in living things.

The Function of Enzymes Biochemical processes, such as digestion (breakdown), synthesis (building up), cellular respiration (energy release),

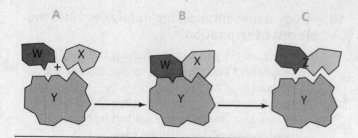

Figure 2-6. Enzymes interact with specific molecules: Enzyme interactions are determined by molecular shape. After the two molecules W and X collide with enzyme Y (A), the enzyme forms a temporary physical connection with them (B) and then separates after a reaction has occurred (C). As a result, the molecules W and X have chemically bonded for the synthesis of the new molecule Z. If the arrows in the illustration were reversed, the reaction would involve splitting molecule Z into two smaller molecules, W and X. This reverse process is digestion.

and photosynthesis (energy capture), are made possible in living things by enzymes.

All living organisms contain enzymes. Enzymes interact with other molecules when they collide. Chemical reactions in living organisms are regulated by many different enzymes that function best at whatever the normal "body" temperature is for the organism.

Importance of Molecular Shape Enzymes and several other molecules, such as hormones, antibodies, and receptor molecules on cell membranes, have specific shapes that influence both how they function and how they interact with other molecules. Many enzymes will interact with some substances, but not others. The enzyme salivary amylase, for example, acts on starches but not proteins. In Figure 2-6, notice how the shapes of W, X, and Y fit together precisely. If the shape of an enzyme is altered, it will not interact with other molecules the way it must to catalyze a reaction, and its function will be impaired.

Enzyme Reaction Rates

Several conditions, such as shape, temperature, and pH, can either speed up or slow down the rate of enzyme action.

Shape Enzymes are chain-like protein molecules that are folded into precise shapes. Each enzyme must have a specific shape to work correctly, and anything that alters that shape will affect the enzyme's ability to function properly. High temperatures and strong <u>acids</u> or <u>bases</u> can change the enzyme's shape either temporarily or permanently. When this happens, the enzyme cannot function, and the reaction rate will decrease in proportion to the number of enzyme molecules that are altered.

Temperature Most enzymes have an <u>optimum</u> temperature at which they function most efficiently and produce the highest reaction rate. For human enzymes, this temperature is typically 98.6°F (37°C). As the temperature of a cell or organism reaches its optimum level, enzymes and the molecules they are interacting with will move faster and collide more often, causing the reaction rate to increase. Beyond the optimum temperature, the rate falls rapidly because the fragile enzyme molecules begin to change shape or break apart. Trace the rise and fall of an enzyme reaction rate in Figure 2-7.

pH The **pH** of a substance is a measure of whether a substance is <u>acidic</u>, <u>neutral</u>, or <u>basic</u>. Placing enzymes in solutions of varying pH values affects their activity. Many enzymes work best in an optimum pH of about 7, which is neutral. This makes sense, since most body fluids and cells maintain a pH of near 7. However, some parts of organisms have typical pH values that are far from neutral. For example, the human stomach is acidic and has a pH of 2 or 3. The small intestine has a pH around 8. Enzymes in these locations typically have optimum rates that correspond to the pH of their environment, as shown in Figure 2-8.

A pH of about 7 is neutral, the same as pure water. A low pH, such as 1 or 2, indicates a strong acid. A high pH, such as 13 or 14, indicates a strong base. In a typical high school biology laboratory, pH is measured with pH paper treated with various indicator dyes.

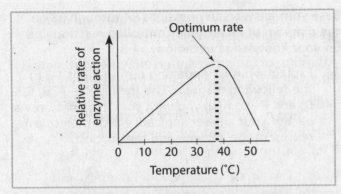

Figure 2-7. **Enzymes and temperature:** Note that the rate of enzyme action is fastest at about 37°C, which is typical of a human enzyme. The reason the rate declines so quickly beyond the optimum is that the higher temperature alters the shape of the enzyme. In this example, by the time the temperature reaches 55°C, all the enzyme molecules have been altered, and as a result, they no longer function.

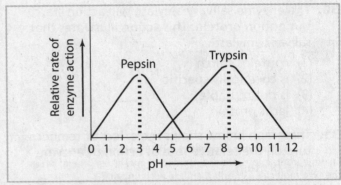

Figure 2-8. **Enzymes and pH:** Pepsin is found in the human stomach and has a pH that matches the acid environment found there. Trypsin is an enzyme located in the small intestine where the pH is close to 8. Notice that each enzyme is less effective if the pH is either raised or lowered from its optimum point.

Review Questions

Set 2.3

23. Only small amounts of enzymes are required for reactions within cells because enzymes are

(1) fragile
(2) reused
(3) small molecules
(4) constantly synthesized

24. Which cell organelle indicated in the diagram below controls the synthesis of enzymes?

(1) A
(2) B
(3) C
(4) D

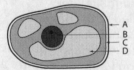

25. In order to survive, all organisms must carry out

(1) autotrophic nutrition
(2) heterotrophic nutrition
(3) enzyme-controlled reactions
(4) the process of reproduction

26. Which group of organic compounds includes the enzymes?

(1) proteins
(2) carbohydrates
(3) sugars
(4) fats

27. Luciferin is a molecule that, when broken down in fireflies, produces heat and light. The rate at which luciferin is broken down in cells is controlled by

(1) a carbohydrate
(2) a simple sugar
(3) an enzyme
(4) a complex fat

28. At which point on the graph below can the rate of enzyme activity be increased by increasing the concentration of sugar molecules?

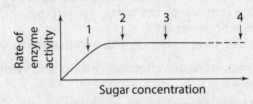

(Enzyme concentration constant)

(1) 1   (3) 3
(2) 2   (4) either 2, 3, or 4

29. Which statement best describes the relationship between enzyme action and temperature shown in the graph below?

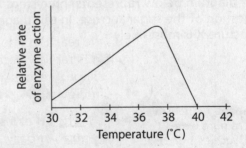

(1) Enzyme synthesis begins at 30°C.
(2) Enzyme activity constantly increases with increasing temperature.
(3) The pH has a greater effect on this enzyme than temperature does.
(4) Enzyme activity increases as the temperature increases from 32°C to 34°C.

30. The enzyme salivary amylase will act on starch but not on protein. This action illustrates that salivary amylase

(1) contains starch
(2) is chemically specific
(3) is not reusable
(4) lacks protein

31. The graph below shows the effect of temperature on the relative rate of action of enzyme X on a protein.

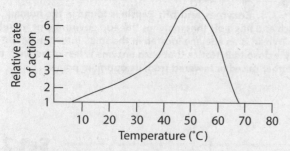

Which change would not affect the relative rate of action of enzyme X?

(1) the addition of cold water when the reaction is at 50°C
(2) an increase in temperature from 70°C to 80°C
(3) the removal of the protein when the reaction is at 30°C
(4) a decrease in temperature from 40°C to 10°C

32. Enzymes influence chemical reactions in living systems by

(1) becoming part of the product after the reactions occur
(2) combining with atmospheric gases to form waste products
(3) affecting the rate at which reactions occur
(4) absorbing water during synthesis and digestion

33. The diagram below represents three steps in the digestion of the sugar sucrose. In this diagram, structure X is most likely

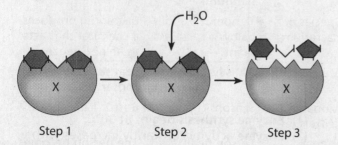

(1) a molecule of oxygen
(2) the end product
(3) an enzyme molecule
(4) the sugar

Base your answers to questions 34 through 36 on the diagram of an enzyme-controlled reaction and on your knowledge of biology.

34. Explain what is happening during Steps 1-3 in the following diagram. Use the labels—A, B, C, D, and E—to help you with your explanation. As part of your answer, indicate which molecules represent the enzyme and the product.

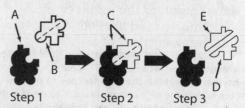

35. Is this reaction an illustration of synthesis or digestion? Support your answer. [1]

36. Explain why heating these molecules might *slow* the rate at which this reaction occurs? [1]

Base your answers to questions 37 through 41 on the diagram and data table below and on your knowledge of biology.

A student is studying the effect of temperature on the action of a protein-digesting enzyme that is contained in stomach fluid. An investigation is set up using five identical test tubes. Each test tube contains 40 milliliters of stomach fluid as well as a 20-millimeter glass tube filled with cooked egg white, as shown in the diagram. After 48 hours, the amount of egg white digested in each tube was measured. The data collected are shown in the following table.

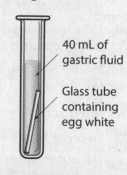

40 mL of gastric fluid

Glass tube containing egg white

Digestion at Different Temperatures		
Tube	Temperature (°C)	Amount of Digestion After 48 Hours
1	4	0.0 mm
2	8	2.5 mm
3	21	4.0 mm
4	37	7.5 mm
5	100	0.0 mm

37. Identify the independent variable in this investigation.

(1) gastric fluid
(2) length of glass tubing
(3) temperature
(4) time

38. State the amount of digestion (in mm) that might be expected after 48 hours in a test tube that is identical to the other 5 test tubes, but at a temperature of 15°C.

  (1) less than 2.5 mm
  (2) between 2.5 and 4 mm
  (3) between 4.0 and 7.5 mm
  (4) more than 7.5 mm

39. The best graph of the results of this investigation would be made by plotting the data on which set of axes?

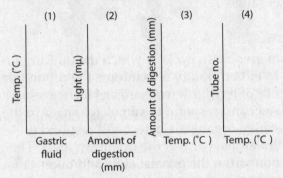

40. The student repeated this same experiment using a glass tube containing potato instead of egg white. After 48 hours, he found no evidence of any digestion.

Explain why no digestion occurred. [1]

41. During the winter, many fish eat very little. Some students thought this might be because less oxygen is dissolved in the cold winter water than in the same water during the warm summer months. The students tested the water and found that cold water holds more dissolved oxygen than warm water. They also discovered that the fish have nearly as much food available during the winter as in the summer.

Explain why the fish eat very little during the winter. [1]

Feedback and Homeostasis

Because an organism's external and internal environment is constantly changing, its homeostasis is constantly threatened. As a result, living things must monitor and respond to changes in the environment. Stability (homeostasis) results when the organism detects <u>deviations</u> (changes) in the environment and responds with an appropriate corrective action that returns the organism's systems to normal. If an organism's monitoring systems or control mechanisms fail, disease or even death can result.

As you go about your daily tasks, your body temperature readjusts, your heart and breathing rates alter slightly, and your blood flow increases or decreases. If your monitoring were to fail, these small adjustments would not be made. Soon, your body's homeostasis would begin to deteriorate. Under extreme conditions, you could become quite ill or even die. However, simple corrective actions usually take care of problems with your homeostasis and life goes on. Some examples of responses organisms have to changes they encounter are shown in Table 2-4.

Dynamic Equilibrium

Organisms have a variety of mechanisms that maintain the physical and chemical aspects of the internal environment within the narrow limits that are favorable for cell activities. The stability that results from these responses is called homeostasis or a "steady state." To many biologists, the phrase *steady state* suggests an

Table 2-4. Responses to Environmental Change

Organism	Change (stimulus)	Response
Species of bacterium	Temperature falls below a certain point.	Bacterium produces a chemical that acts as an antifreeze.
Many plants	Air is hot and dry.	Leaf pores close to conserve water.
Monarch butterflies	Seasons change.	Butterflies migrate.
Human	Person hears a loud noise.	The person becomes alert; heart rate increases for "fight or flight."

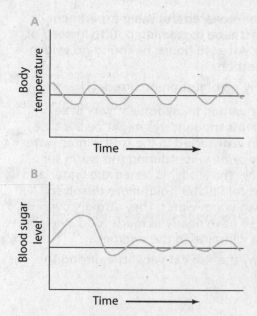

Figure 2-9. Dynamic equilibrium: (A) Temperature: Our body temperature shows a regular pattern of slight changes around a "normal" temperature of about 98.6°F (37°C). The graph represents the slight differences in temperature that are part of a daily cycle. Mechanisms such as shivering and sweating help maintain this range. (B) Blood sugar: Normal blood sugar levels show a rise in blood sugar after a meal, but blood sugar level is quickly restored to equilibrium as the hormone insulin prompts glucose to move from the blood to body cells.

unchanging condition. They prefer to use the term **dynamic equilibrium** to describe the constant small corrections that normally keep the internal environment within the limits needed for survival.

In Figure 2-9, notice that these small corrections include a normal range of variations. Certain microorganisms or diseases can interfere with dynamic equilibrium, and therefore with homeostasis. Organisms, including humans, have mechanisms to deal with such interference and restore the normal state. Homeostatic adjustments have their limits. They can operate only within certain set ranges.

Feedback Mechanisms

A **feedback mechanism** involves a cycle in which the output of a system "feeds back" to either modify or reinforce the action taken by the system. A variety of feedback mechanisms have evolved for helping organisms detect and respond to **stimuli** (changes in the environment). Multi-celled organisms detect and respond to change both at the cellular level and at the organism level. Their systems detect deviations from the normal state and take corrective actions to restore homeostasis.

Feedback responses can be simple or complex. A simple feedback response might involve a hormone that regulates a particular chemical process in a cell. A complex feedback response might be an elaborate behavior, such as bird migration.

Positive Feedback Feedback mechanisms can be either positive or negative. In positive feedback systems, a change prompts a response, which leads to a greater change and a greater response. Childbirth is an example of a positive feedback system. The first contractions push the baby's head against the base of the uterus, which causes stronger contractions in the muscles surrounding the uterus. This increases the pressure of the baby's head against the base of the uterus, which causes stronger contractions and so on. Eventually the baby is born, and the feedback cycle ends.

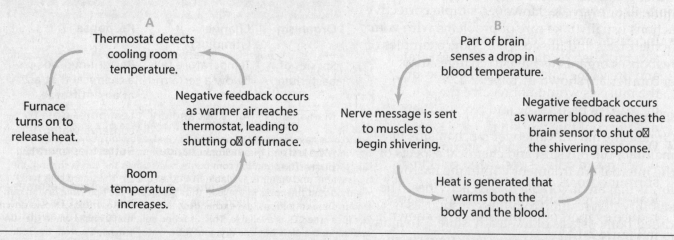

Figure 2-10. Negative feedback systems: (A) The furnace and thermostat in most houses are part of a negative feedback system. (B) Like the household heating system, the regulation of body temperature is a negative feedback system.

Negative Feedback Negative feedback systems are the most common. In this case, a change in the environment can prompt system 1 to send a message (often a hormone) to system 2, which responds by attempting to restore homeostasis. When system 1 detects that system 2 has acted, it stops signaling for further action.

A typical house heating system is an example of negative feedback. The furnace has a thermostat that is set to a specific temperature called the set point. When the room cools below the set point, the thermostat sends a message to turn on the furnace. When the room temperature rises above the set point, the thermostat stops sending the message, and the furnace shuts down. (See Figure 2-10.)

Regulating human body temperature uses a similar system. A structure in the brain detects that the temperature of the blood is too low. This brain structure then sends a signal to muscles, causing them to contract and relax in rapid cycles. The result is shivering, which generates body heat. When shivering has sufficiently warmed the body and blood, <u>sensors</u> in the brain detect the change, and the signal to shiver stops.

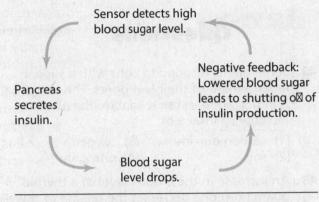

Figure 2-11. **Negative feedback involving blood sugar level**

Negative Feedback and Cell/Organ System Interaction

Maintaining dynamic equilibrium often involves interactions between cells and body organs or systems. For example, certain cells in the body monitor the level of glucose in the blood. When the glucose level is above normal limits, an endocrine organ called the **pancreas** secretes insulin. **Insulin** is a hormone that prompts glucose to move from the blood into body cells, resulting in a lower glucose level in the blood. Another hormone secreted by the pancreas works in the opposite way. When the glucose level in the blood is too low, this hormone prompts the release of glucose stored in the liver. The negative feedback process involving insulin is shown in Figure 2-11.

Other examples of cell/organ feedback interactions include:

- Increased muscle activity is often accompanied by an increase in heart rate and breathing rate. If this did not occur, the muscles would not receive the increase in blood flow and oxygen they need to continue working.
- When plant leaves detect a shortage of water, **guard cells**—specialized cells that surround pores on the surface of the leaf—change shape to close the pores and reduce evaporation. The process is shown in Figure 2-12.

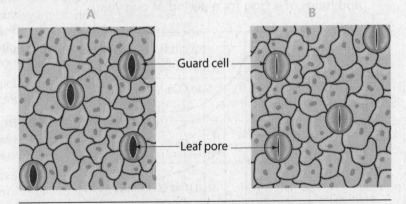

Figure 2-12. **Guard cell activity on the surface of a leaf:** (A) The guard cells have opened the pores in the leaf, allowing gas exchange between the leaf and the environment. Water can exit from the leaf, and CO_2 can enter. This situation commonly exists when the sun is shining, the air is warm, and water is available from the soil. (B) The guard cells have nearly closed the pores in the leaf, thus protecting the leaf from drying out. Under these conditions, gas exchange is limited. Photosynthesis slows down because little CO_2 is available. This situation commonly exists when the sun is shining, the air is hot and dry, and little water is available from the soil.

42. Some plants respond to light with a sudden enlargement of their leaf pores. This response is important because it enables the plant to increase its intake of

(1) carbon dioxide   (3) oxygen
(2) soil   (4) nitrogen

43. An increase in the blood's level of a thyroid gland hormone decreases the release of thyroid-stimulating hormone. This mechanism illustrates

(1) negative feedback
(2) enzyme action
(3) immune response
(4) positive feedback

44. Maintenance of the pH of human blood within a certain range is an example of

(1) chemical digestion
(2) synthesis
(3) respiration
(4) dynamic equilibrium

45. Homeostasis is illustrated in the human body by the effects of insulin on the amount of

(1) proteins digested
(2) amino acids absorbed into the blood
(3) oxygen transport to the lungs
(4) glucose in the blood

46. The chart below shows the amount of oxygen and carbon dioxide exchanged through the skin and lungs of a frog for a period of one year.

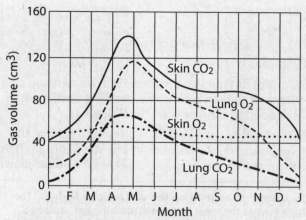

The lowest rate of gas exchange is most likely the result of

(1) increased mating activity
(2) elevated body temperature
(3) environmental conditions
(4) competition with other species

47. A student is frightened by a loud noise, which results in a hormone being released into the blood. The hormone causes the student's heart to beat rapidly. The two systems that work together to cause this reaction are the endocrine system that secretes the hormone and the

(1) nervous system   (3) excretory system
(2) reproductive system   (4) digestive system

48. Which important human process is represented in the diagram below?

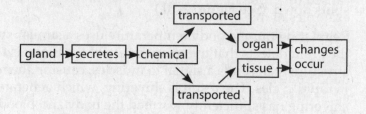

(1) coordination   (3) excretion
(2) digestion   (4) cell respiration

49. Describe what normally happens to a person's blood sugar level soon after he or she eats a meal that contains carbohydrates. [1]

50. Describe the role of insulin in regulating blood sugar levels. [1]

51. On a sheet of graph paper, mark an X and a Y-axis, then draw a line representing the relative blood sugar levels for two individuals (Person A and Person B) over a 5-hour period after a meal. Both people ate the same foods. Person A produces a normal amount of insulin, and Person B does not.

Explain any differences in the lines representing Persons A and B. [1]

52. During hot weather and vigorous exercise, people sweat. As the water on their skin evaporates, the water molecules absorb heat energy.

Explain why this process is important to the individual. [1]

53. Many different feedback mechanisms have evolved over time. These mechanisms allow an organism to respond to changes in both its internal and external environment.

Select an organism from those you have learned about and describe how a specific feedback process works within that organism. Include how the feedback specifically helps the organism maintain homeostasis. [1]

Disease as a Failure of Homeostasis

Disease is any condition that prevents the body from working as it should. As a result, the body may fail to maintain homeostasis. Diseases in humans may result from foreign invader organisms, called **pathogens,** or from abnormal cells in the body that lead to cancer. Disease may also result from <u>toxic</u> substances, poor nutrition, organ malfunction, an inherited disorder, or risky personal behavior. All can lead to a disruption of the body's ability to function normally—that is, to maintain homeostasis.

Sometimes the onset of a disease becomes apparent right away, as in the case of some birth defects or poisoning. Sometimes, however, the disease may not show up for many years, as is the case with lung cancer caused by exposure to tobacco smoke. Some examples of these kinds of diseases are noted in Table 2-5.

Pathogens There are many potentially dangerous disease-causing organisms in the air, water, and food we take in every day. A variety of pathogens—viruses, bacteria, fungi, and other parasites—can interfere with our normal functioning and make us seriously ill. Plants and other animals can also be infected by these and similar organisms. Some examples of pathogens and the diseases they cause are shown in Table 2-6.

Cancer Certain genetic mutations in a cell can result in uncontrolled cell division called cancer. Exposing cells to certain chemicals and radiation increases mutations and thus increases the chance of cancer. In this disease, genes that control and coordinate a cell's normal cycle of growth and division are altered by mutation. As a result, the cell begins to divide abnormally and uncontrollably. The result is a mass of abnormal cells referred to as a <u>tumor</u>.

Table 2-5. Causes of Disease

Cause of Disease	Examples
Inherited disorders	Down syndrome, cystic fibrosis, sickle cell disease
Exposure to toxins	Lead poisoning, radiation poisoning
Poor nutrition	Scurvy (vitamin C deficiency), goiter (iodine deficiency)
Organ malfunction	Heart attack, diabetes
High-risk behaviors	Lung cancer, drug addiction, skin cancer

Table 2-6. Pathogens and Disease

Pathogen	Description of Pathogen	Examples of Disease
Virus	**Viruses** are particles composed of nucleic acid and protein. They reproduce when they invade living cells.	Examples include the common cold, influenza, AIDS, and chicken pox. Immunizations have been developed to combat many viral diseases.
Bacterium	**Bacteria** are one-celled organisms.	Bacterial illnesses include strep throat, syphilis, and food poisoning. **Antibiotics**, drugs like penicillin that we get from microorganisms, are used to treat many bacterial diseases.
Fungus	**Fungi** are organisms made of either one or many cells. They include yeasts and molds. They eat by absorbing organic substances.	Examples include athlete's foot and ringworm. Fungicides and antibiotics are used to fight fungal diseases.
Parasites	Some animals and one-celled organisms are **parasites** that survive by living and feeding on other organisms.	Parasites include leeches and tapeworms. Malaria is a disease caused by a one-celled organism. It is transmitted to humans by mosquitoes. Heartworm is a parasitic worm that lives in dogs and cats. Medicines are available to treat some parasitic diseases. Avoiding exposure to the parasite is also effective.

Once they are identified, often by abnormal proteins on their surfaces, cancer cells may be attacked by the immune system and destroyed. If the immune system is unable to destroy the cancer cells, the disease may become life-threatening.

The Immune System

Humans have many ways of protecting themselves from danger and disease. For example:

- Our eyes, ears, and sense of smell help us detect danger.
- We release hormones that stimulate emergency responses to danger.
- Our muscles allow us to fight off some threats and to flee from others.
- Our skin—when unbroken—keeps out many foreign organisms that could be harmful.
- Our tears, saliva, and other body secretions trap and/or destroy invaders that come into contact with them.
- Our nervous system provides rapid coordination of many of our responses to danger.

Once invaded, however, the body needs an effective way to combat invaders or body cells that malfunction. The **immune system** is the body's primary defense against disease-causing pathogens.

Pathogens, foreign substances, or cancer cells that threaten our homeostasis can usually be identified by molecules on their outer surfaces or membranes. These molecules, called **antigens,** trigger a response from the immune system. Toxins, the poisonous wastes of certain pathogens, can also act as antigens.

All cells have potential antigens on their surfaces. However, the immune system can usually tell the difference between the molecules of "self" cells, which belong to the body, and "non-self" (foreign) cells, which come from outside the body. When cells of our immune system recognize foreign antigens, specialized white blood cells and antibodies attack them and the cells that display them.

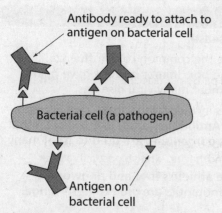

Antibody ready to attach to antigen on bacterial cell

Bacterial cell (a pathogen)

Antigen on bacterial cell

Figure 2-13. Certain white blood cells produce Y-shaped antibodies: The antibodies match the shape of certain antigens on pathogens or abnormal proteins on cancer cells. Note that the antibodies and antigens are not drawn to scale. They would be MUCH smaller than the pathogen cell.

White Blood Cells and Antibodies Some white blood cells are specialized to surround and engulf invading pathogens that are recognized as a threat. Others produce **antibodies**—proteins that either attack the invaders or mark them for killing. The marked invaders may then be destroyed by other white blood cells. In Figure 2-13, notice the Y-shaped antibodies that match the shape of antigens.

Most of the antibodies and white blood cells that attack an invader break down soon after they have defended the body. However, some specialized white blood cells will remain. These cells are capable of quickly dividing and producing more antibodies of the same kind to fight off later invasions of the same **microbes** (microscopic organisms). Antibodies are effective even against microbes that appear years later.

Vaccinations Scientists have discovered that weakened microbes (pathogens) or even parts of microbes can stimulate the immune system to react. The antigens found on the live pathogens are usually present on the weakened or killed ones, too. As shown in Figure 2-14, **vaccines** are made using these weakened, killed, or parts of microbes (pathogens). When vaccines are injected into the body, the immune system responds just as if it had been invaded by a live pathogen. It produces antibodies. These antibodies can attack and destroy any of that pathogen that is still present in the body.

After a vaccination, the immune system "remembers" specific pathogens by leaving behind white blood cells that protect the body for years. The vaccinated body reacts as if it has already defeated the specific pathogen and responds faster in the future than it did when attacked the first time. The second response is so rapid that in most cases the disease will not even have time to develop before the immune system wipes it out.

Damage to the Immune System A person's immune system may weaken with age or other factors. Stress and fatigue, for example, can lower our resistance and make us more vulnerable to disease. Some viral diseases, such as **AIDS,** result from an attack on the immune system. Damage from the disease may leave the person with AIDS unable to deal with infections and cancerous cells. Their weakened immune system is one reason people with AIDS often die of infections that a healthy immune system would easily destroy.

Problems Associated with the Immune Response Although our immune system is essential for our survival, it creates problems for some people. These people have an **allergy**—a rapid immune system reaction to environmental substances that are normally harmless. Examples of such substances include certain foods, pollen, and chemicals from insect bites.

In people with allergies, the immune system reacts by releasing <u>histamines</u>. This leads to anything from a runny nose and sneezing to a rash and swelling. It is the swelling that makes some allergies dangerous: Occasionally, the throat swells, interfering with the victim's ability to breathe. People with allergies often use <u>antihistamines</u> to reduce the effects of the histamines and the symptoms they cause.

Sometimes the immune system fails to recognize the "self" molecules and attacks the body's own cells. For example, in some cases, the immune system attacks and destroys the pancreas cells that produce insulin. The result is one type of diabetes.

Since transplanted organs come from another person, they have foreign antigens on their cells. As a result, the immune system recognizes transplants as "invaders" and attacks them. To avoid "rejection" of their new organ, transplant patients receive injections of special drugs to reduce the effectiveness of their immune system. Of course, because the immune system's ability to protect the transplant patient from normal pathogens is reduced, the patient may become ill from a pathogen that normally would be no threat.

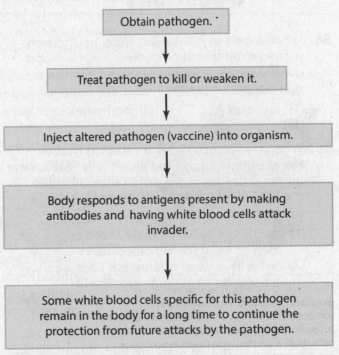

Obtain pathogen.

↓

Treat pathogen to kill or weaken it.

↓

Inject altered pathogen (vaccine) into organism.

↓

Body responds to antigens present by making antibodies and having white blood cells attack invader.

↓

Some white blood cells specific for this pathogen remain in the body for a long time to continue the protection from future attacks by the pathogen.

Figure 2-14. **Preparation and use of a vaccine**

Research and Progress Against Disease Biological research of diseases and their causes has generated a vast amount of knowledge that is used to find ways of diagnosing, preventing, controlling, or curing diseases of plants and animals. Some examples of how medical knowledge has developed are shown in Table 2-7.

Table 2-7. Biological Research of Diseases

Category of Research	Methods Developed
Diagnosing disease	• Culturing (growing) bacteria from the infected person to determine what specific pathogen is responsible for the illness • Using X-rays, CAT scans, ultrasound, blood pressure monitoring devices, and other methods to determine the cause or extent of the illness • Detecting genetic abnormalities that may be present in cells
Preventing and controlling disease	• Promoting improved sanitation measures, including frequent hand washing, safe garbage disposal, and sewage treatment • Sterilizing surgical instruments and treating wounds with antiseptics and other chemicals • Controlling populations of rats, flies, mosquitoes, and other disease-carrying organisms with pesticides or sanitation measures • Treating water, milk, and other foods to reduce the presence of pathogens • Vaccinating to promote the body's immune response to pathogens • Identifying the dangers of risky behaviors such as tobacco use
Treating and curing disease	• Developing antibiotics and other drugs to kill pathogens • Developing medical procedures, including surgical operations and laser techniques, to remove damaged or diseased tissue from the body

Review Questions

Set 2.5

54. When a person is suffering from an infection, such as strep throat or chicken pox, his blood usually shows a significant increase in the number of

(1) enzymes
(2) antibodies
(3) hormones
(4) sugars

55. When microscope slides are stained to show blood cells, the small red blood cells that appear on the slides are much more numerous than the large white blood cells. This supports the concept that

(1) the body's need for white blood cells is less than its need for red blood cells
(2) red cells are more numerous because they are smaller than white blood cells
(3) the nuclei of the white blood cells help them work more efficiently than the red blood cells, which lack nuclei
(4) each kind of cell is present in the numbers best suited to meet the needs of the body

56. Which response usually occurs after an individual receives a vaccination for the influenza virus?

(1) Hormones in the blood stop reproduction of the virus.
(2) Pathogens from the vaccine deactivate the virus.
(3) Enzymes released from antigens digest the virus.
(4) Antibodies against the virus are found in the blood.

57. A patient has just received an organ transplant. Which treatment would be most effective in preventing the patient's body from rejecting the organ?

(1) Treat the patient with medications that decrease the immune system's response.
(2) Treat the patient with antibiotics to fight off a possible viral infection.
(3) Restrict the patient's salt intake.
(4) Give the patient blood transfusions.

58. The body makes chemicals that can help to destroy harmful viruses and bacteria. These chemicals are called

(1) antibodies
(2) vaccines
(3) hormones
(4) antibiotics

59. A vaccine can protect you against a disease because it

(1) destroys toxic substances from bacteria before they can make you sick
(2) stimulates your immune system against the pathogen
(3) kills any pathogenic bacteria in your body
(4) changes pathogenic bacteria into harmless bacteria

60. The body is protected against harmful flu viruses by

(1) red blood cells and hormones
(2) white blood cells and antibodies
(3) white blood cells and enzymes
(4) red blood cells and antibodies

61. In some people, substances such as peanuts, eggs, and milk cause an immune response. This response to usually harmless substances is most similar to the

(1) action of the heart as the intensity of exercise increases
(2) mechanism that regulates the activity of guard cells
(3) action of white blood cells when certain bacteria enter the body
(4) mechanism that maintains the proper level of antibiotics in the blood

62. Parasitic strains of *E. coli* may produce poisonous chemicals that attack living tissue and cause disease in humans. These chemicals are called

(1) antibodies
(2) toxins
(3) viruses
(4) antibiotics

63. Uncontrolled cell division is known as

(1) meiosis
(2) cancer
(3) antibody production
(4) sexual reproduction

64. The resistance of the body to a pathogen is called

(1) immunity
(2) antigen
(3) cancer
(4) infection

65. Diseases can be caused by inherited disorders, exposure to toxic substances, organ malfunction and certain personal behaviors.

Choose *two* of the above causes and *for each one* give a specific example of an associated disease. [1]

66. Our immune system normally helps us resist infection and disease. Sometimes, however, it may actually work against us by attacking certain tissues or organs in the body.

State one example of the immune system attacking the body and explain how we try to counteract the problem. [1]

67. Vaccinations play a major role in medicine today. Explain the role of vaccines in the prevention of disease. Your answer must include at least:

• a description of the contents of a vaccine [1]
• a description of how a vaccine protects the body from disease [1]
• one specific reason certain vaccinations are required for students to attend public schools. [1]

Base your answer to question 68–70 on the information below and on your knowledge of biology.

Stem cells present in an embryo are responsible for the formation of various tissues and organs. Recent research suggests that it may be possible to replicate stem cells from sections of skin taken from adult mice, rather than having to use stem cells from the embryos of mice.

In the future, human stem cells may be used to replace human tissue damaged by diseases such as Parkinson's disease and multiple sclerosis.

68–70. Discuss why the use of stem cells taken from a patient to replace damaged tissues and organs may decrease the potential risk to a patient. In your answer, be sure to:

• identify the major problem that may occur when tissues and organs donated by another individual are used [1]
• explain why this problem may occur [1]
• explain why this problem will not occur if tissues and organs produced by stem cells from the patient are used [1]

Directions

Review the Test-Taking Strategies section of this book. Then answer the following questions. Read each question carefully and answer with a correct choice or response.

Part A

1 Most of the oxygen in our atmosphere comes from processes carried out
   - (1) in the soil
   - (2) by animals
   - (3) in factories
   - (4) by plants

2 Which organism releases oxygen into the atmosphere?
   - (1) mold
   - (2) bird
   - (3) fish
   - (4) tree

3 Plants provide food for animals through the process of
   - (1) respiration
   - (2) digestion
   - (3) photosynthesis
   - (4) excretion

4 Which word equation represents the process of photosynthesis?
   - (1) starch → many glucose molecules
   - (2) glucose + oxygen → carbon dioxide + water + energy
   - (3) carbon dioxide + water → glucose + oxygen
   - (4) fats → sugar molecules

5 Which statement correctly relates the two organisms in the illustration below?

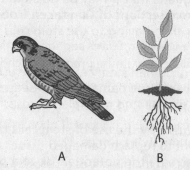

A   B

   - (1) A carries out cell division, but B does not.
   - (2) B transports needed organic materials, but A does not.
   - (3) Both A and B carry out cellular respiration to release energy from organic molecules.
   - (4) Neither A nor B is able to use energy to combine carbon dioxide and water to make organic compounds.

6 A plant cell that lacks chloroplasts will not
   - (1) give off oxygen
   - (2) take in food
   - (3) give off carbon dioxide
   - (4) take in water

7 Which process removes carbon dioxide from the atmosphere rather than adding it?
   - (1) cellular respiration
   - (2) combustion of gasoline
   - (3) photosynthesis
   - (4) deforestation

8 Which process in plants produces carbon dioxide?
   - (1) respiration
   - (2) photosynthesis
   - (3) coordination
   - (4) digestion

9 The size of the openings in a leaf through which gases move in and out is controlled by the
   - (1) root cells
   - (2) chloroplasts
   - (3) chromosomes
   - (4) guard cells

10 What process does the word equation below represent?

enzymes

glucose + oxygen ——→ carbon dioxide + water + energy

   - (1) photosynthesis
   - (2) breathing
   - (3) transport
   - (4) respiration

11 The major source of weight gain in a growing plant is
   - (1) sunlight
   - (2) carbon dioxide
   - (3) oxygen
   - (4) soil

12 Green plants do not release large amounts of CO_2 all the time because they use CO_2 in the process of
   - (1) photosynthesis
   - (2) respiration
   - (3) reproduction
   - (4) evolution

13 The diagram below represents some events that take place in a plant cell. With which organelle would these events be most closely associated?

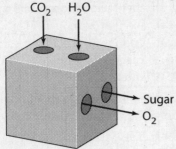

(1) mitochondrion
(2) chloroplast
(3) ribosome
(4) vacuole

14 An enzyme that digests starch will not act upon the sugar sucrose. This fact is an indication that enzymes are
(1) specific
(2) synthetic
(3) starches
(4) generalized

15 Which statement best describes the enzyme represented in the graphs below?

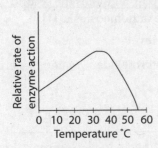 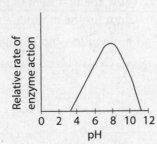

(1) This enzyme works best at a temperature of 37°C and a pH of 8.
(2) This enzyme works best at a temperature of 55°C and a pH of 12.
(3) Temperature and pH have no effect on the action of this enzyme.
(4) This enzyme works best at a temperature near freezing and a pH above 4.

16 The body usually responds to foreign material by forming
(1) hormones   (3) vaccines
(2) antibodies   (4) antigens

17 A sudden increase in the number of white blood cells in a human may be an indication of
(1) growth
(2) color blindness
(3) mental retardation
(4) an infection

Part B

Base your answers to questions 18 and 19 on the equation below and on your knowledge of biology.

$$C_6H_{12}O_6 + 6\,O_2 \rightarrow H_2O + 6\,CO_2 + 36\,ATP$$

(glucose) + (oxygen) → (water) + (carbon dioxide) + ATP

18 The equation represents the process of
(1) excretion   (3) respiration
(2) photosynthesis   (4) coordination

19 Explain the energy connection between the glucose and the formation of ATP in this process. [1]

Base your answers to questions 20 through 23 on the summary equations of two processes below and on your knowledge of biology.

Photosynthesis

water + carbon dioxide $\xrightarrow{\text{enzymes}}$ glucose + oxygen + water

Respiration

glucose + oxygen $\xrightarrow{\text{enzymes}}$ water + carbon dioxide

20 Choose one of the processes and identify the source of the energy in the process you chose. [1]

21 Identify where the energy ends up at the completion of that process. [1]

22 State one reason the processes of photosynthesis is important for living things.[1]

23 State one reason the processes of respiration is important for living things. [1]

Base your answers to questions 24 through 28 on the information and data table below and on your knowledge of biology.

The results of blood tests for two individuals are shown in the data table below. The blood glucose level before breakfast is normally 80–90 mg/100 mL of blood. A blood glucose level above 110 mg/100 mL of blood indicates a failure in a feedback mechanism.

Injection of chemical X, a chemical normally produced in the body, may be required to correct this problem.

Data Table		
Time	Blood Glucose (mg/100 mL)	
	Individual 1	Individual 2
7:00 a.m.	90	150
7:30 a.m.	120	180
8:00 a.m.	140	220
8:30 a.m.	110	250
9:00 a.m.	90	240
9:30 a.m.	85	230
10:00 a.m.	90	210
10:30 a.m.	85	190
11:00 a.m.	90	170

Directions (24–25): Using the information in the data table, construct a line graph on the grid below, following the directions below.

24 Mark an appropriate scale, without any breaks in the data, on each labeled axis. [1]

25 Plot the blood glucose levels for the individual who will most likely need injections of chemical X. Connect the points and surround each point with a small circle.

Example:

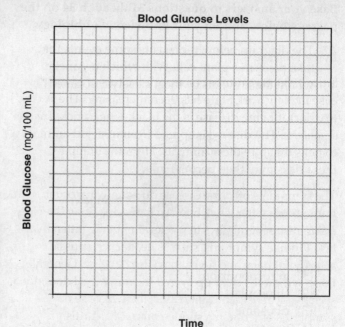

Blood Glucose Levels

Blood Glucose (mg/100 mL)

Time

26 Identify chemical X. [1]

27 State one reason for the change in blood glucose level between 7:00 a.m. and 8:00 a.m. [1]

28 What term refers to the relatively constant level of blood glucose of individual 1 between 9:00 a.m. and 11:00 a.m.? [1]

29 Select one of the paired items below and describe how the first item in the pair regulates the second item for the maintenance of homeostasis. [1]

- insulin—blood sugar level
- CO_2 in blood—breathing rate

Base your answers to questions 31 through 34 on the passage below and on your knowledge of biology.

Lyme Disease

Since 1980, the number of reported cases of Lyme disease in New York State has been increasing. The vector (carrier) of Lyme disease is the black-legged tick, *Ixodes scapularis*. The disease is spread from infected animals to ticks that bite these animals. Humans bitten by these ticks may then become infected.

The symptoms of Lyme disease do not always occur immediately after a tick bite. An individual may develop a skin rash several days to weeks after being bitten by a tick. Flu-like symptoms, such as headaches, muscle aches, joint pain, and fever, may also develop. Generally, these symptoms clear up even if the individual does not seek medical help. In some cases, there may be no symptoms other than a sudden onset of arthritis. However, in a small number of cases, if the infection is not treated, it may lead to chronic arthritis, disorders of the heart and nervous system, or in a few cases, death. A blood test can help to confirm a diagnosis, and antibiotics are effective in treating the infection.

People may take preventive action by frequently checking themselves and their pets for ticks, tucking their pant legs into socks when walking through woods or high grass, wearing light-colored clothing to aid in spotting a tick, and using insect repellent.

30 Describe how Lyme disease is transmitted. [1]

31 State one way people might protect themselves from Lyme disease. [1]

32 State two symptoms that may occur if a person has Lyme disease. [2]

33 State one danger of ignoring any symptoms that may develop after a tick bite. [1]

Base your answers to questions 35 through 37 on the information and data table below and on your knowledge of biology.

Twenty-five geranium plants were placed in each of four closed containers and then exposed to the light conditions shown in the data table. All other environmental conditions were held constant for a period of two days. At the beginning of the investigation, the quantity of carbon dioxide (CO_2) present in each container was 250 cm^3 (cubic centimeters). The data table shows the amount of CO_2 remaining in each container at the end of two days.

Changes in CO_2 Levels			
Container	Color of Light	CO_2 (cm^3) at Start	CO_2 (cm^3) After 2 Days
1	blue	250	50
2	red	250	75
3	green	250	200
4	orange	250	150

34 The independent variable in this investigation was the
(1) type of plant
(2) color of light
(3) amount of CO_2 in each container at the beginning of the investigation
(4) number of days needed to complete the investigation

35 State the problem being investigated in this experiment. [1]

36 Identify the source of the carbon used in photosynthesis. [1]

Part C

Base your answers to questions 38 through 40 on the information below and on your knowledge of biology.

An investigation was performed to determine the effects of enzyme X on three different disaccharides (double sugars) at 37°C. Three test tubes were set up as shown in the diagram below.

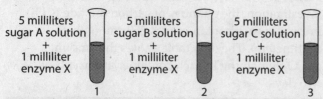

At the end of 5 minutes, the solution in each test tube was tested for the presence of disaccharides (double sugars) and monosaccharides (simple sugars). The results of these tests are shown in the table below.

Result of Sugar Test			
	Test Tube 1	Test Tube 2	Test Tube 3
Monosaccharide	not present	not present	present
Disaccharide	present	present	not present

37 What can be concluded about the activity of enzyme X from the data table? [1]

38 With only the materials list supplied below and common laboratory equipment, design an investigation that would show how a change in pH would affect the activity of enzyme X. Your design must include a *detailed procedure* and a *data table*. [3]

       Materials
       Enzyme *X*
       Sugar *C* Solution
       Indicators
       Substances of various pH values —
            vinegar (acidic)
            water (neutral)
            baking soda (basic)

39 State one safety precaution that should be used during the investigation. [1]

40 Enzyme molecules are affected by changes in conditions within organisms. Explain how a prolonged, excessively high body temperature during an illness could be fatal to humans. your answer must include:
- the role of enzymes in a human [1]
- the effect of this high body temperature on enzyme activity [1]
- the reason this high body temperature can result in death [1]

Base your answer to question 42–44 on the information below and on your knowledge of biology.

41–43 In order to enroll in most schools, students must be vaccinated against certain viral diseases, such as mumps. Even with these vaccinations, many students still suffer from other diseases. Discuss how a vaccination works and why some students still become infected with other diseases. In your answer, be sure to:

- identify what is present in a vaccine that stimulates an immune response [1]
- describe how a vaccine protects against disease [1]
- state why a student vaccinated against mumps can still be infected by the pathogens that cause other diseases, such as chicken pox [1]

44 State one way guard cells of a leaf help to maintain homeostasis in the plant? [1]

Genetic Continuity

Genes in Cells

What do **You** Think?

The genes in my brain cells are different from the genes in my liver cells.

The genes in all of my cells are the same and all of them are turned on and making proteins.

The genes that are turned on in my brain are not the same genes as the ones turned on in my liver.

3 Genetic Continuity

Vocabulary

asexual reproduction	egg	replicate
biotechnology	expressed	selective breeding
body cell	genes	sexual reproduction
bond	genetic engineering	sperm
chromosome	genetic recombination	subunit
clone	heredity	template
DNA	mutation	traits

Topic Overview

When two organisms reproduce, their offspring receive genetic instructions, called **genes**, from each parent. The genes determine which **traits**—or characteristics—each offspring will have. All organisms—whether they are animals, plants, or members of one of the other kingdoms—pass their genetic characteristics along in this manner. Because of this transfer of genetic information, offspring tend to resemble their parents.

Heredity and Genes

Heredity is the passing of genetic information from one generation to the next through reproduction. The hereditary information (**DNA**) is organized in the form of genes located in the **chromosomes** of each cell. Recall that chromosomes, which are found in the cell nuclei, contain the DNA molecules. (See Figure 3-1.) It is the DNA molecules that carry the genetic information of the cell.

A human cell contains many thousands of genes in its nucleus, and each gene carries a separate piece of coded information. The traits inherited by an individual can be determined by one pair of genes or by several pairs of genes. It is also true that a single gene pair can sometimes influence more than one trait. Table 3-1 shows several examples of these variations.

Chromosome

Unwinding

DNA

Figure 3-1. Chromosomes contain DNA: Notice that the chromosome contains one very long double strand of DNA.

Table 3-1. Human Traits Inherited with Different Numbers of Genes	
Trait	**Number of Gene Pairs Needed to Affect Trait**
Cystic fibrosis	Single gene pair
Skin color	Multiple gene pairs
Sickle cell disease	Single gene pair affecting multiple traits

Some traits that an organism inherits are readily observable. These include traits such as hair color, leaf shape, flower scent, and wing structure. The overall structure of the body is also an observable trait that is inherited from the parents. Some children, for example, inherit long, slender toes or large ear lobes.

Other traits are not so obvious. Less obvious traits may involve a defective heart, a single kidney, or how some of the body's chemicals function. Examples include the ability to produce insulin, the types of receptors present on a cell membrane, and whether an individual can make a particular respiratory enzyme.

Methods of Reproduction

There are two common methods of reproduction: asexual and sexual. The major difference between these two methods is whether one or two parents are involved in producing the offspring. **Asexual reproduction** involves one parent or individual (often a single-celled organism); **sexual reproduction** involves two parents.

Asexual Reproduction In organisms that reproduce asexually, all the genetic instructions (genes) come from one individual or parent. Since the genes are all from one parent, offspring are usually identical to the parent.

Because the coded instructions in their cells are the same as the instructions in their parent's cells, asexually produced offspring are genetically identical to their parents. Identical genetic copies are known as **clones.** Because they are asexually produced, entire populations of bacteria—perhaps millions of cells—may be genetically identical clones.

Sexual Reproduction In organisms that reproduce sexually, two parents are required to produce offspring. Each parent produces sex cells. **Sperm** are the sex cells produced by the male; the **egg** is the sex cell produced by the female. Recall that genes in **body cells**—cells other than sex cells—occur in pairs, but each sex cell contains only one gene from each pair. The offspring that results from sexual reproduction therefore receives half of its genetic information from the female parent (via the egg) and half from the male parent (via the sperm).

Genetic Recombination When a sperm and egg combine to form a new cell with a complete set of genetic instructions, a unique combination of genes results. The term for this is **genetic recombination.** This unique combination of thousands of genes produces an offspring that may resemble either or both parents in many ways but will not be identical to either of them.

Review Questions

Set 3.1

1. A cell is represented in the diagram below.

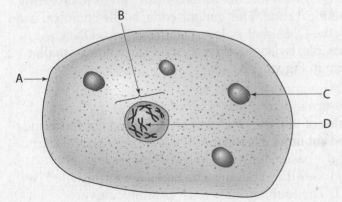

Which statement about the cell is correct?

(1) Structure A synthesizes and secretes cellular products.
(2) Structure B contains chromosomes involved in transmitting genetic information.
(3) Structure C utilizes DNA in the process of photosynthesis.
(4) Structure D is the site of protein synthesis.

2. Which materials are composed of DNA?

(1) proteins   (3) nerve secretions
(2) genes   (4) fluid in vacuoles

3. In an animal cell, DNA is found in the greatest concentration in the

(1) vacuole   (3) nucleus
(2) ribosome   (4) cytoplasm

4. Cystic fibrosis is a genetic disease. Examine the illustration below.

Father with cystic fibrosis	Mother who does not have cystic fibrosis
Father has two abnormal genes for the trait	Mother has ???

Child with cystic fibrosis
Child has two abnormal genes for the trait

The mother's cells most likely contained

(1) a disease-causing virus
(2) one normal gene and one abnormal gene
(3) two normal genes
(4) an abnormal number of chromosomes

5. Bacteria in culture A produce slime capsules around their cell walls. A biologist removed the DNA from some of the bacteria in culture A. He then injected it into bacteria in culture B, which normally do not produce slime capsules. After the injection, bacteria with slime capsules began to appear in culture B. What conclusion could best be drawn from this investigation?

(1) The bacteria in culture A are mutations.
(2) Bacteria reproduce faster when they have slime capsules.
(3) The slime capsules of bacteria in culture B contain DNA.
(4) DNA is most likely involved in the production of slime capsules.

6. The letters in the diagram below represent genes on a particular chromosome.

Gene *B* contains the code for an enzyme that cannot be synthesized unless gene *A* is also active. Which statement best explains why this can occur?

(1) A hereditary trait can be determined by more than one gene.
(2) Genes are made up of double-stranded segments of DNA.
(3) All the genes on a chromosome act to produce a single trait.
(4) The first gene on each chromosome controls all the other genes on the chromosome.

7. Which cell structure includes all of the others?

(1) nucleus   (3) DNA
(2) gene   (4) chromosome

The Genetic Code

The inherited instructions (genes) that are passed from parent to offspring exist in the form of a chemical code. This genetic code, as the chemical code is called, is contained in the DNA molecules of all organisms. DNA molecules resemble a flexible, twisted ladder formed from many smaller repeating units, as shown in Figure 3-2.

DNA Structure

Like other large molecules of life, the DNA molecule is made of thousands of smaller sections called **subunits**. Each subunit has three chemical parts: a sugar, a phosphate, and a base. The subunits vary from one another according to the kind of bases they contain. The bases are represented by the letters A, G, C, and T. The four subunits of DNA molecules are

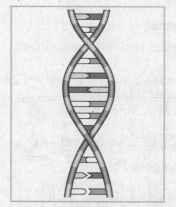

Figure 3-2. Model of a section of a DNA molecule

arranged in pairs, each subunit forming one side and half of one rung of the "twisted ladder." Base A of one subunit always pairs with the base T of another subunit. In a similar way, base G always pairs with base C. Figure 3-3 shows the details of the structure in an untwisted molecule.

Once the chemical and structural properties of DNA were discovered by scientists, it became clear how this molecule could contain a kind of message that functions as a code. Notice in Figure 3-3 that the sequence of bases on this molecule's left strand, reading from top to bottom, is ACAG. A different molecule might have a sequence in the same position reading GCAG or AACG. The specific sequence of bases in a DNA molecule forms a coded message. The message of a single gene is often a sequence of hundreds of bases. The code for an entire human is estimated to be around 3 billion base pairs!

DNA Replication

The ability to copy the coded instructions in the DNA molecule is critical to its function. Knowing the chemical makeup and structure of DNA molecules gave scientists an immediate clue to how the molecule could be copied, or **replicated.** When scientists realized that the bases used weak chemical bonds to pair with each other, they also realized that the DNA could separate at that weak **bond** to form two single strands. Each single strand became a **template**, or pattern, for a new molecule.

The new molecule was built by attaching new subunits to each template strand, always following the base pairing rules of linking A with T and C with G. The result is the formation of two new molecules whose base pair sequences are exactly alike. See Figure 3-4.

When the structure of DNA was determined, scientists finally understood how cells could copy and transfer information to new cells each time they divide and to new offspring during reproduction. Replication produces two identical copies of the cell's genetic information, each ready to be passed from the parent cell to two offspring cells during cell division. Offspring cells are commonly called daughter cells.

Proteins and Cell Functioning

The work of the cell is carried out by the many types of molecules the cell assembles (synthesizes). Many of these molecules are proteins. Protein molecules are long chains. They are formed from various combinations of 20 kinds of amino acids arranged in a specific sequence.

The sequence of amino acids in a particular protein influences the shape of the molecule. This is because some of the amino acid parts are attracted to (and may bond with) other amino-acid parts of the chain. The connections that form between different parts of the chain cause it to fold and bend in a specific way. The final folded shape

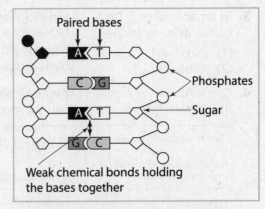

Figure 3-3. **Portion of a DNA molecule:** A single subunit is shown in black. The bases of the DNA molecule are arranged in pairs, represented here by letters. The base pairs form the rungs of the twisted DNA ladder. The sugar and phosphate of each subunit form the sides of the ladder and are connected by strong chemical bonds. The two sides are held together by weak chemical bonds between the paired bases. (Bonds are the links between atoms that hold molecules together.)

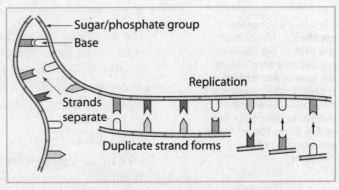

Figure 3-4. **The replication of a DNA molecule:** This is how cells copy their genetic information to be passed on to two offspring cells when cell division occurs. Both strands are replicated at the same time.

of the protein enables it to carry out its function in the cell. Many proteins made by a cell become enzymes that regulate chemical reactions. Remember that an enzyme can interact with a specific molecule because their shapes correspond.

Some of the proteins made in cells become parts of organelles, such as the cell membrane. Other proteins include the hormone insulin or the many antibodies that bind to antigen molecules on pathogens. The color of your eyes and skin are also the result of proteins synthesized by your body.

The DNA-Protein Connection

Cells store vast amounts of coded information in their genes. Much of this coded information is used to make the thousands of proteins that each cell requires for its functions and the structures it contains. The proteins for these structures and functions are made at the ribosomes according to the directions stored in the cell's DNA code.

Because offspring inherit genetic information from their parents, their cells make many of the same proteins. This is what causes the resemblance between some children and their parents. Making many of the same proteins causes both parent and offspring to form similar structures that give them similar features. One example of a protein-dependent trait includes hair texture (curly, straight, or kinky).

If a parent's DNA carries a code for a protein that does not function correctly, the children may also make that defective protein. For example, an albino does not produce the usual amount of eye, hair, or skin color pigment. The condition is caused by a defect in the gene that codes for the protein that produces color pigment. If albino parents pass this gene to their offspring, they, too, may not produce the normal color pigment.

Protein Synthesis The process of synthesizing a protein from DNA begins in the nucleus. There, the DNA code of a particular gene is "read" by a special enzyme and used to produce a "messenger" molecule. This messenger molecule then travels to the ribosomes in the cell's cytoplasm. With the aid of specialized transfer molecules, amino acids are moved to the ribosomes for assembly into protein. They are bonded in the order specified by the messenger molecule. In this way, the sequence of amino acids of any protein, and therefore its overall structure, is determined by the gene's DNA sequence in the nucleus. The process is shown in Figure 3-5.

Figure 3-5. Protein synthesis: Notice that the DNA in the nucleus supplies the instructions for how to assemble the protein to the messenger molecule. The transfer molecules help assemble amino acids. The assembly process occurs at a ribosome.

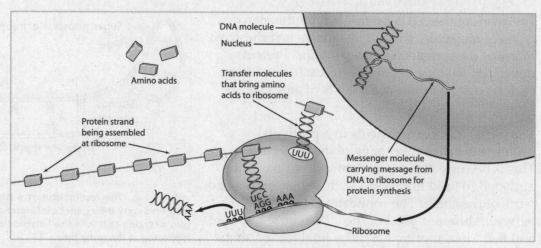

DNA molecule

Nucleus

Amino acids

Transfer molecules that bring amino acids to ribosome

Protein strand being assembled at ribosome

Messenger molecule carrying message from DNA to ribosome for protein synthesis

Ribosome

8. In a DNA molecule, the letters A, T, C, and G represent

(1) bases
(2) sugars
(3) starches
(4) proteins

9. The individuality of an organism is determined by the organism's

(1) amino acids
(2) nitrogen bases
(3) DNA base sequence
(4) order of ribosomes

10. What would most likely happen if the ribosomes in a cell were not functioning?

(1) The cell would undergo uncontrolled mitotic cell division.
(2) The synthesis of enzymes would stop.
(3) The cell would produce antibodies.
(4) The rate of glucose transport in the cytoplasm would increase.

11. The diagram below represents a portion of a DNA molecule.

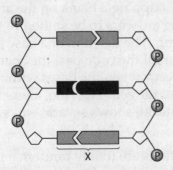

The letter X represents two bases that are

(1) identical and joined by weak bonds
(2) identical and joined by strong bonds
(3) a part of the genetic code of the organism
(4) amino acids used to build folded protein molecules

12. The kinds of genes an organism possesses are dependent on the

(1) type of proteins in the organism's nuclei
(2) sequence of bases in the organism's DNA
(3) number of ribosomes in the organism's cytoplasm
(4) size of the mitochondria in the organism's cells

13. What is the role of DNA molecules in the synthesis of proteins?

(1) They catalyze the formation of bonds between amino acids.
(2) They determine the sequence of amino acids in a protein.
(3) They transfer amino acids from the cytoplasm to the nucleus.
(4) They supply energy for protein synthesis.

14. The diagram at the right represents a molecule of

(1) ATP
(2) protein
(3) carbohydrate
(4) DNA

15. During replication, the strands of a double-stranded DNA molecule separate when the bonds are broken between their paired bases.

Explain why, in terms of the genetic code, it is important that the molecule separate between the bases and not at some other point. [1]

Base your answers to questions 16 and 17 on the diagram below and on your knowledge of biology.

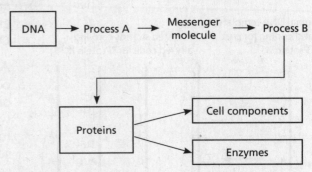

16. Within which organelle does process A occur?

(1) ribosome   (3) vacuole
(2) nucleus   (4) cell membrane

17. Within a living cell, which organelles are directly necessary for process B to occur?

(1) ribosomes   (3) vacuoles
(2) mitochondria   (4) cell membranes

18. In all living cells, DNA controls cellular activities by

(1) determining the order of amino acids in protein molecules
(2) regulating the concentration of molecules on both sides of the cell membrane
(3) varying the rates of starch synthesis
(4) coordinating active and passive transport

19. Which cell organelle indicated in the diagram controls the synthesis of enzymes?

(1) A
(2) B
(3) C
(4) D

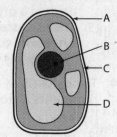

20. The sequence of amino acids that makes up a protein molecule is determined by the sequence of

(1) bases in DNA
(2) glucose in DNA
(3) ribosomes in the cytoplasm
(4) chloroplasts in the vacuoles

21. In DNA, the base represented by an A always pairs with the base represented by

(1) A (2) T (3) C (4) G

22. The presence of DNA is important for cellular metabolic activities because DNA

(1) directs the production of enzymes
(2) is a structural component of cell membranes
(3) directly increases the solubility of nutrients
(4) is a major component of the cytoplasm

Mutations

Genes are actually segments of DNA molecules. Any alteration of the DNA sequence is a **mutation**, which changes the normal message carried by the gene. Many mutations involve the substitution of one base for another. This often causes a different amino acid to be placed in a particular position in the growing protein chain. Some mutations involve the insertion of an additional base into an existing DNA sequence. This affects all of the code past the change, just as skipping a blank on the answer sheet for a test can cause all of the remaining answers to be shifted to the next blank, making almost all of them wrong. The deletion of a base from the normal gene sequence would also alter all the code past the change.

Some mutations occur when the bases within a gene are accidentally rearranged. This, too, alters the genetic code. Figure 3-6 shows several ways that DNA can mutate.

All of these alterations are totally random and can occur anywhere along the molecule, making the result of the change almost impossible to predict. However, when a DNA sequence is changed, it is quite likely that the protein it codes for may be assembled incorrectly. If some amino acids are replaced by others, or if their sequence is different, the folding of the protein may be different. Incorrect folding means that the protein's shape would not be normal. This could cause the protein to malfunction. One mutation caused by a substitution is sickle cell disease. (See Figure 3-7.)

Mutations can cause such serious changes that the cell may die. However, if a mutated cell does survive and can replicate its DNA, its changed instructions will be copied and passed on to every cell that develops from it. In sexually reproducing organisms, only mutations found in sex cells can be inherited by the offspring.

Original DNA template strand coding for part of "Protein X"

Mutated strands carrying altered code for "Protein X"

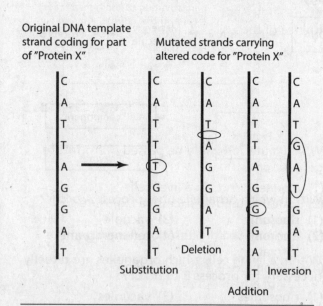

Figure 3-6. Mutation of DNA: The DNA on the left is part of the original template strand that codes for protein X. The four strands on the right show the DNA that would result from several types of mutations.

DNA and Individuality Although an individual's body cells all originally come from a single cell, the body is made up of many types of cells. Each body cell's nucleus—whether it is a nerve cell, skin cell, or bone cell—has a complete set of identical genetic instructions for that individual.

For years, scientists wondered how cells with identical genetic instructions could be so different. The answer is that each kind of cell uses only some of the genetic information it contains. It uses only the instructions it needs to operate its own kind of cell. For instance, information for building all of a person's enzymes is coded in the chromosomes of each cell, but a muscle cell uses only the specific enzymes that are needed by a muscle cell.

Both the internal and external environment of the cell can influence which genes are activated in that cell. Some of this influence may occur during development, leading to the many different types of cells that an organism needs.

The selective activation of genes in a cell may continue as conditions change throughout life. For instance, chemical signals from within the cell or from other cells may activate a particular gene. Hormones are one kind of molecule that can activate parts of a cell's DNA code, leading to the production of a particular protein.

Although genes are inherited, an organism's environment can affect the way some genes are revealed, or **expressed**, in the organism. For example, in some animals, such as the Himalayan rabbit, the outside temperature can cause the activation or inactivation of the genes for fur color. When the rabbit's body area is cold, black fur grows. If the same body area becomes warm, white fur grows instead. (See Figure 3-8.) The environment can also influence human genes. Studies of identical twins (those with identical genetic information) who were raised in different environments show that they have differences that can only be explained by the influence of the environment on gene expression.

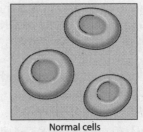

Figure 3-7. **Effects of a substitution mutation:** Normal red blood cells are round. The abnormal cell shapes are due to a substitution mutation that forms a defective protein which changes the cell's shape.

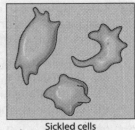

Figure 3-8. **Body temperature and fur color in the Himalayan rabbit:** From what you know about the activation and inactivation of the genes for fur color in this animal, why do you think the ears, feet, nose, and tail are black?

Review Questions

Set 3.3

23. A dog breeder can determine that the sudden appearance of hairlessness in one of the puppies is a mutation if the dog

    (1) is still hairless after 5 years
    (2) shows no change in the hairless condition after its diet is changed
    (3) develops other conspicuous differences from the parent
    (4) is bred and the trait is capable of being inherited

24. Explain how a change in the sequence of nitrogen bases in a DNA molecule could result in a gene mutation. [1]

25. Which mutation could be passed on to future generations?

    (1) a gene change in a liver cell
    (2) cancer caused by excessive exposure to the sun
    (3) a chromosomal alteration during gamete formation
    (4) random breakage of a chromosome in a leaf cell of a maple tree

26. Mutations can be transmitted to the next generation if they are present in

    (1) brain cells   (3) body cells
    (2) sex cells   (4) muscle cells

27. Overexposure of animals to X-rays is dangerous because X-rays are known to damage DNA. A direct result of this damage is cells with

(1) unusually thick cell walls
(2) no organelles located in the cytoplasm
(3) abnormally large chloroplasts
(4) changes in chromosome structure

28. The diagram below shows a portion of a DNA molecule. The base sequence of the unlabeled strand shown in the diagram is *most* likely

(1) G-A-G-T
(2) C-U-C-A
(3) T-C-T-G
(4) G-A-G-U

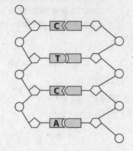

29. The individuality of an organism is determined by the

(1) sequence of bases in DNA
(2) number of amino acids in a cell
(3) position of ribosomes in the cytoplasm
(4) number of bases in the mitochondria

30. In which situation could a mutation be passed on to the offspring of one of the organisms listed in the data table below?

Data Table	
Name of Organism	Number of Chromosomes in a Body Cell
Human	46
Fruit fly	8

(1) Ultraviolet radiation causes fruit-fly wing cells to undergo uncontrolled division, resulting in cells with 9 chromosomes.
(2) A cell in the wall of the human uterus undergoes a change, resulting in cells with 47 chromosomes.
(3) A primary sex cell in a human forms a sperm that contains 23 chromosomes.
(4) A cell in the ovary of the fruit fly undergoes a chromosomal change that results in 5 chromosomes per egg cell.

31. A change in the sequence of bases in a DNA molecule is most accurately referred to as

(1) an insertion, deletion, or substitution
(2) a chromosomal replication
(3) carbohydrate molecule synthesis
(4) selective breeding

Genetic Engineering

Genetic engineering is a new technology that humans use to alter the genetic instructions in organisms. The idea of altering organisms to have more desirable traits, however, is not new. In fact, **biotechnology**—the application of technology to biological science—has been producing useful products for thousands of years. Cheese and bread are just two examples of "biotech" products made with the use of microbes.

Throughout recorded history, humans have also used **selective breeding**—a process that produces domestic animals and new varieties of plants with traits that are particularly desirable. Many meat products, for example, come from animals that have been bred to contain less fat. In addition, many of the fruits and vegetables we consume have been selectively bred to be larger, sweeter, hardier, or even juicier.

To breed a better plant, farmers might select a bean plant that produces many pods and then crossbreed it with a bean plant that resists fungus infections. The farmers would expect to get seeds that would grow into bean plants with both features.

Gene Manipulation

In recent years, plants and animals have been genetically engineered by manipulating their DNA instructions. The result of this genetic manipulation is new characteristics and new varieties of organisms. Consequently, we have been able to produce plants with many beneficial traits. In one instance, plants can now contain genes with the instructions for making chemicals that kill the insects that feed on them. Scientists have also engineered bacteria that can be used to clean up oil spills or that produce human growth hormone.

The basic method that alters genes in organisms uses special enzymes. These enzymes cut DNA segments in a way that allows the segments to be <u>spliced</u>, or moved and attached, to the DNA of a new organism. Once in the new organism, the transferred genes direct the new organism's cells to make the same protein product as the original organism. For example, when we move a human insulin-producing gene into a bacterial cell, the bacterium—and all its offspring—will produce human insulin. This provides a way to produce large quantities of a hormone at low cost. Genes for other human proteins have also been inserted into bacterial cells, as illustrated in Figure 3-9.

Other enzymes have been found that can be used to make many copies of segments of DNA. These can be used to increase the amount of DNA available from a tiny sample. This procedure is helpful even when only a drop of blood or saliva is found at a crime scene. By copying and re-copying the DNA in the sample, criminal investigators can produce a sample that is large enough to test. The test results may identify or clear suspects.

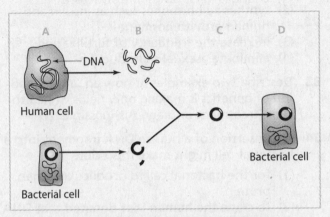

Figure 3-9. **Genetic engineering using bacteria:** On the left (area A), a special enzyme is used to cut a segment of DNA from a human cell and to also cut open a circular piece of DNA from a bacterial cell. When the piece of human DNA is mixed with the open loop of bacterial DNA (area B), they join to form a closed loop (area C). That loop is then taken up by another bacterial cell (area D). The transformed bacterial cell will produce the protein product of the human DNA segment and that DNA loop will be duplicated and passed to all future offspring.

Applications of Biotechnology

The health care field has much to gain through our increasing knowledge of genetics and biotechnology. New methods enable us to locate and decode genes that cause diseases. Once we have a better understanding of the gene's specific defect, we may be able to develop ways to treat the disease. In some cases, we may be able to alter the DNA in affected cells and cure the person.

Due to mutations in their genes, people with genetic diseases are sometimes unable to produce certain hormones, enzymes, or other body chemicals. At times, we can extract these chemicals from animals, such as sheep and cattle. These extractions, however, can be expensive, and the chemicals may contain contaminants that cause side effects. If scientists can produce the chemicals using genetically engineered organisms, we may be able to economically provide the missing chemicals in a pure enough form to avoid the side effects associated with chemicals obtained from animal sources.

32. Genetic engineering is used in the biotechnology industry to

(1) eliminate all infections in livestock
(2) synthesize hormones such as insulin and human growth hormone
(3) increase the frequency of fertilization
(4) eliminate asexual reproduction

33. Describe two examples of how an understanding of genetics is making new fields of health care (treatment or diagnosis) possible. [1]

34. The insertion of a human DNA fragment into a bacterial cell might make it possible

(1) for the bacterial cell to produce a human protein
(2) to clone the human that donated that DNA fragment
(3) for humans to become immune to an infection by this type of bacteria
(4) to clone this type of bacteria

35. In a DNA sample, 15% of the bases are thymine (T). What percentage of the bases in this sample are cytosine (C)?

(1) 15%   (3) 35%
(2) 30%   (4) 85%

Base your answers to questions 36 through 40 on the passage below and on your knowledge of biology.

Advances with Cells and Genes

Recent advances in cell technology and gene transplanting have allowed scientists to perform some interesting experiments, including splicing human DNA into the chromosomes of bacteria. The altered bacteria express the added genes.

Bacteria reproduce rapidly under certain conditions. This means that bacteria with the gene for human insulin could multiply rapidly, resulting in a huge bacterial population capable of producing large quantities of human insulin.

The traditional source of insulin has been the pancreases of slaughtered animals. Continued use of this insulin can trigger allergic reactions in some humans. The new bacteria-produced insulin is actually human insulin. As a result, it does not produce many side effects.

The bacteria used for these experiments are *E. coli*, which are found in the digestive system of humans and many other animals. Some scientists question these experiments and are concerned that the altered *E. coli* may accidentally get into water supplies.

For each of the statements below, write the number 1 if the statement is true according to the passage, the number 2 if the statement is false according to the passage, or the number 3 if not enough information is given in the passage.

36. Transplanting genetic material into bacteria is a simple task. [1]

37. Under certain conditions, bacteria reproduce at a rapid rate. [1]

38. The continued use of insulin from animals may cause harmful side effects in some people. [1]

39. The bacteria used in these experiments are normally found only in the nerve tissue of humans. [1]

40. Bacteria other than *E. coli* are unable to produce insulin. [1]

---

41. The headline "Improved Soybeans Produce Healthier Vegetable Oils" accompanies an article describing how a biotechnology company controls the types of lipids (fats) present in soybeans. The improved soybeans are most likely being developed by the process of

(1) natural selection
(2) asexual reproduction
(3) genetic engineering
(4) habitat modification

42. A product of genetic engineering technology is represented below.

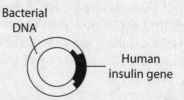

Which substance was needed to join the insulin gene to the bacterial DNA as shown?

(1) a specific carbohydrate
(2) a specific enzyme
(3) hormones
(4) antibodies

43. In the past, diabetics used horse or cow insulin to control their glucose levels. Today, as a result of genetic engineering, human insulin can be synthesized by bacteria. State *one* advantage for a person with diabetes to receive genetically engineered insulin rather than insulin taken from a horse or cow. [1]

Directions
Review the Test-Taking Strategies section of this book. Then answer the following questions. Read each question carefully and answer with a correct choice or response.

Part A

1 Hereditary information for most traits is generally located in
(1) genes found on chromosomes
(2) chromosomes found on genes
(3) the ribosomes of sperm cells
(4) the mitochondria in the cytoplasm

2 An analysis of chromosomes in a culture containing mutated cells may show the loss of one or more bases making up the chromosome. This type of chromosomal change is known as
(1) an addition
(2) an insertion
(3) a deletion
(4) a substitution

3 What is the genetic engineering technique in which DNA is transferred from the cells of one organism to the cells of another organism?
(1) gene splicing   (3) electrophoresis
(2) chromatography   (4) selective deleting

4 A change that alters the base sequence in an organism's DNA is a
(1) mutation   (3) clone
(2) replication   (4) zygote

5 The technique illustrated in the diagram is known as

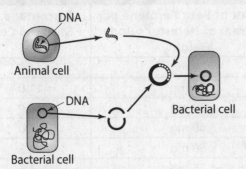

(1) genetic engineering
(2) protein synthesis
(3) internal fertilization
(4) external fertilization

6 The diagram represents a portion of DNA.

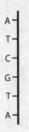

Which DNA strand could correctly pair with the one illustrated?

7 The diagram illustrates what happens to the fur color of a Himalayan rabbit after prolonged exposure to a low temperature.

The change in fur color is most likely due to
(1) the effect of heredity on gene expression
(2) the arrangement of genes on chromosomes
(3) environmental influences on gene action
(4) mutations resulting from a change in the environment

Part B

Base your answers to questions 8 and 9 on the diagram below and on your knowledge of biology. The diagram represents part of a double-stranded DNA molecule.

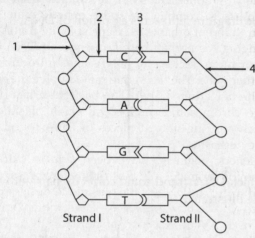

Strand I   Strand II

8 The base sequence of Strand II is most likely
   (1) C–G–G–A   (3) G–T–C–A
   (2) G–A–G–T   (4) T–G–A–C

9 Which event must occur if a nucleus containing this molecule is to undergo mitotic cell division?
   (1) The bonds at point 3 break, and the molecule replicates.
   (2) The molecule separates at point 2, and new bases attach.
   (3) The bonds at point 3 break, and the molecule deletes bases.
   (4) The bonds at points 1, 2, and 4 break, and new sequences of bases form.

10 Identify the process by which information in segments of human DNA can be expressed by a bacterial cell. [1]

Base your answers to questions 11 and 12 on the information below and on your knowledge of biology.

Some geneticists are suggesting the possibility of transferring some of the genes that influence photosynthesis from an efficient variety of crop plant to a less efficient crop plant. The goal is to produce a new variety with improved productivity.

11 To produce this new variety, the project would most likely involve
    (1) genetic engineering
    (2) a gene mutation
    (3) chromatography
    (4) vaccinations

12 Which technique would most likely be used to produce large numbers of genetically identical offspring from this new variety of plant?
    (1) cloning
    (2) sexual reproduction
    (3) electrophoresis
    (4) selective breeding

Base your answers to questions 13 through 17 on the information and data table below and on your knowledge of biology.

Certain chemicals cause mutations in cells by breaking chromosomes into pieces. Cells containing such broken chromosomes are known as mutated cells. Certain nutrients, such as beta carotene (a form of vitamin A), have the ability to prevent chromosome breakage by such mutagenic chemicals.

The results of an investigation of the effect of beta carotene in preventing chromosome damage are presented in the following data table. In the investigation, varying amounts of beta carotene per kilogram of body weight were added to the diets of hamsters. A mutagenic chemical at a constant dose rate was also added to the diets of the hamsters.

The Effect of Beta Carotene Added to Hamster Diet on Cell Mutation	
Amount of Beta Carotene per Kilogram of Hamster's Body Weight	Percentage of Mutated Cells
0 mg	11.5
20 mg	11.0
30 mg	8.0
40 mg	7.0
50 mg	4.5
75 mg	3.5
100 mg	2.0
150 mg	1.2

Using the information in the data table, construct a line graph on the grid provided. Follow the directions given.

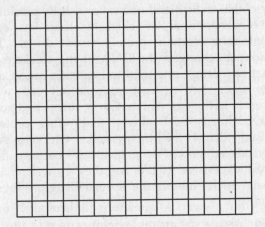

13 Mark an appropriate scale, without any breaks, on each of the axes. [1]

14 Label the axes. [1]

15 Plot the data from the table. Surround each point with a small circle and connect the points. [1]

Example:

16 State an appropriate conclusion for the above experiment regarding the use of beta carotene for the prevention of chromosome damage. Use experimental data to support your conclusion. [1]

17 Vitamins A and E are essential vitamins that can dissolve in oil. A student, knowing this and seeing the above results with beta carotene, suggested that vitamin E will increase the percentage of mutations in the cells of hamsters. State whether or not this is a valid conclusion. Support your statement with an explanation. [1]

18 Animal cells utilize many different proteins. Discuss the synthesis of proteins in an animal cell. Your answer must include at least:

- the identity of the building blocks required to synthesize these proteins [1]
- the identity of the sites in the cell where the proteins are assembled [1]
- an explanation of the role of DNA in the process of making proteins in the cell [1]

Part C

Base your answers to questions 19 through 23 on the passage below and on your knowledge of biology.

Genetic Engineering

Genetic engineering is a technique used by scientists to combine or splice genetic material from different organisms. Gene splicing involves changing the normal base sequences of DNA by removing a section of DNA and introducing another gene. The technique may involve the use of the bacterium *E. coli*. The bacterium has one large chromosome and several small plasmids, which are ring-shaped pieces of DNA found in the cytoplasm.

Genetic engineers have been able to extract plasmids from *E. coli*. Restriction enzymes are used to cut the DNA of the plasmid at designated places in the base sequence. The same enzymes are used to cut a section of human DNA. This section of human DNA is then placed into the space in the cut DNA of the bacterial plasmid. The human DNA codes for the synthesis of a product such as human growth hormone.

The spliced bacterial DNA, which now contains a piece of human DNA, is referred to as a hybrid. This hybridized plasmid is then taken in by *E. coli* cells. When the bacterium reproduces, the hybrid DNA will replicate. The offspring will possess the ability to synthesize the human growth hormone.

19 Describe a bacterial plasmid. [1]

20 Describe a hybrid plasmid. [1]

21 Explain how genetic engineers remove sections from human DNA for splicing into bacterial DNA. [1]

22 State one benefit of gene splicing. [1]

23 Explain why it is not necessary to continue splicing the gene for human growth hormone into *E. coli* once cultures of the bacteria with the spliced gene are established. [1]

Base your answers to questions 24 through 26 on the statement below and on your knowledge of biology.

Selective breeding has been used to improve the racing ability of horses.

24 Define selective breeding.

25 State how selective breeding would be used to improve the racing ability of horses. [1]

26 State *one disadvantage* of selective breeding. [1]

27–28 Knowledge of human genes gained from research on the structure and function of human genetic material has led to improvements in medicine and health care for humans.
- state two ways this knowledge has improved medicine and health care for humans [1]
- identify one specific concern that could result from the application of this knowledge [1]

Base your answers to questions 29 and 30 on the information below and on your knowledge of biology.

A biologist at an agriculture laboratory is asked to develop a better quality blueberry plant. He is given plants that produce unusually large blueberries and plants that produce very sweet blueberries.

29 Describe one way the biologist could use these blueberry plants to develop a plant with blueberries that are both large and sweet. [1]

30 The biologist is successful in producing the new plant. State one method that can be used to produce many identical blueberry plants of this new type. [1]

Base your answer to question 31–34 on the information below and on your knowledge of biology.

Chickens as Drug Factories

Scientists in Scotland have successfully produced five generations of chickens that lay eggs containing certain protein-based drugs. The scientists changed the DNA of the chickens so that two drugs, one used to treat skin cancer and the other used to treat multiple sclerosis, were present in the egg whites. Cows, sheep, and goats have already been altered to produce protein-based drugs in their milk. Chickens are considered good "drug factories" because they are inexpensive to care for, they grow fast, and their chicks inherit the special drug-producing ability.

31–34 Discuss the process scientists used to alter the DNA of the chickens. In your answer, be sure to:
- state one reason why the scientists altered the DNA of the chickens instead of altering a protein already present in the chickens [1]
- identify the type of molecule used to cut the gene from the DNA of another organism and move it into the chicken's DNA [1]
- state one advantage of using chickens for this procedure [1]
- state one reason why some people might not support this method of drug production [1]

35 One variety of wheat is resistant to disease. Another variety contains more nutrients of benefit to humans. Explain how a new variety of wheat with disease resistance and high nutrient value could be developed. In your answer, be sure to:
- identify one technique that could be used to combine disease resistance and high nutrient value in a new variety of wheat [1]
- describe how this technique would be carried out to produce a wheat plant with the desired characteristics [1]
- describe one specific difficulty (other than stating that it does not always work) in developing a new variety using this technique [1]

Reproduction and Development

Genes and Reproduction

What do **You** *Think?*

One parent gives you the genes for some traits while the genes for your other traits come from the other parent.

Boys get most of their genes from their dad and girls get most of their genes from their mom.

Both parents contribute genes for each of the traits you have.

Reproduction and Development

Vocabulary

asexual reproduction	fetus	sex cell
cloning	gamete	sexual reproduction
development	gene expression	species
differentiation	meiosis	sperm
egg	mitosis	testes
embryo	ovaries	testosterone
estrogen	placenta	uterus
expressed	progesterone	zygote
fertilization	recombination	

Topic Overview

A **species** is a group of closely related organisms that share certain
characteristics and can produce new individuals through reproduction.
For any species to survive past a single generation, reproduction is
essential. All individuals eventually die, but the species continues because
individuals reproduce. When individuals reproduce, their offspring begin
a period of **development** that ends in adulthood. Once an individual
reaches adulthood, it is usually able to reproduce and continue the species
for another generation.

Types of Reproduction

Two methods of reproduction are associated with living organisms:
asexual and sexual. **Asexual reproduction** involves just one parent and
results in one or more offspring that are genetically identical to that parent.
Sexual reproduction involves two parents and results in offspring that have
some genetic material (DNA) from each parent. The result is an organism
that may be similar to one or both parents, but is not identical to either.

Asexual Reproduction Organisms that reproduce asexually produce their
offspring in a variety of ways. In some cases they merely divide in two,
producing two new individuals. (The parent in this case *becomes* the
offspring!) Other organisms produce special cells that have a complete set
of genetic information, and these individual cells can develop into new
members of the species. Still others produce an outgrowth of the body that
later detaches to become a separate individual. Many plants can develop
from parts that are either broken off intentionally by humans or separated
naturally from the parent plant. In every case, organisms produced by
asexual reproduction have only one parent, and they have the same genetic
information (in the form of DNA) as the parent. Figure 4-1 shows some
examples of asexual reproduction.

60 Topic 4: Reproduction and Development

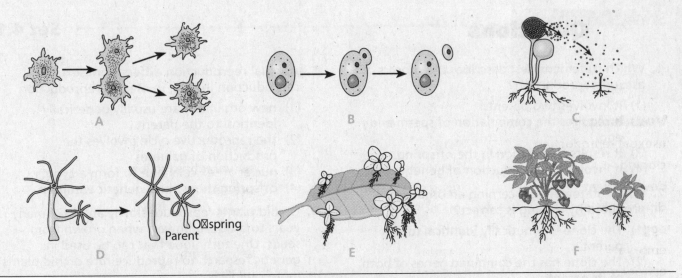

Figure 4-1. Examples of asexual reproduction: (A) An ameba divides to form two new amebas. (B) A yeast cell divides into two cells that are different sizes but genetically alike. (C) Mold spore cells reproduce the mold. (D, E, and F) Some offspring develop attached to the parent, but later separate to become independent individuals.

Parent Offspring

Sexual Reproduction In sexual reproduction, offspring receive half of their genes from one parent and half from the other. The genes are carried on chromosomes in **sex cells** (also known as **gametes** or egg or sperm cells), which join in **fertilization**. Each parent supplies half of the genetic information needed to form a complete individual. The **sperm**, which is the sex cell from the father, provides half of the information; the **egg**, which is the sex cell from the mother, provides the other half.

Offspring produced by sexual reproduction combine genes inherited from each parent's gametes. Since an offspring gets only half of its DNA from each parent, it will not be identical to either of its parents. Also, since each offspring gets a unique combination of genes from its parents, it will differ from its <u>siblings</u> (brothers and sisters).

Cloning **Cloning** is a technique that accomplishes the same end result as asexual reproduction. It is a way of making identical genetic copies. For example, if you cut a piece of stem from a plant and it grows roots and develops into a new plant, you have produced a genetically identical copy of the original plant. This could be called a clone of the plant.

Recently, however, it has also been possible to produce clones of animals that ordinarily only reproduce sexually. This is done by inserting a nucleus from a "parent" organism's cell (one that has a complete set of genetic information from that individual) into an egg cell from which the nucleus has been removed. The result is an egg that now contains not 50%, but 100% of the genetic information from a single parent. If this new egg cell with all of its genes can be made to develop normally, the resulting offspring is a clone of the individual that donated the original cell nucleus. (In mammals, the egg would be implanted and develop inside the body of the female.) Cloning has been accomplished with animals as complex as sheep and pigs.

1. Which statement best describes the process of asexual reproduction?

   (1) It involves two parents.
   (2) It requires the combination of sperm and egg.
   (3) It results in variation in the offspring.
   (4) It involves the production of genetic copies.

2. Which statement concerning an organism produced by cloning is correct?

   (1) The clone is genetically identical to its parent.
   (2) The clone has the combined genes of both of its parents.
   (3) The genetic makeup of the clone will be somewhat different from each of its parents.
   (4) The appearance of the clone will be entirely different from that of its parents.

3. A student using a compound light microscope to observe a cell saw a number of threadlike nuclear structures resembling those shown below.

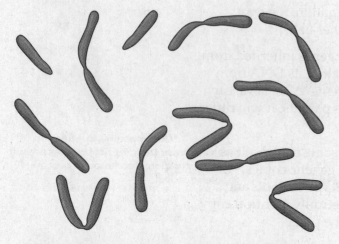

   These threadlike structures are composed primarily of

   (1) fat
   (2) glucose
   (3) DNA
   (4) ATP

4. Plants with desirable qualities can be rapidly produced from the cells of a single plant by

   (1) cloning
   (2) gamete fusion
   (3) meiosis
   (4) immune response

5. Asexual reproduction differs from sexual reproduction in that, in asexual reproduction

   (1) new organisms are usually genetically identical to the parent
   (2) the reproductive cycle involves the production of gametes
   (3) nuclei of sex cells fuse to form a zygote
   (4) offspring show much genetic variation

6. Orchid plants reproduce slowly and take many years to produce flowers when grown from seeds. One technique that can be used in genetic research to reproduce rare orchid plants more rapidly is

   (1) sexual reproduction   (3) selective breeding
   (2) fertilization   (4) cloning

7. Some bacteria produce an enzyme known as penicillinase, which prevents their destruction by penicillin. Since these same organisms reproduce asexually, they normally produce offspring that

   (1) can be killed by penicillin
   (2) have an abnormally high rate of mutation
   (3) have variable numbers of chromosomes
   (4) are resistant to penicillin

8. In plants, one way sexual reproduction differs from asexual reproduction is that in sexual reproduction

   (1) more offspring are produced
   (2) more genetic variation is seen in the offspring
   (3) the offspring and the parents are identical
   (4) more offspring survive to maturity

9. A man cuts some stems from several plants that are growing in his garden. He places the stems in wet sand until they grow roots, and then he transplants them to new pots. This method of reproducing plants is most like

   (1) sexual reproduction
   (2) cloning
   (3) natural selection
   (4) fertilization

10. Compared to the offspring of sexual reproduction in animals, the offspring of asexual reproduction will

    (1) show greater variety
    (2) be more resistant to disease
    (3) be genetically identical to the parent
    (4) grow larger

Cell Division

Cell division is the orderly separation of one cell into two. Before a cell divides, the genetic information in the DNA of the cells is duplicated exactly.

The process, by which a cell's genetic material divides, creating two complete sets of the cell's genetic material, is known as **mitosis.** Mitosis produces two cells that each have a full set of identical genes and chromosomes (unless a mutation occurs somewhere along the way).

During mitosis, one copy of the genetic information is distributed to each new cell. As a result, each new cell has all the information it needs to function properly. One-celled organisms make use of mitosis for asexual reproduction. Multicellular organisms mainly use mitosis for growth and for cell replacement and repair.

A second type of cell division is **meiosis.** This process divides the genetic material in a way that results in the production of the sex cells required by organisms that reproduce sexually. Each sex cell has only half the genetic material needed for a cell to function properly.

Mitotic Division/Mitosis

During the process of mitotic cell division, the double-stranded chromosomes that are visible during mitosis split into two identical single strands and move apart to opposite ends of the cell. This process is shown in Figure 4-3.

The process concludes when the cytoplasm divides, resulting in two smaller, but genetically identical, cells. Mitotic cell division in plants is illustrated in Figure 4-4.

Recall that DNA replication makes an identical copy of all the genetic information in the molecule. The replicated strand carries the instructions for the same proteins as in the original strand. When the DNA replicates, it is actually turning a single-stranded chromosome into a double-stranded one. The double-stranded chromosome then has a duplicate set of instructions to pass on to each of two cells, as shown in Figure 4-2.

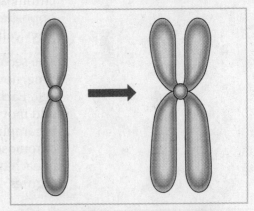

Figure 4-2. Chromosome duplication resulting from DNA replication: As a result of DNA replication, chromosomes become double-stranded.

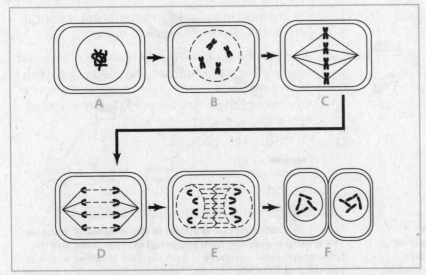

Figure 4-4. Mitotic cell division: The chromosomes in cell A have replicated, forming the double-stranded chromosomes that are finally visible in the cell at stage B. The four chromosomes line up single-file (C). Then the strands separate and move apart (D and E). The final result is two cells (F), each with four single-stranded chromosomes containing identical genetic information in their nuclei.

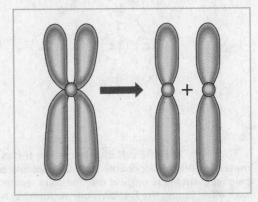

Figure 4-3. Chromosome during mitosis: When cells divide, each double-stranded chromosome separates into two identical single strands.

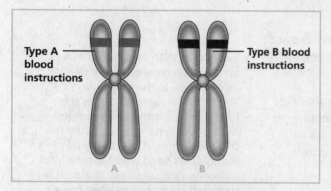

Figure 4-5. Two chromosomes with different information: The two chromosomes of each pair differ in the specific information they carry. For example, chromosome A may have coded gene instructions for type A blood, while the coded gene information on chromosome B may be for type B blood. Information for many other traits coded in the genes of these two chromosomes will be different, too, while some will be the same.

Meiotic Division/Meiosis

The gametes (sperm and eggs) formed during meiotic cell division each have only one half of the organism's genetic information—only one chromosome of each pair that is present in the body cells of that organism. However, a full set of genetic information is needed to produce a complete individual. When sperm and egg combine during **fertilization,** all of the newly paired chromosomes and all of the required genetic information are present in the fertilized egg.

Meiotic division begins with a body cell that has the full number of chromosomes typical of the species. Depending on the species, the cell contains one or more pairs of chromosomes that determine the traits of the organism. Figure 4-5 shows an example.

During the first phase of meiotic division, the double-stranded chromosomes line up in pairs in the center of the cell. The two chromosomes of each pair (still double-stranded) then separate, moving to opposite ends of the cell. Following this separation, the cell divides physically to form two cells.

The second phase involves the division of each of these two new cells. This time, however, the chromosomes line up in single file in the center of each cell. Each chromosome still consists of two strands. The strands separate and move to opposite ends of each of the dividing cells. When the process is complete, four cells have been formed, each having half the number of chromosomes of the organism's body cells. Each contains only one member of each original chromosome pair. Meiotic cell division is illustrated in Figures 4-6 and 4-7.

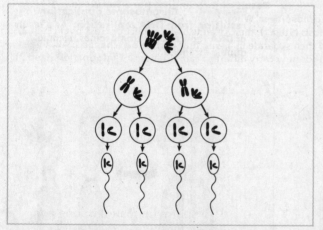

Figure 4-6. Meiotic cell division in the testes of males: Note the *four double-stranded chromosomes* (two pairs) present in the original cell. The pairs separate from each other during the first division—resulting in *two double-stranded chromosomes* in each of two cells. In the next division, the double-stranded chromosomes separate, leaving each final cell with *two single-stranded chromosomes.* These four cells can develop further into sperm cells in the testes of male individuals.

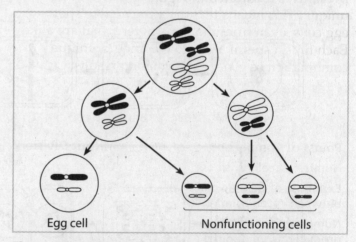

Figure 4-7. Meiotic cell division in the ovaries of females: This process is different from sperm cell formation because the cytoplasm divides unequally in each division, resulting in one large egg cell and three smaller cells that do not function. The egg cell is the one with the most cytoplasm.

Notice that the formation of cells during meiotic division, in which each cell has half the usual number of chromosomes, is very different from the duplication and distribution of a full set of chromosomes that occurs in mitotic division.

Meiotic division in females involves the same number of divisions and chromosome changes as in males. The division of the cytoplasm is where the two differ. The cytoplasm in a cell destined to become an egg cell divides unequally, resulting in one large egg cell and three small nonfunctioning cells. Meiotic division in females is shown in Figure 4-7.

Meiosis as a Source of Variation The events that occur during meiosis do more than simply divide chromosomes into smaller sets and form smaller cells. Meiosis is responsible for much of the genetic variation among the sex cells of each individual. For example, the two members of each pair of chromosomes carry different ways of expressing many of the organism's traits, so the way the different pairs randomly line up *in relation to other pairs* leads to many possible combinations in the sex cells that result. Two combinations are shown in Figure 4-8.

Another way variation can arise is by the exchange of parts of chromosomes, which occurs as they pair up during the first division. The process is sometimes called crossing-over. The result is shown in Figure 4-9. After separation, each set is unique. This means that there are no two sperm or egg cells, even from the same parent, that are alike. Each time a sperm and egg combine, a unique combination of genetic information results.

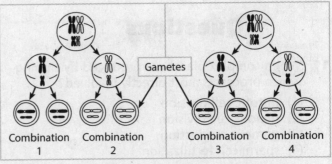

Figure 4-8. Two equally likely combinations of chromosomes lined up for meiotic division: A pair of chromosomes can be arranged in two ways when they pair up at the start of meiosis. This helps increase genetic variation. How many combinations do you see in the gametes? How would more pairs of chromosomes affect the number of possible arrangements?

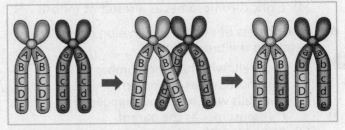

Figure 4-9. Result of exchanging parts between chromosomes: When chromosomes line up in pairs during meiosis (Step 1), their strands may connect or cross over (Step 2) and then separate in a way that parts are exchanged. All four strands now carry different combinations of information (Step 3).

Table 4-1. Summary of Mitotic and Meiotic Cell Division		
Points of Comparison	**Mitotic Division**	**Meiotic Division**
Number of cell divisions	One	Two
Exchange of genetic material between chromosomes	No	Yes
Number of functioning cells produced from original	Two	Four sperm (in males) or one egg (in females)
Genetic makeup of final cells produced	Same as original	Highly variable gametes produced, each containing half of the genetic information of the original
Function of cells produced in multicellular organisms	Growth or replacement of body cells	Combine to form the zygote for reproduction

11. When complex plants are produced by cloning, which process is most directly involved?

(1) mitotic cell division
(2) meiotic cell division
(3) gamete production
(4) sperm cell fertilization

12. If a lobster loses a claw, it is capable of growing a new one. What process makes this possible?

(1) meiosis
(2) fertilization
(3) sexual reproduction
(4) mitosis

13. Organisms that reproduce asexually usually do so by a form of cell division called

(1) meiosis
(2) mitosis
(3) gamete formation
(4) sperm formation

14. A normal body cell of a fruit fly contains eight chromosomes. Each normal gamete of this organism contains

(1) four chromosomes as a result of meiosis
(2) four chromosomes as a result of mitosis
(3) eight chromosomes as a result of meiosis
(4) eight chromosomes as a result of mitosis

15. The process of mitotic cell division normally results in the production of

(1) four cells with half the number of chromosomes as the parent
(2) two cells with the same number of chromosomes as the parent
(3) two cells with only one chromosome from each parent
(4) one cell with a replicated set of matched chromosomes

16. Each of the two daughter (or offspring) cells that result from the normal mitotic division of the original parent cell contains

(1) the same number of chromosomes but different genes than the parent cell
(2) the same number of chromosomes and genes identical to those of the parent cell
(3) one half of the number of chromosomes but different genes than those of the parent cell
(4) one half of the number of chromosomes and genes identical to those of the parent cell

17. All types of asexual reproduction involve the process known as

(1) mitosis
(2) fertilization
(3) meiotic division
(4) aging

18. The diagrams below represent the sequence of events in a cell undergoing normal meiotic cell division.

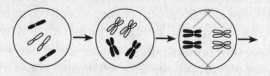

- How many cells will finally be produced? [1]
- How many chromosomes will be in each cell? [1]
- Sketch one of the final cells, showing its chromosomes. [1]

19. The species chromosome number of orangutans is 48. Which diagram represents normal fertilization in orangutans?

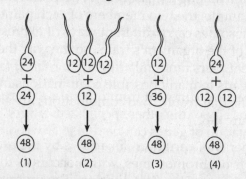

20. Which process is represented in the following photographs?

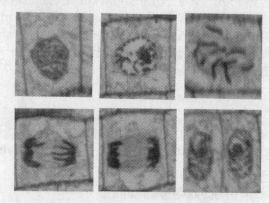

(1) mitotic cell division
(2) zygote formation
(3) fertilization
(4) recombination

21. If the sperm cells of a fish have 12 chromosomes, how many chromosomes would be found in the cells forming the scales of the fish?

(1) 6
(2) 12
(3) 24
(4) 48

Zygote Formation During fertilization, the gametes unite to form a **zygote**—a cell that contains all of the genetic information needed by the offspring. This process is known as **recombination,** since the genes from both parents recombine when fertilization occurs. Since a sex cell contains a unique combination of genetic material, the result of the random combination of any sperm and egg explains the variation found in offspring produced by sexual reproduction. This variation plays a key role in evolutionary change and species survival.

The zygote contains all the information necessary for growth, development, and eventual reproduction of the organism. The zygote divides by mitosis to form a multicellular organism. Fertilization, zygote formation, and some early mitotic divisions that occur in development are shown in Figure 4-10.

Early Development During the early stages of development, the cells that are formed by mitotic division begin to undergo **differentiation,** which simply means that they become different from one another. This leads to the formation of specialized cells, which form the tissues, and then the organs, of multicellular organisms.

In an **embryo,** an organism in an early stage of development, all the genetic information in each cell starts out the same. However, different genes are activated or deactivated in certain cells, causing them to make only some of the many proteins they are capable of synthesizing. As a result, these cells become different from others, and may develop into skin cells, muscle cells, or any of the other specialized cells of the organism. The activation or inactivation of genes can be due to environmental influences from within the cell, from surrounding cells, or from outside the organism.

When a gene is actively producing its protein, scientists say that the gene is **expressed.** There is much evidence that **gene expression,** which is the result of activated genes, can be modified through interaction with the environment. For example, fruit flies that have genes to develop curly wings will develop straight wings instead, if they are raised in a cooler than normal environment. Another example of an environmentally produced gene modification is a plant grown without light. Such a plant is white instead of green, because sunlight is needed to stimulate the gene that produces chlorophyll.

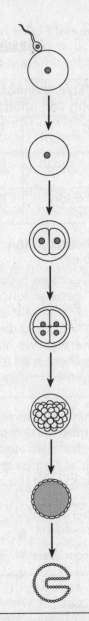

Figure 4-10. Fertilization, zygote formation, and early development: Note that all cell divisions here are by MITOTIC division.

Review Questions

Set 4.3

22. An exact duplication of the complete set of chromosomes of a cell, followed by the separation of these duplicate sets into two new cells, is known as

(1) mitotic cell division (3) meiotic cell division
(2) zygote formation (4) fertilization

23. New cells are produced within the uterus as a direct result of

(1) gamete formation
(2) meiotic cell division
(3) mitotic cell division
(4) ecological succession

24. The data table below summarizes the results of an experiment using primrose plants grown under different temperature conditions.

Data Table: Primrose Color Under Two Growing Conditions

Flower Color	Temperature of 20°C		Temperature of 31°C	
Color coded in DNA	Red	White	Red	White
Actual color expressed	Red	White	White	White

Which conclusion can be drawn from this data table?

(1) Color in primroses is determined only by gene action.
(2) Many traits are not inherited.
(3) Gene exchanges only occur when the plants are grown at lower temperatures.
(4) There is an interaction between environment and heredity.

25. When organisms reproduce sexually, the species number of chromosomes is maintained. This can be demonstrated with a diagram like the one below. Complete the diagram by filling in the blanks with the appropriate information.

Organism with 10 chromosomes in each body cell

Process A ↓ Name of process A: _____

Gamete cell Number of chromosomes in gamete cell: _____

Process B ↓ Name of process B: _____

Zygote Number of chromosomes in zygote: _____

Process C ↓ Name of process C: _____

New multicellular organism Number of chromosomes in new multicellular organism: _____

Base your answers to questions 26 through 29 on the diagrams below and on your knowledge of biology.

Diagram A represents the chromosomes in the nucleus of the body cell of a worm. Diagrams B through G represent chromosomal arrangements that may occur in other cells produced by this worm.

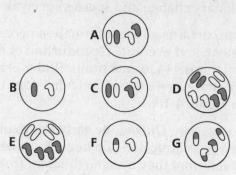

26. If meiosis failed to occur in both male and female worms, the zygote nucleus would resemble diagram

(1) E (2) G (3) C (4) D

27. If genes were exchanged between a single pair of chromosomes during gamete formation, the gamete nucleus would most closely resemble diagram

(1) F (2) B (3) C (4) G

28. The nucleus of a normal zygote formed when fertilization occurs in this species would most likely resemble diagram

(1) E (2) F (3) C (4) D

29. The nucleus of a mature gamete from a female worm would most likely resemble diagram

(1) E (2) B (3) C (4) D

30. In human females, gametes are produced in the

(1) uterus (3) ovaries
(2) testes (4) estrogen

31. Complex organisms produce sex cells that unite during fertilization forming a single cell known as

(1) an embryo (3) a clone
(2) a gamete (4) a zygote

Human Reproduction and Development

Human reproduction and development are carried out by specialized organs. The function of these organs is regulated by hormones from the endocrine system. In humans, as in nearly all mammals, fertilization and development occur internally—within the mother's body. Reproductive organs in other mammals are similar in appearance and function.

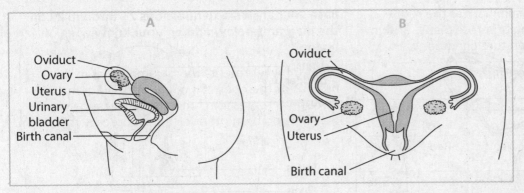

A

Oviduct
Ovary
Uterus
Urinary
bladder
Birth canal

B

Oviduct

Ovary
Uterus

Birth canal

Figure 4-11. **Two views of essential parts of the human female reproductive system and other structures:** View A is from the side; View B is from the front.

Female Reproductive System The human female reproductive system is organized to produce gametes, to support internal fertilization and development, to exchange materials through the placenta, and to provide milk to the offspring.

In human females, the **ovaries** produce egg cells (female gametes) and the hormones **estrogen** and **progesterone.** These hormones are associated with sexual development and the reproductive process. The ovaries are located near the open ends of tubes called oviducts (egg ducts). The egg cell can be fertilized in the oviduct if sperm are present. The oviducts lead to the **uterus,** where the embryo develops into a fetus. The main parts of the female reproductive system are illustrated in Figure 4-11.

After the fertilized egg sinks into the thickened wall of the uterus, a placenta begins to form. The **placenta** is the organ responsible for the passage (by diffusion) of nutrients and oxygen from the mother's blood to the fetus. Wastes from the fetus also diffuse to the mother's blood through the placenta. During birth, the muscular uterus undergoes a series of contractions that eventually push the baby out of the mother's body. The early events of pregnancy are shown in Figure 4-12.

Male Reproductive System The **testes** of the male reproductive system are the organs that produce sperm cells. The testes also produce the hormone **testosterone,** which is associated with male sexual development and reproduction. Other structures associated with the male reproductive system produce the fluids and nutrients that are needed for the proper function and delivery of the male gametes to the female reproductive system. The essential parts of the human male reproductive system are shown in Figure 4-13.

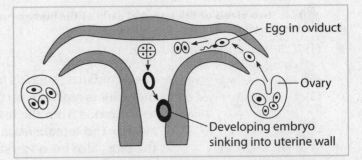

Egg in oviduct

Ovary

Developing embryo sinking into uterine wall

Figure 4-12. **Early events of pregnancy:** The egg released by the ovary travels down the oviduct where fertilization occurs. Mitotic divisions of the zygote begin as it continues to the uterus, where the developing embryo sinks into the uterine wall, and the placenta forms. The placenta will supply essential materials and remove wastes throughout the rest of the pregnancy.

Table 4-2. **The Functions of the Parts of the Human Female Reproductive System**

Structure	Function
Ovary	Produces egg cells; releases the hormones estrogen and progesterone
Oviduct	Site of fertilization; carries egg to uterus
Uterus	Site where embryo and fetus develop in association with placenta
Birth canal (vagina)	Site where sperm enter and swim to egg in oviduct; passageway for the birth of baby

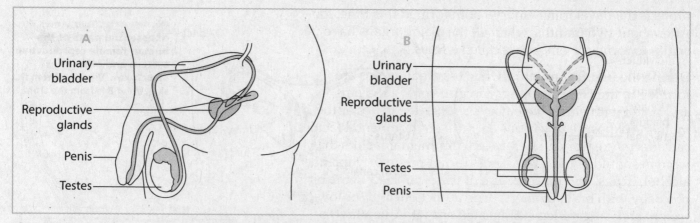

Figure 4-13. **Two views of the essential parts of the human male reproductive system and other structures:** View A is from the side; View B is from the front.

Hormonal Regulation The male reproductive system and other male characteristics, such as facial hair and a deep voice, that develop as sexual maturity is reached are influenced by several hormones, including testosterone from the testes. The development of the female reproductive system and female features, such as breast development and widening of the hips, also involves several important hormones, such as estrogen and progesterone.

Once sexual maturity is reached, females begin a regular cycle of about 28 days, during which an egg is released on about day 14. The timing of the events of this cycle is regulated by two hormones from the ovaries, along with several others from an endocrine gland in the brain. Figure 4-14 illustrates the changes in the level of several hormones associated with regulating this monthly cycle. The cycle varies slightly from individual to individual.

Although the interactions of the hormones are quite complex, estrogen and progesterone play important roles in the female reproductive cycle. Estrogen from the ovaries influences the sexual development of females. Together, estrogen and progesterone influence the preparation of the lining of the uterus so that a fertilized egg that embeds itself there can develop normally. Progesterone also maintains the uterine lining throughout pregnancy. For this reason, progesterone is often called the hormone of pregnancy. At the end of the cycle, if an egg is not fertilized, the levels of estrogen and progesterone decrease, and the lining of the uterus breaks down. Then the cycle begins again.

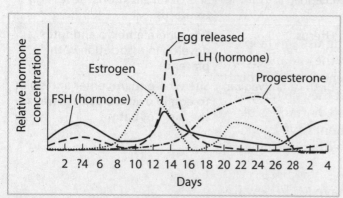

Figure 4-14. **Hormones and events associated with the monthly reproductive cycle in human females:** Notice the rise and fall in hormone levels at various times. These changes influence such events as the release of the egg from the ovary, the preparation of the uterus for a possible pregnancy, and the breakdown of the uterine lining if no pregnancy occurs. Remember that the timing of this cycle is NOT the same for everyone.

Human Development As with most other mammals, embryonic development continues in the uterus. Figure 4-15 shows some of the features of the uterus during pregnancy.

During the first part of pregnancy, cells continue to divide by mitotic division and begin to differentiate, forming tissues and organs. The placenta and a fluid-filled sac that cushions and protects the developing embryo both form at this time, too. After about two months, when all the major organs have begun to form, the embryo is called a **fetus.**

During the first few months, when essential organs are forming in the embryo, things can go wrong. Problems associated with either the embryo's inherited genes or the mother's exposure to various harmful environmental factors can affect the embryo. Harmful environmental factors that a woman should avoid at any time during pregnancy include alcohol, drugs, and tobacco. Use of these can lead to the birth of a baby with brain damage, drug addiction, and/or low birth weight and the problems associated with it. An embryo or fetus may also be harmed if the mother has a poor diet, is exposed to certain toxic substances, or gets certain infections, such as German measles or AIDS.

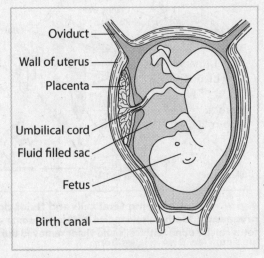

Figure 4-15. **The uterus during pregnancy**

After birth, cell differentiation and body growth continue until adulthood. During adulthood, the structures of the body slowly begin to age. Eventually, the organism weakens and dies. This process of birth, growth, development, aging, and death is a predictable pattern that applies not just to humans, but to all organisms.

Applications of Reproductive Technology

Recent discoveries by scientists have greatly changed the way we can deal with many problems involving the reproduction of humans as well as plants and other organisms. The knowledge we have gained has a variety of agricultural, ecological, and medical applications.

In the field of agriculture, scientists have produced plants that are resistant to insects, weed killers, and even frost. Such altered plants can then be cloned to produce thousands of genetically identical offspring. Using artificial insemination, scientists can generate hundreds of offspring from one farm animal. They can also freeze the sperm or fertilized eggs of an animal and transport them to animals thousands of miles away, at far less cost than transporting the animals themselves.

In the field of ecology, reproductive technology is being used to help build up populations of endangered species. Embryos from the endangered species have been transplanted into related species, who later give birth to offspring that are no different than they would be if they developed in the bodies of the endangered animals themselves. Also, hormones of insects that regulate their reproduction and development have been studied in an attempt to find ways to control insects without using poisonous chemicals.

In the field of medicine, recent scientific discoveries have led to new ways of dealing with reproductive problems in humans, other animals, and plants. Some women cannot become pregnant because of problems with their hormones, ovaries, or other parts of their reproductive systems. Reproductive technologies have enabled doctors to help infertile women become pregnant by using hormone therapy to adjust their hormones to normal levels. Sometimes doctors can extract several eggs from a woman's ovaries and fertilize them with sperm in a laboratory dish. When these

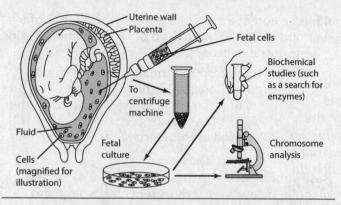

Figure 4-16. **Obtaining fetal cells and fluids during pregnancy:** Biochemical studies and chromosome analysis of the fetus can be done with cells and fluids removed during pregnancy.

fertilized eggs are implanted in the woman's uterus, a successful pregnancy may result.

Ultrasound and miniature video cameras allow doctors to view ovaries, oviducts, and other reproductive structures, or even a developing fetus, to determine if or where problems exist. Methods have also been developed to retrieve fetal cells that are present in the fluids around the developing fetus. (See Figure 4-16.) Doctors can then analyze the cells for chromosome abnormalities and the fluids for biochemical deficiencies that may threaten the health or development of the fetus.

Review Questions

Set 4.4

32. What substances are involved in controlling the production of sperm and eggs in humans?

(1) vitamins   (3) starches
(2) hormones   (4) minerals

33. Which practice is essential to good prenatal care?

(1) increased egg production
(2) frequent dieting
(3) avoidance of drugs
(4) intake of antibiotics

34. Which part of the human male reproductive system produces hormones that influence the development of male sex characteristics?

(1) penis   (3) gametes
(2) testes   (4) ovaries

35. The diagram below represents a sequence of events in a human ovary.

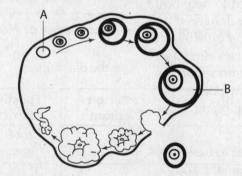

The process that occurs between stage A and stage B is known as

(1) egg formation   (3) mitotic cell division
(2) sperm formation   (4) cell recombination

36. The diagram below represents a series of events that takes place in the life cycle of humans.

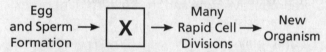

Which term best describes the event taking place in the box labeled X?

(1) fertilization   (3) meiosis
(2) immune response   (4) protein synthesis

Base your answers to questions 37 through 39 on the diagram below and on your knowledge of biology. The diagram represents the human female reproductive system.

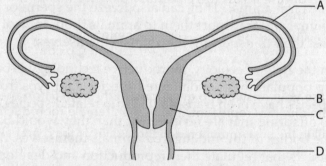

37. Fertilization usually occurs within structure

(1) A   (2) B   (3) C   (4) D

38. A placenta normally develops in structure

(1) A   (2) B   (3) C   (4) D

39. The structure that produces estrogen and progesterone is

(1) A   (2) B   (3) C   (4) D

Base your answers to questions 40 through 42 on the diagram below and on your knowledge of biology. The diagram represents the human male and female reproductive systems.

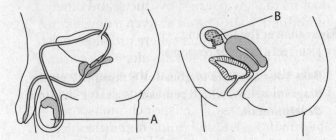

40. Gametes are produced in

(1) A, only   (3) both A and B
(2) B, only   (4) neither A nor B

41. Estrogen and progesterone are produced in

(1) A, only   (3) both A and B
(2) B, only   (4) neither A nor B

42. A substance is produced that influences both the reproductive cycle and the development of sex characteristics in

(1) A, only   (3) both A and B
(2) B, only   (4) neither A nor B

---

43. In humans and other mammals, nutrients are transferred from the mother's bloodstream to the embryo's bloodstream across the

(1) placenta   (3) ovary
(2) uterus   (4) intestine

44. Which substance is a waste that would normally diffuse across the placenta from the embryo to the mother?

(1) glucose   (3) amino acid
(2) oxygen   (4) carbon dioxide

45. The egg of a mammal is smaller than that of a bird because the embryo of the mammal obtains its nutrients from the

(1) placenta through the process of diffusion
(2) mammary glands of the mother
(3) blood of the mother when it mixes with the blood of the embryo
(4) yolk stored in the uterus of the mother

Base your answers to questions 46 and 47 on the diagram below, which represents an experiment, and on your knowledge of biology.

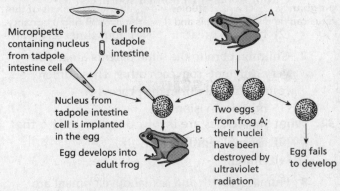

Micropipette containing nucleus from tadpole intestine cell

Cell from tadpole intestine

Nucleus from tadpole intestine cell is implanted in the egg

Egg develops into adult frog

Two eggs from frog A; their nuclei have been destroyed by ultraviolet radiation

Egg fails to develop

46. An inference that can be made from this experiment is that

(1) adult frog B will have the same genetic traits as the tadpole
(2) adult frog A can develop only from an egg and a sperm
(3) fertilization must occur in order for frog eggs to develop into adult frogs
(4) the nucleus of a body cell fails to function when transferred to other cell types

47. Other scientists substituted a nucleus from a frog sperm cell and no adult frog developed. Explain why a sperm cell nucleus would not work in this procedure. [1]

Base your answers to questions 48 through 51 on the diagram below and on your knowledge of biology. The diagram represents the human female reproductive system.

Fill in the boxes numbered 48 through 51 in the chart below using the information from the diagram.

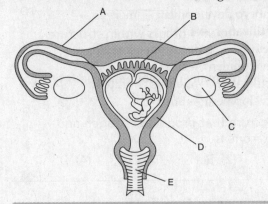

Name of Structure	Letter on Diagram	Function of Structure
48. _____ [1]	**49.** _____ [1]	produces gametes
uterus	D	**50.** _____ [1]
51. _____ [1]	B	transports oxygen directly to the embryo

Directions

Review the Test-Taking Strategies section of this book. Then answer the following questions. Read each question carefully and answer with a correct choice or response.

Part A

1 Compared to the number of chromosomes in a normal human body cell, the number of chromosomes in a normal sperm cell is
(1) the same   (3) half as great
(2) twice as great   (4) four times as great

2 Children born to the same parents are usually very different from each other. These differences result primarily from the process of
(1) mitotic division
(2) meiosis
(3) asexual reproduction
(4) cloning

3 Human growth and sexual development are controlled by
(1) nerves   (3) the digestive system
(2) hormones   (4) the excretory system

4 The diagram below represents the human male reproductive system.

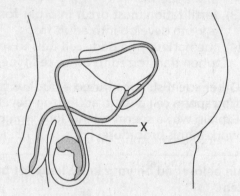

If structure X were cut and tied off at the line, which change would occur immediately?
(1) Hormones would no longer be produced.
(2) Sperm would no longer be produced.
(3) Sperm would be produced but no longer released from the body.
(4) Urine would be produced but no longer released from the bladder

Base your answers to question 5 through 7 on the diagram below, which represents a stage in human development.

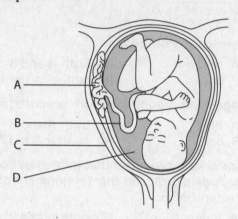

5 The exchange of oxygen, food, and wastes between mother and fetus occurs at
(1) A   (3) C
(2) B   (4) D

6 What is the function of the fluid labeled D?
(1) nourishment
(2) protection
(3) excretion
(4) respiration

7 The structure labeled C, within which development occurs, is known as the
(1) birth canal   (3) ovary
(2) uterus   (4) placenta

8 Which is arranged in the correct sequence?
(1) fertilization → embryo development → meiosis → birth
(2) embryo development → meiosis → fertilization → birth
(3) meiosis → fertilization → embryo development → birth
(4) fertilization → meiosis → embryo development → birth

9 The diagram at the right represents a cell that will undergo mitosis.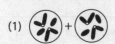

Which of the diagrams best illustrates the daughter cells that result from a normal mitotic cell division of the parent cell shown?

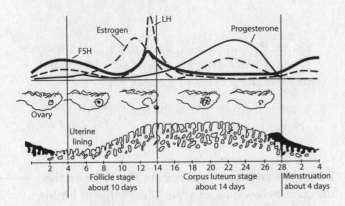

Part B

Base your answers to questions 10 through 14 on the diagram below, which shows some events in the human female reproductive cycle, and on your knowledge of biology.

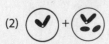

10 During which part of this cycle does the breakdown of the thickened uterine lining occur?
(1) ovulation
(2) corpus luteum stage
(3) menstruation
(4) follicle stage

11 On or about which day is the egg released from the ovary?
(1) day 8
(2) day 14
(3) day 20
(4) day 28

12 What is the average length of this reproductive cycle?
(1) 32 days   (3) 14 days
(2) 28 days   (4) 4 days

13 The hormone FSH stimulates the development of a follicle in the ovary of a human female. As the follicle develops, it secretes estrogen. A high level of estrogen decreases the secretion of FSH. This mechanism is an example of
(1) gamete development
(2) cell differentiation
(3) positive feedback
(4) negative feedback

14 Identify another human reproductive hormone that is *not* shown on this diagram. [1]

15 Compare the number of chromosomes present in the offspring with the number of chromosomes present in the parent organism in the process of cloning. [1]

Base your answers to questions 16 through 19 on the diagram below and on your knowledge of biology. The diagram represents a single-celled organism, such as an ameba, undergoing the changes shown.

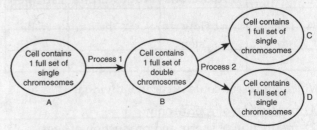

16 As a result of these processes, the single-celled organism accomplishes
(1) gamete production (3) sexual reproduction
(2) energy production (4) asexual reproduction

17 Process 1 is known as
(1) replication   (3) differentiation
(2) meiosis   (4) digestion

18 Process 1 and process 2 are directly involved in
(1) meiotic cell division (3) fertilization
(2) mitotic cell division (4) recombination

19 The genetic content of C is usually identical to the genetic content of
(1) B but not D   (3) D but not A
(2) both B and D   (4) both A and D

Base your answers to questions 20 and 21 on the information below and on your knowledge of biology.

The reproductive cycle in a human female is not functioning properly. An imbalance of hormones is diagnosed as the cause.

20 Identify one hormone directly involved in the human female reproductive system that could cause this problem. [1]

21 Explain why some cells in a female's body respond to reproductive hormones while other cells do not. [1]

22 The data in the table below indicate the presence of specific reproductive hormones in blood samples taken from three individuals. An X in the hormone column indicates a positive lab test for the appropriate levels necessary for normal reproductive functioning in that individual.

Data Table			
Individuals	**Hormones Present**		
	Testosterone	**Progesterone**	**Estrogen**
1		X	X
2			X
3	X		

Which processes could occur in individual 3?

(1) production of sperm, only
(2) production of sperm and production of eggs
(3) production of eggs and embryonic development
(4) production of eggs, only

Base your answers to questions 23 through 25 on the diagram below, which represents some stages in the development of an embryo, and on your knowledge of biology.

23 This entire sequence (A through embryo) started directly after

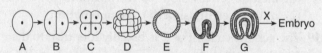

(1) the periodic shedding of a thickened uterine lining
(2) mitotic cell division in a testis
(3) meiotic cell division in the placenta
(4) the process of fertilization

24 If cell A has 46 chromosomes, how many chromosomes will most likely be found in each cell of stage G?
(1) 23　　　　　　(3) 69
(2) 46　　　　　　(4) 92

25 The arrow labeled X represents the process of
(1) meiosis　　　　(3) differentiation
(2) recombination　(4) cloning

26 An incomplete diagram of meiosis in the ovary of an animal is shown below.

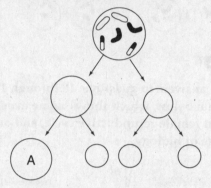

On the diagram below, draw in the chromosomes of cell A. Your drawing should show the usual result of the process of meiosis. [1]

Base your answers to questions 27 and 28 on the diagram below and on your knowledge of biology.

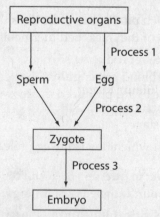

27 State why Process 2 is necessary in sexual reproduction. [1]

28 State one difference between the cells produced by Process 1 and the cells produced by Process 3. [1]

Directions (29–31): The diagrams below represent organs of two individuals. The diagrams are followed by a list of sentences. For each phrase in questions 29 through 31, select the sentence from the list below that best applies to that phrase and record its number.

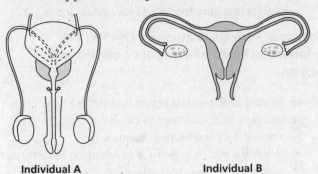

Individual A   **Individual B**

Sentences

1. The phrase is correct for both Individual *A* and Individual *B*.
2. The phrase is not correct for either Individual *A* or Individual *B*.
3. The phrase is correct for Individual *A*, only.
4. The phrase is correct for Individual *B*, only.

29 Contains organs that produce gametes [1]

30 Contains organs involved in internal fertilization [1]

31 Contains a structure in which a zygote divides by mitosis [1]

---

32 Which activity most directly involves the process represented in the diagram below?

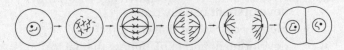

(1) a gamete reproducing sexually
(2) a white blood cell engulfing bacteria
(3) a zygote being produced in an ovary
(4) an animal repairing damaged tissue

Part C

Base your answer to question 33–35 on the information below and on your knowledge of biology.

The Critical Role of the Placenta

The proper functioning of the placenta is critical to the growth and development of a healthy fetus. For example, the placenta appears to act as a nutrient sensor. It regulates the amounts and types of nutrients that are transported from the mother to the fetus.

Improper functioning of the placenta can alter the structure and function of specific cells and organ systems in the developing fetus, putting it at risk for health problems as an adult. For example, in some pregnancies, the placenta develops a resistance to blood flow.

This resistance appears to force the heart of the fetus to work harder. This could result in an increased chance of the individual developing heart disease as an adult. A group of hormones known as glucocorticoids affects the development of all the tissues and organ systems. One of the things this group of hormones does is to alter cell function by changing the structure of cell membrane receptors.

33–35 Discuss the importance of the placenta in the development of a healthy fetus. In your answer, be sure to:
- identify two factors that could influence the nutrients that can pass from the mother to the fetus [1]
- identify the group of hormones that alter cell membrane receptors and explain how this alteration can affect cell function [1]
- state the role of the uterus in the development of the fetus and the placenta [1]

---

36 The production of a normal baby involves protecting the developing embryo from harmful environmental factors. State three ways in which the pregnant woman could avoid exposing the developing embryo to environmental risks. [1]

37 The diagram below shows some steps involved in preparing tissue cultures in plants.

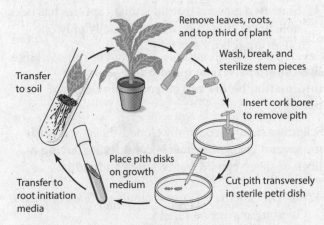

Remove leaves, roots, and top third of plant

Wash, break, and sterilize stem pieces

Insert cork borer to remove pith

Cut pith transversely in sterile petri dish

Place pith disks on growth medium

Transfer to root initiation media

Transfer to soil

Compare the genetic makeup of the offspring plants that are transferred to the soil to that of the parent plant that provided the stem pieces. [1]

38 The process of meiosis followed by fertilization is necessary to maintain the species chromosome number of a sexually reproducing species. For instance, a species with 24 chromosomes in each body cell normally has offspring that also have 24 chromosomes in their body cells.

Explain the specific way that meiotic cell division and fertilization interact to help maintain the species chromosome number. [1]

Base your answers to questions 39 through 41 on the information below and on your knowledge of biology.

Egg Laying vs. Bearing Live Young

Three groups of animals in which most species lay eggs for reproduction are amphibians, reptiles, and birds.

Most female amphibians lay hundreds of eggs in water, which are then fertilized by sperm from the male. Many reptiles lay between 1 and 200 eggs at a time, often in nests on land. The eggs have a leathery shell.

Birds usually lay between one and four eggs at a time in nests on land. Wild bird eggs usually have shells similar to those of the domestic chicken.

Most mammals bear live young. Some of these mammals, humans, for example, usually give birth to one live offspring at a time.

39 State one reason that individuals of some species must lay hundreds of eggs in order for the species to survive. [1]

40 Explain why fertilization in reptiles and birds must be internal. [1]

41 State two reasons that the human species has been able to survive, even though usually only one offspring is born at a time. [1]

Base your answers to question 42–46 on the information below and on your knowledge of biology.

Scientists have successfully cloned sheep and cattle for several years. A farmer is considering having a flock of sheep cloned from a single individual.

42–46 Discuss the process of cloning a flock of sheep. In your answer be sure to:
- state how a cloned flock would differ from an flock of sheep that was not cloned [1]
- state one advantage of having a cloned flock [1]
- state one disadvantage of having a cloned flock [1]

- state one reason the farmer would be able to mate the sheep in his flock with others in the flock [1]
- explain why breeding a sheep from his flock with sheep not in his flock would produce offspring that are not all identical clones [1]

Base your answers to question 47–48 on the information below and on your knowledge of biology.

47–48 Sexual and asexual reproduction are similar in some ways and different in others. Compare the two types. In your answer be sure to:
- Identify which type of reproduction results in genetically identical offspring. Explain why this occurs [1]
- describe one other way the two methods differ from each other [1]

49–53 Base your answers to question 49-53 on the information below and on your knowledge of biology.

A human is a complex organism that develops from a zygote. Briefly explain some of the steps in this process. In your answer be sure to:
- explain how a zygote is formed [1]
- compare the genetic content of the zygote to that of a body cell of the parents [1]
- identify one developmental process involved in the change from a zygote into an embryo [1]
- identify the structure in which fetal development usually occurs [1]
- identify one factor that can affect fetal development and explain how that factor affects fetal development [1]

Base your answers to questions 54 and 55 on the information below and on your knowledge of biology. The reproductive cycle in a human female is not functioning properly. An imbalance of hormones is diagnosed as the cause.

54 Identify one hormone directly involved in the human female reproductive system that could cause this problem. [1]

55 Explain why some cells in a female's body respond to reproductive hormones while other cells do not. [1]

Evolution

What do **YOU** *Think?*   Evolution

Natural selection is a process that allows the best adapted of the species to survive and reproduce.

Evolution is based on natural selection, which is very, very slow.

Natural selection is a process that *gives* organisms what they need when they need it to survive and reproduce.

Evolution explains how life originated on Earth millions of years ago.

Vocabulary

adaptive value	genetic variation	natural selection
evolution	geologic time	overproduction
extinction	mutation	theory
fossil record		

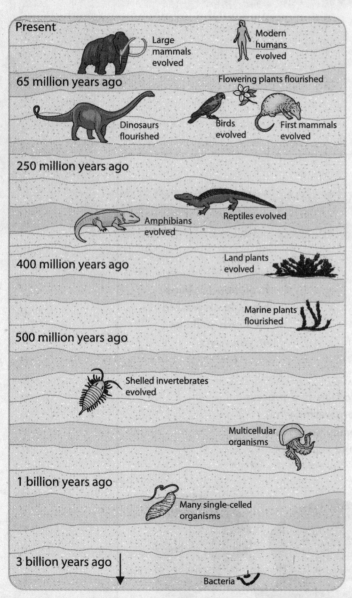

Present

Large mammals evolved

Modern humans evolved

65 million years ago

Flowering plants flourished

Dinosaurs flourished

Birds evolved

First mammals evolved

250 million years ago

Amphibians evolved

Reptiles evolved

400 million years ago

Land plants evolved

Marine plants flourished

500 million years ago

Shelled invertebrates evolved

Multicellular organisms

1 billion years ago

Many single-celled organisms

3 billion years ago

Bacteria

Figure 5-1. Examples from the fossil record

Topic Overview

Extensive evidence indicates that life on Earth began more than three billion years ago. Fossils found in ancient rocks have given us many clues to the kinds of life that existed long ago. The first living organisms were simple, single-celled organisms. Over time, more complex single-celled creatures developed. Then, about a billion years ago, increasingly complex, multicellular organisms began to appear. The idea that explains how this change in species has occurred over time is known as **evolution.**

The Theory of Evolution

The theory of evolution is accepted as the central theme of modern biology. It helps biologists understand how the variations among individuals can lead to changes in an entire species of organism. Since it was first suggested by Charles Darwin, the concept of evolution has been refined by massive amounts of evidence offered by thousands of scientists. So much evidence has been collected that evolution now has the stature of a **theory,** which is a concept that has been tested and confirmed in many different ways and can be used by scientists to make predictions about the natural world.

The theory of evolution helps biologists understand the similarities (such as bone structure and biochemistry) among different organisms. It also helps to explain the history of life that is revealed by the **fossil record,** which is a collection of fossils that provides clues to the history of Earth's organisms.

The fossil record spans much of **geologic time**—the billions of years of Earth's history—revealing many changes in environments as well as species. Figure 5-1 shows examples from the fossil record through geologic time.

Evolution does NOT necessarily produce long-term progress in any set direction. Instead, evolutionary change appears to be more like the growth of a bush. Notice in Figure 5-2 that some branches survive from the beginning with little or no change. Some die out altogether. Others branch repeatedly, with each new branch representing a new species.

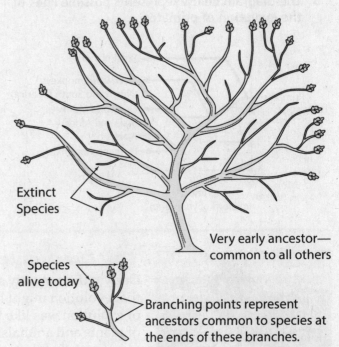

Figure 5-2. **Evolution modeled as the growth of a bush:** Evolutionary changes in species are like the growth of a bush in which some twigs grow and branch, while others die. The tips of the living twigs represent species that are alive now.

Review Questions   Set 5.1

1. Evolution is the process of
   (1) development of one-celled organisms from mammals
   (2) change in species over long periods of time
   (3) embryonic development of modern humans
   (4) changing energy flow in food webs

2. Which phrase best defines evolution?
   (1) an adaptation of an organism to its environment
   (2) a sudden replacement of one community by another
   (3) the isolation of organisms from each other for many years
   (4) a process of change in species over a period of time

3. The study of fossils has allowed scientists to
   (1) describe past environments and the history of life
   (2) study present ocean temperatures at different depths
   (3) analyze the chemical composition of sedimentary rocks and minerals
   (4) describe the details of the process by which life first began on Earth

4. The evolution of species is often represented as a branching tree similar to the one shown in the diagram below. The names shown represent different groups of organisms alive today; the lines represent their evolutionary histories.

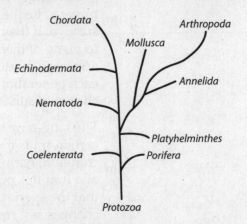

The statement that is best supported by the diagram is that
   (1) *Annelida* and *Arthropoda* have an ancestor in common
   (2) *Echinodermata* are more closely related to *Mollusca* than they are to *Chordata*
   (3) *Mollusca* and *Arthropoda* evolved before *Porifera*
   (4) *Annelida* and *Arthropoda* evolved from *Echinodermata*

5. The diagram below represents possible lines of the evolution of primates.

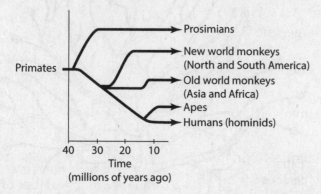

Primates → Prosimians
New world monkeys (North and South America)
Old world monkeys (Asia and Africa)
Apes
Humans (hominids)

40 30 20 10
Time
(millions of years ago)

Which inference can best be made based on the diagram?

(1) Adaptations for living in trees are inherited by all primates.
(2) Humans and apes have a common ancestor.
(3) The embryos of monkeys and apes are identical.
(4) The period of development is similar in most primates.

The Mechanics of Evolution

Darwin did not only suggest that species evolved. He also suggested how that evolution might have occurred. Darwin thought that the mechanism of evolution was like the process of <u>artificial selection</u> practiced by breeders of plants and animals. (See Figure 5-3.) He used the term **natural selection** to indicate that the process of evolution was controlled by "nature" rather than by people. In the process of natural selection, individuals that survive are able to breed and pass their genetic information to the next generation. Those that are not as successful in the environment often die without leaving any offspring.

Figure 5-3. **Racehorses are bred for speed and stamina:** When humans breed plants or animals, they select specific traits, such as speed, flower color, or resistance to insects. In a similar way, "nature" selects any trait that increases an organism's ability to survive and reproduce.

Overview of Evolution

Darwin's ideas are easy to understand: In any environment, an individual may be born with a characteristic that makes it stronger, faster—any sort of advantage that will help it survive and reproduce. The individuals that prove to be the best adapted to their environment will be more likely to survive. If they do survive, their favorable characteristics will be passed on to many of their offspring. As a result, these useful adaptations, which first appeared randomly, are likely to become more and more common with each generation. Similarly, characteristics that reduce an individual's chance of surviving and reproducing will tend to decrease over time.

The long-term result of natural selection is a change in the frequency of certain traits in a population. Beneficial traits tend to become more common; harmful traits tend to become less common. As the frequency of a trait in a population increases or decreases over time, it can be said that the species is evolving. Note that the population—not the individual—changes as a result of evolution. An individual does not evolve; each is born with genetic information that may or may not help it survive and reproduce. As natural selection leads to changes in the composition of a population, that population may have more individuals with a certain favorable characteristic than it did earlier.

Interactions and Evolution

The driving force behind evolution is the interaction between individual organisms and their environment. Conditions that are vital to the process of evolution include

- the potential for a species to increase its numbers, known as **overproduction**
- the <u>finite</u> (limited) supply of resources needed for life
- the genetic variation of offspring due to mutation and genetic "shuffling"
- the selection by the environment of those offspring better able to survive and reproduce

All of these conditions, which are explained below, are involved in the process of evolutionary change.

Overproduction In each generation, a species has the potential to produce more offspring than can possibly survive. Species with high reproductive potential include bacteria, insects, dandelions, and rabbits. (See Figure 5-4.) If all the offspring of these organisms survived, they would overrun Earth. However, that does not happen.

Scientists have learned that, in stable environments, the population of a species remains about the same from one year to the next. For example, no matter how many deer are born in one year, at the same time the next year, there will be about the same number of deer as there was the year before. Similarly, some fish species lay millions of eggs, but by the next year, the population of that species is the same as it was the previous year. This happens because not all of the new individuals that are born or hatched will survive to adulthood.

The Struggle for Survival Overproduction leads to competition among the members of a species. Not all offspring survive long enough to reproduce. In many cases, chance determines which offspring survive. For example, wind may blow a dandelion seed to a patch of fertile soil or into a lake. A deer may be born in a wildlife preserve or in the path of a forest fire.

But chance is not the only factor that determines which offspring will survive and which will die. The offspring all have to cope with environmental conditions, such as temperature, disease, parasites, and predators. They also need resources, such as oxygen, water, food, and shelter. However, the supply of these resources is finite. If they are to survive, organisms of the same species must compete for limited resources. Depending on their success as competitors, individuals will get the resources they need to survive, or they will not. Those that are the best suited to their environment are more likely to survive. Many of the losers in this struggle for resources will die before they have a chance to reproduce.

Variation The new traits that can lead to evolution come from normal variation within species. As shown in Figure 5-5, organisms within a species are never exactly alike. For example, some adult grasshoppers have longer legs than others; some have a lighter body color. In any group of gray squirrels, some have sharper or longer claws,

Rabbit Population Group	
Number of Generations	Number of Rabbits
1	100
72	3,354
100	13,150

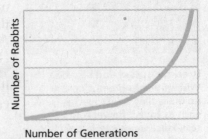

Figure 5-4. Overproduction: Rabbits are known for their high reproductive potential.

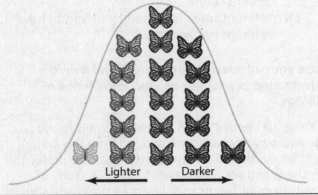

Figure 5-5. Genetic variation: In this example, a species of green butterflies might have individuals that vary in color from very dark green to very light green.

lighter or darker fur, bigger or smaller ears, and so on. The differences among offspring are due to **genetic variation**—the unique combination of traits each organism inherits from its parents.

Some variations give individuals an advantage over others in their struggle for resources. Any trait that helps an organism survive and reproduce under a given set of environmental conditions is said to have **adaptive value.** For example, a rabbit's ability to blend in with its surroundings may allow it to escape capture by a fox. The coloration it inherited has adaptive value for the rabbit, allowing it to escape predators and survive. When the fox population is high, this adaptation may be especially valuable to rabbits that inherited it.

Selection by the Environment As Darwin proposed with his idea of natural selection, traits with an adaptive value in a specific environment give individuals in that environment a competitive advantage. If the beneficial trait is passed to the offspring, they, too, are more likely to survive and reproduce. The proportion of individuals with these advantageous characteristics will increase because they are better able to compete than individuals without the beneficial trait. Eventually, nearly all the individuals in the population will have the beneficial trait. This change in the characteristics present in population over time is evolution.

Although some evolution may occur without much change in the environment, it is usually the adaptation of a species to changes in its environment that brings about evolution. Therefore, a changing environment is often the driving force for evolutionary change.

Review Questions   Set 5.2

6. The process of natural selection is based on the assumption that
   (1) environmental changes will cause changes in body structure in individuals
   (2) most changes from generation to generation are the result of mutations
   (3) part of the population of organisms always remains stable
   (4) different traits inherited by offspring have different survival value.

Base your answers to questions 7 and 8 on the information below and on your knowledge of biology.

A study of beetles on an isolated oceanic island formed by volcanic action and far from any other land shows that all of the beetles that are presently on the island are incapable of flying. A study of fossils from different rock layers of the island shows that the island was once populated with flying beetles. The graph shows the probable change over the last 5,000 years.

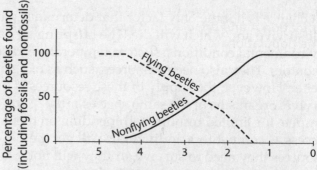

Ages of fossils discovered (in thousands of years)

7. The loss of flying ability by the beetle is most probably the result of
   (1) predators eating the beetles' wings
   (2) beetles not using their wings
   (3) genetic changes in the beetles
   (4) lack of vegetation for the beetle to feed on

8. The graph indicates that the non-flying beetles probably

(1) were better adapted to the environment
(2) arrived from other islands 5000 years ago
(3) mutated and produced flying beetles
(4) became extinct about 1.5 thousand years ago

9. When lions prey on a herd of antelope, some of the antelope are eliminated. Which part of the theory of evolution can be used to describe this situation?

(1) asexual reproduction of the fittest
(2) isolation of the species
(3) survival of the best adapted
(4) new species development due to mutation

10. Every spring, each mature female fish of a particular species produces several million eggs. However, the total population of this species remains at around 10,000 from one year to the next.

State two reasons why the fish population remains approximately the same from one generation to the next. [1]

Base your answers to questions 11 and 12 on the diagram below and on your knowledge of biology.

The diagram represents a small island divided by a mountain range. The mountain range prevents populations A and B from making contact with each other. At one time in the past, however, lowlands existed in the area indicated, and the ancestors of population A and population B were members of the same population.

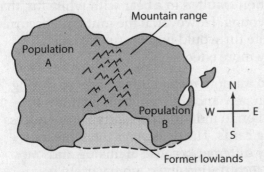

11. Over many years, the climate on the west side of the island has undergone drastic changes while the climate on the east side has remained the same. It is most likely that population B will

(1) migrate and intermix with population A
(2) become extinct
(3) have evolved more than population A
(4) have evolved less than population A

12. The organisms of population A and population B are now incapable of interbreeding and producing offspring. Which biological process most likely caused this situation to occur?

(1) artificial selection   (3) natural selection
(2) cloning   (4) asexual reproduction

Base your answers to questions 13 and 14 on the information and graph below and on your knowledge of biology.

Scientists studying a moth population in a wooded area of New York State recorded the distribution of moth wing color as shown in the following graph. While observing the moths, scientists noted that the moths spent most of the day resting on trees and looking for food during the night. The woods contained trees with a bark color that was predominantly brown.

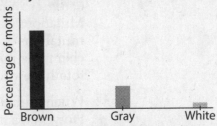

Distribution of moth wing color

13. A fungus infection affected nearly all trees in the woods so that the color of the tree bark was changed to a gray-white color. Which graph shows the most probable results that would occur in the distribution of wing color in this moth population after a long period of time?

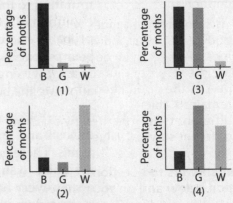

14. As a result of the fungus infection, the change in moth wing color distribution would most probably occur by the

(1) production of sex cells by mitosis
(2) natural selection of favorable variations
(3) eating of pigments in fungus spores
(4) production of mutations as a result of eating the fungus

Sources of Variation

As you may recall, the arrangement of an individual's DNA bases determines all the inherited characteristics of that individual. Any change in bases or their sequence may bring about a change in the individual. But not all of those changes can be passed on to the individual's offspring. In sexually reproducing organisms, only changes in the genes of sex cells can be passed on to the next generation and become the basis for evolutionary change. Other types of variation (such as changes to body cells) die with the individual. For example, a father who has built huge muscles due to exercise does NOT pass those large muscles to his offspring.

There are two major ways an organism can wind up with genes that differ from those of its parents. Some genetic variations arise because of mutations in the genes of an organism. Others are due to "genetic shuffling," the routine sorting and recombination of genes that occurs during sexual reproduction.

Mutation A **mutation** is a change in the base sequence of a DNA molecule. Mutations occur as random, chance events that cannot be predicted. Some mutations occur as errors in DNA as cells function. Radiation and some chemicals can also cause them. Mutations are an important source of totally new forms of genes.

When mutations occur in body cells, they affect only that individual. However, a mutation in a single-celled organism or in the sex cells of a multicellular organism can be passed on to the offspring. In organisms that reproduce sexually, only mutations in the genes of sex cells can become the basis for evolutionary change.

Nearly all mutations are harmful and may affect the offspring so severely that it cannot survive. A few mutations benefit the individual, however, and can increase its chance of surviving, reproducing, and passing the mutation to the next generation. A beneficial mutation may lead to the evolution of a new species. For example, the ancestors of polar bears probably had dark fur. If a mutation resulted in a bear with white fur, that bear probably would have died young. However, if the mutation occurred in a snowy environment, the white fur would be a useful mutation, allowing the bear to stalk its prey more effectively.

Genetic Shuffling The sorting and random recombining of genes during meiosis and fertilization results in new and different combinations of genes. These genes can be passed on to individual offspring. The process is similar to shuffling and dealing cards. The deck stays the same, but nearly every hand will be slightly different because of mixing and rearranging during shuffling. At fertilization, even more variety is introduced because now cards from "two decks" are combined. Although mutations provide new genetic instructions, genetic shuffling is the main source of the variation that exists among the members of any sexually reproducing species.

15. Which statement is basic to the theory of evolution by natural selection?

    (1) In general, living organisms maintain a constant population from generation to generation.

    (2) Changes in living organisms are almost completely the result of mutations.

    (3) Natural variations are inherited.

    (4) There is little competition between species.

16. Which statement is *not* included as part of our modern understanding of evolution?

    (1) Sexual reproduction and mutations provide variation among offspring.

    (2) Traits are transmitted by genes and chromosomes.

    (3) More offspring are produced than can possibly survive.

    (4) New organs are formed when organisms need them.

17. The modern theory of evolution states that a basis for variation within a species is provided by

    (1) mutations

    (2) asexual reproduction

    (3) cloning

    (4) overproduction

18. Sexual reproduction is related to evolution because sexual reproduction

    (1) occurs only in more recently evolved forms of animal life

    (2) increases the chances of extinction of different species

    (3) increases the chances for variations to occur

    (4) is the more usual kind of reproduction

19. Mutations can be transmitted to the next generation if they are present in

    (1) hormones   (3) body cells

    (2) gametes   (4) muscle cells

20. A new chemical was discovered and introduced into a culture containing one species of bacteria. Within a day, most of the bacteria were dead, but a few remained alive. Which statement best explains why some of the bacteria survived?

    (1) They had a genetic variation that gave them resistance to the chemical.

    (2) They were exposed to the chemical long enough to develop a resistance to it.

    (3) They mutated and became a different species after exposure to the chemical.

    (4) They absorbed the chemical and broke it down in their digestive systems.

21. Which characteristics of a population would most likely indicate the lowest potential for evolutionary change in that population?

    (1) sexual reproduction and few mutations

    (2) sexual reproduction and many mutations

    (3) asexual reproduction and few mutations

    (4) asexual reproduction and many mutations

22. Which two factors provide the genetic basis for variation within many species?

    (1) asexual reproduction and meiosis

    (2) mutations and sexual reproduction

    (3) competition and the synthesis of proteins

    (4) ecological succession and mitosis

23. Which statement best describes a current understanding of natural selection?

    (1) Natural selection influences the frequency of an adaptation in a population.

    (2) Natural selection has been discarded as an important concept in evolution.

    (3) Changes in gene frequencies due to natural selection have little effect on the evolution of species.

    (4) New mutations of genetic material are due to natural selection.

The Results of Genetic Variation

The changes that result from mutation or genetic shuffling in the sex cells may affect the offspring in several ways. Most of the changes can be categorized as structural, functional, or behavioral.

Structural Change The structure of any organism is the result of its species' entire evolutionary history. There are millions of examples of variations that have resulted in structural changes. For example, the polar bear (like other bears) has thick fur that keeps it warm in its cold environment.

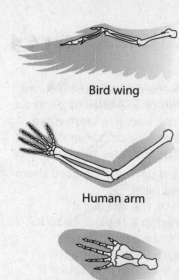

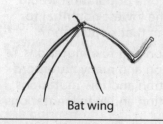

Bird wing

Human arm

Whale flipper

Bat wing

Figure 5-6. Similar bone structure of different species: The limbs shown above are from different species and have different functions, but they share many structural similarities. They are all made of the same type of bones and are attached in a similar way. The whale flipper is actually much larger than the other limbs. Notice that the ulna and radius of the bat wing are almost fused.

Polar bears, however, have evolved an extra protection from the cold. The soles of their feet are also mostly covered with thick fur. This extra fur not only keeps their skin off the ice but also improves traction.

The theory of evolution has helped scientists explain many of the structural variations and similarities found in organisms. For example, in Figure 5-6, notice that each limb has one thick "long" bone, two thinner "long" bones, and a "hand" with five digits. The ancestor of these animals most likely had a similar limb structure. At one point, however, limbs began to vary, evolving into arms, legs, wings, or flippers.

Structures that are no longer used by modern organisms give scientists clues to the evolutionary history of a species. Some snakes, for example, have tiny, nonfunctional leg bones—an indication that they probably evolved from four-legged, lizard-like ancestors.

Functional Change Molecular or biochemical changes affect how an organism works. These are functional changes. For example, all working muscles emit an extremely tiny electrical output. In some eels, however, that electrical output has evolved into an adaptation that helps it find and capture food. The muscles of these eels can produce a massive shock that stuns or kills its prey.

Changes in DNA often lead to functional changes. One example is a mutation in the DNA of certain one-celled organisms that led to their ability to make enzymes that digest wood. Another is the evolution of the ability of some snakes to make a poisonous venom.

Behavioral Change Behaviors have also evolved through natural selection. Many of the specific behaviors we find in species today have become common because they resulted in greater reproductive success.

- Fighting among the males of a walrus population for a harem of females is one evolved behavior. Because of the fighting, the stronger, healthier male mates with the most females.
- The correct rate of "blinking" allows males and females of firefly species to find each other. A different pattern or rate of blinking would isolate the individual from potential mates.

The Importance of Variation

If environmental conditions change, organisms that have adapted to those conditions may die. If all the members of the species had exactly the same combination of characteristics, an environmental change could be disastrous, wiping out the entire species. The variation of organisms within a species increases the likelihood that at least some members of the species will survive in a changed environment. Once the diversity present in a species is lost, it is next to impossible to get it back. Today's endangered species have such small populations that biologists worry that they may not have the genetic diversity to adapt to even slight changes in their environment.

24. The changes in the foot structure in a bird population over many generations are shown in the diagram below.

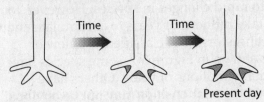

Present day

These changes can best be explained by the concept of

(1) natural selection
(2) extinction
(3) stable gene frequencies
(4) cloning

25. Explain how the lack of genetic diversity found in populations of endangered species might hinder their recovery. [1]

26. The Florida panther, a member of the cat family, has a population of fewer than 100 individuals and has limited genetic variation. Which inference based on this information is valid?

(1) These animals will begin to evolve rapidly.
(2) Over time, these animals will become less likely to survive in a changing environment.
(3) These animals are easily able to adapt to the environment.
(4) Over time, these animals will become more likely to be resistant to disease.

27. Which statement could be used as evidence to show that two different species of organisms most likely developed from a single, common ancestor?

(1) They eat the same types of food.
(2) They have different digestive enzymes.
(3) They lived during the same time period.
(4) They contain similar amino acid sequences.

28. The diagrams below show the bones in the forelimbs of three different organisms.

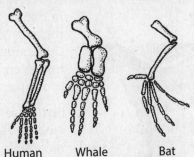

Human   Whale   Bat

Differences in the bone arrangements support the hypothesis that these organisms

(1) are members of the same species
(2) may have descended from the same ancestor
(3) have adaptations to survive in different environments
(4) all contain the same genetic information

29. In most populations, the individuals that produce the greatest number of offspring are

(1) always the strongest
(2) usually the best adapted
(3) those that have only inheritable traits
(4) those that are the most intelligent

30. The best scientific explanation for differences in structure, function, and behavior found in different species of organisms is provided by

(1) carbohydrate electrophoresis
(2) population chromatography
(3) the theory of carrying capacity
(4) the theory of evolution

Patterns of Change

Evolution appears to follow certain patterns that appear repeatedly in the fossil record. For example:

- Changes in species are often related to environmental change.
- Species with short reproductive cycles that produce many offspring tend to evolve more quickly than species with long lifespans and few offspring.
- The failure to adapt to a changing environment may result in the death of the species.

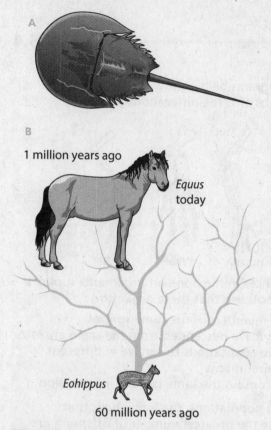

A

B

1 million years ago

Equus
today

Eohippus

60 million years ago

Figure 5-7. **The rate of evolution:** For some species, the rate of evolutionary change has been very slow. For example, the horseshoe crab (A) has shown little change from fossils of its ancestors that lived 300 million years ago. However, the horse (B) has evolved tremendously over the past 60 million years.

The Rate of Evolution

Most of the diversity of life on Earth today is believed to be the result of natural selection occurring over a vast period of geologic time. The amount of change seems to be linked to changes in the environment. Minimal environmental change often results in stable populations. Rapid environmental change often leads to rapid changes in species. However, for any species, it may take millions of years to accumulate enough differences from its ancestors to be classified as a new or different species. As shown in Figure 5-7, some species have hardly changed in many millions of years. Others have changed so much that the relationships may not be obvious.

The rate of evolutionary change may also be influenced by the number of offspring produced by a species. Those that have few offspring and live a long time generally evolve quite slowly. Those that have brief lifespans and numerous offspring can change so quickly that evolution may occur in just a few years.

One example of rapid change involves the evolution of antibiotic resistance by pathogenic bacteria. When a population of millions of bacteria is exposed to an antibiotic, there is a chance that a few might have a gene that makes them resistant to the antibiotic. (This gene probably occurred as a chance mutation at some earlier time. It was most likely present in some of the bacteria before the antibiotic was used, and its appearance was totally unrelated to the presence of the antibiotic.) The antibiotic could kill almost all of the bacteria except for a few that escape exposure to the antibiotic. The ones with the resistance gene would also survive.

Because the antibiotic eliminated most of the competition, the few survivors, including the resistant ones, reproduce quickly, giving rise to a new population of the bacteria. In this new population, a higher proportion of individuals is now resistant to the drug. When the same antibiotic is used on the descendants of this new population, even more resistant bacteria will survive. Now the proportion of resistant bacteria is even higher. In this case, the antibiotic has become an agent of selection. The antibiotic did not cause the original mutation that made the bacteria resistant to the antibiotic. It merely determined which bacteria would live to reproduce. Figure 5-8 shows the process.

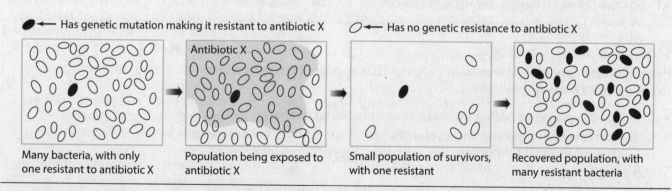

● ← Has genetic mutation making it resistant to antibiotic X   ○ ← Has no genetic resistance to antibiotic X

Antibiotic X

Many bacteria, with only one resistant to antibiotic X

Population being exposed to antibiotic X

Small population of survivors, with one resistant

Recovered population, with many resistant bacteria

Figure 5-8. **How resistance to antibiotics can develop**

Insects also have short reproductive cycles and produce many offspring. Many insect species have changed significantly in response to pesticide use. For example, the widespread use of the pesticide DDT led to insect species becoming resistant in just a few years. As was the case with bacteria and antibiotics, there may have been a few DDT-resistant insects in the population before the chemical was ever used. They probably had a random mutation that had no adaptive value before the use of DDT. Once the DDT was sprayed, nearly all of the nonresistant insects were killed, leaving a high proportion of resistant insects to repopulate the area. Later, if DDT was sprayed again, it was less effective against the resistant offspring of the survivors of the earlier spraying.

As a result of these kinds of rapid evolutionary events, we are finding more and more bacteria that are resistant to antibiotics and more and more insect species that are resistant to our pesticides. This has created many problems in the fields of medicine and agriculture and will continue to be a problem in the future.

Extinction

Extinction is the disappearance of an entire species. Any time the death rate of individuals within a species is greater than the birth rate, extinction is a possibility. Generally, extinction occurs when the environment changes. Temperatures change; sea levels rise and fall. Grasslands become deserts; clear lakes become polluted. The variation of organisms within a species increases the likelihood that at least some members of the species will survive the changing environmental conditions. However, when the adaptive characteristics of a species are insufficient to allow its survival in a new environment, the species will become extinct.

The fossil record shows that throughout geologic time, millions of species have evolved, survived for a while, then failed to adapt successfully, and finally became extinct. It is a surprisingly common process. In fact, from the number of fossils of extinct organisms found, it is apparent that a majority of the species that ever lived on Earth is now extinct. Figure 5-9 shows a fossil of the extinct *Archaeopteryx*, an ancestor of modern birds.

Figure 5-9. An artist's conception of how the extinct *Archaeopteryx* might have looked, and the fossilized skeleton of this animal.

Review Questions

Set 5.5

31. The shark has changed very little in the last 50 million years. Which statement best explains why this is the case?

 (1) The shark is well adapted to its relatively unchanged environment.
 (2) Sharks have a high reproductive rate and show little change in their genetic makeup from one generation to the next.
 (3) Sharks need to change only if humans are present in their environment.
 (4) Sharks have a high mutation and genetic recombination rate.

32. Fossil evidence indicates that many species have existed for relatively brief periods of time and have then become extinct. Which statement best explains the reason for their short existence?

 (1) These organisms lacked the energy to produce mutations.
 (2) Humans modify plant and animal species through the knowledge of genetics.
 (3) These organisms lacked variations having adaptive value.
 (4) Within these species, increasing complexity reduced their chances of survival.

Base your answers to questions 33 through 35 on the diagram below and on your knowledge of biology. The diagram shows an interpretation of relationships based on evolutionary theory. The letters represent different species.

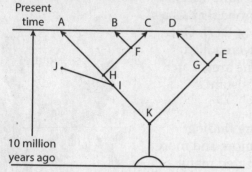

33. Explain why species B and C are more closely related than species A and C are.

34. The diagram indicates that a common ancestor for species C and E is species

    (1) F   (2) G   (3) H   (4) K

35. Which species are least likely to be vital parts of a present-day ecosystem?

    (1) A and E   (3) E and J
    (2) C and D   (4) B and F

Base your answers to questions 36 and 37 on the information below and on your knowledge of biology.

Joshua Lederberg discovered that, in a large population of *Escherichia coli* (*E. coli*) about 1 in 10 million of the offspring was naturally resistant to the antibiotic streptomycin. When these naturally resistant bacteria were isolated and grown separately, they soon formed a larger population. The entire population so formed was also naturally resistant to streptomycin.

36. The formation of the large streptomycin-resistant population is based on

    (1) variations and survival of the fittest
    (2) mutations and asexual reproduction
    (3) sexual reproduction and no mutations
    (4) survival of the fittest and cloning

37. According to modern evolutionary theory, the resistance to streptomycin probably resulted directly from

    (1) culturing the *E. coli*
    (2) changes in temperature under which *E. coli* are grown
    (3) a change in the DNA of *E. coli*
    (4) the presence of streptomycin in the environment of *E. coli*

38. A large population of cockroaches was sprayed with a newly developed, fast-acting insecticide. The appearance of some cockroaches that are resistant to this insecticide supports the concept that

    (1) species traits tend to remain constant
    (2) variation exists within a species
    (3) insecticides cause mutations
    (4) the environment does not change

39. Compounds like the pesticide DDT may bring about the evolution of new strains of organisms by

    (1) destroying food producers
    (2) acting as a natural selecting agent
    (3) mixing two different sets of genes
    (4) creating new ecological niches

40. Some evolutionary pathways are represented in the diagram below.

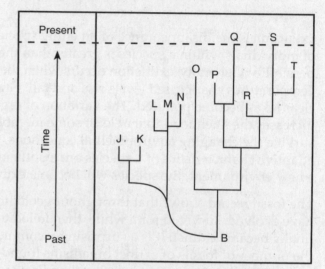

An inference that can be made from information in the diagram is that

    (1) many of the descendants of organism B became extinct
    (2) organism B was probably much larger than any of the other organisms represented
    (3) most of the descendants of organism B successfully adapted to their environment and have survived to the present time
    (4) the letters above organism B represent members of a single large population with much biodiversity

41. Explain why changes in climate can result in the extinction of a species. [1]

Practice Questions
for the New York Regents Exam

TOPIC 5

Directions

Review the Test-Taking Strategies section of this book. Then answer the following questions. Read each question carefully and answer with a correct choice or response.

Part A

1 How does natural selection operate to cause change in a population?
   (1) The members of the population are equally able to survive environmental change.
   (2) The members of the population differ so that only some survive when the environment changes.
   (3) The members of the population cause environmental changes and adapt to them.
   (4) All the members of the population adapt to environmental changes.

2 Which mutation could be passed on to future generations?
   (1) a gene change in a liver cell
   (2) cancer caused by excessive exposure to the sun
   (3) a chromosomal alteration during gamete formation
   (4) random breakage of a chromosome in a leaf cell of a maple tree

3 A trait with low survival value to the members of a population will most likely
   (1) undergo a series of mutations in succeeding generations
   (2) cause the reproductive rate of the individual to increase
   (3) decrease in frequency from one generation to the next
   (4) remain unchanged in frequency through many generations

4 A change in the genetic material that produces variation in a species may be the result of
   (1) the struggle for survival
   (2) the overproduction of a species
   (3) a mutation
   (4) competition

5 The DNA sequences found in two different species are 95% the same. This suggests that these species
   (1) are evolving into the same species
   (2) contain identical proteins
   (3) may have similar evolutionary histories
   (4) have the same number of mutations

6 The process by which a species passes out of existence is known as
   (1) endangerment
   (2) deforestation
   (3) extinction
   (4) adaptation

7 The diagram below illustrates the change that occurred in the frequency of body pattern traits shown by an insect population over ten generations.

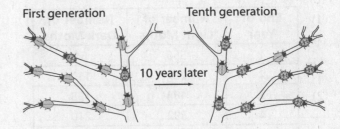

First generation   Tenth generation

10 years later

A probable explanation for this change would be that over time there was
   (1) a decrease in the adaptive value of the spotted trait
   (2) an increase in the adaptive value of the spotted trait
   (3) an increase in the population of the insect
   (4) a decrease in the mutation rate of the gene for body pattern

8 The fact that a healthy deer can outrun a timber wolf is an example of
   (1) mutation
   (2) isolation
   (3) non-random mating
   (4) natural selection

9 A maple tree releases hundreds of seeds in a single season. This is an example of
   (1) a mutation
   (2) isolation
   (3) overproduction
   (4) non-random mating

Part B

Base your answers to questions 10 through 15 on the information below and on your knowledge of biology.

The bark of trees around Manchester, England, was mostly light in color before the Industrial Revolution. Light-colored peppered moths that rested on the trees were camouflaged from bird predators, while dark-colored peppered moths were easily preyed upon. After a few years of industrialization, the tree bark became darkened from pollution. The table below represents a change in the number of light- and dark-colored moths within the peppered moth population over a period of six years from the beginning of industrialization.

End of Year	Number of Light Moths	Number of Dark Moths
1	556	64
2	237	112
3	484	198
4	392	210
5	246	281
6	225	357

Using the information in the data table, construct a line graph on the grid provided. Follow the instructions below.

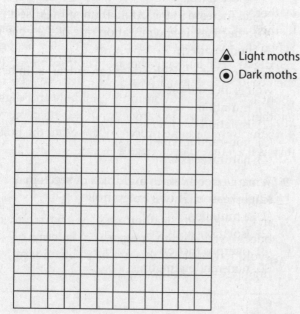

Changes in Peppered Moth Population

▲ Light moths
◉ Dark moths

Number of moths

End of year

10 Mark an appropriate scale, without any breaks, on each axis. [1]

11 Plot the data for the number of dark moths on the grid. Surround each point with a small circle and connect the points. [1]

Example: ◉——◉——◉

12 Plot the data for the number of light moths on the grid. Surround each point with a small triangle and connect the points. [1]

Example: ▲——▲——▲

13 At the end of which year of study was the number of dark-colored moths closest to the number of light-colored moths?
(1) 1   (2) 2   (3) 5   (4) 6

14 Which aspect of the evolutionary process is suggested by the information provided?
(1) The light-colored moths will eventually increase in number.
(2) The darker moths appeared when the tree trunks became lighter.
(3) The changing environment caused a darkening of the pigments of the moths.
(4) The darker moths increased in number when the environment became more favorable for their traits.

15 The biological concept that is most closely associated with the changes in the peppered moth population in England is known as
(1) natural selection   (3) asexual reproduction
(2) positive feedback   (4) homeostatic control

Base your answers to questions 16 through 19 on the paragraph below and on your knowledge of biology.

Two different species of crickets inhabited a meadow. One species of cricket had a straw-colored body and made up 90% of the total cricket population. The other species of cricket had a dark red body and made up 10% of the population. This proportion between the species had been constant for many years.

A new variety of grass with purple blades appeared in the meadow. The purple grass was better adapted to the meadow environment than the native green grass and replaced the green grass within a period of 50 years.

16 The appearance of the purple grass was most likely the result of
(1) asexual reproduction (3) cloning
(2) genetic engineering (4) mutation

17 Which graph most likely indicates the percentages of the straw-colored crickets (%S) over the 50-year period after the appearance of purple grass?

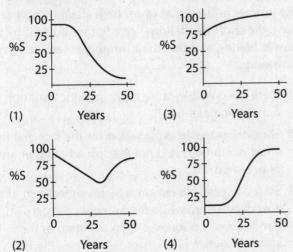

18 The evolutionary concept that would explain the changes taking place during the 50-year period in both the crickets and grasses is called
(1) common ancestry
(2) natural selection
(3) homeostatic balance
(4) selective breeding

19 What is the most likely reason for the large proportion of straw-colored crickets in the original population?
(1) The straw-colored crickets were larger and killed off most of the red crickets.
(2) Few natural enemies of the straw-colored crickets lived in the meadow.
(3) More straw-colored crickets than red were able to survive in the green grass.
(4) Red-colored crickets were not a part of the fossil record for the meadow.

20 State what could happen to a species in a changing environment if the members of that species do not express any genetic variations. [1]

Part C

21 Genetic variation is the raw material of evolution. Identify two different sources of genetic variation in a plant or animal population. [1]

Base your answers to questions 22 through 25 on the information below and on your knowledge of biology.

A hawk has a genetic trait that gives it much better eyesight than other hawks of the same species in the same area. Explain how this could lead to evolutionary change within this species of hawk over a long period of time. In your answer, be sure to include an explanation of:

- competition within the hawk population [1]
- survival of various individuals in the population [1]
- how the frequency of the better-eyesight trait would be expected to change over time within the population [1]
- what would most likely happen to the hawks having the better-eyesight trait if they also had unusually weak wing muscles [1]

Base your answers to questions 26 and 27 on the information below and on your knowledge of biology.

Scientists have observed thousands of female leatherback turtles during egg laying. Every female leatherback exhibits the same remarkable behavior. When she first comes up on the beach to lay her eggs, she digs a deep hole, lays her eggs in the hole, and then covers the eggs with sand. She then travels about 100 meters away from the first hole and digs another. She doesn't lay any eggs in this hole, but goes through the same process of covering the hole just as if there had been eggs present.

26 Write a hypothesis to explain why the female leatherback digs two holes. [1]

27 In the past, some leatherbacks may have only dug one hole and laid their eggs in it. In terms of evolution, how can this modern behavior of digging two holes be explained? [1]

Base your answers to questions 28 and 29 on the information below and on your knowledge of biology.

Two adaptations of the monarch butterfly that aid in its survival are the production of a certain chemical and a distinctive coloration that other animals can easily recognize. When a monarch butterfly is eaten, the presence of the chemical results in a bad taste to the predator. Although the viceroy butterfly does not contain the chemical that tastes bad to a predator, it does resemble the monarch in size, shape, and coloration.

28 Explain how the combination of this chemical and the distinctive coloration aid in the survival of the monarch butterfly. [1]

29 Explain how the characteristics of the viceroy butterfly aid in its survival. [1]

Base your answers to question 30–33 on the information below and on your knowledge of biology.

In the past, a specific antibiotic was effective in killing a certain species of bacteria. Now, most members of this bacterial species are resistant to this antibiotic.

Explain how this species of bacteria has become resistant. In your answer be sure to include the concepts of:

- overproduction [1]
- variation [1]
- natural selection [1]
- adaptation to the environment [1]

Base your answers to questions 34 through 37 on the passage below and on your knowledge of biology.

Dandelions are weeds that are very common in many grassy areas of New York State. Dandelion flowers first open up in a bright-yellow stage, and later turn a fluffy white when they are ready to release their seeds. The seeds are carried by the wind, and can sometimes travel great distances before landing and growing into new plants.

The stems of dandelions are usually very long, typically about 20–30 centimeters (cm), and stand high above the surrounding grass.

A science teacher in Niagara County discovered an area in her lawn where nearly every dandelion had a

stem less than 1 cm long. These short dandelions were replacing large amounts of grass in the lawn surrounding her house. They were growing much more thickly than the taller dandelions in other nearby areas. The short dandelions appeared to be growing very successfully in one area of her lawn, but did not appear to have spread to other areas of her lawn.

The teacher noticed that every time she mowed her lawn, the short dandelions were left untouched by the mower blades, and that their numbers were steadily increasing.

34 State *one* possible cause of the genetic variation in dandelion height. [1]

35 State *one* possible explanation for the fact that the short dandelions had not yet spread to other areas of her lawn. [1]

36 State *one* possible reason why the amount of grass was decreasing, while the number of short dandelions was increasing in the lawn of the science teacher. [1]

37 State *one* possible advantage the short dandelions may have over the tall dandelions in this yard. [1]

Base your answers to question 38 through 40 on the information below and on your knowledge of biology.

Growers of fruit trees have always had problems with insects. Insects can cause visible damage to fruits, making them less appealing to consumers. As a result of this damage, much of the fruit cannot be sold. Insecticides have been useful for controlling these insects, but, in recent years, some insecticides have been much less effective. In some cases, insecticides do nothing to stop the insect attacks.

38 Identify the original event that resulted in the evolution of insecticide resistance in some insects [1]

39 Explain why the percentage of resistant insects in the population has increased [1]

40 Describe one alternative form of insect control, other than using a different insecticide, that fruit growers could use to protect their crops from insect attack [1]

Ecology

Topic Overview

What do You Think?

Succession

Succession is the changes that occur in a species as it evolves into a series of new species.

Succession is the series of changes that take place in plant and animal communities as the habitat changes.

Succession is the series of changes a species makes as it adapts to new conditions.

6 Ecology

Vocabulary

abiotic	ecological niche	herbivore
autotroph	ecological succession	heterotroph
biodiversity	ecology	host
biosphere	ecosystem	limiting factors
biotic	energy pyramid	parasite
carnivore	environment	population
carrying capacity	finite	predator
community	food chain	prey
competition	food web	producer
consumer	habitat	scavenger
decomposer		

Topic Overview

Our Earth is home to trillions of different organisms. None of these organisms can survive alone. All organisms—including humans—must interact with both the living and nonliving things around them. **Ecology** is the study of how organisms interact with the living and nonliving things that surround them.

Organisms and Their Environment

As you read this book, you are surrounded by your environment, which includes this book and perhaps your chair, light streaming through the window, a dog barking outside, and a pretzel on the table. If you're in class, your environment may include other students reading nearby, your teacher pacing the aisles, the drone of an airplane, the smell of the lunchroom, sunlight coming in the window, and the unseen mite picking skin flakes off your arm. In short, the **environment** is every living and nonliving thing that surrounds an organism.

Parts of an Ecosystem

Ecosystem is a short way of saying "ecological system." Scientists use the term to describe any portion of the environment. An ecosystem is made up of all the living things, such as bacteria, plants, and animals, that interact with one another. These interacting living things are termed **biotic** factors. When scientists study ecosystems, they also study the nonliving things, such as soil, water, physical space, and energy, that influence the organisms. Nonliving influences are termed **abiotic** factors.

A decaying log, a pond, a field of corn, and even a fish tank are ecosystems. In each of these ecosystems, organisms interact with both the biotic and abiotic parts of their environment. For example, frogs in a pond ecosystem may interact with insects, fish, hawks, and children chasing them with nets. They are also affected by abiotic factors, such as rainfall, the acidity of their pond, temperature, and the amount of light. Some biotic and abiotic parts of an ecosystem are shown in Figure 6-1.

Because the world contains a wide variety of physical conditions, many different kinds of environments are available to organisms. Some are shown in Figure 6-2. Most species, however, have a specific environment that is their "home." That specific environment is known as the species' **habitat.** Familiar habitats include fields, forests, oceans, streams, and deserts.

All the organisms of a species that live in the same area make up a **population.** Ants in a single anthill would be one population. All the different populations are combined to form a <u>community.</u>

Collectively, all of Earth's ecosystems make up the **biosphere**—the biologically inhabited portions of the planet. Earth's biosphere extends from the deepest ocean troughs to high above the surface of the planet. It includes all the water, land, and air in which organisms live. Throughout the biosphere, organisms interact and compete for vital resources, such as food, space, and shelter.

The fundamental concept of ecology is that all living organisms are interdependent, and they interact with one another and with the physical environment. These interactions result in a flow of energy and a cycling of materials essential for life.

Environmental Limits on Population Size

In any ecosystem, the growth and survival of organisms depends on the physical conditions and on the resources available to the organism. If they had unlimited resources, living things could produce populations of <u>infinite</u> (unlimited) size. Within any ecosystem, however, resources, such as oxygen and carbon dioxide, water, nutrients, space, and sunlight, are

Abiotic Factors

Biotic Factors

Figure 6-1. **Parts of an ecosystem: The biotic part of the ecosystem includes all the living things that make up the community.**

Figure 6-2. **Some ecosystems in Earth's biosphere:** In each ecosystem, the organisms interact with one another and with their environment. The degree to which each abiotic factor is present determines the types of organisms that can live there.

Ocean

Woodland

Pond

finite (limited). This has a profound effect on the interactions among organisms: Because the resources are finite, organisms must compete with one another to survive.

Competition is the struggle for resources among organisms. Within any one species, competition keeps the size of that species' population in check. In established ecosystems, populations tend to increase or decrease depending on the resources that are available at the time. This variation in population size tends to follow a predictable cycle. Many populations, for example, vary with the seasons. Over time, however, the size of the population remains stable.

Factors in the environment that limit the size of populations are known as **limiting factors.** Some limiting factors are abiotic; others are biotic. For example, abiotic factors, such as the amount of dissolved oxygen in a pond, may limit the kinds and numbers of fish that can live there; the amount of sunlight filtering through a forest may limit the number of green plants living on the forest floor. Some other specific limiting factors include the intensity of light, the temperature range in the environment, minerals that are available in the water or soil, the type of rock or soil in the ecosystem, and the relative acidity (measured according to the pH scale).

An important biotic factor that limits population sizes is the relationship between **predators,** which kill and eat other organisms, and **prey,** which are killed for food. As predators kill and eat their prey, they limit the growth of the prey population. If too many prey animals are killed, predators begin to starve, and their population is reduced. With fewer predators, the size of the prey population begins to recover.

The number of organisms of any single species that an ecosystem can support is referred to as its **carrying capacity**. It is determined not only by the available energy, water, oxygen, and minerals (and the recycling of such minerals), but also by the interactions of its organisms. For example, a field's carrying capacity for a population of foxes is affected not only by the climate, but also by the number and kinds of other populations present. If there are many mice for the foxes to eat, the fox population may boom. If there are many viruses affecting the health of the foxes, their population may crash. Figure 6-3 shows the population increase that normally occurs until the carrying capacity is reached.

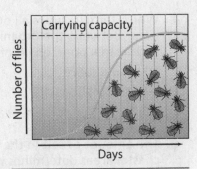

Figure 6-3. Carrying capacity: This population of insects increased until it neared its carrying capacity. Then the population became approximately stable.

Review Questions

Set 6.1

1. All of Earth's water, land, and atmosphere within which life exists is known as
   (1) a population
   (2) an ecosystem
   (3) the biosphere
   (4) a biotic community

2. In the biosphere, what are some of the major abiotic factors that determine the distribution and types of plant communities?
   (1) temperature, sunlight, and rainfall
   (2) humidity, location, and humans
   (3) soil type, soil bacteria, and soil water
   (4) insects, carbon dioxide, and nitrogen in the air

Base your answers to questions 3 and 4 on the two graphs below and on your knowledge of biology. The first graph shows the number of days of snow cover from 1940–1960. The second graph shows the percentage of white mice in a population that was sampled during the same period.

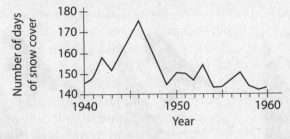

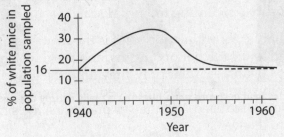

3. The appearance of the greatest percentage of white mice occurred
   (1) before the maximum number of days of snow cover
   (2) at the same time as the maximum number of days of snow cover
   (3) after the maximum number of days of snow cover
   (4) both before and after the maximum number of days of snow cover

4. Which statement is supported by the data in the graphs?
   (1) The percentage of brown mice was greatest during the years of longest snow cover.
   (2) The percentage of mice with white fur was greatest during the years of longest snow cover.
   (3) The actual number of white mice was greatest during the years of least snow cover.
   (4) The actual number of brown mice was greatest during the years of longest snow cover.

5. The fact that an organism cannot live without interacting with its surroundings is a basic concept in the field of study known as
   (1) ecology
   (2) evolution
   (3) behavior
   (4) technology

6. When two different species live in the same area and use the same limited resources, which of the following will occur?
   (1) competition
   (2) succession
   (3) parasitism
   (4) industrialization

7. Which term includes all of the interactions that occur between the organisms and the physical factors in a pond environment?

(1) population
(2) ecosystem
(3) abiotic
(4) competition

8. The amount of salt in the air and water of coastal areas determines which species can exist there. In these areas, salt functions as a

(1) source of energy
(2) biotic factor
(3) food source
(4) limiting factor

9. This graph shows the changes in two populations of herbivores in a grassy field.

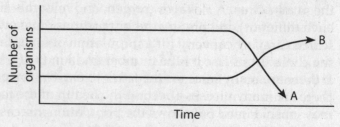

A possible reason for these changes is that

(1) all of the plant populations in this habitat decreased
(2) population B competed more successfully for food than population A
(3) population A produced more offspring than population B
(4) population A consumed members of population B

Population Interactions

There is a wide diversity of interacting species in most ecosystems. Most of the interactions occur as organisms obtain their food. Every population is linked, directly or indirectly, with all of the other populations in the ecosystem. Each population has one or more specific roles in the ecosystem. As a result, maintaining the ecosystem's diversity is essential to its stability.

Roles in the Ecosystem

The role that each species plays in an ecosystem is called its **ecological niche.** Only one species at a time can occupy a particular niche. If two species attempt to fill the same role in an ecosystem, competition results. Usually, one species will be more suited to the niche, which forces the other species to move on or face elimination. Eventually, only one species will occupy each niche.

Figure 6-4. **Feeding patterns among warblers:** Several warbler species feed in spruce trees, but they actually occupy different niches because each species feeds in a different part of the spruce tree.

Sometimes it appears as if different populations occupy the same niche. For example, deer and moose often live in the same area and seem to eat the same plants. A closer examination reveals that the deer and moose have different food preferences and only compete when food is very scarce. Similarly, several bird species may seem to nest and feed in the same tree. In reality, it is more probable that the birds are nesting in different parts of the tree and eating different insects. For example, the northeastern United States is home to several species of warblers. Five of those species feed on the insects that live in spruce trees. As shown in Figure 6-4, each species feeds in a different part of the tree.

Competition for a particular ecological niche often occurs when a foreign species enters an area. The new species may be more successful than the native species, partly because the newcomer may not have any natural enemies to control its population. Humans frequently bring foreign species into an area either on purpose or accidentally. One example is the zebra mussels that were brought to the Great Lakes on cargo ships. The zebra mussel has become a major problem in New York waterways.

Relationships in an Ecosystem

In every ecosystem, populations of different species are linked together in a complex web of interactions. Sometimes these relationships are competitive; occasionally they are cooperative. For example, termites have one-celled organisms in their intestinal tracts. These unicellular organisms help the termites digest their food. The tiny organisms gain a place to live and plenty of food, and the termites can make use of a food supply that they would not be able to digest without this cooperative relationship.

Other relationships benefit one organism and have no effect on the other. For example, when a shark attacks and eats its prey, small pieces of the food drift downward. Smaller fish swimming below the shark feed on these scraps. The small fish benefit, but the shark is unaffected.

Food Chains Among the most common relationships in any ecosystem are the predator-prey relationships. **Food chains,** such as those shown in Figure 6-5, illustrate the relationships between prey and predator. In simple terms, the food chain shows what eats what.

Organism's niches are partly defined by how they obtain their food. For example, photosynthetic organisms make their own food and in the process, store the sun's energy. They are known as **autotrophs** (self-feeders) or **producers.** They provide a source of food energy for almost all other living things.

Heterotrophs must acquire food by consuming other organisms. **Herbivores** are heterotrophs that survive on plant tissues; **carnivores** are heterotrophs that eat other animals. Heterotrophs are also known as **consumers.**

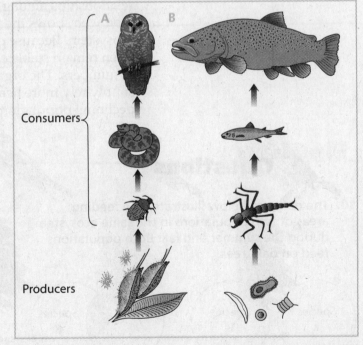

Figure 6-5. Typical food chains: A field ecosystem (A) and a pond ecosystem (B)

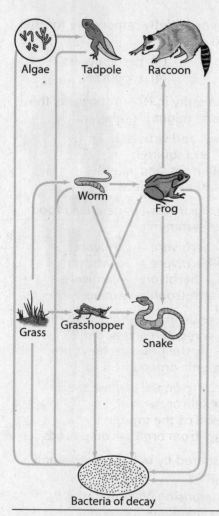

Figure 6-6. **A simplified food web near a pond**

The wastes and dead bodies of all these organisms are consumed by the **decomposers.** The decomposers recycle materials that can then be reused by producers.

Two other feeding relationships between organisms do not fit into the typical predator-prey categories. These organisms are similar to predators in that they feed on other organisms, but different in that they do not kill the organisms for food. **Scavengers,** such as vultures, are consumers that eat dead organisms. They are nature's "clean-up crew." Scavengers, however, are not decomposers. Dead bodies and wastes still have to be broken down by decomposers. **Parasites** are organisms that attack other live organisms (called **host** organisms), but rarely kill them. Parasites usually live on or in the body of their host. Ticks, for example, may live on a dog and also feed on its blood.

Notice in Figure 6-5 that both food chains begin with autotrophs—the photosynthetic producers—and end with consumers. The intermediate heterotrophs (the herbivores and carnivores that rely on others for food) are often, but not always, part of food chains. All of the organisms in a food chain, if not eaten by others, are eventually consumed by decomposers. So a food chain may be as simple as: grass → decay bacteria.

Decomposers may be included at the end of a food chain, but it is important to remember that they actually consume and break down the chemical materials in all dead organisms and in the wastes of all living organisms.

Food Webs Normally, each organism feeds on more than one kind of organism. Because organisms normally have more than one food source, food chain diagrams are oversimplified. **Food webs,** as shown in Figure 6-6, are diagrams that show the more complex feeding relationships among producers, consumers, and decomposers. The food web shows the many interconnected food chains that exist in the ecosystem. Because organisms have several food choices, ecosystems often remain stable even when one population shows a major decline in numbers. The organisms that feed on the declining population simply rely more heavily on one of their other food choices until the declining population recovers.

Review Questions   Set 6.2

10. The diagram below illustrates the feeding areas of two populations in the same ecosystem during the summer and fall. Both populations feed on oak trees.

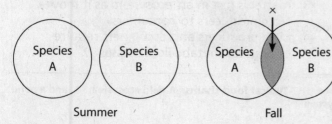

The portion of the diagram labeled X most likely indicates that

(1) these populations compete for food in the fall, but not in the summer
(2) the species are separated by a geographic barrier in the summer
(3) the supply of oxygen is greater in the summer than in the fall
(4) mating occurs between the species in the fall, but not in the summer

11. An earthworm lives and reproduces in the soil. Through its feeding, excretion, and tunneling activities, the worm adds nutrients and allows air to enter the soil. Together, these statements describe the earthworm's

(1) habitat
(2) nutrition
(3) niche
(4) environment

12. Among the populations of any natural community, the basic food supply is always a critical factor because it is

(1) produced by all organisms
(2) synthesized from oxygen
(3) a means of transferring energy
(4) present in surplus amounts

13. A consumer–producer relationship is best illustrated by

(1) foxes eating mice
(2) leaves growing on trees
(3) rabbits eating clover
(4) fleas living on a cat

Base your answers to questions 14 through 16 on the food chain below and on your knowledge of biology.

rosebush→aphid→beetle→spider→toad→snake

14. Which organism in this food chain can transform light energy into chemical bond energy?

15. At which stage in this food chain will the population with the smallest number of organisms probably be found?

(1) spider
(2) aphid
(3) rosebush
(4) snake

16. If all of the aphids were killed off due to the spraying of pesticides, what would happen to the number of toads this ecosystem could support?

17. Which group of organisms is *not* represented in the food web below?

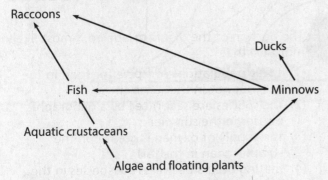

(1) consumers
(2) carnivores
(3) producers
(4) decomposers

18. Which organisms are chiefly responsible for the recycling of dead matter?

(1) parasites
(2) viruses
(3) decomposers
(4) producers

19. In a natural community in New York State, the producer organisms might include

(1) bacteria, fungi, and viruses
(2) deer, rabbits, and squirrels
(3) grasses, maple trees, and weeds
(4) trout, peas, and earthworms

20. Which sequence illustrates a generalized food chain in a natural community?

(1) autotroph → herbivore → carnivore
(2) autotroph → herbivore → autotroph
(3) heterotroph → herbivore → carnivore
(4) consumer → autotroph → carnivore

21. In a food chain consisting of photosynthetic organisms, herbivores, carnivores, and organisms of decay, the principal function of the photosynthetic organisms is to

(1) capture energy from the environment
(2) provide material for decay
(3) prevent erosion of the topsoil
(4) release energy from organic compounds

22. A characteristic shared by both predators and parasites is that they

(1) feed on decomposing plant material
(2) capture and kill animals for food
(3) live inside their hosts
(4) attack a living food source

23. As you drive down the highway, you may see crows feeding on dead animals. As a result of this nutritional pattern, crows may be classified as

(1) scavengers
(2) predators
(3) herbivores
(4) producers

24. When the food relationships in a habitat are illustrated by means of a diagram, the result is always a complicated weblike pattern. This is due to the fact that

(1) many consumers are adapted to use more than one food source
(2) producer organisms always outnumber the consumer organisms
(3) matter is lost in an ecosystem as it moves from producers to consumers
(4) both producers and consumers require oxygen for metabolic processes

25. Although three different butterfly species all inhabit the same flower garden in an area, competition between the butterflies rarely occurs. The most likely explanation for this lack of competition is that the butterflies

(1) occupy different niches
(2) have a limited supply of food
(3) share food with each other
(4) are able to interbreed

26. In the diagram below, which organisms are components of the same food chain?

(1) trees, mountain lion, snake, and hawk
(2) trees, rabbit, deer, and shrubs
(3) grasses, cricket, frog, and mouse
(4) grasses, mouse, snake, and hawk

27. In the diagram of a food chain below, what do the arrows indicate?

(1) the direction in which organisms move in the environment
(2) the direction of energy flow through a series of organisms
(3) the order of importance of the various organisms
(4) the return of chemical substances to the environment

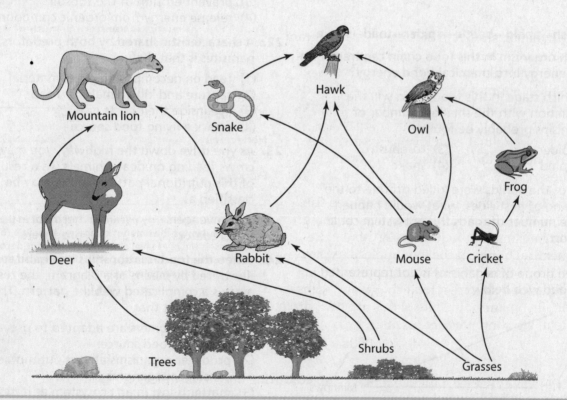

Energy Flow Through an Ecosystem

Almost all organisms use the solar energy stored in food to power their life processes. That energy, however, does not remain in the organism forever. Every second of every day, an animal that is not eating has less energy in its tissues than it had a few seconds before. This energy loss occurs because the organism is continually breaking the chemical bonds in food to use the energy to live. As it is released to make ATP and then used in the cells, much of the energy is converted to heat and is lost to the environment. Only a small amount can actually be used by the cells. As a result, each next step in the food chain has less of the original solar energy available to it.

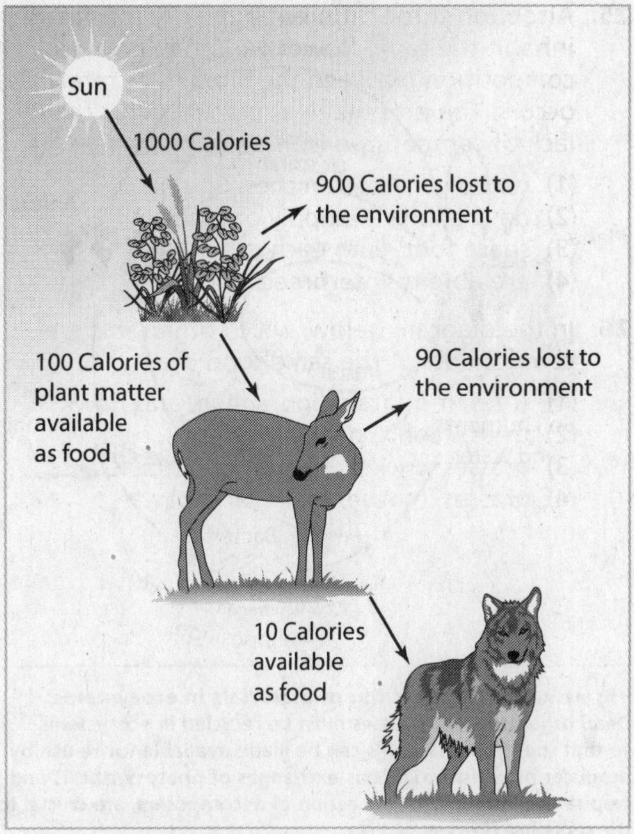

Figure 6-7 shows how the energy is lost. Only the energy stored in the body tissues of each organism is passed to the next consumer in the chain. Because of the energy loss described above, most of the original stored energy is lost in just a few steps of the food chain. For this reason, food chains are usually quite short.

An **energy pyramid,** shown in Figure 6-8, is a diagram that illustrates the transfer of energy through a food chain or web. Each block of the energy pyramid represents the amount of energy that was obtained from the organisms below it. Only this amount of energy is available to the organisms in the next higher block. Notice that each level is smaller due to the loss of heat as the organisms carry on their life activities.

A continual input of energy, typically from the sun, is required to start the process and to keep it going. Producer organisms capture this energy and store it in the chemical bonds of the food molecules they make. The flow of energy that accompanies the transfer of the food shown in food chains and webs is essential to life on Earth. In spite of this constant drain of energy to the environment, life continues because the sun continues to provide energy.

Recycling and Reusing Materials

The parts of dead organisms that are not consumed during one of the other steps in the food chain are not wasted. Decomposers extract the last bit of energy contained in the dead organisms (as well as the energy in the waste products from living organisms) and use it to sustain their life processes. As they do so, they return the raw materials contained in the once-living matter to the soil. This process of breaking down dead organisms, as well as the wastes produced by living organisms, into their raw materials and returning those materials to the ecosystem is known as <u>decomposition</u>.

Figure 6-7. **As energy is transferred, much of it is lost to the environment as heat.**

Sun
1000 Calories
900 Calories lost to the environment
100 Calories of plant matter available as food
90 Calories lost to the environment
10 Calories available as food

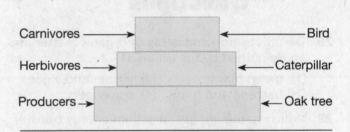

Carnivores — Bird
Herbivores — Caterpillar
Producers — Oak tree

Figure 6-8. **An energy pyramid:** Each block in the energy pyramid illustrates the amount of energy available for use by organisms at the next level above it. (Energy for decomposers actually comes from organisms at all the levels, so they are not shown in this simplified pyramid.)

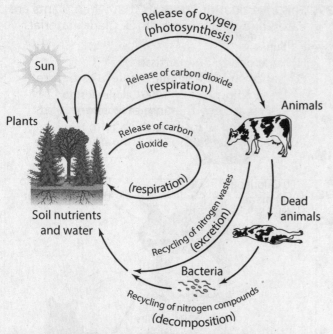

Release of oxygen (photosynthesis)

Release of carbon dioxide (respiration)

Sun

Plants

Release of carbon dioxide

(respiration)

Soil nutrients and water

Animals

Recycling of nitrogen wastes (excretion)

Dead animals

Bacteria

Recycling of nitrogen compounds (decomposition)

Figure 6-9. **The recycling of materials in ecosystems:** Dead organisms and wastes must be recycled in ecosystems so that their raw materials can be made available for re-use by producer organisms. The gas exchanges of photosynthesis and respiration, along with the action of decomposers, are crucial to the recycling process.

Two examples of organisms that fill the role of decomposers are bacteria and fungi. Because of the actions of decomposers, the atoms and molecules in living things cycle through both the nonliving and living parts of the biosphere. As they do, chemical elements, such as carbon, hydrogen, oxygen, and nitrogen, that make up the bodies of living things pass through food webs and are combined and recombined in different ways in different living organisms. For example, plants trap carbon dioxide and water molecules in energy-rich compounds (such as glucose and starch) during photosynthesis. When plants need energy to power their cell processes or are eaten by a consumer, these molecules may be broken down and used by the organism. During respiration, energy is released by the cells and molecules of carbon dioxide and water returned to the environment.

Much of the cycling of materials in ecosystems is carried out by decomposers. Figure 6-9 shows some of the ways matter cycles throughout the ecosystem.

Review Questions

Set 6.3

28. Decomposition and decay of organic matter are accomplished by the action of
   (1) green plants
   (2) bacteria and fungi
   (3) viruses and algae
   (4) scavengers

29. Which statement best describes energy transfer in a food web?
   (1) Energy is transferred to consumers, which convert it to nitrogen and use it to make amino acids.
   (2) Energy from producers is converted into oxygen and transferred to consumers.
   (3) Energy from the sun is stored in green plants and transferred to consumers.
   (4) Energy is transferred to consumers, which use it to produce food.

30. Organisms that eat goats obtain less energy from the goats than the goats obtain from the plants they eat. This is because the goats
   (1) pass on most of the energy to their offspring
   (2) convert solar energy to food energy
   (3) store all of their energy in milk
   (4) use energy for their own metabolism

Base your answers to questions 31 and 32 on the energy pyramid below and on your knowledge of biology.

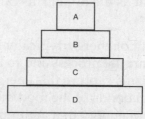

31. If birds eat insects that feed on corn, which level on this pyramid would birds occupy?
   (1) A   (2) B   (3) C   (4) D

32. Which statement concerning the energy in the pyramid is correct?
   (1) The producer organisms contain the least amount of energy.
   (2) Stored energy decreases as it is passed from consumer to consumer.
   (3) Consumers contain more energy than producers.
   (4) Decomposers are the source of energy for this pyramid.

33. Most green algae are able to obtain carbon dioxide from the environment and use it to synthesize organic compounds. This activity is an example of

(1) cellular respiration
(2) autotrophic nutrition
(3) heterotrophic nutrition
(4) heterotrophic respiration

Base your answers to questions 34 through 37 on the activities described in the paragraphs below and on your knowledge of biology.

A tomato plant was placed under a sealed bell jar and exposed to light. Carbon dioxide containing radioactive carbon was introduced into the bell jar as shown in the following diagram. After an hour, the inlet valve was closed. Later, the entire plant was removed from the soil and cleaned by rinsing it in water.

A Geiger counter indicated radioactivity in the roots. These roots were then dried and chopped into very small pieces. The chopped roots were sprinkled into an aquarium containing a very hungry goldfish that was *not* radioactive.

Four days later, the fish was removed from the aquarium and a tissue section of the fish was tested with the Geiger counter. The counter indicated an above-normal level of radioactivity in the fish tissues.

34. Which cycle is primarily being studied by means of this investigation?

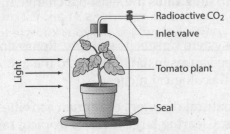

(1) oxygen   (3) nitrogen
(2) carbon   (4) water

35. A control setup for this investigation would be identical to the one described except for the replacement of the

(1) tomato plant with a geranium plant
(2) goldfish with a tadpole
(3) radioactive carbon dioxide with atmospheric carbon dioxide
(4) soil with distilled water

36. By which process was the radioactivity incorporated into the material that was transported to the roots?

(1) growth   (3) photosynthesis
(2) mitosis   (4) respiration

37. This investigation suggests that when plants are eaten by animals, some of the plant materials may be

(1) changed to animal tissue
(2) separated into smaller molecules before being digested
(3) eliminated by the animal in a form that allows the plant to grow again
(4) used in regulating the animal's digestive processes

38. A cycling of materials is represented in the diagram below.

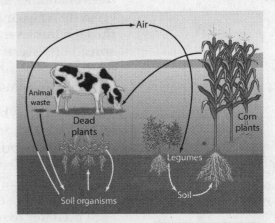

Which statement is supported by the events shown in the diagram?

(1) Materials are cycled between living organisms only.
(2) Materials are cycled between heterotrophic organisms only.
(3) Materials are cycled between the living and nonliving components of the environment only.
(4) Materials are cycled between autotrophic organisms only.

39. Which ecological principle is best illustrated by the diagram below?

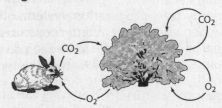

(1) In an ecosystem, material is cycled among the organisms and the environment.
(2) In an ecosystem, the number of producers and consumers is equal.
(3) Competition within a species results in natural selection.
(4) An ecosystem requires a constant source of energy.

Diversity Benefits Species and Habitats

As a result of evolution, there is a great diversity of species on Earth. Almost every ecosystem is populated by many species, each occupying its own special niche. The interrelationships and interdependencies of these species help to keep ecosystems stable, and the diversity of species increases the chance that at least some organisms will survive in the face of large environmental changes.

Biodiversity is a measurement of the degree to which species vary within an ecosystem. There is a strong connection between biodiversity and the stability of an ecosystem. A natural forest, for example, contains many different species of trees. If disease or insects attack one population, nearby trees of another species are likely to survive. The mix of species in the ecosystem also makes it difficult for the disease organisms to move quickly through this environment. Here, biodiversity serves as a barrier to the spread of disease or insect attack. In contrast, on a tree farm where all of the trees are planted and are of a single species, the entire population could be seriously damaged by a single disease or insect attack.

The interactions between organisms may allow an ecosystem to remain stable for hundreds or thousands of years. In established, stable ecosystems, populations tend to increase and decrease in size in a predictable pattern. Over time, however, the size of the population remains relatively stable. For example, when the prey population increases, a large food supply causes the size of the predator population to rise. Because each predator requires many prey to meet its energy needs, the prey population rapidly decreases. Soon, with the decline in a prey population, some of the predators begin to starve. When only a few predators remain alive, the prey population reproduces and greater numbers of prey survive. The cycle begins anew. Figure 6-10 illustrates the seasonal change in a rabbit population.

The loss of biodiversity in an ecosystem upsets its stability. Removing species from an environment often causes instability due to the loss of organisms that were filling critical ecological niches.

Many species may be lost when natural disasters or human activities cause large-scale destruction to habitats. Clearing large areas of tropical rain forest, for example, has disrupted many ecosystems; some may never recover. Although some species may be able to return to a damaged ecosystem, others with critical roles may be totally lost. The interdependencies between populations in the original ecosystem may have been so great that if biodiversity is lost, the ecosystem may never be restored to its original state.

Species can also be lost when humans do not consider the environmental impact of their actions. For example, offering bounties for the removal of predatory mountain lions from some environments sounded like a good idea at one time, but it led to population explosions of deer herds. Soon the deer overpopulated the area, and their overgrazing reduced the food supply so much that many deer starved. The overgrazing also led to soil erosion that caused permanent environmental damage.

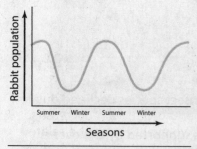

Figure 6-10. Rabbit populations: Rabbit populations may rise and fall over the course of a year, but from year to year they follow the same pattern if the environment is stable.

When humans clear land for agricultural purposes, the loss of biodiversity may also lead to an unstable environment. Disease and insect pests present major problems to farmers whose crops are genetically similar. For these farmers, any disruption threatens to affect the entire crop. Farmers are constantly in search of ways to control insect pests and diseases in their crops, because they have created an environment that is always in danger of serious disruption. In natural ecosystems, the diversity of species provides no such concentration of one kind of food, making it far less likely that any single pest or disease will cause problems.

Biodiversity Benefits Humans

Biodiversity also represents one of the greatest resources known to humans. It ensures the availability of a rich variety of genetic material, some of which may prove valuable to humans. Though still largely untapped, the genetic diversity found in rain forests has provided humans with medicines, insecticides, and other useful resources. If we destroy ecosystems, we lose much of the biodiversity they hold. As diversity is lost, potentially valuable resources are lost with it.

Review Questions

Set 6.4

Base your answers to questions 40 and 41 on the information and graph below and on your knowledge of biology.

During the 1970s, Canadian forests in New Brunswick were heavily sprayed to control the spruce budworms that were damaging the spruce trees. Ecologists discovered that, along with the budworm, bees of many species—including sweat bees and bumblebees—had also been killed. All of the bees were important for pollinating flowers so the plants could produce fruit. Miles away from the spruce forests, blueberry growers were devastated when their blueberry yield declined by 75 percent over the same time period as the spraying was taking place. The graph shows the biodiversity present in the Canadian spruce forests prior to, during, and after the spraying.

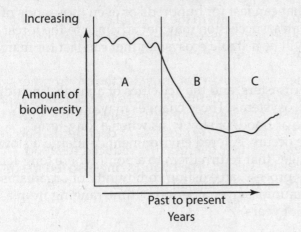

40. As the number of insect species declined due to spraying, the blueberry production decreased. Explain how these two events might be related even though the pesticide did not land directly on the blueberry plants. [1]

41. On the graph provided below, draw a line that shows the relationship of ecosystem stability to changes in biodiversity. [1]

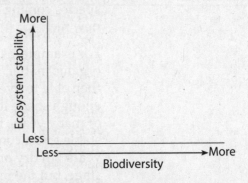

42. Explain why medical researchers are concerned when the biodiversity of an ecosystem decreases. [1]

43. The color, taste, and juiciness of a particular variety of strawberry makes it very popular. Growers are able to plant hundreds of acres of this variety, and all the plants are exactly the same, since they reproduce asexually. Explain why this lack of diversity in the strawberry field could prove to be a problem for the growers. [1]

44. The graph shows the biodiversity present in four different species living in the same area.

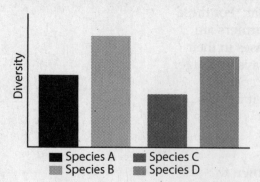

Species A
Species B
Species C
Species D

If the environment were to change dramatically or if a new plant disease were to be introduced, which plant species would be the most likely to have individuals that could survive the disease?

(1) Species A   (3) Species C
(2) Species B   (4) Species D

45. A forest community is made up of thousands of species of organisms and can exist practically unchanged for hundreds of years. This stability is due to the

(1) diversity of organisms present
(2) abundance of insects that feed on plants
(3) changes in the climate of the area
(4) lack of decomposers in the forest

Environmental Changes

Many environments, such as the bare rock on a mountaintop, have few resources that can provide homes for living organisms. Through natural processes, these environments will change over long periods of time to become habitats for many diverse species. The series of changes by which one habitat changes into another is called **ecological succession.**

In the process of ecological succession, each community causes modifications to its environment. The modifications result in changes that make it more suitable for another community. The original species that lived there may find it harder to adapt to these changes, while the new species coming in may be able to compete more successfully for the new niches.

For example, as grasses grow in an area with very shallow soil, they add organic matter, making the soil deeper and more fertile. Shrubs are then able to live in this modified environment and will eventually produce enough shade to eliminate the grasses growing below them. Over a period of many years, these gradual changes may result in the formation of a stable forest community that can last for hundreds or even thousands of years. (In dry or cold climates, succession may not advance to the forest stage, but the final stage will be a stable ecosystem that can last for many years.)

Climatic changes, natural disasters, and the activities of animals (including humans) can alter stable ecosystems. These changes may occur rapidly, perhaps due to a forest fire or flood, or slowly, as when a long-term drought or climate change occurs. Altered environments undergo a slow series of successional changes that return them to a point where long-term stability is possible. In this process, an existing community of organisms is replaced by different communities over a period of time ranging from a few decades to thousands of years.

Time

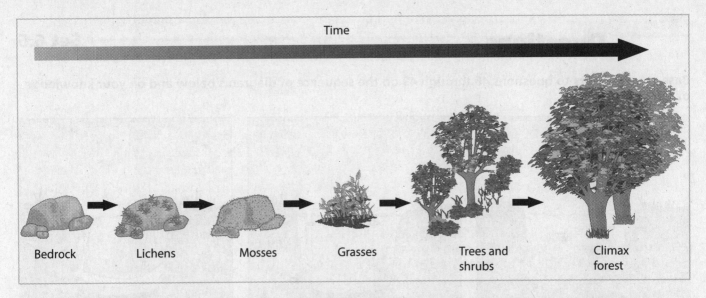

Figure 6-11. **Succession from bare rock to a forest:** As the depth of the soil increases, it can support the root systems of larger plants.

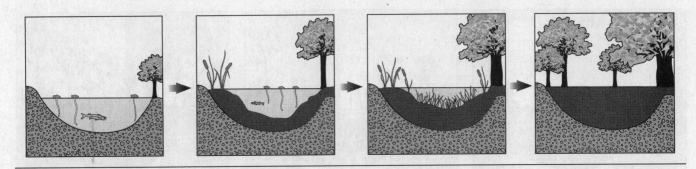

Figure 6-12. **Succession from a lake to a forest**

There are two commonly observed patterns of succession. A community of mostly bare rock will gradually accumulate soil, leading to a progression of vegetation types from grasses to shrubs, and eventually a forest. This process is seen in Figure 6-11.

Another commonly observed example of ecological succession is the change from a lake community to a forest. The lake will gradually accumulate sediments from erosion and the buildup of organic debris from plants and dead organisms. As the lake fills in, it becomes shallower. After many years, it may become a swamp. The filling-in continues, and eventually a mature forest may result. Successional changes from lake to forest are shown in Figure 6-12.

Base your answers to questions 46 through 49 on the sequence of diagrams below and on your knowledge of biology.

1840

1870

1900

1930

1960

1990

46. This sequence of diagrams best illustrates

(1) succession
(2) evolution
(3) the effects of acid rain
(4) a food chain

47. If no human intervention or natural disaster occurs, by the year 2050 this area will most likely be a

(1) lake   (3) desert
(2) swamp   (4) forest

48. The natural increase in the amount of vegetation from 1840 to 1930 is related to the

(1) decreasing water depth
(2) increasing amount of sunlight
(3) presence of bottom-feeding fish
(4) use of the pond for fishing

49. Describe what would happen over the fifty years following 1990 if a fire burned off all of the vegetation in the area. [1]

Base your answers to questions 50 and 51 on the information below and on your knowledge of biology.

If you travel inland from the shores of the present Lake Michigan, which was once much larger than it is today, you would travel through the following areas:

1. the present sandy beach
2. grasses
3. a cottonwood forest
4. a pine forest
5. an oak forest
6. a beech-maple forest (where the original shoreline was located)

50. The sequence of plant growth is an illustration of

(1) succession
(2) a food chain
(3) evolution
(4) an autotroph pyramid

51. Describe why the plants growing in the area of the old shoreline are beech and maple trees and no longer the grasses observed near the new shoreline. [1]

52. When a stable forest community is destroyed by fire, the community usually is

(1) not restored
(2) restored in a series of successive changes
(3) restored only if humans reforest the area
(4) changed into a permanent grassland

53. The conditions that existed in a forest before a fire will be established mainly by

(1) the water cycle
(2) the carbon cycle
(3) succession
(4) evolution

54. Which statement accurately describes ecological succession?

(1) The lack of animals in an altered ecosystem speeds up the process of natural succession.
(2) Abrupt changes in an ecosystem only result from human activities.
(3) After a major disaster, stable ecosystems can never become established again.
(4) An abrupt change in an ecosystem can lead to a long-term gradual change.

55. When Mount St. Helens erupted in 1980, a portion of the surrounding area was covered by lava, which buried all of the vegetation. Four months later, *Anaphalis margaritacea* plants were found growing out of lava rock crevices. The beginning of plant regrowth in this area is a part of the process known as

(1) species preservation
(2) evolution
(3) biotic competition
(4) succession

Base your answers to questions 56 through 58 on the diagram below, which represents the changes in an ecosystem over a period of 100 years, and on your knowledge of biology.

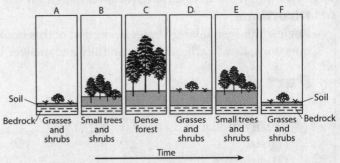

56 State one biological explanation for the changes in types of vegetation observed from *A* through *C*. [1]

57 Identify one human activity that could be responsible for the change from *C* to *D*. [1]

58 Predict what would happen to the soil and vegetation of this ecosystem after stage *F*, assuming no natural disaster or human interference. [1]

59 The diagrams below show some changes in an environment over time.

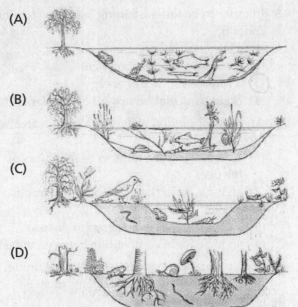

(A)

(B)

(C)

(D)

Which phrase best describes this sequence of diagrams?

(1) the path of energy through a food web in a natural community
(2) the altering of an ecosystem by a natural disaster
(3) natural communities replacing each other in an orderly sequence
(4) similarities between an aquatic ecosystem and a terrestrial ecosystem

Directions

Review the Test-Taking Strategies section of this book. Then answer the following questions. Read each question carefully and answer with a correct choice or response.

Part A

1 The members of an animal community are usually similar in
   (1) size
   (2) structure
   (3) food requirements
   (4) environmental requirements

2 Which is a biotic factor that affects the size of a population in a specific ecosystem?
   (1) the average temperature of the ecosystem
   (2) the number and kinds of soil minerals in the ecosystem
   (3) the number and kinds of predators in the ecosystem
   (4) the concentration of oxygen in an ecosystem

3 In order to be self-sustaining, an ecosystem must contain
   (1) a large number of organisms
   (2) a warm, moist environment
   (3) a constant source of energy
   (4) organisms that occupy all of the niches

4 An overpopulation of deer in a certain area will most likely lead to
   (1) a decrease in the number of predators of the deer
   (2) an increase in the number of autotrophs available for food
   (3) a decrease in the incidence of disease
   (4) an increase in competition between the deer

5 For a natural ecosystem to be self-sustaining, many essential chemical elements must be
   (1) converted to energy
   (2) changed into fossil fuels such as oil and coal
   (3) permanently removed from the environment
   (4) cycled between organisms and the environment

6 A food chain is illustrated below.

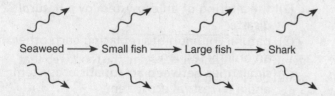

Seaweed ⟶ Small fish ⟶ Large fish ⟶ Shark

The arrows represented as ∿⟶ most likely indicate
   (1) energy released into the environment as heat
   (2) oxygen produced by respiration
   (3) the absorption of energy that has been synthesized
   (4) the transport of glucose away from the organism

Part B

Base your answers to questions 7 and 8 on the information and graph below and on your knowledge of biology.

The Effect of pH on Survival Rates of Selected Species in Certain Adirondack Lakes

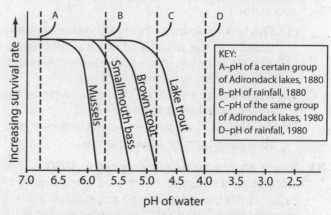

KEY:
A–pH of a certain group of Adirondack lakes, 1880
B–pH of rainfall, 1880
C–pH of the same group of Adirondack lakes, 1980
D–pH of rainfall, 1980

–*National Geographic* (adapted)

7 State how the pH of these Adirondack lakes changed between 1880 and 1980. [1]

8 State the effect that the pH change in these Adirondack lakes had on lake trout, brown trout, smallmouth bass, and mussels. [1]

9 Which types of organisms must be present in an ecosystem if the ecosystem is to be maintained?
   (1) producers and carnivores
   (2) producers and decomposers
   (3) carnivores and decomposers
   (4) herbivores and carnivores

10 Although three different bird species all inhabit the same type of tree in an area, competition between the birds rarely occurs. The most likely explanation for this lack of competition is that these birds
(1) have different ecological niches
(2) eat the same food
(3) have a limited supply of food
(4) are unable to interbreed

11 Identify one abiotic factor that would directly affect the survival of the fish shown in the diagram below. [1]

12 Which pair of terms would most likely apply to the same organism?
(1) heterotroph and herbivore
(2) heterotroph and autotroph
(3) autotroph and parasite
(4) producer and predator

13 A food chain is represented below.

corn plants → field mice → garter snakes → red-tailed hawks

The most abundant organisms in the food chain would be the
(1) corn plants
(2) field mice
(3) garter snakes
(4) red-tailed hawks

Base your answers to questions 14 through 16 on the food web and graph and on your knowledge of biology. The graph represents the interaction of two different populations, A and B, in the food web.

Food Web

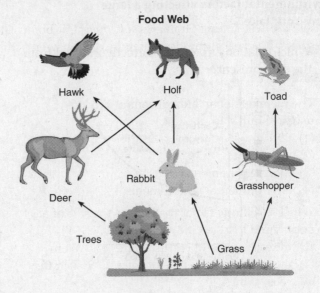

Graph

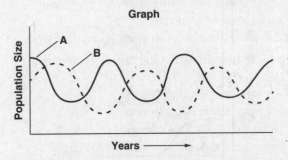

14 Population A is made up of living animals. The members of population B feed on these living animals. The members of population B are most likely
(1) scavengers   (3) predators
(2) autotrophs   (4) parasites

15 Identify one heterotroph from the food web that could be a member of population A. [1]

16 An energy pyramid is shown below.

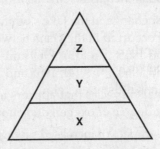

Identify one organism shown in the food web that would be found at level X. [1]

Base your answers to questions 17 through 20 on the graphs below that show data on some environmental factors affecting a large New York lake.

17 Which relationship can be correctly inferred from the data present?

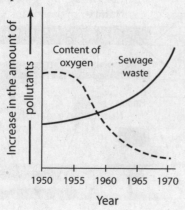

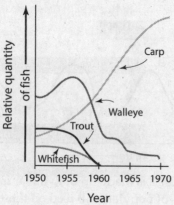

(1) As sewage waste increases, the oxygen content decreases.
(2) As sewage waste increases, the oxygen content increases.
(3) As oxygen content decreases, the carp population decreases.
(4) As oxygen level decreases, the trout population increases.

18 The greatest change in the lake's whitefish population occurred in the years between
(1) 1950 and 1955   (3) 1960 and 1965
(2) 1955 and 1960   (4) 1965 and 1970

19 Identify the fish species that appears to withstand the greatest degree of oxygen depletion. [1]

20 Explain the impact of increased sewage levels on the biodiversity of the lake ecosystem. Support your answer with specific examples from the graph. [1]

Base your answers to questions 21 through 24 on the information below and data table.

A field study was conducted to observe a deer population in a given region over time. The deer were counted at different intervals over a period of 40 years. During this period, both ranching and the hunting of deer and their predators increased in the study region. A summary of the data is presented in the table.

Deer Population Changes 1900-1940

Year	Deer Population (thousands)
1900	3.0
1910	9.5
1920	65.0
1924	100.0
1926	40.0
1930	25.0
1940	10.0

Using the information in the data table, construct a line graph on the grid following the directions below.

Deer Population Changes 1900-1940

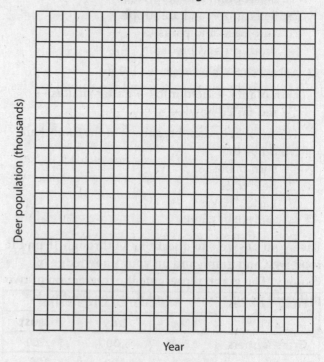

21 Mark an appropriate scale, without any breaks in the data, on each labeled axis. [1]

22 Plot the data for the deer population on the grid. Connect the points and surround each point with a small circle.

Example: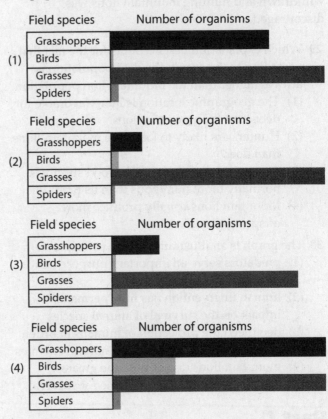

23 During which 10-year period did the greatest increase in the deer population occur?
   (1) 1900–1910   (3) 1920–1930
   (2) 1910–1920   (4) 1930–1940

24 State one possible action that could have been taken to help maintain a more stable population of deer in the area. [1]

Base your answers to questions 25 through 28 on the information below and on your knowledge of biology.

For 25 years, hay was cut from the same 10 acres on a farm. During these years, shrews, grasshoppers, spiders, rabbits, and mice were seen in this hayfield. After the farmer retired, he no longer cut the hay, and the field was left unattended.

25 Which description best matches the events in the former hayfield over the next few decades?
   (1) The plant species will change, but the animal species will remain the same.
   (2) The animal species will change, but the plant species will remain the same.
   (3) Neither the plant species nor the animal species will change.
   (4) Both the plant species and the animal species will change.

26 The grasshoppers, spiders, shrews, and other organisms, along with the soil minerals, amount of rainfall, and other factors, constitute
   (1) an ecosystem   (3) a biosphere
   (2) a species   (4) a food web

27 Just before he retired, the farmer determined the population size of several of the field species during the months of May, July, and August. The results are recorded in the table below.

Field Species	Number of Organisms		
	May	**July**	**August**
Grasshoppers	1,000	5,000	1,500
Birds	250	100	100
Grasses	7,000	20,000	6,000
Spiders	75	200	500

Draw a food chain that represents the most likely feeding relationships among four of the organisms (grasshoppers, birds, grasses, and spiders) that live in the field. [1]

28 Which graph best represents the relative population size of the field species for May?

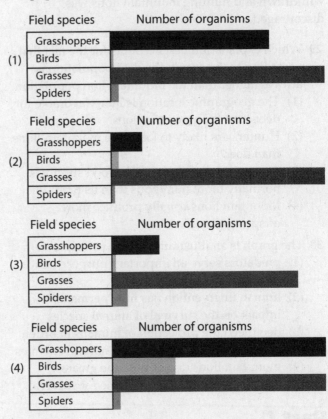

Base your answers to questions 29 and 30 on the information below and on your knowledge of biology.

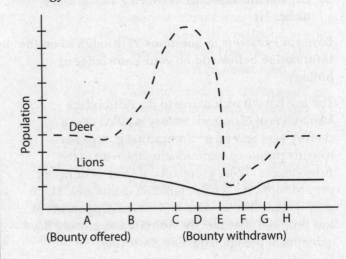

The graph shows the relative populations of mountain lions and deer in a certain geographic area that is generally favorable to both animals. At the time indicated by point A, hunters were offered a bounty payment for each mountain lion killed. Later, at the time indicated by point E, these bounties were withdrawn and hunting mountain lions was discouraged.

29 Which explanation best accounts for the fact that, according to the graph, the deer population is always higher than the mountain lion population?
   (1) The geographic location is more favorable for deer than for mountain lions.
   (2) Hunters are likely to kill more mountain lions than deer.
   (3) The organism serving as the food supply is normally more numerous than its predator.
   (4) Mountain lions usually produce more offspring than deer.

30 The graph is an illustration of the principle that
   (1) predators serve an important purpose in a balanced ecosystem
   (2) human intervention has little permanent impact on the survival of animal species
   (3) deer need the protection of humans in order to survive the attacks of their natural enemies
   (4) mountain lions do not pose the greatest danger to deer in their struggle for survival

Part C

31 State *two* reasons why it is important to preserve biodiversity. [1]

32 Explain the difference between a habitat and a niche. [1]

Base your answers to questions 33 through 35 on the information below and on your knowledge of biology.

The last known wolf native to the Adirondack Mountains of New York State was killed over a century ago. Several environmental groups have recently proposed reintroducing the wolf to the Adirondacks. These groups claim there is sufficient prey to support a wolf population in this area. These prey include beaver, deer, and moose. Opponents of this proposal state that the Adirondacks already have a dominant predator, the Eastern coyote.

33 State one effect the reintroduction of the wolf may have on the coyote population within the Adirondacks. Explain why it would have this effect. [1]

34 Explain why the coyote is considered a limiting factor in the Adirondack Mountains. [1]

35 State one ecological reason why some individuals might support the reintroduction of wolves to the Adirondacks. [1]

Base your answers to questions 36 and 37 on the information and graph below and on your knowledge of biology. The graph contains information about an ecosystem.

The graph below shows the carrying capacities of an ecosystem for three different species, 1, 2, and 3, that inhabit an area and the actual population sizes of these three different species in the area.

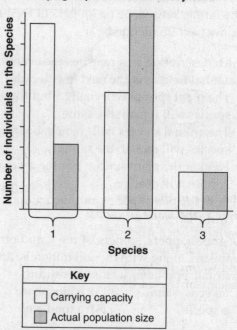

36 Identify which species population would most likely have the greatest competition among its members. Support your answer using information from the graph. [1]

37 Explain how an ecosystem can have three different carrying capacities. [1]

Human Impact on Ecosystems

Global Warming

The hole in the ozone layer is the cause of global warming since it lets in more heat from the sun and warms the polar regions of the Earth.

Global warming is really a natural process. The Earth was first very cold and it has been getting warmer ever since.

Plants are a major cause of global warming since they give off so much carbon dioxide.

Global warming is partly the result of our burning so much fossil fuel like coal and gasoline.

7 Human Impact on Ecosystems

Vocabulary

carrying capacity	global warming	pollution
deforestation	industrialization	renewable resource
direct harvesting	nonrenewable resource	technology
energy flow	nuclear fuel	trade-off
fossil fuel	ozone shield	water cycle

Topic Overview

All living things affect the environment around them. Porcupines chew the bark from trees; squirrels break twigs as they leap from branch to branch. Generally, the changes to the environment are small. Humans, however, have made impressive technological achievements in the past few hundred years. As a result, we are now making significant changes in Earth's diverse environments. As the human population grows and our need for the resources to sustain our technology expands, the possibility that we will harm Earth's ecosystems increases. Our decisions about how to use—or misuse—Earth's resources will have a profound impact on all the organisms that depend on those resources.

Need for Awareness and Understanding

Human activities can create ecological problems that must be avoided or corrected. If we are to find solutions to those problems, we must encourage everyone to become environmentally literate. That means people need to understand the causes and effects of environmental problems as well as the possible solutions that could lead to environmental stability. Because environmental issues often concern many countries, resolving environmental issues frequently requires global awareness, cooperation, and action.

Our Environment

Like all living things, humans are part of Earth's natural ecosystems. We depend on our ecosystem to supply the food we eat, the water we drink, and the air we breathe. As long as our ecosystem functions normally, those essential resources will be available. We can continue to depend on the plants in the ecosystem to provide food and oxygen and to recycle the carbon dioxide we exhale. We will also be able to rely upon our ecosystem to maintain the quality of our water.

Limited Resources

Earth has a finite supply of resources. Some of Earth's resources, such as our food supply and solar energy, are renewable. Given sufficient time,

renewable resources can be replaced. Other resources, such as fossil fuels and minerals, are **nonrenewable resources.** Once they're used, they cannot be replaced. Decisions we make today and tomorrow will determine whether or not we increase our consumption of Earth's limited resources. One way to reduce our use of resources is to control the growth rate of our population. An ever-increasing human population accelerates the use of Earth's limited resources. Making the right decisions about these issues will affect you as well as the future generations of all the organisms that share the biosphere.

Figure 7-1. **A commercial fishing trawler**

Renewable Resources Although many resources are renewable, they must be used carefully. Increased consumption can stress the natural processes that renew some resources. As a result, the resource might be unable to renew itself. For example, the fish we eat are a renewable resource. Even if many fish are captured, over time the fish populations can reproduce and recover their losses. Today, however, modern, commercial fishing (see Figure 7-1) can remove so many fish so quickly that specific populations may not have time to recover. In some cases, the reduction can be so severe that the fish population may fail to reproduce. At that point, the fish would no longer be a renewable resource.

Nonrenewable Resources Our increasing consumption of resources that cannot be replaced naturally is becoming a serious problem. Most metals, such as the aluminum we use for packaging, and other minerals, such as the silicon we use for computer chips, are nonrenewable resources. Fossil fuels, such as the gas that runs our cars and the coal that powers many factories, are also nonrenewable resources. Using too many nonrenewable resources will cause their <u>depletion</u> (serious reduction) within a relatively short time.

Preserving Our Resources Individuals can help maintain our supply of both renewable and nonrenewable resources by practicing the three R's: Reduce, Reuse, and Recycle. Suggestions are included in Table 7-1.

Natural Processes in Ecosystems

Several natural processes that occur in ecosystems affect the life and health of humans as well as all the other organisms that rely on the ecosystem. Some activities of humans affect these processes, and most of the changes are likely to be <u>detrimental,</u> or damaging, to the ecosystems. For example,

The 3 R's	Action	Example
Reduce	Avoid using the resource.	Use energy efficiently; walk, bike or carpool instead of driving.
Reuse	Use the same product over and over, instead of throwing it away after one use.	Use dishes rather than paper plates. Instead of discarding your paper lunchbag, take it home and use it again.
Recycle	Don't throw it in the trash. Instead, discard the product in a way that it can be used again, or to make another product.	Paper, metal, plastic, and glass are all easily recycled. Donate unwanted clothing, books, and furniture to charitable organizations.

Table 7-1. How Individuals Can Preserve Resources

if **pollution**—a harmful change in the chemical makeup of the soil, water, or air—spreads to a particular habitat, some of the species that live in that habitat will suffer. The stability of the ecosystem and the variety of species that live in it might be threatened.

Maintaining Atmospheric Quality Throughout the biosphere, animals take in oxygen during respiration and release carbon dioxide. Plants and algae take in carbon dioxide during photosynthesis and release oxygen. Through the biotic processes of respiration and photosynthesis, the levels of carbon dioxide and oxygen in the atmosphere are kept in the range that is suitable for life.

Abiotic factors also help maintain the quality of the atmosphere. For example, as it falls, rain cleans the air of particles and soluble gases. The rainfall also helps maintain humidity in the atmosphere.

Soil Formation Soils form when weathering breaks down rocks and when organic materials from decaying plants and animals accumulate. Such soils support the growth of many producer organisms and serve as a habitat for decomposers. The root systems of plants hold the soil in place. If the vegetation that covers the ground is removed, the soil can be washed away by rain or blown away by wind. Soil erosion sometimes occurs during a drought when many plants die, leaving bare soil.

The Water Cycle Water continuously evaporates from the surface of the land and water and from the leaves of plants. The water vapor rises into the atmosphere and collects as clouds that can move long distances. Eventually, the vapor condenses as precipitation, which is distributed over many areas of Earth. The water collects as runoff or groundwater or evaporates. The process by which water continually moves from Earth's surface to the atmosphere and back is called the **water cycle,** and is shown in Figure 7-2. Many ecosystems maintain a supply of fresh water, which is available to all organisms, including humans.

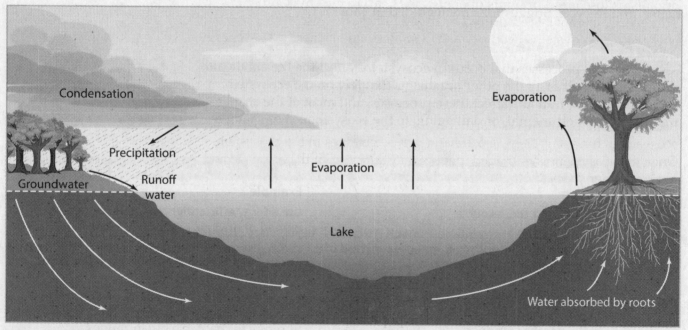

Figure 7-2. The water cycle

Waste Removal and the Recycling of Nutrients Plants that live in the soil use the soil's minerals as they grow. Nutrients are transported from one organism to another through the food chains in the ecosystem. Those that are not released into the atmosphere are eventually contained in the dead bodies and wastes of organisms. Decomposers break down the wastes and the dead bodies of organisms, removing the nutrients in the process. The nutrients are then restored to the soil, where they can then be used by other plants, continuing the cycle.

Without this natural recycling, much of the abiotic materials needed by living organisms would remain "locked up" in the bodies of dead organisms. Minerals and other nutrients would not be available for new organisms. In tropical forests, where heavy rains are frequent, decomposition and the recycling process must take place rapidly. Otherwise, the frequent rains strip the land of minerals before new plants can absorb and use them. In areas where the Amazon rain forest has been cleared and burned for planting, many nutrients have been washed away, leaving the soil unfertile.

Humans sometimes make use of this natural recycling process when they mix decaying lawn and garden wastes to make compost, which is a natural fertilizer and soil conditioner. Adding compost to the soil recycles wastes naturally and reduces the need for chemical fertilizers. It also reduces the amount of waste material in landfills and eliminates the need to burn yard waste, which pollutes our atmosphere.

The Flow of Energy Food chains, food webs, and energy pyramids illustrate the **energy flow** through ecosystems. Each organism has a role in the process and contributes to the overall stability of the ecosystem. As a result, losing all or most of the members of any species of an ecosystem could upset the stability of the whole ecosystem.

Energy is passed through the environment, but unlike nutrients, it does NOT recycle. Instead, at each feeding level in an energy pyramid, organisms lose large amounts of energy (as heat) to the environment. This energy cannot be recaptured by living things. Because of this constant energy loss, ecosystems need a constant source of new energy. That energy source is usually the sun.

People and the Environment

Because humans are part of Earth's ecosystems, they affect the way ecosystems function. They also are affected by changes in the ecosystem. Once the ecosystem is damaged, people may suffer from that damage just like any other species.

Population Growth

Most species in new environments can have a period of rapid population growth. The population increase levels off as it approaches the ecosystem's **carrying capacity,** which is the number of individuals of a species the environment can support. For example, as rabbits move into a field, their population may boom. Eventually, the food supply dwindles, and the scarcity of food leads to a reduction in the population of rabbits. Those that do not get enough to eat may become too weak to escape predators or

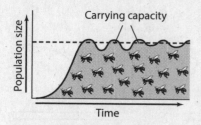

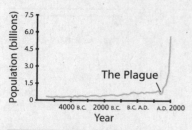

Figure 7-3. A population growth curve: In a new environment, the population usually increases quickly, but it stabilizes when it reaches the carrying capacity of that environment.

Figure 7-4. Growth curve for the human population worldwide

recover from diseases. Some may even die of starvation. The population growth levels off when the number of rabbits is balanced by the availability of food and the presence of limiting factors, such as predators. The relationship between population and the carrying capacity of an environment is shown in Figure 7-3.

Earth can only support a certain number of people. Our planet has a carrying capacity for humans just as it does for other species. The more people there are, the more resources they need. These resources come from the environment. More people also produce more waste, which must be disposed of or recycled. Overcrowding and lack of food also become problems when populations are very large.

For thousands of years, the human population grew slowly. Then about 300 years ago, our food supply began to increase, and improvements in health care and hygiene led to dramatic increases in our population. At present, the population curve inclines steeply upward. To many population scientists, the sharp increase suggests that the human population is growing at a dangerously fast rate. Compare Figure 7-4, the growth curve for the human population, with Figure 7-3, the growth curve typical for animals in an ecosystem.

If the human population continues to grow at the rate shown in Figure 7-4, Earth's carrying capacity could be reached soon. That result could be catastrophic. With no controls, the human population might even overshoot Earth's carrying capacity for our species. There might not be enough food, water, space, and/or oxygen. The resulting deaths from famine, disease, or wars over resources could reduce the human population to a small fraction of its present level. Finding ways to slow our population growth so that the growth rate levels off before Earth's carrying capacity is reached could save future generations from suffering the consequences of unlimited population growth.

Review Questions

Set 7.1

1. Which of these resources is renewable?

(1) wood
(2) oil
(3) iron
(4) coal

2. The best way to ensure that there will be enough aluminum for all future needs is to

(1) dig more mines and process more aluminum ore
(2) buy more aluminum from other countries and save our own
(3) recycle and reuse aluminum
(4) increase space exploration and search for new sources of aluminum

3. Some ecologists are concerned that the human population has outgrown the capacity of many of Earth's ecosystems. The natural limiting factor that will most likely prevent further human population growth in many parts of the world is

(1) habitat destruction
(2) political intervention
(3) food supply
(4) social intervention

4. Which of these human activities is quite often responsible for the other three human activities?

(1) increasing demand on limited food production
(2) rapid increase of loss of farmland due to soil erosion
(3) rapid increase of human population
(4) increasing levels of air pollution

5. The graphs on the right show the size of the human population in relation to food production per acre in four different countries over the same period of time.

Which country's population appears to have reached—and is now maintaining—its population close to its carrying capacity? Explain how you can tell. [1]

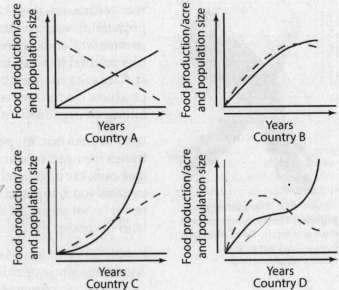

Key ——————— Population size
      – – – – – Food production/acre

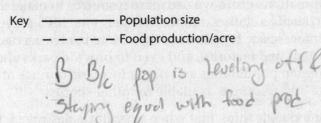

B B/c pop is leveling off &
staying equal with food prod

Human Activities and the Loss of Diversity

Some human activities that destroy habitats and degrade ecosystems do far more than damage individual organisms. They also destroy diversity in both the living and nonliving parts of the environment. For example, when humans use land to build a parking lot, the organisms that lived on that land are likely to die. Other organisms that ate the plants, burrowed through the ground, or nested in the nearby trees are also affected. There will be fewer resources available for a variety of species.

Many deliberate human activities, such as clearing land to plant a single crop, can change the equilibrium in an ecosystem. So can some accidents, such as inadvertently or unknowingly adding a species to an ecosystem.

Direct Harvesting The destruction or removal of species from their habitats is known as **direct harvesting.** It can sometimes lead to the extinction of a species. For example, some species that live in distant parts of the world (rain forests or deserts) are removed from their native habitats and sold to people who want them as unusual pets, ornaments, or house or garden plants. That cute monkey or beautiful parrot in the pet shop may not have been born in captivity. Instead, it may have been captured in the wild and shipped here. Many animals die in the process.

Other organisms are killed to collect a specific body part. For example, baby harbor seals are killed for their pelts, and elephants are killed for the ivory in their tusks, which people carve into jewelry or other trinkets. Direct harvesting can threaten the existence of the entire population of a species. Due to over-harvesting, some species of plants and animals have been taken from their native habitats in such large numbers that those species are now endangered. So many whales have been slaughtered that some species are now in danger of extinction.

In the past, humans have caused the extinction of several species. For example, in the early 1800s, billions of passenger pigeons lived in

Figure 7-5. **The passenger pigeon:** The passenger pigeon, once present in huge numbers, is now extinct because of uncontrolled hunting.

North America. (See Figure 7-5.) Each year hunters shot millions, until the population was greatly reduced. By the time people realized that the species was endangered, it was too late to save it. The last passenger pigeon died in a zoo in Cincinnati, Ohio, in 1914. Today, some endangered species are protected by law. However, because there may be a demand for products made from endangered species, poaching (illegally capturing or killing an organism) is a continuing problem.

Land Use As human populations grow, we use more resources to make the things we need or want, such as clothes, homes, refrigerators, MP3 players, and cars. We also need more space for places to live. More land is needed to grow food, to build roads and factories, and even to provide parks and recreational areas. As human populations and needs increase, our use of land decreases the space and resources available for other species.

Habitat Destruction Many people think that when a habitat is destroyed, the organisms simply find a new home. However, because other parts of the ecosystem are already occupied, displaced animals seldom find a new place to live. Habitat destruction occurs when people take over land for their own use. It is an important way that species can become endangered. They simply have nowhere to live! As habitats are destroyed, whole ecosystems can be damaged and entire species may become extinct. For example, pandas are endangered today because humans have greatly reduced the size of their habitat.

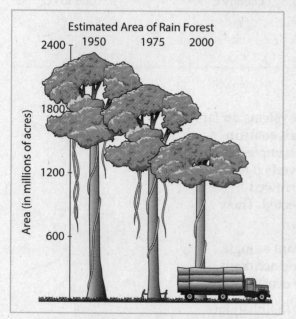

Figure 7-6. **Habitat destruction:** The destruction of rain forests, an example of deforestation, eliminates many ecosystems.

Deforestation, or the destruction of forests resulting from human activity, is a land use decision that causes widespread habitat destruction. People clear the forest by burning or cutting down the trees. Deforestation can provide people with land for farming and places to live. It also provides resources to use in building or manufacturing. Due to deforestation, the area covered by the world's rain forests is only about half as large as the area covered 150 years ago. (See Figure 7-6.) The wetlands, fields, and forests of New York are also threatened by development.

Biodiversity When a wide variety of different species live together in an ecosystem, it is said to have biodiversity. A reduction in biodiversity occurs when species are lost. This lost biodiversity can affect the health of whole ecosystems and food webs. It can even affect the proportion of gases in the atmosphere. Our future ability to find new medicines for treating diseases or to discover new sources of genes that could be genetically engineered into more productive and pest-resistant crops is threatened when biodiversity is lost.

Habitat destruction, such as deforestation, can lead to loss of biodiversity, but it is not the only way that human activities threaten biodiversity. For example, a farmer might plow under a meadow that is home to many species. Then the farmer might plant a single crop, such as corn or wheat, on many continuous acres of land. This practice greatly reduces the biodiversity of the area. (See Figure 7-7.) In addition, it creates an ideal environment for insects that feed on that crop. To control the insects, the farmer may need to use pesticides, which could harm other organisms living in the same or nearby environments.

Figure 7-7. **Loss of biodiversity:** The corn in this field provides habitats for only a few species. The meadow that once grew here was home for hundreds of species of flowers, shrubs, trees and small animals such as insects, mice, and birds.

Imported Species Biodiversity is often reduced when people import and release a species from one environment into another. The release may be inadvertent or intentional. For example, before 1859, there were no rabbits in Australia. Then two dozen rabbits were released in Australia. By 1953, more than a billion rabbits occupied 1.2 million square miles of the continent. These rabbits ate massive amounts of vegetation ordinarily available to the native species.

Many species become pests when they are added to a new environment. Because the new organisms are not part of an existing food web in the area, they often have no natural enemies in their new environment and rapidly overpopulate the area. They then crowd out, feed on, or otherwise eliminate native species. Two examples are Japanese beetles and gypsy moths, which were accidentally released in the U.S. (See Figure 7-8.) Now they are serious pests in New York.

Once an imported species becomes a pest, it is very difficult to solve the problem. If another species is imported to control it, the second species may choose to feed on native organisms, adding another problem. Using pesticides or poisons can kill other organisms in addition to the imported one. Sometimes scientists find a disease organism that only affects the imported species. The rabbits that overran Australia were eventually controlled by a disease organism. However, there is always a risk that the species may become resistant to the disease and overpopulate again.

Because imported species are such a problem, many states and countries have laws to restrict the transport of fruits and vegetables. The goal of these laws is to avoid introducing diseases or insects that might damage local crops. Some countries require the <u>quarantine</u> (confined isolation) of certain animals and plants until officials are sure they are free of any pests that could escape into the new environment.

Scientists are working to find safer methods of pest control. One safe pest control method is setting traps that use chemical scents to attract insects. With this method, no other species are harmed and the population of the pest species can be reduced to a safe level. Breeding and releasing native predators of a pest species has also sometimes been used successfully and without harm to other species.

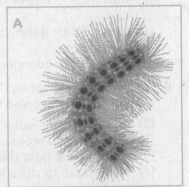

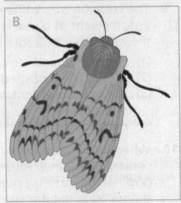

Figure 7-8. **Imported species:** (A) During the larval stage, the gypsy moth consumes vast quantities of leaves. (B) The adult moth lays hundreds of eggs, continuing the problem.

6. Ladybugs were introduced as predators into an agricultural area of the United States to reduce the number of aphids feeding on grain crops. This action is an example of

(1) preservation of endangered species
(2) conservation of natural resources
(3) protection of watershed areas
(4) use of a nonchemical means of pest control

7. An example of a human activity that has had a positive effect on the environment is the

(1) disruption of natural habitats through deforestation
(2) capture and sale of rare South American birds
(3) use of reforestation to control erosion in the mountains
(4) hunting of endangered species of animals

controls insect pop without chem

8. The trees in a forest aid in reducing flood damage chiefly because their

(1) branches store water in the form of sap
(2) leaves absorb moisture from the air
(3) root systems hold the soil in place
(4) stems serve to store food

9. The creation of wildlife refuges and the enforcement of game laws are conservation measures that promote increased

(1) use of chemicals to control pests
(2) preservation of species
(3) use of natural controls to limit pest populations
(4) exploitation of wildlife species

10. When land is cleared for agriculture or home construction, small isolated sections of the original habitat may remain. Explain how this reduction in habitat size and the isolation of small sections of habitat might lead to species endangerment. [1] *Many would die as there is less room to feed & live*

11. A method of agriculture presently used throughout the world where one crop is grown on many acres of land has created serious insect problems. This is primarily because this method

(1) increases soil erosion
(2) provides concentrated areas of one kind of food for insects
(3) increases the effectiveness of insecticides used over long periods of time
(4) involves the growing of crops in former desert areas

12. The least ecologically damaging method for controlling the mosquitoes that spread the diseases malaria and encephalitis is by

(1) draining the swamps where mosquitoes breed
(2) spraying swamps with chemical pesticides
(3) spreading oil over swamps
(4) introducing local fish species to the swamps where mosquitoes breed

13. Many people place bat boxes on their property to provide housing that attracts insect-eating bats. Explain how this activity has a positive effect on the environment. [1]

14. In 1859, a small colony of 24 rabbits was brought to Australia. By 1928 it was estimated that there were 500 million rabbits in a 1-million square mile section of Australia. Which statement describes a condition that probably contributed to the increase in the rabbit population?

(1) The rabbits were affected by many limiting factors.
(2) The rabbits reproduced by asexual reproduction.
(3) The rabbits were unable to adapt to the environment.
(4) The rabbits had no natural predators in Australia.

15. Humans are responsible for some of the negative changes that occur in nature because they

(1) have controlled the use of many pesticides and other environmentally damaging chemicals
(2) have passed laws to preserve the environment
(3) are able to preserve scarce resources
(4) are able to modify their physical environment to provide for human needs

16. Which of the following human activities would be the most likely to prevent certain species from becoming extinct?

(1) Pass laws to place all endangered species in zoos.
(2) Increase the hunting of predators.
(3) Increase wildlife management and habitat protection.
(4) Mate organisms from different species to create new and stronger organisms.

17. In the Cochella Valley in California, much of the desert has been converted into golf courses, housing developments, and hotels. The habitat of the Cochella Valley fringe-toed lizard is rapidly being lost. This lizard is adapted to life on fine, windblown sand. Environmentalists want to save the lizard, and developers want to continue construction. Which action would be the best long-term solution?

(1) Land in the Cochella Valley should be purchased and set aside as a preserve for the lizards.
(2) The fringe-toed lizards should be crossed with a species adapted for survival in a different habitat.
(3) The land should be developed as planned and the lizards relocated to a different valley.
(4) The land should be developed as planned and the lizards monitored to see if they can adapt to the new conditions.

18. Refer to the chart below, which illustrates some methods of pest control.

Methods of Insect Pest Control
Insect pests can be repelled or attracted with sex hormones.
Insect populations can be controlled by releasing males sterilized with X-rays.
New plant varieties can be produced and grown that are resistant to insect pests.
Insect pests can be controlled by introducing their natural enemies.

One likely effect of using these methods of pest control will be to

(1) prevent the extinction of endangered species
(2) increase water pollution
(3) reduce pesticide contamination of the environment
(4) harm the atmosphere

The Impact of Technology and Industrialization

Humans modify ecosystems through population growth, consumption, and technology. As human populations grow, they take up more space, consume more resources, and produce more wastes. The expansion of **technology** (using scientific knowledge and technical processes to meet human needs) also increases the quantity of resources people use. All these activities lead to changes in ecosystems, including the way they function. The equilibrium of stable ecosystems can be upset by human actions.

Industrialization

Industrialization is the development of an economy in which machines produce many of the products people use. These products may add to the quality of life, but their manufacture can harm the environment. In addition to contributing to pollution of the air and water, industrialization increases the demand for energy, water, and other resources, including fossil and nuclear fuels.

Higher energy demands in an industrialized society mean that more power plants must be built. Additional power plants—especially those that burn coal—add to the pollution of our air and water. **Nuclear fuel** is an energy source that results from splitting atoms. Nuclear power plants do not pollute the air or water with toxic chemicals, but they can cause thermal pollution of waterways. Also, the disposal of radioactive nuclear wastes presents a huge environmental problem.

Another problem with increased industrialization is that most factories use a lot of water. Large wells drilled for factories sometimes dry up the nearby smaller wells that individuals use to supply their homes. In some cases, withdrawing large quantities of water causes the ground to collapse, forming sinkholes. In dry climates, reducing the supply of groundwater can have serious consequences for native plants and the consumers that depend on them for food.

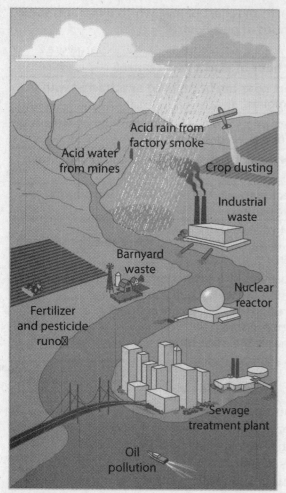

Figure 7-9. Water pollution: Water pollution, which can damage an ecosystem, comes from many sources.

Labels in figure:
Acid rain from factory smoke
Acid water from mines
Crop dusting
Industrial waste
Barnyard waste
Nuclear reactor
Fertilizer and pesticide runoff
Sewage treatment plant
Oil pollution

Just as conservation (the three R's) can help preserve our resources, it can also help to limit the negative impact of industrialization. We can REDUCE our demand for energy and manufactured goods that we don't really need. We can REUSE manufactured products rather than discard them, and we can RECYCLE as many products as possible, conserving both energy and resources in the process.

Water Pollution

Rivers, lakes, and oceans are easy places for people to dispose of wastes, including sewage, wastes from homes and factories, and animal wastes from farms. The addition of pollutants to natural environments causes water pollution, which can change the abiotic conditions in ecosystems. For example, sewage and animal wastes can act as fertilizer, increasing the growth of plants, algae, and bacteria in aquatic systems. Plants consume oxygen all the time, day and night. However, photosynthesis, the primary source of oxygen, stops at night because it requires light. As a result, oxygen production also stops. Then, oxygen levels drop and many organisms suffocate. When these organisms die, oxygen-using decomposers begin their decay activity, which further decreases the oxygen supply. Eventually, all the organisms in this oxygen-reduced ecosystem may be lost. Figure 7-9 shows several ways water pollution can affect a natural habitat.

Toxic Wastes Many wastes dumped into waterways from cities, farms, or industries can be toxic (poisonous) to the organisms that use or live in the water. Chemical fertilizers and weed and insect killers can be washed off farmlands into streams or rivers. The chemicals can collect in the cells of organisms living in the water and along the shore. These toxic materials then move through the food chain and eventually damage or kill many kinds of organisms.

Although the level of toxic substances in the water might be low, scientists have learned that the concentration of a toxin increases as it moves through the food chain. For example, small quantities of toxic substances are absorbed into the cells of algae and other producers living in the water. When those producers are eaten by small herbivores, the toxins are stored in the herbivore's fatty tissue. There it stays until the herbivore is eaten by the next consumer in the food chain. At each level of the chain, larger and larger amounts of toxic material collect in the fatty tissue. Organisms at or near the top of the food chain are most likely to accumulate enough of these chemicals in their bodies to cause them harm. (See Table 7-2.)

For example, farmers used to spray the pesticide DDT on their crops. Rain washed some of the DDT off the land and into streams and rivers. In the water, the DDT moved up through the food chain. Soon, fish-eating birds at the top of the food chain produced eggs with very thin shells. The shells were so thin that they broke easily, which killed the next generation of birds before it even hatched.

Table 7-2. Accumulation of a Toxic Substance by Organisms in a Food Chain				
Food Chain Organisms	Plant —>	Herbivore —>	Carnivore 1 —>	Carnivore 2
Relative concentration of the toxic substance	.000003	0.04	0.5	2.0
Magnification factor (compared to the amount in the plant)	0	1,333 times as much	16,667 times as much	66,667 times as much

Thermal Pollution Some power plants and industries use water to cool their machines or materials. The warmed water is then released into a river or lake, and the water temperature in the river or lake rises. Because warm water cannot hold as much dissolved oxygen as cold water, the oxygen level in the river or lake drops as the water temperature rises. Some species may suffocate as a result of <u>thermal</u> pollution; others may be forced to try to find a new home.

The solution to most of these problems is to find better ways to deal with wastes and to reduce the need for power. Sewage can be treated before it is discharged into waterways. Toxic wastes can be separated from other materials and either recycled or stored safely. People could conserve energy by using less power. Methods could be developed for cooling industrial processes that would reduce their damage to the environment.

Air Pollution

Just as wastes dumped into rivers and oceans cause water pollution, harmful substances released into the air cause air pollution. Early in the industrial age, people thought that burning wastes just disappeared into the atmosphere, and that they didn't have to worry any more about the wastes. We now know this is not true! Most of the pollutants released into the atmosphere eventually wind up in the water cycle and return to the water or land. Like water pollution, air pollution can damage habitats and harm the organisms that live in them. Figure 7-10 shows how air pollution can affect a natural habitat.

Burning Fossil Fuels Fuels such as the coal and gas that formed from the remains of organisms that lived millions of years ago are known as **fossil fuels.** Factories, cars, and most electrical power-generating plants burn fossil fuels. When fossil fuels are burned, carbon dioxide and other gases— some containing sulfur and/or nitrogen—are added to the air.

Acid Precipitation Sulfur and nitrogen compounds that are produced when fossil fuels burn can combine with moisture in the atmosphere. When this moisture falls to Earth as <u>acid rain</u>, snow, or other precipitation, it has a low pH level and is much more acidic than normal precipitation. Some acid precipitation can be as acidic as lemon juice. When highly acidic rain or snow touches plants, it may damage them and disrupt the way they function. The damaged plants may be more susceptible to attacks by fungi or insects.

Acid precipitation can also fall into lakes and streams or run off the land into the water. In lakes, the lower pH levels can be deadly to algae, the eggs of some fish, and other organisms. Producer organisms, such as algae, are killed. Without algae suspended in it, the water looks crystal clear and pure. However, the food chains in the ecosystem have been disrupted, and

Figure 7-10. Air pollution: Trees can be damaged—or killed— by polluted air.

populations of fish and other organisms have died. Some lakes have become so acidic that nothing can live in them.

Smog Other air pollutants are produced by automobile exhaust and by industrial processes. Some of these pollutants can be toxic when inhaled. This kind of pollution becomes more serious when weather conditions trap the gases in an area for hours or even days. <u>Smog</u> is a kind of air pollution that results when certain pollutants react with sunlight. It looks like a gray or brown haze and contains many airborne pollutants. People with respiratory diseases are especially sensitive to air pollution and may be in danger when air pollution is intense.

Global Atmospheric Changes

Some pollutants in the air harm living things directly, like the trees in Figure 7-10. Others can cause worldwide atmospheric changes that threaten many habitats and the organisms that live in them.

Global Warming Sunlight passes through the gases in the atmosphere to reach Earth. But some of these atmospheric gases, called <u>greenhouse gases,</u> also trap and absorb the infrared radiation that bounces off Earth's warmed surface. For thousands of years, this process—called the <u>greenhouse effect</u>—has kept Earth warm. In recent years, however, the amount of greenhouse gases in the atmosphere has increased. As Figure 7-11 shows, the increased amount of greenhouse gases in Earth's atmosphere traps some of the heat that would normally radiate into space. The result is that Earth's average temperature is rising. This increase in temperature, called **global warming,** could lead to changes in climate patterns and even to the melting of the ice caps at the North and South Poles. Most of the recent increase in greenhouse gases has been caused by burning fuel for transportation and industry.

Carbon dioxide, a major greenhouse gas, is released when fossil fuels are burned. (See Figure 7-12.) If the greenhouse effect causes climate change, the world's food supply may suffer. Another effect could be that the ice

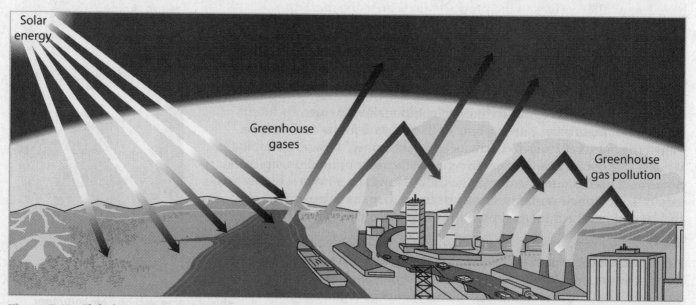

Solar energy

Greenhouse gases

Greenhouse gas pollution

Figure 7-11. Global warming: Pollution caused by human activity is increasing the amount of greenhouse gases in the atmosphere. This increase can intensify the greenhouse effect, causing global warming.

caps could melt, leading to a rise in sea level and flooding in many coastal habitats.

Finding and using energy sources that do not add carbon dioxide to the atmosphere is one way to prevent further global warming. Because trees remove large quantities of carbon dioxide during photosynthesis and store it in their tissues as carbon compounds, growing more long-lived trees could also help solve the problem.

Ozone Depletion Ozone depletion is another atmospheric problem that we must solve. Like global warming, ozone depletion is a worldwide problem, and international cooperation is needed to find an effective long-term solution.

The release of certain industrial gases into the atmosphere has led to destruction of much of the **ozone shield,** the layer of ozone gas in the upper atmosphere that protects Earth from some of the sun's radiation. (See Figure 7-13.) The thinning "hole" in the ozone shield allows above normal amounts of ultraviolet radiation from the sun to reach Earth's surface. Ultraviolet radiation can cause genetic mutations and can kill cells that are exposed to it. An increase in ultraviolet radiation at Earth's surface could result in more cases of skin cancer. It could also destroy many of the producer organisms in the oceans. This would disrupt food chains and reduce the amount of oxygen released by the producers.

The main cause of ozone depletion is the release of gases called chlorofluorocarbons, or CFCs, into the atmosphere. CFCs have been used as coolants in refrigerators and air conditioners, as propellants in aerosol cans, and in the manufacture of plastic foam. Some steps have been taken to reduce the release of these gases. Researchers have found alternatives to the products that cause the most damage, and international agreements to reduce emissions of the harmful gases have been made.

Individual Choices and Societal Actions

Many people hope technology will help solve some of our environmental problems. In fact, technology has led to some improvements. For example, advances in technology have allowed farmers to greatly increase the crop yield of an acre of land. Larger crop yields mean a greater supply of food. However, some kinds of technology, such as pesticides and fertilizers, can cause pollution and have other harmful effects on the environment.

If technology cannot solve all our environmental problems, people will need to take some difficult steps to save our ecosystem. For some problems, solutions are now available, but they affect our quality of life. For example, we know how to reduce the air and water pollution caused by factories, power-generating plants, and automobiles, but the solutions are expensive and would make the

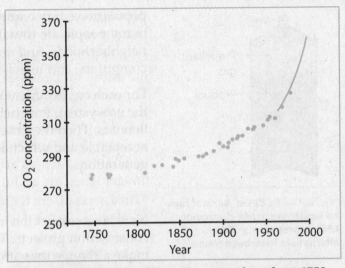

Figure 7-12. Carbon dioxide in the atmosphere from 1750 to 2000: The amount of carbon dioxide in the atmosphere has increased greatly since the beginning of the Industrial Revolution. The dots are data from ice core samples; the solid line represents direct measurements.

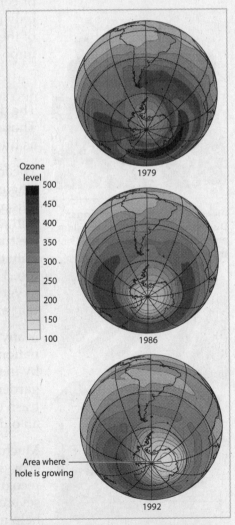

Figure 7-13. The "hole" in the ozone shield: These satellite maps show how much the "hole" in the ozone shield above the South Pole grew in just over a decade.

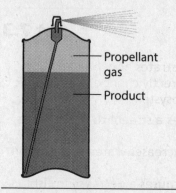

Figure 7-14. **CFCs:** Aerosol cans no longer use ozone-destroying CFCs as propellants. Safer alternatives have been found.

Propellant gas
Product

products we buy cost more. We also know how to conserve energy, but many people are unwilling to give up their large cars, brightly lit neighborhoods, and air-conditioned comfort and to turn off their radios, computers, and televisions.

For each environmental problem, people must learn to assess the risk to the ecosystem. For each solution, they must learn to analyze the costs and benefits. Then they must determine which **trade-off,** or compromise, is acceptable and which is simply too dangerous to the welfare of future generations.

The Impact of New Technologies

New laws restrict the introduction of certain new technologies or major construction projects. The individual or company seeking permission to make a change that affects the environment must prepare a statement known as an environmental impact statement. This statement includes an analysis of how the project or technology will affect the environment and is usually discussed at public hearings. Then members of the public or their elected representatives vote on whether or not to allow the new technology or construction project to go forward. Appropriate decisions can be made only if the public is environmentally literate and has a clear understanding of the ecological issues. If an incorrect decision is made, it may be impossible to undo the damage that might result.

Figure 7-15. **Public hearings:** Discussion can be held to consider environmental issues and the trade-offs involved.

Today's Decisions Affect the Next Generation

The decisions we make today can have a huge impact on our environment. Those decisions, right or wrong, will affect the people living today as well as future generations.

The loss of some species may seem unimportant. However, the loss of that single species might have a huge impact on the ecology of an area. If the loss of species continues, large-scale destruction of natural environments will result, with serious consequences for the future. For example, the destruction of large forests or the loss of algae in ocean waters affects not only the organisms that live in those ecosystems but organisms elsewhere too. Those losses may compromise Earth's ability to produce enough oxygen and remove enough carbon dioxide to maintain an atmosphere that meets the needs of all of its inhabitants, including humans.

Many important decisions about the environment are made by states and nations, but a surprising number of important decisions are made each day by individuals. For example, individuals decide whether to burn their garden waste or turn it into compost, whether to toss the soda can into the trash or recycle it, whether to grab a fresh sheet of paper or write a note on an old envelope.

Figure 7-16. **Recycling:** Decisions on recycling are made by individuals and their communities.

Much of the impact of our technology and population growth on Earth's ecosystems has been detrimental. If our environmental problems are not recognized and solved, the long-term damage will be irreversible and severe. On the other hand, cooperation by individuals and nations can help maintain the stability of the ecosystems upon which all life depends. Making people aware of the successful results of the collective actions of many separate individuals may be the most promising approach to solving ecological problems.

19. Car exhaust has been blamed for increasing the amount of carbon dioxide in the air. Some scientists believe this additional carbon dioxide in the air may cause

    (1) global warming
    (2) increased biodiversity
    (3) habitat preservation
    (4) ozone destruction

20. Deforestation will most directly result in an immediate increase in

    (1) atmospheric carbon dioxide
    (2) atmospheric ozone
    (3) wildlife populations
    (4) renewable resources

21. Which human activity has probably contributed *most* to lake acidification in the Adirondack region of New York State?

    (1) passage of environmental protection laws
    (2) reforestation projects in lumbered areas
    (3) production of chemical air pollutants by industry
    (4) use of biological insect controls to eliminate pests

22. A major reason that humans can have such a significant impact on an ecological community is that humans

    (1) can modify their environment through technology
    (2) reproduce faster than most other species
    (3) are able to increase the amount of finite resources available
    (4) remove large amounts of carbon dioxide from the air

23. Explain how the runoff waters from farm land and golf courses might be dangerous to organisms living in ponds, rivers, or streams. [1]

24. Explain why water shortages occur frequently in parts of New York State even though the water supply is nearly constant. [1]

25. The number of industries along New York State's rivers is increasing. What is the most likely consequence of increased industrialization?

    (1) a decrease in the amount of water needed by industry
    (2) a decrease in the amount of water pollution
    (3) an increase in the destruction of natural ecosystems
    (4) an increase in the amount of water available for recreational use

26. Which statement illustrates how human activities can most directly change the dynamic equilibrium of an ecosystem?

    (1) A hurricane causes a stream to overflow its banks.
    (2) Increased wind increases water evaporation from a plant.
    (3) Water pollution causes a decrease in fish populations in a river.
    (4) The ozone shield helps prevent harmful radiation from reaching the surface of Earth.

27. Which illustrates the human population's increased understanding and concern for ecological interrelationships?

    (1) importing organisms in order to disrupt existing ecosystems
    (2) allowing the air to be polluted only by those industries that promote technology
    (3) removing natural resources from the Earth at a rate equal to or greater than the needs of an increasing population
    (4) developing animal game laws in order to limit the number of organisms that may be killed each year

28. When living organisms obtain water and food from their environment, they may also take in toxic pesticides. Low concentrations of some pesticides may not kill animals, but they may damage reproductive organs and cause sterility. The data table below shows concentrations of a pesticide in tissues of organisms at different levels of a food chain.

Concentration of Pesticide in Tissues	
Organisms	**Pesticide Concentration (parts per million)**
producers	0.01 — 0.03
herbivores	0.25 — 1.50
carnivores	4.10 — 313.80

What does this information suggest to a person who is concerned about health and is deciding on whether to have a plant-rich or an animal-rich diet? Support your answer using the information provided. [1]

Directions

Review the Test-Taking Strategies section of this book. Then answer the following questions. Read each question carefully and answer with a correct choice or response.

Part A

1 Today's lifestyles have led to increased demands for disposable products. The packaging of these products has caused environmental problems most directly associated with
(1) food web contamination
(2) atmospheric depletion
(3) solid waste disposal
(4) the use of nuclear fuels

2 Some modern agricultural methods have created serious insect problems, primarily because these methods
(1) increase soil loss
(2) provide concentrated areas of food for insects
(3) aid in the absorption of water
(4) grow crops in areas where formerly only insects could live

3 The decline and extinction of many predatory animal species is most probably the result of
(1) an overabundance of prey species
(2) the introduction of a new species of animal into an area
(3) the disruption of natural food chains
(4) the decreased use of chemical pesticides

4 Modern methods of agriculture have contributed to the problem of soil depletion because many of these methods
(1) require smaller amounts of mineral and fertilizer application
(2) interfere with the natural cycling of elements
(3) use many varieties of cloned plants
(4) depend on the practice of planting and harvesting

5 Which action that humans have taken in attempting to solve an ecological problem has had the most negative effect?
(1) seeking better means of birth control in the human population
(2) applying scientific farming techniques to oceans
(3) producing stronger and more effective pesticides
(4) developing new techniques for the disposal of sewage and industrial and chemical wastes

6 Japanese beetles, a major insect pest in the United States, do relatively little damage in Japan because they
(1) are kept in check by natural enemies
(2) are kept in check by effective pesticide sprays
(3) hibernate during the winter months
(4) have gradually adapted to the environment

7 Gypsy moths were accidentally introduced into North America. The most probable reason these insects have become serious pests in North America is that they
(1) were bred by research scientists and are resistant to all pesticides
(2) are protected by environmental laws and feed on other insect species
(3) have few natural enemies and reproduce successfully
(4) are affected by natural controls and feed on plants

8 The survival of many plants and animals has been aided most by
(1) increasing the height of industrial smokestacks to spread air pollutants away from the immediate vicinity of combustion
(2) reduction in the number of restrictive pollution control laws
(3) heavy use of pesticides to kill all of the insect pests that compete with humans for food sources
(4) development of research aimed toward the preservation of endangered species

9 DDT is an insecticide that accumulates in the fatty tissues of animals and is transferred through food chains. Its concentration increases at each link of a food chain. Which organism in a food chain is most likely to accumulate the highest concentration of DDT?
   (1) rabbit (a herbivore)
   (2) corn (a producer)
   (3) field mouse (a consumer)
   (4) owl (a predator)

10 What is the most likely cause of the change in life expectancy shown in the graph below?

Changes in Average Life Expectancy (1910-1970)

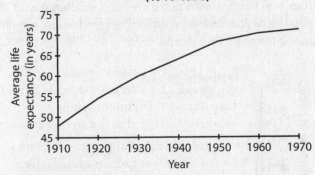

   (1) poor land-use management that has affected the quality of the topsoil
   (2) technological oversights that have had an impact on air quality
   (3) a decrease in natural checks, such as disease, on the population
   (4) widespread use of pesticides, such as DDT, in water supplies

11 As water flows downhill, its energy can be used to generate electricity. Later, this water may evaporate, fall as rain, and be used again to generate electricity in the same way. This explains why electricity generated with water is considered
   (1) a source of water pollution
   (2) a renewable form of energy
   (3) more expensive than nuclear energy
   (4) responsible for global warming

Part B

Base your answers to questions 12 through 15 on the passage below and on your knowledge of biology.

Keystone Species

A keystone species is one whose presence contributes to the diversity of life and whose extinction would lead to the extinction of other forms of life. A keystone species helps to support the ecosystem of which it is a part.

An example of what can happen when a keystone species is removed occurred when fur hunters eliminated sea otters from some Pacific Ocean kelp beds. Otters eat sea urchins, which eat kelp. With its major predator gone, sea urchin populations exploded and consumed most of the kelp. Fish, snails, and other animals associated with the kelp beds disappeared.

The grizzly bear is another example of a keystone species. Grizzlies transfer nutrients from the ocean ecosystem to the forest ecosystem. The first stage of this transfer is performed by salmon that swim up rivers, sometimes for hundreds of miles. Salmon are rich in nitrogen, sulfur, carbon, and phosphorus. The bears capture the salmon and carry them onto dry land, scattering nutrient-rich feces (wastes) and partially eaten salmon carcasses. It has been estimated that the bears leave up to half of the salmon they harvest on the forest floor.

12 One action humans can take that might ensure that these sea otters will continue their function as a keystone species in their environment is to
   (1) establish a sea otter wildlife refuge in the Atlantic Ocean
   (2) pass laws to regulate the hunting of sea otters
   (3) plant kelp in the Pacific Ocean
   (4) destroy sea urchins found living in the kelp beds

13 Some people feel the grizzly bear should be eliminated from parts of its natural range. Describe the impact of this proposed action on the forest ecosystems in these areas if the bears are eliminated. Support your answer with information from the passage. [1]

14 Which organism is most likely *not* functioning as a keystone species in its ecosystem?
(1) beaver — transforms its territory from a stream to a pond or swamp, maintaining the habitat for a variety of native species
(2) elephant — destroys trees, making room for grass species and preventing the environment from becoming a woodland
(3) black-tailed prairie dogs — burrows act as homes to other creatures, including burrowing owls, badgers, rabbits, snakes, salamanders, and insects
(4) zebra mussels — compete with native species, reducing the biodiversity of the Great Lakes ecosystem

15 Which sequence best represents the feeding relationships in a kelp ecosystem that has not been disturbed by humans?
(1) sea urchins → kelp → fish
(2) kelp → sea urchins → sea otters
(3) kelp → sea otters → sea urchins
(4) sea urchins → snails → kelp

Base your answers to questions 16 through 19 on the diagram below and on your knowledge of biology. The diagram represents the growth rate of a mouse population introduced into an abandoned field ecosystem.

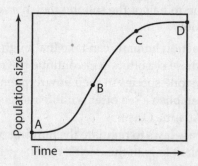

16 At what points is food most likely a limiting factor in the rate of mouse population growth?
(1) A and B   (3) C and D
(2) B and C   (4) B and D

17 At what point is the rate of population growth the greatest?
(1) A   (2) B   (3) C   (4) D

18 At what point would the mouse population be the greatest in the ecosystem?
(1) A   (2) B   (3) C   (4) D

19 Compare the growth rate of the mouse population in the abandoned field to the growth rate of the human population. In your comparison be sure to identify
• how it is similar [1]
• how it is different [1]

Base your answers to questions 20 and 21 on the information and graph below and on your knowledge of biology.

The screw-worm fly is a destructive parasite of livestock. The graph shows the results of an experiment in which one population of screw-worm flies was treated with pesticides and another group of equal size was treated with ionizing radiation, which made the male flies sterile.

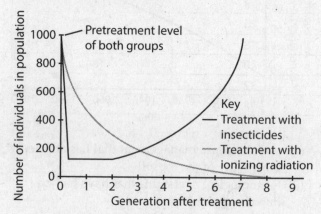

20 At what point after treatment will the group treated with pesticide probably reach its pretreatment population?
(1) first generation   (3) third generation
(2) seventh generation   (4) eighth generation

21 At what point after treatment will the sterility method be more successful against screw-worm flies than the pesticide method?
(1) immediately   (3) third generation
(2) second generation   (4) sixth generation

Base your answers to questions 22 and 23 on the information in the paragraph below and on your knowledge of biology.

A single protist (a one-celled organism) was placed in a large test tube containing nutrient broth. The tube was kept at room temperature for 24 hours. Samples from the tube were observed periodically during the 24 hours, using the low power of a compound light microscope. The data are summarized in the table below.

Age and Number of Protists in Culture	
Age of the Population in Hours	**Number of Protists in the Population**
0	1
6	2
8	3
10	4
13	8
16	16
18	32
20	64
22	128
24	256

22 Which graph best represents the data given in the table?

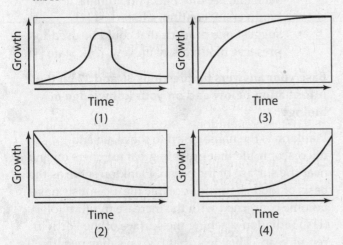

23 Which graph most resembles the growth of the human population at the present time?
(1) 1   (2) 2   (3) 3   (4) 4

Base your answers to questions 24 and 25 on the graph below which shows pollution from nitrogen-containing compounds (nitrates) in a brook flowing through a deforested and a forested area between 1965 and 1968.

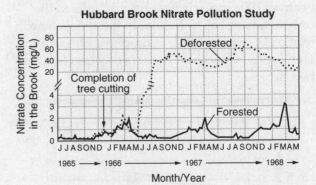

24 State how nitrate pollution in the brook changed after the brook flowed through the deforested area. [1]

25 Explain how deforestation contributed to this change. [1]

Part C

Base your answers to questions 26 through 29 on the information and graphs below, and on your knowledge of biology.

For over 100 years scientists have monitored the carbon dioxide concentrations in the atmosphere in relation to changes in the atmospheric temperature. The graphs below show the data collected for these two factors.

Concentration of Carbon Dioxide in the Atmosphere

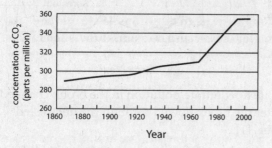

Average Atmospheric Temperature Change per Year

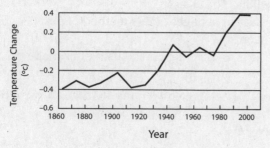

26 State the overall relationship between the concentration of carbon dioxide and changes in atmospheric temperature. [1]

27 State one way in which humans have contributed to the increase in atmospheric carbon dioxide. [1]

28 Identify one specific *negative* effect the continued rise in temperature would be likely to have on an ecosystem. [1]

29 Describe one way humans could try to reduce the problem of global warming. [1]

Base your answers to questions 30 and 31 on the information below and on your knowledge of biology.

Cattail plants that grow in freshwater swamps in New York State are being replaced by an imported species of plant called purple loosestrife. The two species have very similar environmental needs.

30 Since cattails and loosestrife occupy the same niche, it is predicted that eventually only one of the two species will exist in New York freshwater swamps. State one reason why loosestrife will probably out-compete the cattails and be more successful. [1]

31 Explain why loosestrife plants replacing the native cattails could potentially cause a decrease in many swamp wildlife populations and perhaps even lead to the elimination of some species from New York State. [1]

32 Describe two ways in which the destruction of the rainforest in South America could affect a hospital patient in New York State? [1]

Base your answer to questions 33–35 on the information below, and on your knowledge of biology.

Human activities continue to place strains on the environment. One of these strains on the environment is the loss of biodiversity.

33–35 Explain what this problem is and describe some ways humans are involved in both the problem and the possible solutions. In your answer be sure to:
- state the meaning of the term *biodiversity* [1]
- state one *negative* effect on humans if biodiversity continues to be lost [1]
- suggest one practice that could be used to preserve biodiversity in New York State [1]

Base your answers to questions 36 and 37 on the information below and on your knowledge of biology.

Plankton is the name given to the algae and microscopic life that grow in great numbers on and near the surface of the ocean. Plankton serve as the basis of food chains for oceanic life. Scientists have become concerned with the increase in ultraviolet (UV) radiation reaching the surface of the Earth in recent years. They fear that UV rays may negatively impact the plankton.

36 Explain why the amount of UV radiation reaching the surface may be on the increase, especially near the North and South Poles. [1]

37 Describe the effect any large-scale plankton destruction will have on larger species living in these same areas of the ocean where the UV levels have been increasing. [1]

38 Destruction of the ozone shield is generally considered a negative aspect of human involvement with the ecosystem. Explain how solving this problem will require increasing global awareness and cooperation [1]

Base your answers to questions 39 and 40 on the diagram below and on your knowledge of biology. The diagram represents a part of a food web in a Long Island ecosystem.

The numbers in the diagram show the concentration of the insecticide DDT in parts per million (ppm) in the body tissues of the various organisms.

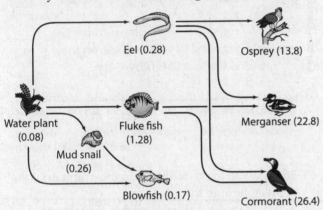

39 Explain why the water plant contains the pesticide DDT. [1]

40 Explain why the amounts of DDT in the three bird species are so much higher than in the other organisms of this food web. [1]

Base your answers to questions 41 through 43 on the information below and on your knowledge of biology.

The planning board of a community held a public hearing in response to complaints by residents concerning a waste-recycling plant. These residents claim that the waste-hauling trucks were polluting air, land, and water and that the garbage has brought an increase in rats, mice, and pathogenic bacteria to the area. The residents were insistent that the waste-recycling plant be closed permanently.

Other residents recognized the health risks but felt that the benefits of waste recycling outweighed the health issues.

41 Identify *two* specific health problems that could result from living near the waste recycling plant. [1]

42 State *one* cause of a health problem that can be associated with the presence of the waste recycling plant. [1]

43 State *one* ecological benefit of recycling wastes. [1]

Base your answers to questions 44–45 on the information below and on your knowledge of biology.

44–45 Ladybugs were introduced as predators into an agricultural area of the United States to reduce the number of aphids (pests that feed on grain crops). Describe the positive and negative effects of this method of pest control. Your response must include at least:
- *two* advantages of this method of pest control [1]
- *two* possible dangers of using this method of pest control [1]

Base your answers to questions 46 through 48 on the information below and on your knowledge of biology.

In the 1980s, global deforestation was estimated at 17 to 20 million hectares per year, an area the size of Great Britain. Today, the area affected by deforestation has decreased significantly in some regions of the world through the use of sustainable forest management. However, there are still regions of the world affected by wide-scale deforestation, because of the short-term economic benefits. The harmful effects of deforestation on regional and worldwide climate and ecology continue as forest areas are destroyed.

46 State one short-term economic benefit of deforestation. [1]

47 Explain how deforestation decreases biodiversity. [1]

48 Explain how wide-scale deforestation may contribute to global warming. [1]

Base your answer to questions 49 through 52 on the information below and on your knowledge of biology.

Zebra mussels have caused several major changes in the ecosystem in the Hudson River. Native to Eurasia, zebra mussels were accidentally imported to the Great Lakes in ships during the late 1980s and first appeared in the Hudson in 1990.

In regions of the Hudson north of West Point, zebra mussels have depleted the levels of dissolved oxygen to the point where many native organisms either die or move to other waters. In addition, large amounts of phytoplankton (small photosynthetic organisms) are consumed by the zebra mussels.

Before the introduction of zebra mussels, one typical food chain in this part of the Hudson was:

phytoplankton → freshwater clams →
   other consumers

49 As a result of the introduction of zebra mussels into the Hudson River, state one likely change in the population of each of two different species (other than the zebra mussels) found in the river. [1]

50 Identify one gas in this ecosystem and state how a change in its concentration due to the effects of zebra mussels would affect organisms other than the zebra mussels. [1]

51 State how the death of many of the native organisms could affect the rate of decay and how this would affect the amount of material being recycled. [1]

52 Explain why the size of the zebra mussel population would decrease after an initial increase. [1]

Base your answer to questions 53–56 on the information and graph below and on your knowledge of biology.

At an observatory in Mauna Loa, Hawaii, scientists have been measuring and collecting data related to changes in the atmosphere since the 1950s. The remote location of the observatory makes it ideal for studying atmospheric conditions that can cause climate change. One specific measurement taken is the amount of atmospheric carbon dioxide. Information for a 7-year period is shown in the graph below.

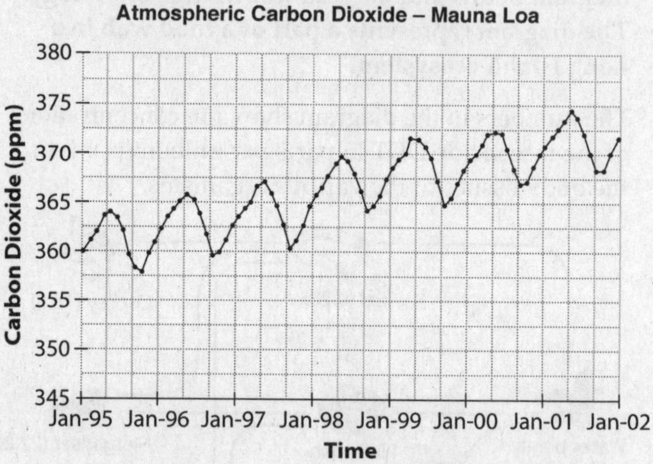

Atmospheric Carbon Dioxide – Mauna Loa

Source: www.mlo.noaa.gov

53–56 Analyze the data shown in the graph. In your answer, be sure to:
 • state the overall relationship between time and carbon dioxide levels [1]
 • state *one* possible cause for the overall change in the carbon dioxide levels shown in the graph [1]
 • identify the biological process that might account for the decreases in carbon dioxide levels [1]
 • identify *two* actions carried out by humans that could lower carbon dioxide levels [1]

Scientific Inquiry and Skills

What do You Think?

Experimental Design

I am doing an experiment to determine the effect of different colors of light on photosynthesis. The dependent variable will be how fast the plants use carbon dioxide.

I am doing an experiment to determine the effect of temperature on the activity of a starch-digesting enzyme. The independent variable will be how fast the enzyme breaks down starch.

I am doing an experiment to determine the effect of different amounts of fertilizer on plant growth. My control group will get the most fertilizer.

Scientific Inquiry and Skills

Vocabulary

assumption	dependent variable	model
bias	evidence	observation
conclusion	experiment	opinion
control	hypothesis	peer review
controlled experiment	independent variable	research plan
data	inference	scientific literacy

Topic Overview

Science is both a body of knowledge and a way of knowing things. Through intellectual and social activities, human thinking is applied to discovering and explaining how the world works. Science originates when people ask questions. Scientists use scientific inquiry and skills to seek answers to questions about the world. This involves formulating hypotheses, designing and conducting experiments, collecting data, and analyzing the data to form conclusions. Scientists also rely on peer review by other scientists to confirm the validity of their results.

What Is Science?

At one time, "scientific" knowledge was just a collection of opinions and unrelated ideas attempting to explain observations. For example, many people gazing out over the ocean were certain that Earth was flat as shown in Figure 8-1. A few individuals were equally sure that Earth was round. The topic was hotly debated. Those believing that Earth was flat offered for **evidence** (support for the idea that something is true) the fact that some ships never returned home. They believed that these ships had been destroyed when they sailed over Earth's edge. Those who believed that Earth was round also had evidence. They had observed boats approaching land and noticed that the tops of the sails were visible before the hull of the boat.

Another common idea once was that living organisms could come from nonliving things. Some people believed that when conditions were just right, frogs formed from the mud, water, and gases in the bottom of a pond. People also thought that if you left some grain and a dirty shirt in a wooden box, mice would develop after a period of time. Many people were certain that reproduction was not necessary for life to form. This idea, too, was discussed and debated.

Today, scientists do more than debate whether or not a new opinion or idea seems to make sense. They develop explanations using observations as evidence. New information is combined with what people already

Figure 8-1. **Ships at sea: At one time a flat Earth seemed to make sense.**

know. Learning about the historical development of scientific concepts and about the individuals who have contributed to scientific knowledge helps people understand the thinking that has taken place. At first, it might seem silly to believe that Earth is flat, but based on observations made at the time and the tools available at the time, it's not surprising that many people believed in a flat Earth. The emergence of life from pond mud seemed equally reasonable.

Scientific Inquiry

Scientific investigation involves the following:

- questioning
- observing and inferring
- experimenting
- collecting and organizing data
- finding evidence and drawing conclusions
- repeating the experiment several times
- peer review

Questioning is at the heart of science. Progress in science depends on people who not only wonder how the world works but who also take the time to develop questions that can be tested and answered.

Observations and Inferences

Observations are things or events that are made using any of the senses or tools, such as thermometers, graduated cylinders, balances, or rulers. As more and better tools are developed, the ability of scientists to observe the natural world increases. For example, the invention of both the microscope (Figure 8-2) and, later, the electron microscope increased our ability to observe the structure of living organisms. This led to the realization that all living things are composed of cells.

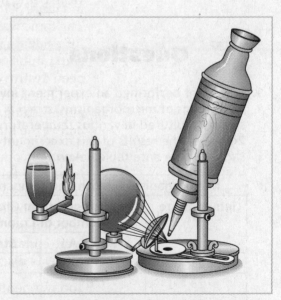

Figure 8-2. **The microscope: With the invention of the microscope, scientists could finally observe microorganisms.**

Inferences Conclusions or deductions based on observations are **inferences**. Inferences may be very subtle. An inference can also be thought of as an idea or conclusion based on the results of an experiment or observation. For example, you may infer that a slug that remains motionless for several hours is dead.

Assumptions A good experiment keeps assumptions to a minimum. An **assumption** is the belief that something is true. Assumptions also may be very subtle, and at first you may be unaware you are making them. For example, when doing a seed germination experiment, you might assume that all 100 seeds planted will germinate when watered and kept under favorable conditions. The idea that 100% of the seeds will grow is an assumption. An assumption that could be made during a slug feeding experiment is that slugs will eat every day if provided with desirable food.

Opinions Ideas people have that may or may not have any basis in fact are **opinions**. Opinions are often **biased**, or influenced by an assumption that may or may not be correct. Although everyone has opinions, which should be respected, a good way to avoid bias is to leave opinions out of data collection and analysis.

The Scientific View Understanding the scientific view of the world is essential to personal, societal, and ethical decision making. To think scientifically, you must critically analyze events, explanations, and ideas. You should use these skills—as well as ideas from other disciplines—to develop personal explanations of natural events. You should also create visual models and mathematical formulations to represent your thinking.

Keep in mind that asking questions to develop an explanation is a continuing and creative process. Sometimes conflicting explanations arise from the same body of evidence. For example, plants seem to grow better when talked to daily. Some explain this by crediting the voice or words. Others point out that simply breathing carbon dioxide on the plant helps it grow. Science is a search for the truth. Scientific thinking can keep you from being misled and making poor judgments.

Review Questions

Set 8.1

1. A student performed an experiment involving two strains of microorganisms, strain A and strain B, cultured in various temperatures for 24 hours. The results of this experiment are shown in the data table below.

Microorganism Growth and Temperature		
Temperature (°C)	Microorganism Growth (Number of Colonies)	
	Strain A	Strain B
25	10	11
28	10	7
31	11	3
34	12	0

Based on the results of the experiment, the student inferred that strain A was more resistant to higher temperatures than strain B was. What, if anything, must the student do for this inference to be considered a reasonable conclusion?

(1) nothing, because this inference is a valid scientific fact
(2) repeat this experiment several times and obtain similar results
(3) repeat this experiment several times using different variables
(4) develop a new hypothesis and test it

2. The graph below represents the results of an investigation of the growth of three identical bacterial cultures incubated at different temperatures.

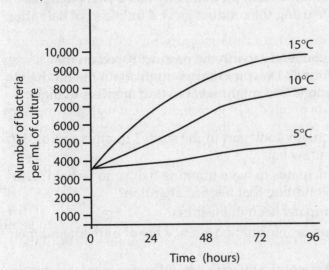

Which inference can be made from the graph?

(1) Temperature is unrelated to the reproductive rate of bacteria.
(2) Bacteria cannot grow at a temperature of 5°C.
(3) Life activities in bacteria slow down at high temperatures.
(4) Refrigeration will most likely slow the growth of these bacteria.

3. A student prepared the following list of steps for performing a laboratory investigation. She omitted one important step for completing the investigation.

Steps to Follow in an Experiment
Define a problem.
Develop a hypothesis.
Select suitable lab materials and perform a controlled experiment to test the hypothesis.
Collect, organize, and graph the experimental data.
?

State the procedure that is missing in the chart. [1]

4. When heavy rains occur while apple orchards are in bloom, the apple crop the following fall is much smaller than normal. This information can best be described as

(1) an inference   (3) a prediction
(2) a hypothesis   (4) an observation

5. Which of the steps listed below would be first in a scientific investigation?

(1) Perform the experiment.
(2) Analyze the experimental data.
(3) Formulate a hypothesis.
(4) Define the problem to be investigated.

Inquiry Skills and Understandings

Everyone needs to understand certain concepts about science and inquiry. **Scientific literacy** involves applying critical thinking skills to everyday life, particularly to claims related to health, technology, and advertising. For example, imagine you are watching a television commercial with your family. The advertiser claims its company has developed a cream that makes hair grow when applied to the scalp. According to the commercial, people with thin hair or no hair have both used the cream with success.

Before rushing out to buy this product, you should think about the claims and begin to question some of what you heard. Next, think about how you can get answers to your questions. Then you should evaluate whether or not the information is to be believed. Here is a way to approach the problem:

1. *Inquiry involves asking questions, and locating, interpreting, and processing information from a variety of sources.*

You may begin by thinking about the following questions:

- How many people were tested?
- What is in the product?
- How long do you have to use it to get results?
- Does it have any side effects?

Next, you ask your friends, and no one knows anything about the product. You also find that your state's consumer product information agency has no information about the company or the hair growth product. Then, you may go to the Internet and find that the company has a Web page that claims 50% of the people using the product grew a full head of hair after ten applications.

Now ask yourself: Are you ready to use the product based on the information you have found? Do you know enough about the product to make an informed decision? You might want to find answers to more questions.

- How many people actually took part in the study? In other words, 50% of how many people grew hair?
- What caused the participants to have thinning hair or to be bald? Did they have a medical condition that needed attention?
- How long has the company been in business?
- Why hasn't the consumer information agency heard of them and their product?
- Was the cream tested scientifically with careful experimental techniques and design?

Keep in mind that careful scientific inquiry involves doing research to find answers to questions and explanations of natural phenomena. Much of the research in the hair product example was done by finding information without actually doing a laboratory investigation.

2. *Inquiry involves making judgments about the reliability of the source and relevance of information: Scientific explanations are accepted when they are consistent with experimental and observational evidence.*

When evaluating evidence and making decisions about how useful your information is, keep the following in mind.

- All scientific explanations are tentative. They can be changed or updated as new evidence emerges. What seems to be true today may be disproved tomorrow.
- Each new bit of evidence can create more questions than it answers. This leads to an increasingly better understanding of how things work.
- Good scientific explanations can be used to make accurate predictions about natural phenomena.
- Beyond the use of reasoning and consensus, scientific inquiry involves the testing of proposed explanations using conventional techniques and procedures. In other words, logic is not enough. Questions should be answered using a good experimental design and thoughtful interpretation.

For example, suppose you read in a magazine about a newly developed HIV vaccine that is said to be effective on monkeys. You should ask:

- Are these results preliminary and tentative, or are they the final results of extensive studies?
- How was the testing done? How many animals were used? For how long have they remained healthy?

- Is HIV in monkeys the same as HIV in humans? Is this the solution to the HIV epidemic in humans or just an early step?

3. *Answers can be found through a research plan and hypothesis testing.*

Figure 8-3. **Research:** A review of the literature must be done before the investigation can be designed. Useful resources include primary science journals, professional Web sites, and library databases.

Developing a Research Plan A **research plan** involves finding background information, developing a hypothesis, and devising an experimental process for testing a hypothesis. Before investing time and resources on research, it is important to find out what others have already learned. (See Figure 8-3.) Most research plans begin with a thorough library search. This search may include the use of electronic information retrieval (the Internet and library databases), a review of the literature (scientific journals), and feedback from the investigator's peers. This background work is done so that the researcher has a thorough understanding of the major concepts being investigated and any similar investigations.

Making Hypotheses Inquiry involves developing and presenting proposals, including formal hypotheses, to test explanations. A good **hypothesis** attempts to explain what has been observed in a way that can be tested. It is a tentative answer to a question. Experiments cannot prove a hypothesis; they can only either support the hypothesis or fail to support it.

Most hypotheses would make sense if the words "I think that" were added to the beginning of the statement. Try adding "I think that" to the beginning of each hypothesis in the following chart.

A good hypothesis can also help determine the organization of an experiment as well as what data to collect and how to interpret those data. Testing a hypothesis is valuable even when the

Examples of Hypothesis Statements
This hormone will make plants grow faster.
The presence of this chemical in our drinking water does not harm us.
If this hormone is applied to plant leaves, then the plant will grow faster.
If this chemical is safe, then it will not harm us when it is added to our drinking water.

hypothesis is not supported by experimental results, since new information is gained in the process of testing any hypothesis.

Designing an Experiment

Once the background work has been done and the hypothesis developed, the actual experiment must be designed. An **experiment** is a series of trials or tests that are done to support or <u>refute</u> (disprove) a hypothesis.

Let's say that you suspect that applying the chemical IAA (a growth hormone) to plant leaves will increase the growth rate of the plant. Your hypothesis might read as follows: *If IAA is applied to the leaves of plants, then the plants will grow more rapidly than those that do not have IAA applied to their leaves.* Once you have written your hypothesis, you must make decisions about variables and experimental techniques.

The Dependent Variable What is it that you will measure? In this experiment, you will measure the effect of IAA on plants. What you will measure is called the **dependent variable,** since it depends on what you do to the plants. Since you asked about how the plants will grow, you will need to measure how large the plants are at the beginning as well as at regular intervals until the conclusion of the experiment. You will also have to decide how to make the measurements. Will you measure only the height of the stem, or will you also measure the size of the leaves? What units will you use?

Independent Variables Factors that might influence the dependent variable are **independent variables.** This is the variable the investigation manipulates. If you are investigating the effect of IAA being applied to the leaves, you must decide on the concentration of IAA. How often will it be applied to the leaves, and how will you apply it? You may even decide to test several concentrations of IAA. In this example, the frequency of applications and the concentration of IAA are independent variables.

Controlling Variables How will you control the independent variables that might affect your interpretation of the results? A **control** is an established reference point used as a standard of comparison. It allows you to make comparisons that generate valid information. For example, you should start with plants that are of the same kind and are about the same age and size as in Figure 8-4. All of the plants should be healthy, grown in the same kind of soil, and provided with the same amount of water and light. If you neglect to control all independent variables, one or more of them may affect plant growth, and you may reach a false conclusion concerning IAA.

A **controlled experiment** is one in which the possible variables have been carefully considered and regulated so the results are due only to the independent variable you are testing.

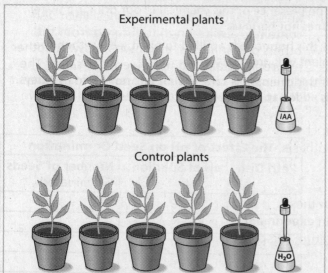

Figure 8-4. Experimental controls: The control group will have distilled water applied to their leaves in place of IAA. It is important to apply something to the leaves of the control group or they would be treated differently in two ways from the experimental group. The plants will be the same type, size, and age as those in the experimental group. They will be grown in the same soil, with the same amount of light and water.

Keep in mind that there should only be one variable being tested at one time. You can test different concentrations of IAA, or you can test the frequency of applying IAA, but you cannot test both on the same plants at the same time. You also cannot test both the impact of fertilizer AND the impact of IAA on the same plants at the same time.

Developing Experimental Techniques Selecting, acquiring, and building apparatus, as well as considering safety precautions and planning how to avoid bias, are important parts of this stage in the development of the research plan. For example, in the IAA study, you need to decide how many plants to use. Would one plant for each concentration of IAA be enough? Should you use 100 plants for each concentration? Think about these possibilities. With only one plant, genetic differences could cause variations in growth. Could one of the plants have been infected with a fungus while still an embryo? Would using multiple plants help to cancel out this type of problem? How many trials will you need?

Is one trial enough, or would five or six trials be better? Large sample sizes with repeated trials provide much more accurate information, and there is less probability of error due to chance. Large sample sizes and multiple trials are more likely to produce valid results.

When designing an experiment, think of the steps in the following Experimental Design Guide as a way to assist you in your planning. Remember that you should first formulate the question you want to answer or the problem you want to solve. Then review the literature to learn about the topic you are investigating.

Experimental Design Guide	
What is your hypothesis?	The hypothesis is a testable statement. It should suggest a possible answer to the question you are investigating.
What is your dependent variable?	What should change and/or be measured as a result of the experiment? Make a data table to record the data as they are collected.
What is your independent variable?	What is the treatment? Are you only changing one factor at a time to see its effect? Will there be several groups, with each testing one treatment—such as several pH values, colors of light, or temperatures?
Describe how you will control the experiment.	What other possible factors may vary that could also affect the results and make your experiment inconclusive?
What steps will you take to conduct this experiment?	Make a list of procedures and materials needed to conduct the experiment. Be sure to address safety issues.

Review Questions

Set 8.2

6. A drug company tested a new medication before putting it on the commercial market. Pills without medication were given to 500 test subjects in group A, and pills with medication were given to 500 subjects in group B. In this experiment, the individuals in group A served as the
   (1) host group
   (2) dependent variable
   (3) control
   (4) hypothesis

7. In order to find the percentage of organic matter in soil from several different locations, a student collected the samples, weighed them immediately, roasted them for several minutes in a flame to burn off organic matter, and weighed them again. The student concluded that the difference between the first and second weights represented the weight of the organic matter in the soil. The most serious mistake that the student made in this experiment was in
   (1) taking large samples
   (2) weighing the samples before roasting them
   (3) failing to dry the samples before first weighing them
   (4) assuming that roasting could remove the organic matter

8. In an investigation to determine the effects of environmental pH on the germination of dandelion seeds, 25 dandelion seeds were added to each of five petri dishes. Each dish contained a solution that differed from the others only in its pH, as shown below. All other environmental conditions were the same. The dishes were covered and observed for 10 days. The data table the student designed is shown below.

The Effect of pH on Seed Germination		
Petri Dish	pH of Solution	Number of Seeds Germinated
1	9	
2	8	
3	7	
4	6	
5	5	

State the independent variable in this investigation. [1]

Base your answers to questions 9 through 11 on the information below and on your knowledge of biology.

A student placed five geranium plants of equal size in five environmental chambers. Growing conditions were the same for each plant except that each chamber was illuminated by a different color of light of the same intensity. At the end of 20 days, plant growth was measured.

9. State a possible hypothesis for this experiment. [1]

10. What control should be used in this experiment? [1]

11. Describe one modification you would make in the design of this experiment to make the results more reliable. [1]

---

12. A new drug for the treatment of asthma is tested on 100 people. The people are evenly divided into two groups. One group is given the drug, and the other group is given a glucose pill. The group that is given the glucose pill serves as the

    (1) experimental group (3) control
    (2) limiting factor   (4) indicator

13. As part of a laboratory experiment, a thin slice of peeled raw potato weighing 10 grams is placed in an oven at 80°C. After 5 hours, the potato sample is removed from the oven and weighed again. The purpose of this experiment might be to

    (1) test for the presence of starch in living tissues
    (2) isolate cells in various stages of cell division
    (3) determine the water content of potato tissue
    (4) study the rate of photosynthesis in potatoes

14. Describe the function of a control group in an experiment. [1]

15. A student wants to shorten the ripening time for tomatoes. He predicts that the more water the seedlings receive, the faster the tomatoes will ripen. To test this prediction, he grows 20 tomato plants in a garden in full sunlight that has dry soil and 20 in a garden in a shadier location where there is greater moisture content in the soil. He then records the time it takes for fruit to develop and ripen on the plants in each garden location.

State a serious error the student made with the design of this experiment. [1]

16. In attempting to demonstrate the effectiveness of a new vaccine, a scientist performed these experimental procedures:

    • One hundred genetically similar rats were divided into two groups of 50 rats each (group A and group B).
    • Each rat in group A was given an injection of the vaccine in a glucose-and-water solution.
    • Each rat in group B was given an injection of the glucose-and-water solution containing no vaccine.
    • After several weeks, all rats in both groups were exposed to the disease for which the vaccine was developed.

Identify the dependent variable that was studied in this experiment. [1]

17. Scientists breed mice to be as genetically alike as possible to use in experiments. Explain why scientists would want mice that are genetically alike.

In your answer be sure to explain:
    • The advantage of using genetically alike mice [1]
    • Why cloned mice would be even better [1]

Collecting and Organizing Data

In science, **data** generally refers to the results of trials, or tests, completed during experiments such as that in Figure 8-5. Scientific inquiry involves the ability to use various methods of recording, representing, and organizing data. Data can be organized into diagrams, tables, charts, graphs, equations, and matrices. Scientists must then be able to interpret the organized data and make inferences, predictions, and conclusions based on those data.

A data table is an important initial stage in making sense of the information you will collect while doing an experiment. When constructing a table to record your data, keep the checklist in mind.

Data Table Checklist

✓ Title the table in a way that relates the independent variable to the dependent variable. For example: The Effect of Fertilizer Concentration (the independent variable) on Plant Growth (the dependent variable).

✓ Column headings include the dependent and independent variables. They may also include trial or setup numbers or other information.

✓ Column headings need to indicate units of measurement.

✓ The independent variable is typically recorded in increasing order.

✓ The dependent variable is recorded to correspond with the independent variable.

Figure 8-5. Data collection: Making measurements and carefully recording data are important parts of doing an experiment.

The next step is to construct a graph like the one in Figure 8-6 that allows you to see trends or patterns in your mathematical data. Almost every day you interpret graphs. Television, newspapers, and other media often use graphs to illustrate ideas. Advertisers use graphs to convince us to use their pain reliever or allergy medication. They know that a carefully constructed graph can provide us with a large amount of information quickly. Examining columns of numbers in a data table is time consuming and sometimes difficult. Looking at a graph allows us to make comparisons quickly and to draw conclusions.

Graph Construction Checklist

Title
✓ Title your graph so that the reader knows what it is illustrating. You can often use the same title you used on the data table.

Vertical axis
✓ Dependent variable is on the vertical axis.

✓ Vertical axis is labeled, including units of measure.

✓ Scale on the vertical axis is appropriate, without any breaks, and spaced at even intervals.

Horizontal axis
✓ Independent variable is on the horizontal axis.

✓ Horizontal axis is labeled, including units of measure.

✓ Scale on the horizontal axis is appropriate, without any breaks, and spaced at even intervals.

Points
✓ Points are plotted accurately.

Data
✓ Data points are connected, and the line does not go beyond. (You only know what you measured; beyond that is speculation.)

Legend
✓ Legend indicates the meaning of each line if there is more than one. Often you are expected to surround data points with small circles or triangles.

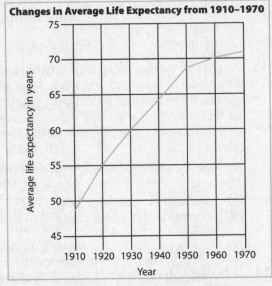

Figure 8-6. Everyday use of graphs: Interpreting graphs like this one is part of everyday life.

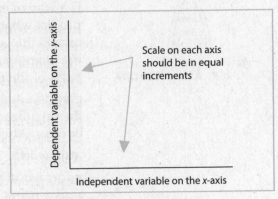

Figure 8-7. Rules for a line graph

There are four basic types of graphs:

- pie or circle graph
- bar graph
- histogram
- line graph

A scientist must decide which type of graph will be the most effective for presenting data so that the conclusion will be clear. Different rules are used in drawing each type of graph. However, there are a few rules common to all line and bar graphs.

Rule 1: The dependent variable is plotted on the vertical, or y-axis. Remember that the dependent variable is what you find out as a result of doing the experiment. It is what you measure during the experiment.

Rule 2: The independent variable is plotted on the horizontal, or x-axis. This is the factor you varied to find its effect on the test organisms or situation.

Rule 3: The spacing between the numbers on both axes must be in equal increments, without any breaks. Figure 8-7 shows how to apply the three rules to a line graph. Use the Graph Construction Checklist when constructing a graph.

The Results

A careful examination of the experimental results involves the ability to look at relationships between the predicted result contained in the hypothesis and the actual result.

Drawing Valid Conclusions After carefully considering how well the predicted result and the actual result of the experiment correspond, a decision about the outcome—a **conclusion**—can be made. A scientist needs to determine whether the hypothesis has been supported.

Scientists often use statistical analysis techniques to find the likelihood that their results were produced by chance. If the results differ only slightly, errors in measurement, genetic differences among the test organisms, or chance may be the reason. Once a significant pattern or relationship has been discovered as a result of data analysis, a scientist next tries to explain why these results were obtained.

A **model** can often be used to explain the results of an experiment. A model is a way of explaining or demonstrating what might be happening and to predict what will occur in new situations. A model explains how DNA carries the genetic code and how traits are passed from one generation to the next. As more is learned about the structure and function of DNA, parts of the model are confirmed or changed. See Figure 8-8.

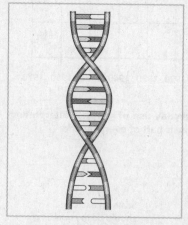
Figure 8-8. A model of DNA

Reporting Results One assumption of science is that other individuals could arrive at the same explanation if they had access to similar evidence. Experiments that cannot be repeated exactly with the same results have little worth.

Research must be shared in such a clear manner that other scientists can repeat the investigation and try to get the same results. When reporting the results of an experiment, a scientist must pay close attention to details. The experimental results may be used by hundreds of other scientists to repeat the experiment. Thus, each step of the experiment must be described accurately and in exact detail.

If you wanted to repeat an experiment done by a friend, would you be able to do it if your friend told you to heat the mixture "for a little while"? Or if you had to add some soap powder to the mixture, would it be acceptable for your friend to tell you to "add two pinches"? If you expect to obtain the same results, your friend must provide precise instructions, such as to heat the mixture at a temperature of 75°C for 5 minutes, and then add 2 grams of a certain kind of soap powder.

Scientific inquiry also requires the ability to develop a written report for public scrutiny. Scientists report their findings in scientific journals or during presentations at professional meetings. The report describes the hypothesis, including a literature review of previous studies, the experiment performed, its data and the scientist's conclusion, and suggestions for further study. Based on the results of the experiment and public discussion and review, inquiry may also require the scientist to revise the explanation and think about additional research. A **peer review,** in which several scientists examine the details of an experiment, is an important part of the scientific process. Scientists are expected to question explanations proposed by other scientists. Peers analyze the experimental procedures, examine the evidence, identify faulty reasoning, point out statements that go beyond the evidence, and suggest alternative explanations for the same observations. Peer review is one of the systems of checks and balances in science.

Figure 8-9. Peer review: Scientists examine one another's work to ensure that the results are correct.

Keep in mind that all scientific explanations are subject to change as more is learned. Scientists know and accept this as a part of the way they work. With new information, they must be willing to change their thinking and, therefore, their explanations.

Evidence is a collection of facts offered to support the idea that something is true. Scientists accept evidence when it is supported by many facts. Until they have a large collection of evidence to support their thinking, scientists must remain neutral.

Sometimes claims are made that are not supported by actual evidence. Scientific claims should be questioned if

- the data are based on samples that are very small, biased, or inadequately controlled
- the conclusions are based on the faulty, incomplete, or misleading use of numbers

For example, enough organisms must be used in an experiment and the difference in data between the control and experimental group must be significant enough so that genetic differences, random chance, and inaccuracies in measurement cannot be responsible for the results. Wherever appropriate, a statistical analysis of the results should be done. This could be something as simple as finding the average, calculating the percentage of difference, or determining the frequency. Claims should also be questioned if

- fact and opinion are intermingled
- adequate evidence is not cited
- conclusions do not follow logically from the evidence given

Further Science Understandings

Well-accepted scientific theories are supported by many different scientific investigations, often involving the contributions of individuals from different disciplines. In developing a theory, scientists carry out many investigations. They may vary in degree of complexity, scale, and focus. Research by different scientific disciplines can bring to light multiple views of the natural world. The resulting theory can encompass many different aspects of natural events. For instance, the theory of evolution began with the observations of one naturalist. But over the years scientists—including botanists, biologists, geologists, oceanographers, and others—researched numerous aspects of the theory to reach one general scientific idea.

Review Questions   Set 8.3

18. A student conducted an original, well-designed experiment, carefully following proper scientific procedure. In order for the conclusions to become generally accepted, the experiment must

(1) contain several experimental variables
(2) support the original hypothesis
(3) be repeated to verify the reliability of the data
(4) be conducted by a scientist

19. A student tossed a coin five times and observed results of four tails and one head. He concluded that when a coin is tossed, there is an 80% chance of getting a tail and a 20% chance of getting a head. The conclusion would be more valid if

(1) only two tosses of the coin had been used
(2) the weight of the coin had been taken into consideration
(3) a greater number of tosses had been used
(4) the surface the coin landed on had been taken into consideration

Base your answers to questions 20 through 22 on the experiment described below and on your knowledge of biology.

After watching the behavior of earthworms in soil, a biology student suggested that the penetration of air into the soil promotes the root development of plants. The student then set up the following experiment.

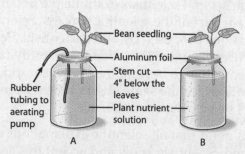

20. The important data to be recorded in this experiment will come from the observation of the increase in

(1) leaf size   (3) number of leaves
(2) stem size   (4) number of roots

21. State the hypothesis being tested in this experiment. [1]

22. State one way this experiment could be improved to make the results more reliable. [1]

Base your answers to questions 23 through 25 on the experiment described below and on your knowledge of biology.

A group of 24 frogs was separated into two equal groups. Group A was placed in an environment in which the temperature was a constant 35°F. Group B was placed in a similar environment, except the temperature was a constant 65°F.

Equal amounts of food were given to each group at the start of the experiment and again every 24 hours. Immediately before each daily feeding, the excess food from the prior feeding was removed and measured. This allowed the scientist to determine the daily amount of food each group of frogs consumed. Each day, the heart rate and breathing rate of the frogs were checked. At the end of the experiment, the following bar graphs were prepared:

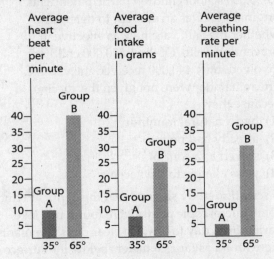

23. Using one or more complete sentences, state the hypothesis the scientist was most likely investigating in this experiment.

24. After examining the graphs, the scientist could reasonably assume that at a low temperature the frogs would

(1) become more active
(2) produce less carbon dioxide
(3) eat more food
(4) use more oxygen

25. The independent variable in this experiment was

(1) heart rate
(2) breathing rate
(3) amount of food consumed
(4) temperature of the environment

Base your answers to questions 26 through 29 on the information below and on your knowledge of biology.

A student was working on an investigation to measure the relative activity of an enzyme at various pH values. He collected the following data: pH 2, enzyme activity 10; pH 8, enzyme activity 50; pH 12, enzyme activity 10; pH 4, enzyme activity 20; pH 6, enzyme activity 40; pH 10, enzyme activity 40

26. Identify the independent variable in this experiment. [1]

27. Organize the data by filling in the data table provided. Follow these directions when completing your data table.

- Provide an appropriate title for the data table. [1]
- Fill in the first box in each column with an appropriate heading. [1]
- Arrange the data so that pH values are in increasing order. [1]

Title:	

28. Using the information in the data table, construct a line graph on the grid provided, following the directions below:

- Provide an appropriate title for the graph. [1]
- Make and label an appropriate scale, without any breaks, on each axis. [1]
- Plot the data on the grid. Surround each data point with a small circle and connect the points. [1]

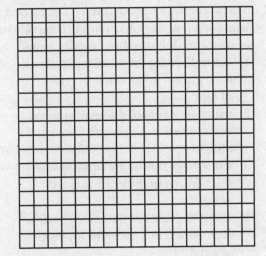

29. According to the data, this enzyme would probably work best at what pH values?

(1) 7 and 8   (3) 6 and 7
(2) 2 and 12   (4) 4 and 10

Directions

Review the Test-Taking Strategies section of this book. Then answer the following questions. Read each question carefully and answer with a correct choice or response.

Part A

1 One ounce each of protein, carbohydrate, and fat are burned separately in a calorimeter to determine Caloric content. The results are shown in the data table.

Caloric Content of Substances	
Organic Compound	Number of Calories Produced
Protein	147
Fat	271
Carbohydrate	152

Which statement represents a valid conclusion based on the data?
(1) An ounce of fat contains about twice as many Calories as an ounce of protein.
(2) Protein is a better energy food than carbohydrate.
(3) Carbohydrates, fats, and proteins all yield approximately the same number of Calories per unit of weight.
(4) Proteins and carbohydrates provide the most Calories per ounce.

2 Which laboratory procedure would be best for demonstrating the effect of light intensity on the production of chlorophyll in pea plants?
(1) using 10 plants of different species, each grown in the same intensity of light
(2) using 10 plants of different species, each grown in a different intensity of light
(3) using 10 plants of the same species, each grown in the same intensity of light
(4) using 10 plants of the same species, each grown in a different intensity of light

3 In an early trial of the Salk vaccine for polio, 1,830,000 school children participated. This original trial was an attempt to determine whether the Salk vaccine was effective in preventing polio. Of the 1,830,000 children involved, only 440,000 received the vaccine. The remainder were not given the vaccine because they
(1) had a natural immunity
(2) already had polio
(3) served as a control
(4) were allergic to the vaccine

4 A scientific study showed that the depth at which some microscopic plants were found in a lake varied from day to day. On clear days, the plants were found as far as 6 meters below the surface of the water but were only 1 meter below the surface on cloudy days. Which hypothesis would these observations support?
(1) Light intensity affects the growth of microscopic plants.
(2) Wind currents affect the growth of microscopic plants.
(3) Nitrogen concentration affects the growth of microscopic plants.
(4) Precipitation affects the growth of microscopic plants.

5 A scientist tested a hypothesis that white-tailed deer would prefer apples over corn as a primary food source. The findings of the test, in which the scientist claimed that the deer preferred apples, were published. Which research technique, if used by the scientist, might result in this claim being questioned?
(1) The scientist observed four deer in different locations at various times of the day.
(2) The scientist observed a total of 500 deer in 20 different locations at various times of the day.
(3) The scientist observed 200 deer in various natural settings, but none in captivity.
(4) The scientist observed 300 deer in various locations in captivity, but none in natural settings.

6 Conclusions based on an experiment are most likely to be accepted when
(1) they are consistent with experimental data and observations
(2) they are derived from investigations having many experimental variables
(3) scientists agree that only one hypothesis has been tested
(4) hypotheses are based on one experimental design

Part B

Base your answers to questions 7 through 10 on the information below, and on your knowledge of biology.

The list represents different procedures involved with a scientific experiment and are in no special order. For statements 7 through 10, identify the procedure being described by the appropriate letter.

Experimental Procedures
A. *Test the hypothesis with an experiment.*
B. *State the results.*
C. *Draw a conclusion from the results.*
D. *Form a hypothesis.*

7 Beans will grow faster if you fertilize them at regular intervals than if you only fertilize the ground once before you plant them. [1]

8 If I add more catalyst to the reaction, the reaction will speed up. [1]

9 A scientist took saliva from his dog's mouth and mixed it with a solution of starch and warm water. He took the same amount of saliva from his own mouth and mixed it with the contents of a second tube of starch and warm water. One hour later, the contents of both tubes were checked for sugar. [1]

10 In an experiment, caterpillars consumed 8 grams of lettuce leaves and 0.4 grams of tomato leaves. [1]

11 The data table below shows an effect of secondhand smoke on the birth weight of babies born to husbands and wives living together during the pregnancy.

Effect of Secondhand Smoke on Birth Weight

	Wife: Nonsmoker Husband: Nonsmoker	Wife: Nonsmoker Husband: Smoker
Number of Couples	837	529
Average Weight of Baby at Birth (Kg)	3.2	2.9

Based on these data, a reasonable conclusion that can be drawn about secondhand smoke during pregnancy is that secondhand smoke
(1) is unable to pass from the mother to the fetus
(2) slows the growth of the fetus
(3) causes mutations in cells of the ovaries
(4) blocks the receptors on antibody cells

12 A student studied how the amount of oxygen affects ATP production in muscle cells. The data for amount X are shown in the graph below.

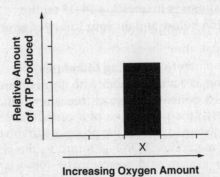

If the student supplies the muscle cells with less oxygen in a second trial of the investigation, a bar placed on the graph to represent the results of this trial would most likely be
(1) shorter than bar X and placed to the left of bar X
(2) shorter than bar X and placed to the right of bar X
(3) taller than bar X and placed to the left of bar X
(4) taller than bar X and placed to the right of bar X

13 A student studied the location of single-celled photosynthetic organisms in a lake for a period of several weeks. The depth at which these organisms were found at different times of the day varied greatly. Some of the data collected are shown in the table below.

Data Table	
Light Conditions at Different Times of the Day	Average Depth of Photosynthetic Organisms (cm)
Full light	150
Moderate light	15
No light	10

A valid inference based on these data is that
(1) most photosynthetic organisms live below a depth of 150 centimeters
(2) oxygen production increases as photosynthetic organisms move deeper in the lake
(3) photosynthetic organisms respond to changing light levels
(4) photosynthetic organisms move up and down to increase their rate of carbon dioxide production

Part C

Base your answer to question 14–17 on the information below and on your knowledge of biology.

Help for Aging Memories
As aging occurs, the ability to form memories begins to decrease. Research has shown that an increase in the production of a certain molecule, BDNF, seems to restore the processes involved in storing memories. BDNF is found in the central nervous system and seems to be important in maintaining nerve cell health. Researchers are testing a new drug that seems to increase the production of BDNF.

14–17 Design an experiment to test the effectiveness of the new drug to increase the production of BDNF in the brains of rats. In your answer, be sure to:
- state the hypothesis your experiment will test [1]

- describe how the control group will be treated differently from the experimental group [1]
- identify two factors that must be kept the same in both the experimental and control groups [1]
- identify the dependent variable in your experiment [1]

Base your answer to question 18–21 on the information below and on your knowledge of biology.

An Experimental SARS Vaccine Works in Animals
Scientists reported that they had protected animals from the effects of the SARS virus by using an experimental vaccine. The SARS virus causes an acute respiratory illness in humans and other animals.

This vaccine was sprayed once into the nostrils of each of four African green monkeys. Four weeks later, these monkeys were exposed to the virus that causes SARS. The monkeys showed no sign of the disease in their respiratory tracts. Blood tests confirmed the presence of proteins known as neutralizing antibodies that indicate protection against disease. The scientists also sprayed a placebo (a substance that did not contain the vaccine) into the nostrils of each of four other African green monkeys. After exposure to the virus that causes SARS, all of these monkeys developed symptoms of this condition.

18–21 Briefly explain the nature of a vaccine and some steps that should be taken before a vaccine is available for public use. In your answer, be sure to include:
- a description of what a vaccine is [1]
- an explanation of why one group had a placebo sprayed into their nostrils before exposure to the virus [1]
- an explanation of why scientists used monkeys to test the SARS vaccine [1]
- a statement of what could be done to verify the results [1]

Base your answer to questions 22 and 23 on the information and diagram below, and on your knowledge of biology.

A laboratory setup for a demonstration is represented in the diagram below.

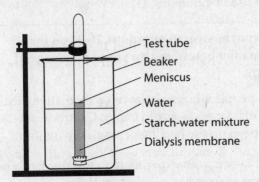

22–23 Describe how an indicator can be used to determine if starch diffuses through the membrane into the beaker. In your answer, be sure to include:
- the procedure used [1]
- how to interpret the results [1]

Base your answers to questions 24 through 26 on the information below and on your knowledge of biology.

In an investigation, plants of the same species and the same initial height were exposed to a constant number of hours of light each day. The number of hours per day was different for each plant, but all other environmental factors were the same. At the conclusion of the investigation, the final height of each plant was measured.

The following data were recorded:

8 hours, 25 cm; 4 hours, 12 cm; 2 hours, 5 cm; 14 hours, 35 cm; 12 hours, 35 cm; 10 hours, 34 cm; 6 hours, 18 cm

24 Organize the data by completing both columns in the data table provided, so that the hours of daily light exposure increase from the top to the bottom of the table. [1]

Data Table	
Dally Light Exposure (hours)	Final Height (cm)

25 State one possible reason that the plant exposed to 2 hours of light per day was the shortest. [1]

26 If another plant of the same species had been used in the investigation and exposed to 16 hours of light per day, what would the final height of the plant probably have been? Support your answer. [1]

Base your answers to questions 27 and 28 on the information and data table below and on your knowledge of biology.

Trout and black bass are freshwater fish that normally require at least 8 parts per million (ppm) of dissolved oxygen (O_2) in the water for survival. Other freshwater fish, such as carp, may be able to live in water that has an O_2 level of 5 ppm. No freshwater fish are able to survive when the O_2 level in water is 2 ppm or less.

Some factories or power plants are built along rivers so that they can use the water to cool their equipment. They then release the water (sometimes as much as 8°C warmer) back into the same river.

The Rocky River presently has an average summer temperature of about 25°C and contains populations of trout, bass, and carp. A proposal has been made to build a new power plant on the banks of the Rocky River. Some people are concerned that this will affect the river ecosystem in a negative way.

The data table below shows the amount of oxygen that will dissolve in fresh water at different temperatures. The amount of oxygen is expressed in parts per million (ppm).

Data Table	
Temperature (°C)	Fresh Water Oxygen Content (ppm)
1	14.24
10	11.29
15	10.10
20	9.11
25	8.27
30	7.56

27 State one effect of temperature change on the oxygen content of fresh water. Support your answer using specific information from the data table. [1]

28 Explain how a new power plant built on the banks of the Rocky River could have an environmental impact on the Rocky River ecosystem downstream from the plant.

Your explanation must include the effects of the power plant on:
- water temperature [1]
- dissolved oxygen [1]
- fish species [1]

Base your answers to questions 29 and 30 on the information in the newspaper article below and on your knowledge of biology.

Patients to test tumor fighter

Boston—Endostatin, the highly publicized experimental cancer drug that wiped out tumors in mice and raised the hopes of cancer patients, will be tested on patients this year.

"I think it's exciting, but ... you always have the risk that something will fail in testing," said Dr. Judah Folkman, the Harvard University researcher whose assistant, Michael O'Reilly, discovered endostatin.

Endostatin and a sister protein, angiostatin, destroy the tumors' ability to sprout new blood vessels. This makes cancer fall dormant in lab animals, but no one knows if that will happen in humans.

The Associated Press

29 Explain why it is necessary to test these experimental drugs on human volunteers as well as on test animals. [1]

30 State one reason that mice are often used by scientists for testing experimental drugs that may be used by humans. [1]

Base your answer to questions 31–34 on the information below and on your knowledge of biology.

Many people who are in favor of alternative medicine claim that large doses of vitamin C introduced into a vein speed up the healing of surgical wounds.

31–34 Describe an experiment to test this hypothesis. Your answer must include at least:
- the difference between the experimental group of subjects and the control group [1]
- two conditions that must be kept constant in both groups [1]
- data that should be collected [1]
- an example of experimental results that would support the hypothesis [1]

What do **You** _Think_?

Laboratory Procedures

When you are looking at cells with a microscope always start focusing with the high power objective lens, then if the cells appear too large, switch to a lower power.

You shouldn't eat food or drink soda in a classroom laboratory unless you make sure you wash your hands first.

Paper chromatography is used to separate mixtures of molecules that are of different sizes.

Gel electrophoresis is used to cut DNA into smaller fragments.

9 Laboratory Skills

Vocabulary

balance

chromatography

compound light microscope

dichotomous key

dissection

electronic balance

electrophoresis

graduated cylinder

indicator

magnification

mass

metric ruler

microscope

stain

stereoscope

triple-beam balance

volume

Topic Overview

Biologists are always trying to add to our understanding of the world in which we live. To do this, they make observations and do experiments. To help them collect data from these observations and experiments, they rely on a variety of tools and techniques. These tools, like microscopes, extend our senses, allowing us to collect data that would otherwise be unavailable. Scientists have also developed specific techniques that give us valuable information about the cells, molecules, and processes of living organisms.

Tools for Measurement

During laboratory investigations, you are often required to make measurements of length, mass, and volume. You need to know the proper pieces of equipment to select and the appropriate procedures and units to use.

Measuring Length Typically a **metric ruler** is used to determine the length of an object. To measure length, use either centimeters (cm) or millimeters (mm). You should know how to convert millimeters to centimeters and vice versa.

The metric ruler shown in Figure 9-1 is <u>calibrated</u>—or scaled—in centimeters (cm). The lines indicated by the numbers 1, 2, 3, and so on each represent a distance of 1 centimeter. The smaller divisions each equal 1 millimeter (10 mm = 1 cm). A line equal to 5 cm is shown above the ruler in Figure 9-1.

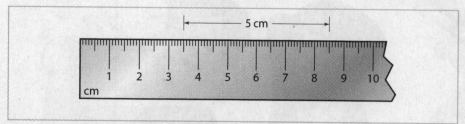

Figure 9-1. Metric ruler: The tool used for measuring length in centimeters and millimeters (not shown to scale)

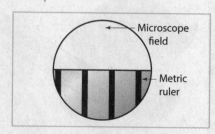

Figure 9-2. Microscope field with metric ruler (not shown to scale)

Micrometers (μm), are very tiny units that are used to measure objects through the microscope. One thousand micrometers equal one millimeter.

Figure 9-2 shows a metric ruler as seen under the low-power objective of a microscope. The distance across the field of view is approximately 3.2 millimeters, or 3,200 micrometers (since 1.0 mm = 1,000 μm).

If the cells observed on the slide in Figure 9-3 are being viewed through the same low-power objective, the field of view is still 3.2 millimeters. The approximate length of each cell is therefore about 1 millimeter or 1,000 micrometers, since about 3 cells fit across the diameter (widest part) of the field.

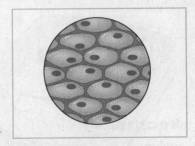

Figure 9-3. **Microscope field with cells**

Measuring Volume A **graduated cylinder** is often used to measure a liquid's **volume**, or the space it occupies. Liters and milliliters are typically used to indicate volume in the metric system, while quarts and ounces are used in the English system. Graduated cylinders are calibrated in milliliters (mL).

Water and many other fluids form a meniscus (curving surface) when placed in the narrow tube of a graduated cylinder. To correctly read the volume of the liquid, place the cylinder on a flat surface. Then read from the bottom of the curved meniscus at eye level. The volume of liquid in the graduated cylinder in Figure 9-4 is 13 mL.

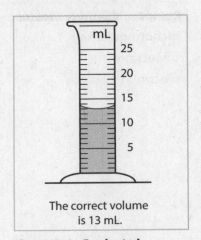

The correct volume is 13 mL.

Figure 9-4. **Graduated cylinder: You can find the volume of a liquid using a graduated cylinder.**

Measuring Temperature In the biology laboratory, temperature is often measured in degrees Celsius. The freezing point of water is 0°C; the boiling point is 100°C. Human body temperature is 37°C, which is the temperature indicated on the thermometer in Figure 9-5.

Measuring Mass In the biology laboratory, **mass**—the quantity of matter in something—is often measured with a **balance**, which is a tool that works by comparing an object of unknown mass with an object of known mass. The triple-beam balance or an electronic balance is typically found in a high school laboratory.

A **triple-beam balance** (Figure 9-6) has a single pan and three bars (beams) that are calibrated in grams. One beam, the 500-gram beam, is divided into five 100-gram units. Another beam is divided into ten units of 10 grams totaling 100 grams. The front beam is divided into 10 major units of 1 gram each. Each of these divisions is further divided into 0.1-gram units.

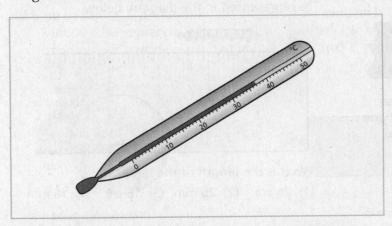

Figure 9-5. **Thermometer: This Celsius thermometer shows human body temperature.**

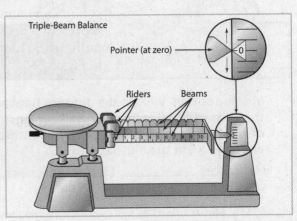

Triple-Beam Balance

Pointer (at zero)

Riders   Beams

Figure 9-6. **Triple-beam balance**

Before using a balance, make sure that the pan is empty and that the pointer and all of the <u>riders</u> (devices that are moved along the beams) are on zero. To determine the mass of an object, it is first placed on the pan. Then, starting with the 500-gram beam, the masses on the beams are adjusted until the pointer is again pointing to zero. The mass of the object is equal to the sum of the readings on the three beams.

An **electronic balance** measures mass automatically. To use an electronic balance, first turn it on and wait until it shows a zero mass. (This may require using the re-zero button shown on Figure 9-7.) Place the object with the unknown mass on the pan. Read the mass.

Never place a substance directly on a balance pan. Instead, protect the balance with a weighing paper or dish. With a triple-beam balance, first find the mass of the weighing paper. Then find the mass of the substance AND the weighing paper. Subtract the mass of the weighing paper from the total mass of the paper plus the substance. The remainder is the mass of the substance.

For an electronic balance, put the weighing paper on the balance and then use the re-zero button to set the balance to zero. Next, put the substance on the paper and read the mass. The re-zero button automatically subtracts the mass of the weighing paper from the total. The reading on the balance is the actual mass of the substance.

Review **Questions**   Set 9.1

1. The crab shown in the illustration below has four pairs of walking legs and one pair of pincer legs. The crab is shown in its normal walking position.

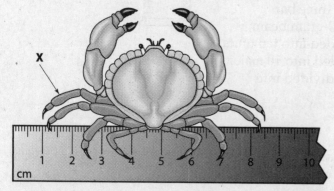

In this position, what is the distance between the ends of the front pair of walking legs? (One of the front pair of walking legs is identified with an "X" in the illustration.)

(1) 8.5 cm   (3) 7.5 cm
(2) 85 cm   (4) 75 cm

2. Identify which piece of laboratory equipment you would use to accurately measure 10 grams of glucose. [1]

3. Which piece of laboratory equipment would be used to most accurately measure the volume of a liquid?

(1) beaker   (3) test tube
(2) balance   (4) graduated cylinder

4. A student measured a larva using a metric ruler, as represented in the diagram below.

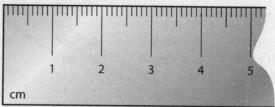

What is the length of the larva?

(1) 26 cm   (2) 26 mm   (3) 16 cm   (4) 16 mm

5. Which of the graduated cylinders below contains a volume of liquid closest to 15 mL?

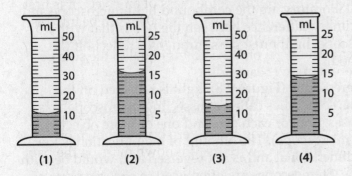

(1)   (2)   (3)   (4)

6. Which diagram below shows a correct measurement?

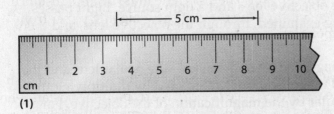

|← 5 cm →|

(1)

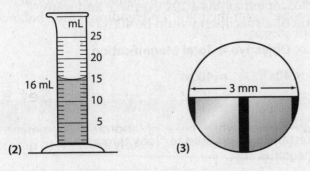

(2)   (3)

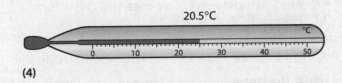

20.5°C

(4)

7. The diagram below shows a triple-beam balance with a mass on the pan.

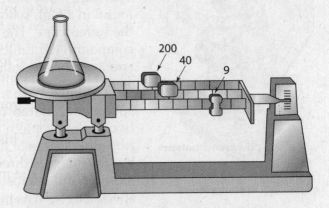

200   40   9

With the riders in the positions indicated, what is the mass of the object on the pan of the balance?

(1) 9 grams   (3) 249 grams
(2) 200 grams   (4) 942 grams

8. Draw a meniscus to represent a water level of 6 mL on the diagram below of a graduated cylinder. [1]

Microscope Skills

The **microscope** is a tool that uses a lens or a combination of lenses to make an object easier to see. It allows for the examination of objects too small to be seen with the unaided eye. Microscopes also permit the close observation of fine details. For example, without a microscope you can see the legs and wings of a fly. With a microscope you can also see the hairs covering the fly's body, the pads and clawlike structures on its feet, and the framework of its wings. This is possible for two reasons. A microscope magnifies the specimen and also allows you to distinguish between objects that are close together. **Magnification** is the ability of a microscope to make an object appear larger.

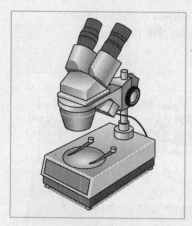

Figure 9-8. **A stereoscope**

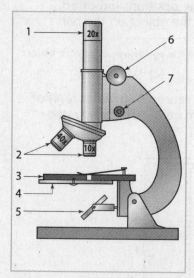

Figure 9-9. **A compound microscope:** Each part is labeled with a number. The names and functions of the parts are given in Table 9-1.

Types of Microscopes

There are many different types of microscopes. The two most commonly found in a high school laboratory are the compound light microscope and the stereoscope. The primary difference between the two is that with a compound light microscope, light must pass through or reflect off the specimen being examined.

Stereoscopes With a stereoscope (Figure 9-8), light is reflected off the specimen. A **stereoscope**, sometimes called a dissecting microscope, has two ocular eyepiece lenses, one for each eye, and one or more objectives (the other lenses of the microscope). The amount of magnification is low, but the image is three-dimensional and is not reversed as it would be with a compound microscope. Stereoscopes are often used to observe parts of specimens such as insects, worms, or flowers.

Compound Microscopes The typical **compound light microscope** has one ocular lens, at least one objective lens, and a light source. Light passes through the object being examined, through the objective lens, and then through the eyepiece.

The image you see is magnified by both lenses—the ocular lens and the objective lens. The total magnification is calculated by multiplying the magnification of the ocular by the magnification of the objective. For example, if you use a microscope that has a 10x eyepiece and a 40x objective, the magnification of a specimen would be 400x.

Eyepiece × Objective = Total Magnification

10x   × 40x   = 400x

Table 9-1. Names and Functions of Parts of a Compound Microscope	
1 Eyepiece or Ocular Lens	• lens nearest the eye and used to "look through" • usually magnifies 10x
2 Objective Lenses	• lenses located closest to specimen • usually 2 or 3 • commonly magnify at 4x, 10x, and 40x
3 Stage	• flat surface (platform) on which the slide is placed • stage clips hold the slide in place
4 Diaphragm	• located under the stage • controls the amount of light passing up through the specimen
5 Light Source	• might be a mirror or a light bulb • provides light that passes up through the specimen and makes it visible
6 Coarse Adjustment	• used to focus only under low power (up to 100x) • never used when the high-power objective is in place for viewing • usually the larger knob; causes a large amount of movement of the lenses
7 Fine Adjustment	• the only focus you should use with high power • used to sharpen the image under low power • also used to see different layers of a specimen • usually the smaller of the focus knobs; causes a small amount of movement of the lenses

Microscope lenses may get dirty from contact with fingers, specimens, stains, and so on. Do not use paper towels or your shirt to clean them! Only use lens paper to clean the lenses of a microscope. Lens paper will not scratch the soft glass of the lens.

Techniques for Using Microscopes

Due to the action of microscope lenses, there are a number of things you need to remember when viewing objects through a compound light microscope.

Figure 9-10. **Microscope view:** The letter "e" as seen on a slide (A) and as seen through the microscope (B). (Only the change in position of the letter is shown, not magnification.)

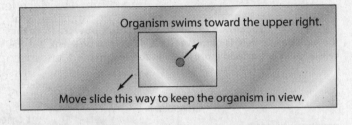

Figure 9-11. **Moving the slide to follow a moving object**

- The image will be upside-down and backwards, as shown in Figure 9-10.
- You must move the slide in the direction that is opposite the way the organism appears to be moving. In other words, if the organism appears headed toward the upper right side of your field of view, you must move the slide down and to the left to keep it in view. See Figure 9-11.
- The field becomes darker as you increase the magnification. You will need to increase the amount of light passing through the specimen as you go from low power to high power. The diaphragm, located under the stage, can be used to do this.
- Since the field becomes smaller under high power, center the object you are viewing before switching to a higher power. Otherwise the object may be outside of the field of view.

Focusing When observing specimens through the compound light microscope, first use the low-power objective. Do this even if higher magnification is needed to make your observations.

1. First, place the slide on the stage of your microscope. Position the slide so that the specimen is over the opening in the stage. Anchor the slide with the stage clips.
2. Move the coarse adjustment so that the low-power objective is as close to the slide as you can get it without touching the slide. Some microscopes have a built-in "stop" that prevents you from getting the objective lens too close to the slide. You should look at the objective and the slide while doing this. Never lower the objective while looking through the eyepiece.
3. Look through the eyepiece with both eyes open and turn the coarse adjustment so that the low-power objective and slide move apart. The specimen should come into view.
4. Next, turn the fine adjustment to bring the specimen into sharp focus.
5. To focus the specimen under higher magnification after locating it under low power, move the slide so that what you are interested in seeing is located in the center of your field of view. Remember that as you increase the magnification, the object appears larger, but you see less of its edge. The field of view becomes smaller when you

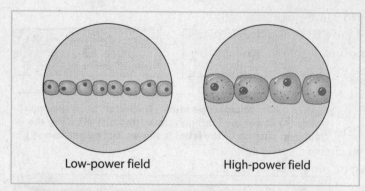

Low-power field   High-power field

Figure 9-12. **Specimen under low and high power:** Note that the high power field is narrower (only 4 cells can be seen), but the cells appear larger, and more detail is visible.

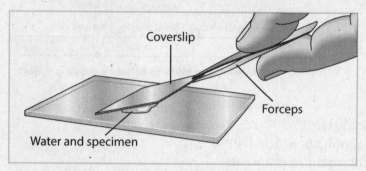

Coverslip

Forceps

Water and specimen

Figure 9-13. **Preparing a wet-mount slide**

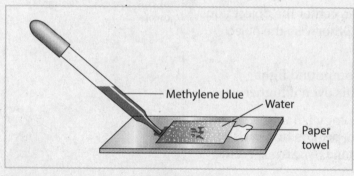

Methylene blue

Water

Paper towel

Figure 9-14. **Staining a wet-mount slide**

switch from low power to a higher power. See Figure 9-12.

6. Watch from the side of the microscope and slowly turn the high-power objective into place. Be sure that the high-power objective is not going to touch the slide. High-power objectives are longer than low-power objectives and can easily hit the slide—be careful.

7. If the objective is not going to hit the slide, click it into position. As you look through the eyepiece, the specimen should be visible. Use the fine adjustment to sharpen the focus. Remember never to use the coarse adjustment when using the high-power objectives. You could damage the microscope lens and break the slide.

Preparing Wet-Mount Slides Only specimens that are small and thin can be seen through a compound light microscope. However, thin slices may quickly dry and shrivel. To avoid this, a temporary wet-mount slide can be prepared by using the following steps:

1. Using a <u>pipette</u> (eye dropper), add a small drop of water to the center of a clean, glass slide.

2. Place the object to be viewed in the water. (It should be lying flat rather than folded over.)

3. Use <u>forceps</u> to position a <u>coverslip</u>, as shown in Figure 9-13. Using forceps will keep you from getting fingerprints on the coverslip. Fingerprints could interfere with your ability to view the image clearly.

4. Lower the coverslip slowly. This technique will prevent the formation of air bubbles under the coverslip.

Staining Specimens When you examine cells and cell parts through a microscope, they often appear to be transparent. You need to adjust the light and the focus so that you can see differences in thickness and density. Although adjusting the amount of light passing through the specimen may help, stains are often used to create greater contrast. Different types of cells and cell parts vary in their ability to soak up various stains. For example, certain cell parts turn darker in the presence of iodine stain. Other parts do not become darker.

To add a stain, such as methylene blue, to a wet-mount slide, place a drop of the stain beside one edge of the coverslip. Next touch a small piece of paper towel to the opposite edge of the coverslip. The towel absorbs water and draws the stain across the slide under the coverslip. This technique allows you to keep the slide on the stage of the microscope. You do not need to prepare a new slide. See Figure 9-14.

Identifying and Comparing Cell Parts It is important to remember that cells have specific structures that perform specific jobs. Many of these structures in Figures 9-15 and 9-16 are visible through a compound light microscope. Some of the parts you can either expect to see or see evidence of are the following:

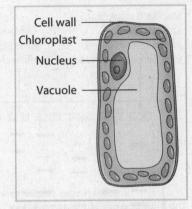

Figure 9-15. **Typical plant cell:** Structures that can be seen through a microscope

- **Nucleus**—usually observed as a rounded, dense, dark-staining structure. It can be located anywhere in the cell, not just in the middle.

- **Cytoplasm**—typically fills the cell. It appears to be clear in some cells and very grainy in others. Cell organelles, which may or may not be visible, are suspended in the cytoplasm.

- **Cell membrane**—found surrounding the cytoplasm. It is the outer boundary of animal cells and is located between the cell wall and the cytoplasm in plants and some other organisms.

- **Cell wall**—The nonliving cell wall on the outside of the cell membrane in plant cells is a supportive structure. Many bacteria form a different type of protective cell wall.

- **Chloroplasts**—green, oval structures found in the cytoplasm of some plant cells and photosynthetic one-celled organisms.

- **Vacuoles**—often seen as clear areas in the cytoplasm. Plant cells contain very large fluid-filled vacuoles that occupy much of the inside of the cell. Some single-celled organisms may contain specialized vacuoles for digestion and for regulating water balance.

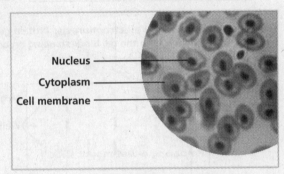

Figure 9-16. **Animal cells:** As seen through a compound light microscope

- **Chromosomes**—most easily observed in cells undergoing mitosis or meiosis as in Figure 9-17. They are usually dark-staining and threadlike.

Additional Laboratory Techniques

There are many techniques that are useful in the biology laboratory. Some of the most common are electrophoresis, chromatography, and the application of stains and indicators. Dichotomous keys are especially useful for field research.

Electrophoresis Gel **electrophoresis** is a very powerful tool and is widely used by scientists in many disciplines—not just biologists. It allows scientists to separate mixtures of large molecules according to size. DNA and proteins are the two types of molecules most often separated by gel electrophoresis.

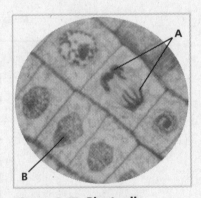

Figure 9-17. **Plant cells undergoing mitotic cell division:** A indicates chromosomes, and B indicates a nucleus before the cell undergoes mitosis.

When setting up a protein gel, a sample of biological material containing proteins is prepared by breaking open the cells in order to release the proteins. Next, the proteins are treated with both chemicals and heat. One of the chemicals used coats the protein molecules and gives them a negative charge. Then, very small amounts of the prepared sample are placed in wells at the top of a special gel positioned in a gel electrophoresis apparatus. (The wells are similar to the holes you would get by pressing the teeth of a comb part way into a block of gelatin dessert.) The gel is placed between two electrodes that are connected to a power supply. This causes one end of the gel to take on a positive charge and the other to take on a negative charge.

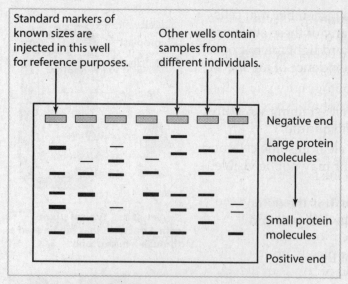

Standard markers of known sizes are injected in this well for reference purposes.

Other wells contain samples from different individuals.

Negative end

Large protein molecules

Small protein molecules

Positive end

Figure 9-18. **Protein gel electrophoresis:** Protein gels are typically run vertically, with the gel block standing on end.

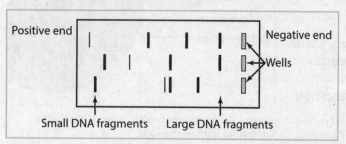

Positive end

Negative end

Wells

Small DNA fragments   Large DNA fragments

Figure 9-19. **DNA gel electrophoresis:** DNA gels are typically run horizontally, with the gel block lying flat.

Positively charged molecules in the sample move toward the negative electrode, while negatively charged protein molecules move toward the positive electrode. The type of gel used in protein electrophoresis is made up of long molecules that form a tangled mesh. Smaller molecules are able to work their way through the gel more quickly than larger molecules. Therefore, molecules are separated by both their size and electrical charge. See Figure 9-18.

DNA gel electrophoresis is a little different. The analysis of an individual's DNA begins with the use of special enzymes to cut the DNA at specific points in the sequence of bases. This produces fragments of DNA that are of different lengths. These pieces of DNA will vary in size and number from one individual to another due to the uniqueness of each genetic code.

Next, small amounts of the DNA samples are placed in wells located on one side of a semisolid gel. See Figure 9-19. Typically the DNA gel is made of <u>agarose</u>—the same gelatine-like substance used to culture bacteria but without the nutrients. The gel is located between two electrodes that are connected to a power supply. This causes one end of the gel to take on a positive charge and the other to take on a negative charge when the current is turned on. The negatively charged DNA fragments move toward the positive electrode.

As with the protein gel, the smaller the fragment, the more rapidly it moves through the gel. Small pieces of DNA will travel farther and be located farther from the well where they were initially injected. This allows the DNA fragments to form a distinct pattern that becomes visible through staining or a variety of other techniques.

The information provided by both DNA and protein gels looks very much like a bar code. The patterns formed from different protein samples or the DNA of different individuals can provide information about relatedness. DNA has been used to determine who the father and/or mother of a child actually is in paternity cases or in instances where a couple suspects that the child given to them in the hospital is not their child. It has also been used to determine guilt or innocence during criminal investigations. The source of blood, semen, or skin can be identified with this technique. DNA left at a crime scene can be compared to a suspect's DNA to determine if the suspect was at the crime scene.

In the case of endangered species, scientists can use DNA electrophoresis to learn which groups are being devastated by poachers, since skins from members of the same group will have similar DNA patterns. Gel electrophoresis can also be used to determine and to identify the genes responsible for specific genetic diseases such as sickle cell disease.

Chromatography Like gel electrophoresis, **chromatography** is a technique used for separating mixtures of molecules. In one type of chromatography commonly used in the biology laboratory, the mixture being separated is placed on a paper to which it sticks. For example, chlorophyll extract from plant leaves is placed on filter paper or special chromatography paper. It is done by placing a small dot of the concentrated chlorophyll extract near one end of a strip of the paper. Then, the end of the paper nearest the dot of extract is placed in a solvent. In the case of chlorophyll, the <u>solvent</u> could be alcohol. The solvent cannot touch the dot when it is initially set up, or the chlorophyll would simply wash away into the solvent.

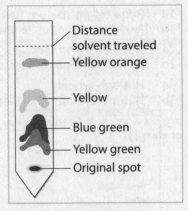

Figure 9-20. Chlorophyll chromatography

As the solvent soaks into the paper and moves upward, substances in the mixture that do not stick tightly to the paper will be picked up by the solvent and moved along quickly. Substances that are more tightly held to the paper and less attracted to the solvent will also be picked up but will move along more slowly. This results in the formation of bands of the different substances on the chromatography paper. If the substances in the mixture are colorless, they can be viewed by combining them with reactive chemicals that will give them color. The chlorophyll extract consists of several plant pigments that are very colorful and easy to distinguish.

In summary, the rate at which a substance moves along the paper in a given solvent can be used to separate it from other substances. By comparing the distances moved with those of known substances in the same solvent, the unknowns can be identified. See Figure 9-20.

Stains and Indicators **Stains** can be used to make cell structures more visible. In fact, chromosomes were so named for the fact that they are easily stained. Commonly used stains are iodine and methylene blue. Iodine darkens certain cell structures. It is especially useful when examining plant cells through the microscope. Methylene blue stains structures in the nucleus. It is useful when observing many types of cells.

An **indicator** is a substance that changes color when it contacts certain chemicals. The examples in Table 9-2 represent only a few of the indicators commonly used in the biology laboratory.

Other indicators can be used to determine how much sugar there is in a solution or the amount of carbon dioxide present. Swimming pool owners use indicators to tell them how much chlorine is in the water. Some of the pregnancy test kits that pharmacies sell also use indicators.

Table 9-2. Indicators Used in the Biology Laboratory

Indicator	What It Tests
pH paper	A piece of pH paper is dipped in the solution to be tested. Its color is then matched to a color scale. Specific colors indicate whether the solution is acidic (pH values from 0 to 6), neutral (pH 7), or basic (pH values from 8 to 14).
Iodine (Lugol's) solution	A color change from golden brown to blue-black indicates the presence of starch in the tested solution.

Dichotomous Keys A key is used to sort, name, and/or classify a particular organism. By working through a series of steps, organisms are eliminated until the one of interest is finally identified. Each step of a **dichotomous key** typically consists of two statements that divide the things being identified/classified into two groups. Each statement is followed by a direction that indicates either what step to go to next or the name of the organism.

To make your own dichotomous key, you would need to start out with two statements that divide the organisms being classified into two groups.

1a	Requires petroleum fuel	go to Step 2
1b	Requires only muscle power	bicycle
2a	Has wings and flies	jet
2b	Has no wings and does not fly	go to Step 3
3a	Has two wheels	motorcycle
3b	Has more than two wheels	car

Figure 9-21. A dichotomous key is used to sort, name, or classify.

Each statement would be followed with a direction about the next step to take. At the next step, you again divide the organisms into two groups that are again followed by directions about the next step to go to or the identity of the organism or object. For example, Figure 9-21 shows how you might construct a key to classify a bicycle, car, jet, and motorcycle.

Pretend that you do not know a motorcycle from a bicycle from a jet, from a car. All you could do is examine each one of the objects, make observations, and determine how they work. Once you did that, you would be ready to place names on each of the four items.

Notice that if you did not work through the key step by step, it would be very easy to misname an object. If you thought about a bicycle as having two wheels and scanned down the list with no attention to following the steps, you could easily mistake the bicycle for a motorcycle. You would spot step 3a, which says, "Has two wheels" and say to yourself, "Yep, that's the bicycle." You would totally miss the fact that the object in step 3a must run on petroleum fuel. Always start at the beginning of a key.

Review Questions

Set 9.2

Base your answers to questions 9 through 11 on the diagram and information below, and on your knowledge of biology.

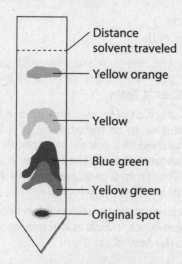

- Distance solvent traveled
- Yellow orange
- Yellow
- Blue green
- Yellow green
- Original spot

Several drops of concentrated green pigment extract obtained from spinach leaves were placed near the bottom of a strip of highly absorbent paper. When the extract dried, the paper was suspended in a test tube containing solvent so that only the tip of the paper was in the solvent. As the solvent was absorbed and moved up the paper, the various pigments within the extract became visible, as shown in the diagram.

9. A valid conclusion that can be drawn from this information is that spinach leaves
   (1) contain only chlorophyll
   (2) contain pigments in addition to chlorophyll
   (3) contain more orange pigment than yellow pigment
   (4) are yellow-orange rather than green

10. The technique used to separate the parts of the extract in the diagram is known as
    (1) staining   (3) chromatography
    (2) dissection   (4) electrophoresis

11. In which organelle would most of these pigments be found?
    (1) nucleus   (3) ribosome
    (2) mitochondrion (4) chloroplast

12. A student observed a one-celled organism in the field of view of a compound light microscope as shown in the adjacent diagram.

On the diagram, draw an arrow to indicate the direction the organism would seem to move if the student moved the slide on the stage to the left and down. [1]

13. To test for the presence of glucose, a student added the same amount of Benedict's solution to each of four test tubes. (Benedict's is a glucose indicator that is a royal blue color when no glucose is present. To determine if glucose is present, Benedict's must be mixed in the unknown solution and heated for several minutes.)

Two of the test tubes contained unknown solutions. The other two test tubes contained known solutions. The chart below shows the color results obtained after the solutions were heated in the four test tubes in a hot water bath.

Data Table		
Tube	Contents	Color After Heating
1	Unknown solution + Benedict's solution	Royal blue
2	Unknown solution + Benedict's solution	Red orange
3	Water + Benedict's solution	Royal blue
4	Glucose + water + Benedict's solution	Red orange

The student could correctly conclude that

(1) all of the tubes contained glucose
(2) tubes 1 and 2 contained glucose
(3) tube 1 did not contain glucose, but tube 2 did
(4) tube 2 did not contain glucose, but tube 1 did

14. A student viewing a specimen under the low-power objective of a compound light microscope switched to high power and noticed that the field of view darkened considerably.

Which microscope part identified on this microscope would the student adjust to brighten the field of view?

(1) A   (2) B   (3) C   (4) D

15. A student studied the upper layer of cells of a tissue sample on a slide, using the high-power objective of the compound microscope shown.

Which part of the microscope should the student adjust to observe the lower layer of the sample?

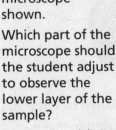

(1) A   (2) B   (3) C   (4) D

16. State the purpose of using stains in a wet-mount slide preparation. [1]

17. The eyepiece of a compound light microscope has a magnification of 10X and the low-power objective and high-power objective lenses have magnifications of 10X and 30X, respectively. If the diameter of the low-power field measures 1500 micrometers, the diameter of the high-power field will measure either 4500 micrometers or 500 micrometers.

Select the correct diameter. Support your answer. [1]

Base your answers to questions 18 and 19 on the diagram below of some internal structures of an earthworm and on your knowledge of biology.

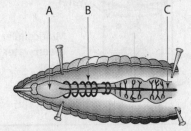

18. Which laboratory equipment should be used to observe the surface details of structures A, B, and C of the earthworm?

(1) stereoscope
(2) compound light microscope
(3) graduated cylinder
(4) triple-beam balance

19. Structure A has a diameter of 3 millimeters. What is the approximate diameter of the blood vessel indicated by C?

(1) 2.5 mm   (3) 1.5 mm
(2) 2.0 mm   (4) 0.5 mm

Base your answers to questions 20 and 21 on the illustration below and on your knowledge of biology. The image is a representation of an animal cell as it would appear when viewed with compound light microscope

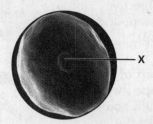

20. Identify the organelle indicated by letter X. [1]

21. What technique could be used to make the organelle indicated by letter X more visible? [1]

22. While focusing a microscope on high power, a student crushed the coverslip. The student probably

    (1) shut the light off
    (2) turned up the light intensity
    (3) rotated the eyepiece
    (4) used the coarse adjustment

23. An experimental setup is shown in the diagram below.

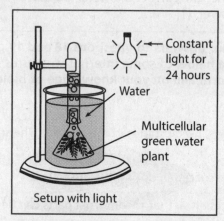

Setup with light

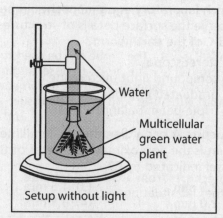

Setup without light

Which hypothesis would most likely be tested using this setup?

(1) Green water plants release a gas in the presence of light.
(2) Roots of water plants absorb minerals in the absence of light.
(3) Green plants need light for cell division.
(4) Plants grow best in the absence of light.

Base your answers to questions 24 through 27 on the photograph below and on your knowledge of biology. The photograph shows onion root-tip tissue viewed under the high-power objective of a compound light microscope.

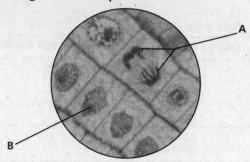

24. The photograph illustrates stages in the process of

    (1) meiosis in root tips
    (2) mitotic cell division in plants
    (3) water conduction in onions
    (4) chlorophyll production in chloroplasts

25. Identify the structure indicated by arrow A. [1]

26. Identify the structure indicated by arrow B. [1]

27. Describe one adjustment that could be made to the microscope to make the field of view brighter. [1]

28. Pieces of pH paper were used to test the contents of three test tubes. The results are shown in the diagram below.

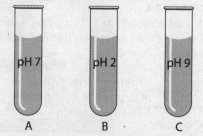

Which statement about the tubes is correct?

(1) Tube A contains a base.
(2) Tube B contains a base.
(3) Tube B contains an acid.
(4) Tube C contains an acid.

29. When viewed with a compound light microscope, which letter would best illustrate the way in which the microscope inverts and reverses the image?

(1) A   (2) W   (3) F   (4) D

30. Gel electrophoresis is a technique used to
(1) cut DNA into pieces of various sizes
(2) separate DNA fragments by charge and size
(3) move DNA fragments from one species to another
(4) make copies of chromosomes

Observing Plant and Animal Specimens

Classroom experiences involving plants and animals range from observation to dissection. Opportunities to observe plants and animals require consideration and appreciation for the organism. The abuse of any live organism for any purpose is intolerable.

Dissection and Preserved Specimens

The dissection of plant and animal specimens provides a framework upon which to organize biological knowledge. **Dissection** (or the examination of preserved specimens) provides a way to

- observe similarities and differences that exist among species
- understand the relationship between biological form and function
- expose and identify the internal structures of organisms

To dissect a specimen correctly, you need:

- the knowledge of what equipment to use and how to use it properly
- a work area that is clean and well organized both before and after the activity

Equipment commonly used during dissection activities is described in Table 9-3.

Table 9-3. Dissection Equipment

Equipment	Use
Dissecting pan	Resembles a cake pan but has a wax or a rubber-like substance in the bottom. The specimen is placed on the waxy surface.
Dissecting pins	Large pins with a "T" shape used to anchor the specimen during the dissection
Scalpel	A sharp instrument used to slice open the specimen so that the internal parts can be observed
Scissors	Used for cutting open the specimen and to remove parts. May have two sharp points or one blunt and one sharp point.
Probe/ Teasing needle/ Dissecting needle	Used to move structures around while they are still intact. The probe can be used to lift some organs so that others located below them are observable. The probe or dissecting needle is also used to point out different structures when showing specific features to someone else. Another function is to "tease" or gently tear apart structures such as muscle tissue.
Tweezers/ Forceps	Used to lift out small parts, to move structures, and to pry parts open
Safety goggles	Wrap-around shatter-proof glasses used to protect eyes from accidental splashes of preservative when dissecting as well as in other lab situations.

31. State one scientific purpose for dissecting an organism. [1]

32. For what purpose would the equipment in the following illustration most likely be used?

   (1) dissecting an earthworm
   (2) removing cell organelles
   (3) identifying and classifying a single-celled organism
   (4) observing mitosis on prepared slides

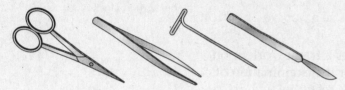

33. Along with a dissecting pan, which group of equipment would be most useful to a student planning to dissect a preserved specimen?

   (1) dissecting pins, compound light microscope, and pH paper
   (2) pH paper, eye dropper, and safety goggles
   (3) safety goggles, scissors, and compound light microscope
   (4) safety goggles, stereoscope, and scissors

34. What is the best use for the dissection instrument illustrated in the diagram below?

   (1) cutting through bones
   (2) spreading apart muscle tissue
   (3) cutting through thick muscles
   (4) removing blood plasma

Laboratory Safety

Laboratory investigations are, for some students, the most exciting part of the Living Environment course. However, they sometimes involve potentially dangerous activities and materials. As a result, careful attention to safety procedures is critical.

Using Safety Equipment

You should know how to properly use the safety equipment located in your biology laboratory. It is critical to be aware of the location in your laboratory of each of these:

- fire extinguisher
- safety shower
- eye wash station
- fire blanket
- emergency gas shutoff

Use the safety equipment provided for you. Goggles should be worn whenever a lab calls for the use of chemicals, preserved specimens, or dissection. If indicated by your teacher, you should also wear a safety apron when using chemicals. Some activities, such as those involving chemicals or live or preserved organisms, also require the use of special gloves.

Safety in the Laboratory

Read all of the directions for an investigation before you start to work. If you are unsure about any part of the lab procedures, check with your teacher. As a general rule, do not perform activities without permission; do only what the instructions and your teacher direct you to do.

- Do *not* eat or drink in the laboratory.
- When you are heating a test tube, always slant it so that the open end of the tube points away from you and others. Never heat a closed container, such as a test tube that has been closed with a stopper.
- Never inhale or taste any of the chemicals you are using in a laboratory. This includes the specimens you are dissecting.
- If you spill a chemical or get any on your skin, wash it off immediately. Also, report the incident to your teacher.
- Tell your teacher about any personal injury no matter how minor it may seem.
- Tie back long hair, and keep loose clothing away from laboratory equipment, chemicals, and sources of heat and fire.
- Never expose flammable liquids to an open flame. Use a hot water bath (such as a large beaker of water heated on a hot plate) if you need to heat flammable liquids (such as alcohol). See Figure 9-22.
- Know what equipment to use when handling hot glassware. Do not use bare fingers to pick up hot test tubes or beakers. Use test tube holders and beaker tongs.
- Do not use glassware that has cracks or large chips. Tell your teacher about the damage and get a replacement.
- Do not pour chemicals back into stock bottles or exchange stoppers on the stock bottles.
- Use laboratory apparatus as it is intended to be used. For example, do not stir a solution using a thermometer, plastic ruler, or your pen.
- Do not use electrical equipment around water. If electrical cords seem to have exposed wires or if you get a shock handling electrical equipment, notify your teacher immediately. Do not attempt to disconnect the equipment yourself.

Figure 9-22. Hot water bath: A hot water bath is used to heat test tubes that contain a flammable liquid such as alcohol.

Cleaning Your Work Area

- Turn off the gas and water after you are done with them. Disconnect any electrical devices.
- Clean your work area by returning materials to their appropriate places, washing glassware according to your teacher's instructions, and wiping off the lab surface.
- Dispose of chemicals according to the instructions provided by your teacher.
- Wash your hands thoroughly!

Review Questions   Set 9.4

35. If a student spills nitric acid on her arm, she should *first*

(1) report the accident to the school nurse
(2) report the spill to her teacher
(3) rinse her arm with water
(4) allow the acid to evaporate

36. When they are not being used during a laboratory investigation, electrical devices should be

(1) put away
(2) turned off
(3) unplugged
(4) covered

37. A student performing an experiment noticed that the beaker containing the water being heated had a small crack. It was not leaking. What should the student do?

(1) Stop heating the beaker and try to fix the crack.

(2) Stop heating the beaker and report the crack to the teacher.

(3) Stop heating the beaker and immediately take the beaker to the teacher.

(4) Continue heating as long as the liquid does not start to leak out of the crack.

38. The diagram below shows a student conducting a laboratory experiment. Describe one safety procedure the student should be following that is *not* represented in the diagram. [1]

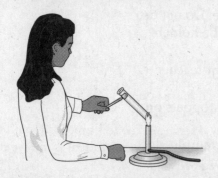

39. The diagram below shows a student heating some test tubes with chemicals in them during a laboratory activity. Describe one error in the laboratory procedure shown in the diagram. [1]

40. An *unsafe* procedure for heating a nutrient solution in a flask would be to

(1) heat the solution at the lowest temperature on a hot plate

(2) stopper the flask tightly to prevent evaporation of the solution

(3) use a Bunsen burner to heat the solution

(4) stir the solution while it is heating

41. Chlorophyll can be removed from leaves by boiling them in alcohol, a flammable solvent. In addition to wearing safety goggles, which is the safest procedure to follow?

(1) A stoppered test tube of leaves and alcohol should be held over the Bunsen burner.

(2) A stoppered test tube of leaves and alcohol should be placed in a large beaker of alcohol and heated on a hot plate.

(3) A beaker of leaves and alcohol should be placed on a tripod over a Bunsen burner.

(4) A beaker of leaves and alcohol should be placed into a larger beaker of water and heated on a hot plate.

42. Which safety procedure should a student follow during a dissection?

(1) The student should wear gloves and hold the specimen in the palm of her hand while cutting the specimen open.

(2) The student should cut the specimen open while holding it under running water.

(3) The student should apply additional preservative to the specimen.

(4) The student should direct the cutting motion away from her body.

Directions

Review the Test-Taking Strategies section of this book. Then answer the following questions. Read each question carefully and answer with a correct choice or response.

Part A

1 The diagram below shows a wasp positioned next to a centimeter ruler.

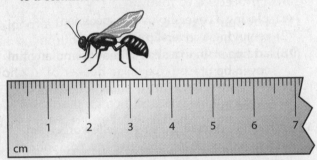

What is the approximate length of a *wing* of this wasp?
(1) 10 mm   (3) 3.5 cm
(2) 1.4 cm   (4) 35 mm

2 When preparing a wet-mount slide of onion cells, a student put a drop of Lugol's iodine stain on the slide. Lugol's iodine stain was added to
(1) prevent the formation of air bubbles
(2) make cell structures more visible
(3) increase the magnification
(4) increase the rate of photosynthesis in the cells

3 A student views some cheek cells under low power. Before switching to high power, the student should
(1) adjust the eyepiece
(2) center the image being viewed
(3) remove the slide from the stage
(4) remove the coverslip from the slide

4 Bromthymol blue turns yellow in the presence of carbon dioxide. This characteristic makes it possible for bromthymol blue to function as
(1) a measure of volume
(2) an indicator
(3) a catalyst
(4) an energy source

5 Which statement describes two unsafe laboratory practices represented in the diagram below?

(1) The flame is too high, and the test tube is unstoppered.
(2) The opening of the test tube is pointed toward the student, and the student is not wearing goggles.
(3) The test tube is unstoppered, and the student is not wearing goggles.
(4) The beaker has water in it, and the flame is under the tripod.

6 A student sees the image shown below when observing the letter "f" with the low-power objective lens of a microscope.

Which of the four diagrams below most closely resembles the image the student will see after switching to high power?

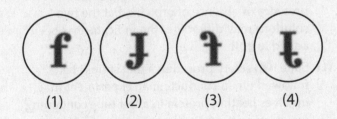

(1)   (2)   (3)   (4)

Part B

7 The diagram below represents the field of view of a compound light microscope. Three single-celled organisms are located across the diameter of the field.

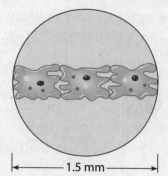

|← —— 1.5 mm —— →|

Knowing that 1 mm = 1000 micrometers, what is the approximate length of each single-celled organism?
(1) 250 micrometers
(2) 500 micrometers
(3) 1000 micrometers
(4) 1500 micrometers

8 Electrophoresis is a method of
(1) separating DNA fragments
(2) changing the genetic code of an organism
(3) indicating the presence of starch
(4) separating colored compounds on a strip of paper

9 A student, not wearing safety goggles, gets some unknown chemical in his eye. What is the most appropriate action he should take?
(1) Put on safety goggles immediately.
(2) Ask his lab partner to see if his eye looks OK.
(3) Go to the eyewash station and use it to rinse his eye thoroughly.
(4) Rub the eye gently and see if it hurts or stings.

10 An indicator for a protein is added to a solution that contains protein and to a solution that does not contain protein. State one way, other than the presence or absence of protein, that the two solutions may differ after the indicator has been added to both. [1]

11 State two safety procedures that should be followed when conducting an experiment that involves heating protein in a test tube containing water, an acid, and a digestive enzyme. [1]

12 Which laboratory procedure is represented in the diagram below?

Paper towel

(1) placing a coverslip over a specimen
(2) removing a coverslip from a slide
(3) adding stain to a slide without removing the coverslip
(4) reducing the size of air bubbles under a coverslip

13 A student is viewing a single-celled organism under the low-power objective of a compound light microscope. Describe an adjustment the student would need to make to see the organism clearly *after* switching from low power to high power. In your description include the name of the part of the microscope that would be used to make the adjustment. [1]

14 What is the volume of the liquid in the graduated cylinder shown below?

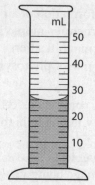

(1) 23 mL   (2) 26 mL   (3) 27 mL   (4) 28 mL

15 The diagrams below show four different one-celled organisms (shaded) in the field of view of the same microscope using different magnifications. Which illustration shows the largest one-celled organism?

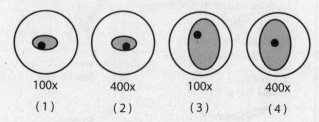

| 100x | 400x | 100x | 400x |
| (1) | (2) | (3) | (4) |

Base your answers to questions 16 through 18 on the information below, the key, and on your knowledge of biology.

Biologists use keys to accurately classify unknown organisms such as the unidentified female mosquito shown in the following diagram. These keys are designed to categorize organisms according to structural characteristics. The key shows various characteristics used to identify the differences among *Anopheles*, *Deinocerites*, *Culex*, *Psorophora*, and *Aedes* mosquitoes.

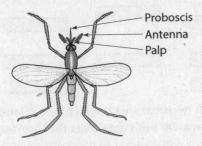

— Proboscis
— Antenna
— Palp

Unknown female mosquito

1a Antennae very bushy — Male mosquito	**1b** Antennae not bushy — Go to 2
2a Palps much shorter than proboscis — Go to 3	**2b** Palps as long as proboscis — Female *Anopheles*
3a Tip of abdomen blunt, without points — Go to 4	**3b** Tip of abdomen with points — Go to 5
4a Antennae much longer than proboscis — Female *Deinocerites*	**4b** Antennae shorter than proboscis — Female *Culex*
5a Many long scales present on hind legs — Female *Psorophora*	**5b** Hind legs without long scales — Female *Aedes*

16 According to the key, which feature distinguishes male from female mosquitoes?
  (1) palp length
  (2) leg scales
  (3) abdomen points
  (4) antennae appearance

17 According to the key, which characteristics are necessary to identify a female *Anopheles* mosquito?
  (1) antennae, palps, and proboscis
  (2) wings, proboscis, and scales on legs
  (3) eyes, scales on legs, and abdomen tip
  (4) palps, abdomen tip, and wings

18 According to the key, the unknown female mosquito belongs to the group known as
  (1) *Deinocerites*   (3) *Psorophora*
  (2) *Culex*   (4) *Aedes*

Base your answers to questions 19 through 22 on the information and diagram below and on your knowledge of biology. The diagram represents some of the steps in a procedure used in a specific laboratory activity.

Samples of DNA from an eye-color gene of four individuals, W, X, Y, and Z, were cut into pieces using a type of chemical. The results of this procedure are shown below.

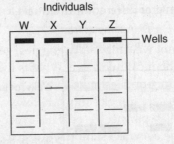

Individuals

W X Y Z

— Wells

19 Identify the specific type of chemical used to cut the DNA in this procedure. [1]

20 Which two individuals have DNA base patterns for this gene that are the most similar? Support your answer. [1]

21 The diagram represents the results of the procedure known as
  (1) cloning
  (2) chromatography
  (3) gel electrophoresis
  (4) protein sequencing

22 State where the smallest fragments of DNA would be located on the gel in the illustration. [1]

23 A chromatography setup is shown below.

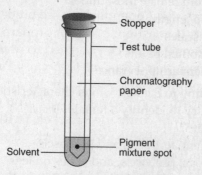

Identify one error in the setup. [1]

Part C

24 Some students did a lab to test the vitamin C content of several fruits. They squeezed the juice from some of the fruits and cut others up and placed them in a blender to obtain a juice sample. Juice for each fruit was kept in a clean, labeled beaker. Pipettes were used to transfer the juices to test tubes for analysis.

During the laboratory cleanup, one student drank some of the juice left in one beaker. State why this was an unsafe procedure. [1]

25 Below is a drawing of a hypothetical electrophoresis gel. Included on the gel are some bands for several different individuals.

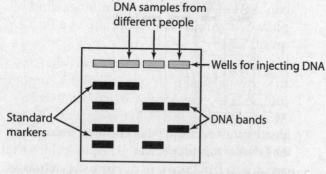

- Decribe where the smallest fragments of DNA would be located on the gel in the illustration. [1]

- Discuss two practical applications of information that can be obtained through this process. [1]

Base your answers to questions 26 through 28 on the information and diagram below and on your knowledge of biology.

The diagram below shows the results of a test that was done using DNA samples from three bears of

different species. Each DNA sample was cut into fragments using a specific enzyme and placed in the wells as indicated below. The DNA fragments were then separated using gel electrophoresis.

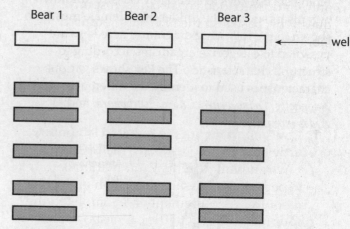

26 Which two bears are most closely related? Support your answer with data from the test results. [1]

27 Identify one additional way to determine the evolutionary relationship of these bears. [1]

28 Identify one procedure, other than electrophoresis, that is used in the laboratory to separate the different types of molecules in a liquid mixture. [1]

---

29 The dichotomous key begun below should allow users to classify the organisms illustrated. Complete the key using only information shown in the illustration. [3]

Dichotomous Key
1a. Wings present...............................Fly 1b. No wings present............................. go to 2

Part D of The Living Environment Regents Examination, is composed of multiple-choice and/or open-ended constructed-response questions, based on the NY State-required laboratory activities.

Questions and Answers About Part D of the Regents Examination

1. **How important are the required laboratory activities?** Everyone taking the Living Environment Regents Examination is expected to have satisfactorily met the laboratory requirement and completed the four laboratory activities. Questions on Part D of the Regents Examination assess content and skills related to these required laboratory activities. Everyone who has completed these activities should have available for review the *Student Laboratory Packet* supplied by the Regents for each of the labs. The packet contains background information, procedures, questions, and answers that were filled in as you carried out the laboratory activity. These packets should be used for review purposes, along with the information provided in this Appendix.

2. **How do the required labs help me in the Living Environment course?** Performing the required laboratory activities accomplishes two basic things. First, you learn and/or practice important laboratory skills associated with the biological sciences. Second, the lab activities are each associated with specific concepts contained in the *Living Environment Core Curriculum*, helping you better learn, understand, and apply those concepts.

3. **How can this Appendix help me prepare for the Part D questions?** To best prepare for the questions on Part D, you need to review your completed *Student Laboratory Packet* for each required laboratory activity along with the information presented here. You should have all four completed packets (with correct answers) available as you work through this Appendix.

4. **What should I know about each of the Required Laboratory Activities?** The most critical thing is that you have actually completed each activity and observed firsthand the results of each part. The next thing is to review the content and skills associated with each activity by working through the rest of this Appendix. In many cases, the content or skills are already found elsewhere in this book. References and notes are provided to show you where to look. Specific information and skills related to each activity is provided in this section.

The questions on Part D may be *applications* of the skills and content associated with the activity. For example, although red onion cells are used in the diffusion laboratory activity, a question involving the basic concepts of diffusion using another kind of plant cell would be appropriate as a Part D question.

It is important to note that you do *not* have to know, for test purposes, all of the content information provided with each activity. Much of it is included in the activity so that you can understand the important concepts. Only a few concepts in the required labs that are not in the Core Curriculum are actually testable. Each of these will be clearly noted in this Appendix.

Laboratory Activity #1: Relationships and Biodiversity

In this activity, you conducted a number of tests to compare various characteristics of a hypothetical "endangered plant species" with 3 other species that were related to it. From the data, you then determined which species might be the most likely to produce the substance "Curol" that has important medical uses. The final segment of the activity focused on biodiversity, both its benefits and how the loss of biodiversity can be an environmental problem.

Skills and/or content associated with the laboratory activity	Procedures and suggestions for review Note: Pages noted below are either in *Brief Review in the Living Environment* (BR) or in your *Student Lab Packet* (SLP).
Making/recording observations of plant tissues	See pages 146–148 and page 179 (BR) for information about observations, inferences, assumptions, and opinions.
Making/recording observations of tissue samples with a microscope	Review focusing and other microscope skills on pages 169–172 (BR). In this activity you examined plant tissues with the microscope to look for similarities and differences.
Comparing samples to determine similarities and differences	You compared the flowers, leaves, seeds, and stem cross-sections in an attempt to determine which one was most closely related to *Botana curus (B. curus)*. If a Regents question illustrates parts of specific organisms, you could be asked to use your observations to determine relationships between them.
Use of paper chromatography	Review what you did during the laboratory activity on pages 2–3 (SLP). Review the process on page 175 (BR). Be prepared to answer questions about why goggles were required or about correct vs. incorrect technique related to chromatography, such as: What if the water (solvent) level was above the pigment spots when the paper was put in the cup? (answer: the pigment would wash away and not go up the paper)
Use of an indicator (to test for enzyme M)	You were testing for an enzyme that was present in *B. curus* to see if any of the other plants also produced it. The presence of this enzyme in any of the other plants might suggest a closer relationship to *B. curus*. Review information about indicators on page 175 (BR).
Use of simulated gel electrophoresis of DNA from plant samples	Review what you did during the laboratory activity on pages 3–4 (SLP), then review the technique of electrophoresis on pages 173–174 (BR). Be prepared to answer questions about how enzymes are used to cut the DNA into fragments as described in the lab activity. Also know how to interpret gel electrophoresis results: e.g., what do the bands represent and what information do they convey, or, where would the smallest fragments be on a gel?
Translating the DNA code to a particular protein sequence	Review what you did during the laboratory activity on page 7 (SLP). You first used the base pairing "rule" for DNA to RNA transcription—G goes with C, and A goes with U (not T) to get the mRNA sequences. Then you used the Universal Genetic Code Table provided by your teacher to look up which amino acid each three-letter mRNA sequence represented. This enabled you to get a particular amino acid sequence for each species, so that you could compare them and determine possible genetic relationships. Similar DNA suggests common ancestry. Review the information on pages 47–48 (BR) regarding proteins and DNA in cells.
Using branching tree diagrams to show relationships	Review question 6 on page 6 (SLP), then review Figure 5–2 on page 81 (BR). Read pages 87–88 (BR). Read the information about Practice Questions 13–14 on pages x–xi (BR).
Human actions and biodiversity	Re-read the passage on page 7 (SLP), then review your answers to questions 8–10. Review pages 110–111 (BR) and pages 127–129 (BR) regarding the benefits of biodiversity, and the section: *Extinction*, on page 91 (BR).

Questions and comments regarding Laboratory Activity #1

After reviewing your *Student Lab Packet* and the sections of this book as noted above, check yourself by answering the following questions found in this book on the pages noted.

p. 49; 8, 9, 13, 16, 17
p. 50; 18, 20, 21, 22
p. 54; 35
p. 55; 1, 6
p. 56; 8
p. 81; 4
p. 82; 5
p. 89; 27, 30
p. 101; 5
p. 111; 40, 41, 42
p. 112; 44, 45

p. 120; 32
p. 143; 36
p. 176; 9, 10, 11
p. 177; 13, 14, 15
p. 178; 22
p. 179; 29, 30
p. 183; 3
p. 184; 12, 13
p. 185; 20
p. 186; 22, 23, 24

You should also be able to:

- explain how you used your lab data to determine which plant species is the closest relative to *B. curus.*
- explain why finding a close relative to *B. curus* is important.
- list several forms of structural evidence that can be used to indicate biological relationships (such as similarities in embryos, flower form, or leaf shape).
- explain why structural evidence is often less useful than molecular evidence to determine biological relationships.
- use a genetic code table to convert a DNA sequence, to a mRNA sequence, to an amino acid sequence. (Ask your teacher for a copy of the table you used in the activity and practice with it.)
- explain why closely related species often share many molecular/biochemical similarities.
- answer questions related to why and how biodiversity may be lost, why such a loss is important, and how human activities often play a role in the loss of biodiversity.
- discuss why tradeoffs must be considered when the destruction of habitats/native species is involved.

Part D Review Questions: Lab 1

Base your answers to questions 1 through 4 on the information below and on your knowledge of biology.

To demonstrate techniques used in DNA analysis, a student was given two paper strip samples of DNA. The two DNA samples are shown below.

Sample 1:
ATTCCGGTAATCCCGTAATGCCGG
ATAATACTCCGGTAATATC

Sample 2:
ATTCCGGTAATCCCGTAATGCCGGA
TAATACTCCGGTAATATC

The student cut between the C and G in each of the shaded CCGG sequences in sample 1 and between the As in each of the shaded TAAT sequences in sample 2. Both sets of fragments were then arranged on a paper model of a gel.

1. The action of what kind of molecules was being demonstrated when the DNA samples were cut? [1] *enzymes*

2. Identify the technique that was being demonstrated when the fragments were arranged on the gel model. [1] *gel electrophorisis*

3. The results of this type of DNA analysis are often used to help determine
   (1) the number of DNA molecules in an organism
   (2) if two species are closely related
   (3) the number of mRNA molecules in DNA
   (4) if two organisms contain carbohydrate molecules

4. State one way that the arrangement of the two samples on the gel model would differ. [1]
   number of bands

5. R, S, and T are three species of birds. Species S and T show similar coloration. The enzymes found in species R and T show similarities. Species R and T also exhibit many of the same behavioral patterns.

   Show the relationship between species R, S, and T by placing the letter representing each species at the top of the appropriate branch on the diagram to the right. [1]

Base your answers to questions 6 through 8 on the diagram below and on your knowledge of biology. Letters A through L represent different species of organisms. The arrows represent long periods of geologic time.

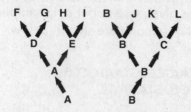

6. Which two species are the most closely related?
   (1) J and L
   (2) G and L
   (3) F and H
   (4) F and G

7. Which species was best adapted to changes that occurred in its environment over the longest period of time?
   (1) A
   (2) B
   (3) C
   (4) J

8. Which two species would most likely show the greatest similarity of DNA and proteins?
   (1) B and J
   (2) G and I
   (3) J and K
   (4) F and L

Base your answers to questions 9 through 11 on the information below and on your knowledge of biology.

Paper chromatography can be used to investigate evolutionary relationships. Leaves from a plant were ground and mixed with a solvent. The mixture of ground leaves and solvent was then filtered. Using a toothpick, twenty drops of the filtrate (material that passed through the filter) were placed at one spot on a strip of chromatography paper.

This procedure was repeated using leaves from three other species of plants. A separate strip of chromatography paper was prepared for each plant species. Each of the four strips of chromatography paper was placed in a different beaker containing the same solvent for the same amount of time. One of the laboratory setups is shown below.

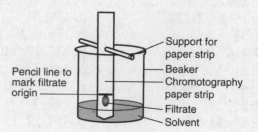

9. State one reason for using a new toothpick for the filtrate from each plant. [1] Sanitation

10. State one way the four strips would most likely be different from each other after being removed from the beakers. [1] Different colors

11. State how a comparison of these resulting strips could indicate evolutionary relationships. [1]

Base your answers to questions 12 through 14 on the information below and on your knowledge of biology.

Scientists found members of a plant species they did not recognize. They wanted to determine if the unknown species was related to one or more of four known species, A, B, C, and D. The relationship between species can be determined most accurately by comparing the results of gel electrophoresis of the DNA from different species.

The chart below represents the results of gel electrophoresis of the DNA from the unknown plant species and the four known species.

Results of Gel Electrophoresis of DNA from Five Plant Species

Unknown Species	Species A	Species B	Species C	Species D

Key
—— = Band in the gel

12. The unknown species is most closely related to which of the four known species? Support your answer. [1]

13. Identify one physical characteristic of plants that can be readily observed and compared to help determine the relationship between two different species of plants. [1]

14. Explain why comparing the DNA of the unknown and known plant species is probably a more accurate method of determining relationships than comparing only the physical characteristic you identified in question 13. [1]

Laboratory Activity #2: Making Connections

In Part A of this activity, you learned to take your pulse rate. Then you compared pulse rate data for the class. You next experienced muscle fatigue by rapidly squeezing a clothespin. In Part B, you designed a controlled experiment to determine which of two claims about exercise and pulse rate is correct.

Skills and/or content associated with the laboratory activity	Procedures and suggestions for review **Note:** Pages noted below are either in *Brief Review in the Living Environment (BR)* or in your *Student Lab Packet (SLP)*.
Taking pulse rate	You should be familiar with the procedure to find a person's pulse rate on page 2. (SLP) Review the information on human systems on pages 10–13 (BR).
Data tables and graphs	Review the data table and histogram you prepared on page 3 (SLP). Also review the questions and your answers on page 4 (SLP). Review the information about collecting and organizing data on pages 154–156 (BR).
Muscle fatigue	Review the information, questions, and your answers to them on pages 5 and 6 (SLP).
Designing a controlled experiment and a report on the findings	Review the background information on page 7 (SLP) to help you recall how you determined the hypothesis your experiment tested. Review the steps for the design of a controlled experiment and how to organize the final report on pages 8–9 (SLP), then read over your final laboratory report for this activity, noting how you addressed each step of the design and report organization. Review the information on pages 149 through 158 (BR) regarding experimental design and the reporting of results and conclusions.

Questions and comments regarding Laboratory Activity #2

After reviewing your *Student Lab Packet* and the sections of this book as noted above, check yourself by answering the following questions found in this book on the pages noted.

p. 14; 38
p. 16; 15
p. 149; 3, 5
p. 153; 6, 8
p. 154; 9, 10, 11, 12, 14, 15, 16

p. 158; 18, 19
p. 159; 23, 24, 25, 26, 27, 28
p. 161; 7, 8, 9, 10, 11, 12, 13
p. 162; 14

You should also be able to:

- explain what your pulse rate tells you about activities occurring within your body.

- explain why a higher level of activity would affect a person's pulse rate. Be sure to state specifically how the functioning of muscle cells is affected by blood flow through various parts the body including the respiratory and digestive systems.

- explain what muscle fatigue is, what happens to cause it, and how it can eventually be overcome—see page 5 (SLP).

- explain why different individuals may have different resting pulse rates and that not all people experience muscle fatigue with the same amount of muscle activity.

- explain why evidence is important in determining whether or not a claim someone makes is true.

- describe your actual experiment, including the question, hypothesis, independent and dependent variables, and your conclusions. You should also be able to suggest at least one additional experiment that could be done to answer a question that came about as a direct result of the experiment you conducted. (Such a question might involve the effect of more activity on the test subjects, having more test subjects, or choosing a greater variety of test subjects.)

Part D Review Questions: Lab 2

15. On a television talk show, a guest claims that people who exercise vigorously for 15 minutes or more every day are able to solve math problems more rapidly than people who have no vigorous exercise in their daily routine.

    Describe a controlled experiment that could be conducted to test this claim. In your description be sure to:

    - state the purpose of the experiment [1]
    - state why the sample to be used should be large [1]
    - describe how the experimental group will be treated and how the control group will be treated [2]
    - state the specific data to be collected during the experiment [1]
    - state one way to determine if the results support the claim [1]

16. A student measures his pulse rate while he is watching television and records it. Next, he walks to a friend's house nearby and when he arrives, measures and records his pulse rate again. He and his friend then decide to run to the mall a few blocks away.

On arriving at the mall, the student measures and records his pulse rate once again. Finally, after sitting and talking for a half hour, the student measures and records his pulse rate for the last time. Which graph below best illustrates the expected changes in his pulse rate according to the activities described above?

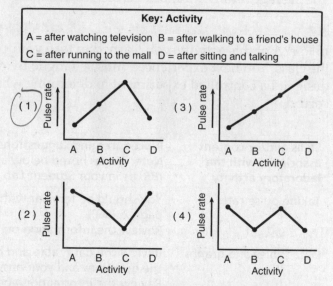

Key: Activity

A = after watching television B = after walking to a friend's house
C = after running to the mall D = after sitting and talking

17. A student squeezed a clothespin as many times as possible in a 30-second time period. The student repeated this procedure nine more times in quick succession. The data obtained are in the chart below.

Trial	Number of Squeezes in 30 Seconds
1	32
2	29
3	28
4	27
5	26
6	25
7	23
8	21
9	19
10	17

State one hypothesis that this data would support concerning the relationship between number of trials and number of squeezes in 30 seconds. [1]

Base your answers to questions 18 and 19 on the information below and on your knowledge of biology.

In an investigation, 28 students in a class determined their pulse rates after performing each of three different activities. Each activity was performed three times during equal time intervals. The average results are shown in the graph below.

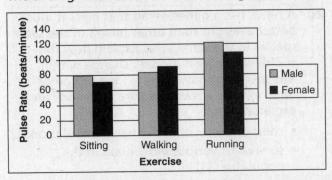

18. Before constructing the graph it would have been most helpful to organize the results of the investigation in
   (1) a research plan   (3) a data table
   (2) an equation   (4) a generalization

19. Some students concluded that males always have a higher pulse rate than females. Does the graph support this conclusion? Justify your answer. [1]

Laboratory Activity #3: The Beaks of Finches

The Beaks of Finches lab is a simulation of how natural selection works. Various tools are used in this activity to represent some beak variations that might be present in a population. Competition between participants leads to finding which tool(s) are best suited for obtaining enough food for the individuals with that tool (beak variation) to survive. The activity concludes with data about actual beak variations present today in different species of finches—the result of competition over many years on the Galapagos Islands.

Skills and/or content associated with the laboratory activity	Procedures and suggestions for review Note: Pages noted below are either in *Brief Review in the Living Environment* (BR) or in your *Student Lab Packet* (SLP).
Predicting	Review the procedures and questions on page 2 (SLP) to recall why you could expect a particular tool to be useful for the job specified.
Collecting and organizing data, making predictions	Review what you did during the Round One competition on page 3 (SLP). You could be asked to place data in a data table provided, as you did in this activity. Review the information on p. 154–156 (BR).
Analyzing and interpreting data	Review what you did during the Round Two competition on page 3 (SLP). The competition in Round Two was expected to make it harder to collect as many seeds in the same time interval as you had in Round One. State whether or not your results supported this expectation. Include data from the table in your answer. Read the introduction to The Mechanics of Evolution and Overview of Evolution on page 82 (BR) and on pages xiii–xiv (BR) about data table question strategies.
Summarizing results	Review questions 1–9 and your answers on pages 4–6 (SLP). Read the information on page 82 (BR), then on page 83–84 (BR) read the three sections and review the information in figures 5–4 and 5–5. Read pages 99–101 (BR); *Environmental Limits on Population Size*.
Galapagos Island Finches—Interpreting charts	Review the chart on page 6 (SLP), noting the "design" of each beak compared with the way it functions and the preferred food. Review the questions about the chart along with your responses to them. Be prepared to answer similar questions in association with this chart or a similar chart or diagram.

Questions and comments regarding Laboratory Activity #3

After reviewing your *Student Lab Packet* and the sections of this book as noted above, check yourself by answering the following questions found in this book on the pages noted.

p. 84; 6   p. 101; 6
p. 85; 11, 12   p. 102; 9
p. 87; 16   p. 104; 10
p. 93; 1, 3, 5, 7   p. 158; 19

You should also be able to:

- identify a specific procedure or action you carried out in this lab that is directly associated with *each* of the following concepts associated with evolution: variation, competition, survival, adaptation, and the role of the environment as an agent of natural selection. For help, see question #9 on page 6 (SLP).
- describe how being assigned a tool is more like how adaptations occur in nature than being allowed to choose a particular tool for the task.
- predict how the addition of small pebbles to the dish (that could not be used as food) could affect the results as the (food) seeds were being collected.
- explain how the characteristics of a particular bird's beak could affect its survival.
- explain why a bird has no control over the type of beak it has.
- explain how a particular beak could be useful in one environment and nearly useless in another.
- explain why migration to a new environment may enable an individual who cannot successfully compete in its original location to survive.
- explain why an individual with a beak that does not enable it to compete successfully for food cannot simply get a new beak that would make it better adapted.
- describe two characteristics of a bird, other than its beak, that would vary among individuals in the population and be a factor in the ability of individual birds to survive. Select one of these characteristics and state

how it would specifically be important to the individual's survival.

- name two species on the beak chart, on page 6 (SLP), that would be likely to compete when food is scarce. Explain the basis for your answer.

Part D Review Questions: Lab 3

20. A hawk has a genetic trait that gives it much better eyesight than other hawks of the same species in the same area. Explain how this could lead to evolutionary change within this species of hawk over a long period of time. In your answer, be sure to include an explanation of:

- competition within the hawk population [1]
- survival of various individuals in the population [1]
- how the frequency of the better-eyesight trait would be expected to change over time within the population [1]
- what would most likely happen to the hawks having the better-eyesight trait if they also had unusually weak wing muscles [1]

21. In members of a bird species living on a remote island, the greatest number of beak variations in the population would most likely be found when

(1) there is a high level of competition for limited resources
(2) homeostasis is limited by a severe climate
(3) they have a large and varied food supply
(4) they are prey for a large number of predators

22. The different tools used during the beaks of finches lab represented

(1) feeding adaptations in finches
(2) nest construction adaptations
(3) variations in seed size
(4) variations in ecosystems

Base your answer to question 23 on the portion of the mRNA codon chart and information below.

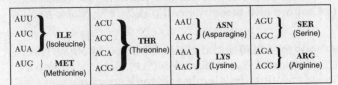

Series I represents three mRNA codons. Series II includes a mutation of series I.

Series I AGAUCGAGU
Series II ACAUCGAGU

23. How would the amino acid sequence produced by the mutant strand (series II) compare to the amino acid sequence produced by series I?

(1) The amino acid sequence would be shorter.
(2) One amino acid in the sequence would change.
(3) The amino acid sequence would remain unchanged.
(4) More than one amino acid in the sequence would change.

Base your answers to questions 24 through 26 on the passage below and on your knowledge of biology.

When Charles Darwin traveled to the Galapagos Islands, he observed 14 distinct varieties of finches on the islands. Darwin also observed that each finch variety ate a different type of food and lived in a slightly different habitat from the other finches. Darwin concluded that the finches all shared a common ancestor but had developed different beak structures.

24. The 14 varieties of finches are most likely the result of

(1) absence of biodiversity
(2) biological evolution
(3) asexual reproduction
(4) lack of competition

25. The second sentence best describes

(1) an ecosystem
(2) a predator/prey relationship
(3) a niche
(4) a food web

26. The different beak structures mentioned in the last sentence were most likely influenced by

(1) selection for favorable variations
(2) environmental conditions identical to those of the common ancestor
(3) abnormal mitotic cell division
(4) characteristics that are acquired during the bird's lifetime

Laboratory Activity #5: Diffusion Through a Membrane

The Diffusion Through a Membrane activity initially focuses on making a model "cell" and determining how certain materials move through the membrane surrounding it. Indicators are then used to test various solutions to determine which materials moved and where they ended up. Red onion cells were treated with salt solution and distilled water to determine the effect of such substances on live cells.

Skills and/or content associated with the laboratory activity	Procedures and suggestions for review **Note:** Pages noted below are either in *Brief Review in the Living Environment (BR)* or in your *Student Lab Packet (SLP)*.
Making a model "cell"	Review the procedures by which you made a model "cell" out of dialysis tubing (or a plastic bag). The "cell" contained both glucose and starch while the beaker contained starch indicator solution and water—see p. 2 (SLP). Read pages 5–8 (BR) regarding cell organelles, including the cell membrane. Read p. 166–168 (BR), *Tools for Measurement*.
Using starch and glucose indicator solutions	Review the procedures (p. 3 SLP, Table One) for testing for starch and glucose using the indicator. Notice that, in each case, a color change indicated the presence of the substance, and that the glucose test required heating before a result could be observed.

Determining indicator results	Table 2 (p. 3 SLP) summarizes the tests and results for each indicator. Be sure you can explain why it is necessary to test both the substance you want the indicator to "find" and any other substances that are also present. Read p. 175 (BR); *Stains and Indicators*.
Observing and interpreting results	Review your Model Cell Observations (p. 4 SLP) and the diagrams you filled in. Then carefully review your answers to questions 1–7 on pages 4–5 (SLP). Be sure you now understand which molecules moved through the membrane and know how you could tell. Also be sure you know how this information was used to determine the relative sizes of the molecules.
Making a wet-mount slide (of onion cells)	Review the procedures for making a wet mount slide. (p. 6 SLP) Read pages 169–172 (BR); *Microscope Skills*.
Drawing and labeling microscope images	Review the drawings you made for questions 6, 10, and 15. (p. 7 SLP) Note the differences in each drawing and review what you did each time to cause the changes you observed and drew.
Adding liquids to wet-mount slides	Review the procedure for this technique. (p. 6 SLP) You should be able to describe this process and predict the effect a substance being added would have on the cells.
Applying skills and concepts	Review the Analysis Questions and your answers to them. (p. 8–9 SLP) Just as you did for these questions, you should be able to apply the main concepts from this activity to questions like these if they appear on Part D of the Regents examination.

Questions and comments regarding Laboratory Activity #5

After reviewing your *Student Lab Packet* and the sections of this book as noted above, check yourself by answering the following questions found in this book on the pages noted.

p. 6; 11	p. 168; 3, 4
p. 9; 22, 23, 25, 26, 27, 28	p. 169; 5, 6, 8
p. 10; 30, 31, 32, 33, 35	p. 177; 13, 14, 15,
p. 15; 4, 5, 6, 7, 8, 9, 10	16, 17
p. 16; 11	p. 178; 22
p. 18; 28, 29	p. 183; 2, 4

You should also be able to:

- explain why dialysis tubing or a plastic bag could be used to simulate a cell membrane in this activity.
- identify a particular indicator and explain how it is used to indicate whether or not a specific substance is present.
- explain why it was important to keep the onion skin material as flat as possible when making the wet-mount slide.
- describe the direction that particles move during the process of diffusion relative to the concentration of a substance or substances.
- describe how the size of a molecule can affect whether or not it can pass across (through) a membrane.
- provide several examples of cells being affected by the process of diffusion. The effects may be on the appearance of the cell, the contents of the cell, and/or the functioning of the cell.
- provide several specific examples of the process of diffusion occurring within the human body. For each example be able to identify the substance(s) diffusing and the effect of this process on body functioning.
- describe the effect of salt on the water content of cell cytoplasm.
- describe how distilled water can be used to counteract the effect of salt on living cells on a wet-mount microscope slide.
- predict the effect of an error in procedure by students doing this particular laboratory activity, such as putting a substance in the wrong place, using salt solution instead of water, using the wrong indicator, and so on.
- Understand that osmosis, the diffusion of water through a membrane, is a kind of diffusion and therefore follows the same general "rules" as for the diffusion of other substances.

- explain how the process of digestion is related to the process of diffusion—see question 6 on p. 9 (SLP).

Part D Review Questions: Lab 5

27. An investigation was set up to study the movement of water through a membrane. The results are shown in the diagram below.

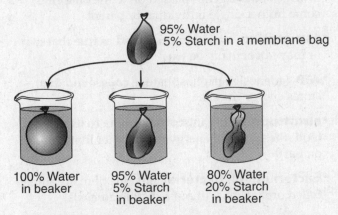

95% Water
5% Starch in a membrane bag

100% Water in beaker

95% Water 5% Starch in beaker

80% Water 20% Starch in beaker

Based on these results, which statement correctly predicts what will happen to red blood cells when they are placed in a beaker containing a water solution in which the salt concentration is much higher than the salt concentration in the red blood cells?

(1) The red blood cells will absorb water and increase in size.

(2) The red blood cells will lose water and decrease in size.

(3) The red blood cells will first absorb water, then lose water and maintain their normal size.

(4) The red blood cells will first lose water, then absorb water, and finally double in size.

28. Molecules A and B are both organic molecules found in many cells. When tested, it is found that molecule A cannot pass through a cell membrane, but molecule B easily passes through. State one way the two molecules could differ, that would account for the difference in the ability to pass through the cell membrane. [1]

29. Elodea is a plant that lives in freshwater. The diagram below represents one Elodea leaf cell in its normal freshwater environment.

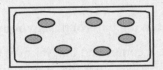

Elodea cell in freshwater

Predict how the contents of the Elodea cell would change if the cell was placed in saltwater for several minutes by completing the diagram, "Elodea cell in saltwater" below. Label the location of the cell membrane. [2]

Elodea cell in saltwater

30. The photos below show two red onion cells viewed with the high power of a compound light microscope. Describe the steps that could be used to make cell A resemble cell B using a piece of paper towel and an eyedropper or a pipette without removing the coverslip. [3]

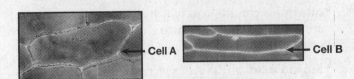

Cell A   Cell B

31. An indicator for a protein is added to a solution that contains protein and to a solution that does not contain protein. State one way, other than the presence or absence of protein, that the two solutions may differ after the indicator has been added to both. [1]

Glossary

Glossary items with asterisk are required vocabulary for the Regents Examination.

*abiotic nonliving parts of the environment

acid/acidic a compound that releases hydrogen ions when dissolved in water; a substance, such as vinegar, with a sour taste. Any pH below 7 indicates an acid, the lower the pH, the stronger the acid. The lowest pH possible is pH 0. Strong acids are usually harmful to living cells.

acid rain rain that is more acidic than normal

*active transport the process by which cells use energy to transport molecules through the cell membrane from areas of low concentration to areas of high concentration

*adaptive value any trait that helps an organism survive and reproduce under a given set of environmental conditions

agarose a gel-like substance used in bacterial cultures

*AIDS (acquired immunodeficiency syndrome) the disease that results when the HIV virus attacks the human immune system

*allergy a condition in which a person's immune system is overly sensitive to environmental substances that are normally harmless

*amino acid any one of several building blocks of protein

animal a complex, multicellular organism with specialized tissues and organs, but no cell walls; a heterotroph that obtains energy by consuming other organisms

*antibiotic a medicine produced by microorganisms used to destroy pathogens in humans and domestic animals

*antibody (pl. **antibodies**) a protein, produced by the immune system, that either attacks invading pathogens or marks them for killing

*antigen a molecule found on the outer surfaces of cells that the immune system recognizes as either part of the body or an outside invader

antihistamine a substance that reduces the effects of histamines and the symptoms they cause

artificial selection the process of breeding two organisms with desirable characteristics to produce offspring that have the advantages of both parents

*asexual reproduction a method of reproduction in which all the genes passed on to the offspring come from a single individual or parent

*assumption something accepted as true that may or may not actually be true

*ATP (adenosine triphosphate) a compound that stores energy in cells

*autotroph an organism that produces its own food; the source of energy for all other living things on Earth

*bacterium (pl. **bacteria**) any one of many single-celled organisms without a distinct nucleus

*balance a tool that measures mass by comparing the unknown mass of an object with an object of known mass

base a compound that produces hydroxide ions when dissolved in water, raising the pH above 7; the higher the pH, the stronger the base; strong bases are usually harmful to living cells

*bias a tendency to favor something; prejudice

*biochemical process a chemical process that occurs in a living thing

*biodiversity the variety of species in an area

biome large groups of ecosystems with similar climates and organisms; examples include the tundra, taiga, temperate forest, chaparral, tropical rain forest, desert, temperate grassland, tropical savanna grassland, and polar and high-mountain ice

*biosphere all of Earth's ecosystems, collectively; the biologically inhabited portions of Earth, including all of the water, land, and air in which organisms survive

*biotechnology the combination of technology and biological sciences

*biotic the living parts of the environment

*body cells non-reproductive cells in an individual such as skin, liver, and muscle cells; body cells contain the full number of chromosomes typical of the species

*bond the chemical link between atoms that hold molecules together

calibrate to adjust the scale of a measurement tool

*carnivore an organism that survives by eating animals

*carrying capacity the largest population of any single species that an area can support

*catalyst a substance that can speed up the rate of a chemical reaction without being changed or used up during the reaction

*cell the basic unit of structure and function that makes up all organisms

*cell membrane the thin boundary between the cell and its environment

*cellular respiration the process in which nutrients are broken apart, releasing the chemical energy stored in them

Celsius a temperature scale based on 100 equal units, with 0 as the freezing point of water and 100 as the boiling point of water

*chloroplast the green organelle that contains chlorophyll; where photosynthesis takes place

chlorophyll the molecules in chloroplasts that help convert light energy to chemical bond energy

*chromatography a laboratory technique used to separate mixtures of molecules

*chromosome a thick, threadlike structure that contains genetic information in the form of DNA

*circulation the flow of materials within a cell as well as between parts of a multicellular organism

classify to group things based upon their similarities

climax community a relatively diverse and stable ecosystem that is the end result of succession

*clone an organism that is genetically identical to the organism from which it was produced

*cloning a technique used to make identical organisms

*community a combination of all the different populations that live and interact in the same environment

*competition the struggle between organisms for the same limited resources in a particular area

*compound light microscope a tool that uses more than one lens and a light source to magnify an object

*conclusion the decision made about the outcome of an experiment; usually based on how well the actual result matches the predicted result

*consumer an organism that obtains its energy from producers

*control that group in an experiment in which everything—except the variable to be tested—is identical; the standard of comparison in an experiment

*controlled experiment an experiment in which all variables—except for the one being tested—are exactly the same

coverslip a thin slice of glass that covers the specimen on a slide

*cytoplasm the jellylike substance that is between the cell membrane and the nucleus and that contains specialized structures

*data the results of specific trials or tests completed during experiments

*decomposer an organism, generally a bacterium or fungus, that consumes dead organisms and organic waste

decomposition the process whereby dead organisms, as well as the wastes produced by living organisms, are broken down into their raw materials and returned to the ecosystem

*deforestation forest destruction that results from human activity

*dependent variable the part of an experiment that is changed to test a hypothesis

depletion a serious decline or reduction

detrimental damaging; harmful

*development the changes that occur from the fertilized egg to a complete individual; occurs by mitosis and differentiation of cells

deviation a change from normal circumstances

*dichotomous key a guide that compares pairs of observable traits to help the user identify an organism

*differentiation the process that transforms developing cells into specialized cells with different structures and functions

*diffusion the movement of molecules from areas of high concentration to areas of low concentration

*digestion the process that breaks down large food molecules into simpler molecules that the organism can use

*direct harvesting the destruction of an organism, or the removal of an organism from its habitat

*disease a condition, other than injury, that prevents the body from working as it should

*dissection the act of cutting apart a dead organism to examine its internal structure

*DNA (deoxyribonucleic acid) the material found in all cells that contains genetic information about that organism

*dynamic equilibrium the constant small corrections that normally occur to keep an organism's internal environment within the limits needed for survival

*ecological niche the specific role played by an organism or a population of organisms in the ecosystem

*ecological succession the process by which an existing community is replaced by another community

*ecology the study of how living things interact with one another and with their environment

*ecosystem all the living and nonliving things that interact in a specific area; a subdivision of the environment

*egg a sex cell produced by a female

*electronic balance a balance that measures mass automatically

*electrophoresis a tool that allows scientists to separate mixtures of molecules according to size

*element a substance consisting of only one kind of atom

*embryo an organism in the early stages of development (prior to birth)

endocrine glands various hormone-producing glands that secrete substances directly into the blood or lymph

endoplasmic reticulum an organelle that transports proteins and other materials from one part of the cell to another

*energy flow the movement of energy through an ecosystem

*energy pyramid a diagram showing how food energy moves through the ecosystem

*environment every living and nonliving thing that surrounds an organism

environmental impact statement a statement that includes an analysis of how a new project or technology might affect the environment

*enzymes proteins that speed up the rate of chemical reactions in living things

*equilibrium a state of balance and stability

estrogen a hormone (produced by the ovaries) that controls female sexual development and the reproductive process

*evidence support for the idea that something is true

*evolution the process by which species have changed over time

*excretion the removal of all the wastes produced by the cells of the body

*experiment a series of trials or tests that are done to support or refute a hypothesis

*expressed the way that an unseen gene is seen in an organism as an actual physical trait

*extinction the disappearance of all members of a species from Earth

Fallopian tubes that part of the female reproductive system where the egg cell is fertilized by the sperm cell; also called oviducts

*feedback mechanism a cycle in which the output of a system either modifies or reinforces the first action taken by the system

*fertilization the process that combines a sperm cell and an egg cell

*fetus the unborn, developing young of an animal during the later stages of development

*finite limited; able to be used up; opposite of infinite

flow of energy the movement of energy through an ecosystem

*food chain a representation that identifies the specific feeding relationships among organisms

food web a representation of many interconnected food chains that shows the feeding relationships among producers, consumers, and decomposers

forceps a tool used mainly during dissection to lift out small parts, to move structures, and to pry parts open

fossil the preserved remains of ancient organisms

fossil fuel a fuel, such as coal and gas, that comes from the remains of organisms that lived millions of years ago

fossil record a collection of fossils used to represent Earth's history

fungus (pl. **fungi**) the kingdom of organisms that are mostly multicellular, have cell walls made of chitin, and are heterotrophic

gamete an egg or sperm cell; a sex cell

gas exchange the process of obtaining oxygen from the environment and releasing carbon dioxide

gene (pl. **genes**) a segment of DNA (on a chromosome) that contains the code for a specific trait

gene expression see *expressed*; the result of activated genes

genetic engineering a set of technologies that humans use to alter the genetic instructions of an organism by substituting DNA molecules

genetic recombination the formation of a new combination of genes during sexual reproduction

genetic variation the normal differences found among offspring

geologic time Earth's history as revealed by layers of rock

global warming a increase in Earth's average surface temperature caused by an increase in greenhouse gases

glucose a sugar that is a major source of energy for cells

graduated cylinder a tool used to measure the volume of a liquid

greenhouse effect the trapping of heat by gases in the atmosphere

greenhouse gas an atmospheric gas that traps heat

growth an increase in the size or number of cells

guard cells specialized cells that control the opening and closing of the pores on the surface of a leaf

habitat the place where an animal or plant lives

herbivore an organism that eats only plants

heredity the passing of traits from parent to offspring

heterotroph organism that cannot make its own food; a consumer

histamine a chemical that is released as the immune system's reaction to an allergy

homeostasis the ability of an organism to maintain a stable internal environment even when the external environment changes

hormone a chemical produced in the endocrine glands

host the organism in a parasitic relationship that provides a home and/or food for the parasite

hot water bath in the science laboratory, usually a large beaker of water heated on a hot plate; used to heat test tubes that contain a flammable liquid, such as alcohol

humerus the long bone in the upper part of the arm

hypothesis a statement that predicts a relationship between cause and effect in a way that can be tested

immune system the body's primary defense against disease-causing pathogens

immunity the body's ability to destroy pathogens before they cause disease

independent variable a factor that might influence the dependent variable in an experiment

indicator a substance that changes color when it encounters certain chemical conditions

industrialization the process of converting an economy into one in which large-scale manufacturing is the primary economic base

inference a conclusion or deduction based on observations

infinite without limits or bounds

inorganic a type of molecule that does not contain both carbon and hydrogen but can contain any other combination of elements

insulin a hormone that prompts glucose to move from the blood into body cells, resulting in a lower glucose level in the blood

limiting factor any factor in the environment that limits the size of a population

lipid any one of a group of organic compounds that includes oils, fats, and waxes

*magnification the ability of a microscope to make an object appear larger

*mass a measure of the quantity of matter in an object

*meiosis the process that results in the production of sex cells (sperm and egg)

*meniscus the curved surface at the top of a column of liquid

*metabolism all the chemical reactions that occur within the cells of an organism

*metric ruler a tool used to measure the length of an object

*microbe any microscopic organism

micrometer a unit of length equal to one millionth of a meter

*microscope a tool that uses a lens or a combination of lenses to magnify an object

*mitochondria pod-shaped organelles that contain enzymes used to extract energy from nutrients

*mitosis the process that divides the cell's nucleus into two, each with a complete set of genetic material from the parent cell

*model a representation used to explain or demonstrate a process or structure; also used to predict what might occur in a new situation

molecule a particle in which two or more atoms combine to form a single unit; the smallest unit of a compound

muscular system a body system comprised of tissue that contracts when it is stimulated; the combination of muscles that enables the body to move

*mutation any alteration in the sequence of DNA

*natural selection the process by which the organisms that are best adapted to a specific environment survive and produce more offspring than organisms that are not as well adapted

neutral a solution with a pH of 7 that is neither acidic nor basic; the tissues of many living things maintain a pH within 1 or 2 units of this neutral point

*niche the specific role played by an organism in its ecosystem

nitrogen cycle the movement of nitrogen from the atmosphere to the soil and organisms and then back to the atmosphere

nitrogen fixation the process by which nitrogen forms compounds that can be used by living things

*nonrenewable resource any resource, such as fossil fuels and minerals, that cannot be replaced

*nuclear fuel an energy source that results from splitting atoms

*nucleus a large structure within a cell that controls the cell's metabolism and stores genetic information, including chromosomes and DNA

nucleic acids large, complex organic molecules that contain the instructions cells need to carry out their life processes

nutrient a substance that provides the body with the materials and energy needed to carry out the basic life of cells

objective one of the lenses of a microscope

*observation any information that is collected with any of the senses

ocular the eyepiece lens of a microscope

*opinion ideas people have that may or may not be based in fact

optimum the most favorable condition

*organ a body structure made of different kinds of tissues combined to perform a specific function

*organ system several organs that work together to perform a major function in the body

*organelle a structure within the cell that carries out a specific function

*organic term used to describe molecules that contain both hydrogen and carbon

*organic compound a compound that contains both hydrogen and carbon

*ovary (pl. **ovaries**) the organ of the human female reproductive system that produces an egg cell, the female gamete

*overproduction the potential for a species to increase its numbers beyond the area's carrying capacity

oviduct the part of the female reproductive system where the egg cell is fertilized by the sperm

oxygen-carbon dioxide cycle the movement of oxygen and carbon dioxide between living things and the environment

*ozone shield the layer of ozone gas in the upper atmosphere that protects Earth from some of the sun's radiation

*pancreas an endocrine organ that secretes insulin

*parasite an organism that survives by living and feeding on other organisms

parasitic relationship an arrangement in which one organism lives in or on a host organism, deriving some or all of its nourishment from the host, to the host's detriment

*pathogen an organism that invades the body, causing disease

*peer review the process by which scientists carefully examine the work of other scientists to look for possible flaws in their experimental design or their interpretation of results

*pH a measure of whether a substance is acidic, neutral, or basic

*photosynthesis the process by which some organisms are able to capture light energy and use it to make food from carbon dioxide and water

pioneer species the first organisms to become established in a new habitat

pipette a laboratory tool that looks like a slender tube but works something like an eyedropper

*placenta the organ that enables nutrients and oxygen to pass from the mother's blood to the fetus, and waste products to pass from the fetus to the mother's blood

plant any complex, multicellular organism that obtains energy through photosynthesis and consists of cell walls and specialized tissues and organs

poaching illegally capturing or killing an organism

*pollution a harmful change in the chemical makeup of the soil, water, or air

*population all the individuals of a single species that live in a specific area

*predator an animal that hunts and kills other animals for food

predator-prey relationship the connection between predators and prey that limits the growth of both populations

*prey an animal that is hunted and killed by predators

primary succession the first group of communities that moves into a previously lifeless habitat

*producer an organism that makes its own food from light energy and inorganic materials

*progesterone a hormone associated with sexual development and the reproductive system

proportion the relationship of one thing to another in terms of size, number, amount, or degree

protist a single-celled organism with both its genetic materials and its organelles enclosed in membranes

quarantine confined isolation

radius one of the two long bones of the lower forearm

*receptor molecule certain protein molecules in the cell membrane that can receive chemical messages from other cells

*recombination the additional mixing of genetic material from a sperm and egg which results in a unique combination of genes

refute to disprove

*replicate to copy

*renewable resource Earth's resources, such as our food supply and solar energy, which, given time, can be replaced

*research plan the initial stage of an experiment that involves finding background information, developing a hypothesis, and devising an experimental method for testing the hypothesis

*respiration the process by which the chemical bond energy stored in nutrients is released for use in cells

*reproduction the process by which organisms produce new organisms of the same type

*ribosome one of the tiny structures in the cell that is the site of protein production

rider one of the devices that is moved along the beam of a balance

*scavenger a carnivore that feeds on the bodies of dead organisms

science a way of learning about the natural world and the knowledge gained through that process

*scientific literacy a basic knowledge of the natural world combined with an understanding of the diverse ways that scientists gain knowledge

scientific theory a concept, which has been tested and confirmed in many different ways, that explains a wide variety of observations

secondary succession a type of change that occurs when a disturbance empties an existing habitat without destroying the soil

*selective breeding the process of choosing a few organisms with desirable traits to serve as the parents of the next generation

sensor a structure that reacts to stimuli by sending a nerve impulse to the brain

*sex cell an egg (female) or a sperm (male)

*sexual reproduction a method of reproduction that involves two parents to produce offspring that are genetically different from either parent

sibling a brother or sister

*simple sugar the result of the digestion of starches. Glucose is a simple sugar.

skeletal system the body system that contains the bones, provides shape and support, and protects internal organs

smog a kind of air pollution that results when certain pollutants react with sunlight

*species a group of organisms that share certain characteristics and can mate with one another, producing fertile offspring

sperm the male sex cell

splice to join two things together

*stain a chemical used to make cell structures more visible when viewed under a microscope

steady state the condition in which something remains relatively constant in spite of minor fluctuations

*stereoscope a microscope that uses two eyepieces; often used for dissections; also called a dissecting microscope

*stimulus (pl. **stimuli**) any change in the environment that causes an organism to react

stomata tiny pores found on the underside of most leaves

*subunit the section of a DNA molecule that contains a sugar, a phosphate, and a base

symbiotic a kind of long-term association between members of different species in which at least one species benefits and neither species is harmed

*synthesis a life process that involves combining simple substances into more complex substances

tare button a function on an electronic balance that returns the mass reading to zero

*technology all of the practical scientific knowledge that has been used to meet human needs

*template the pattern for a new molecule

*testes the male reproductive organ that produces sperm and the hormone testosterone

*testosterone a hormone associated with male sexual development and reproduction

*theory an explanation, supported by many observations and/or experiments, that can be used to accurately explain related occurrences

*thermal pollution a kind of water pollution in which the temperature of the water increases

*tissue a group of specialized cells that perform a specific function

toxic poisonous

*trade-off an exchange or agreement made to reach a compromise

*trait a characteristic that is passed from parent to offspring through the genes

transpiration the process whereby plants absorb water through their roots and eliminate it through tiny pores on the undersides of their leaves

*triple-beam balance a tool, with a single pan and three bars calibrated in grams, used to measure mass

tumor a clump of cells that develops when cancerous cells divide uncontrollably

ulna one of the two long bones in the lower forearm

*uterus the organ, in female animals, where the embryo develops into a fetus

*vaccine a substance made of weakened, killed, or partial pathogens and designed to protect the body from future invasions of that pathogen

*vacuole storage sacs within the cytoplasm of a cell that may contain either wastes or useful materials, such as water or food

vertebrate an animal with a backbone

*virus a nonliving particle of protein and genetic material that reproduces by invading the cell of a living organism

*volume the space occupied by something

*water cycle the process by which water continuously moves from Earth's surface to the atmosphere and back

*zygote the cell that results from the joining of the egg and sperm

Index

abiotic (environmental) factors 98–100

acid 4, 26, 27, 99–100, 132–134, 175

acid precipitation 133–134

active transport 7–8

adaptations 87–88
  behavioral 88
  and evolution 82–84
  functional 88
  structural 87–88

agriculture
  environmental impact 111, 128, 135
  reproductive technology 71

AIDS 35

air pollution 133–135

alleles 45

allergies 35

Amazon rain forest 125

amino acids 47–48

amniocentesis 72

animals
  observing specimens 179

antibiotics 90–91

antibodies 34–35

antigens 34

antihistamines 35

asexual reproduction 45, 60–61

assumptions
  in science 148

ATP 21–24

autotrophs 103–104

bacteria 6, 33
  antibiotic resistance 90–91, 96
  and genetic engineering 53, 57

base 4, 26, 175

biochemical processes 20–27

biodiversity 110–111, 127–129

biosphere 99

biotechnology 52–53

biotic (environmental) factors 98–100, 124

blood sugar 30

body cell 45, 51

body systems, human 10–13

cancer 33–34

carbohydrates 21–22, 23

carbon cycle 108

carbon dioxide
  and global warming 134–135

carrying capacity 101, 125–126

catalysts 25

cell division 63–65
  meiotic 64–65, 67
  mitotic 63, 67, 173

cell membrane 7, 11, 13, 173

cell parts 173

cell respiration 3, 20–21, 23–24

cells 2–8
  differentiation 67
  organization of living things 2–4
  parts 173
  and proteins 47–48
  staining 172, 175

cell wall 7, 173

CFCs 135

change, evolutionary
  behavioral 88
  functional 88
  structural 87–88

chemistry
  of life 3–4, 8, 20–27

chlorofluorocarbons (CFCs) 135

chlorophyll 6, 67, 175

chloroplasts 6, 21, 173

chromatography 175

chromosomes 44, 63–65, 173
  damage 57

circulation 11

circulatory system 11

classification
  changes in 3

clones 45, 61

cloning 61

communication
  among body systems 10–11
  in science 156–157

community 99

competition
  and environmental resources, 100, 102–103
  and evolution 83, 90

compost 125

compound microscope 170–171

conclusions 156–157

conservation 132

consumers 103–104

control, experimental 152

cooperation
  among organisms 103

crossing over (genetics) 65

cytoplasm 5–6, 13, 173

data
  collection 154–155
  organization 154–157

DDT 91, 132

decomposers 104, 107–108, 125
  in polluted water 132

deforestation 128

dependent variable 152–153, 155

development 60, 67–71

diabetes 35

dichotomous key 175–176

differentiation 67

diffusion 5–6

digestion 8, 10–11

digestive system 10–12

direct harvesting 127–128

disease 33–36
  and biodiversity 110
  prevention 35–36
  treatment 36, 53

dissecting microscope 170

dissection 179

diversity
  in ecosystems 110–111
  loss of 127–129
  of organisms 3

DNA 13, 44, 46–48
  and electrophoresis 174
  and evolution 86
  manipulation 52–53
  mutations 50–51
  replication 47, 63–65

dynamic equilibrium 30–31

ecological succession 112–113

ecology 98–113

ecosystems 98–113
  energy in 107–108
  human impact on 122–136
  relationships in 103–104

egg cell 61, 65, 69–70, 86

electrophoresis 173–174

embryo 67, 70

endangered species 71, 88, 128, 174

endocrine system 11, 31

energy
  for cell processes 21–22

Acknowledgments

Photographs:

Unless otherwise acknowledged, all photographs are the property of Savvas Learning Company LLC. Photo locators denoted as follows: Top (T), Center (C), Bottom (B), Left (L), Right (R), Background (Bkgd)

Cover Betty Shelton/Shutterstock **i** Betty Shelton/Shutterstock; **66** Comstock Images/Thinkstock; **91** DK Images; **123** DK Images; **173** (B) Comstock Images/Thinkstock, (CR) Duncan Smith/Photodisc/Thinkstock; **178** (R) Comstock Images/Thinkstock, (L) Crestock; **A-11 (L)** Ed Reschke/Photolibrary/Getty Images; **A-11** (R) Michael Abbey/Science Source **Regents Exams: January 2020: 004:** AP Images; **008:** Popperfoto/Getty Images; **019:** EFK Kenya; 020: Alfred Eisenstaedt/The Life Picture Collection/Shutterstock; **028L:** Bartosz Budrewicz/Shutterstock; **028R:** Volodymyr Burdiak/Shutterstock **Regents Exams: August 2019: 010:** AP Images; **021:** Our Living World: An Artistic Edition of the Rev. J.G. Wood's Natural History of Animate Creation – Mammalia Vol. 1, John George Wood, p. 163, published 1885, in this hand-colored version, by Selmer Hess. Originally published in black-and-white in Wood's Illustrated Natural History, Volume I: Mammalia, p. 203, by Routledge, Warne & Routledge, London, 1853.; **022:** Bob Benson; **Regents Exams: June 2019: 002:** Cosmin Manci/Shutterstock; **006:** Arthur Anker; 020: Original Art by Natalie Rowe; **023:** Sang-Youl Park, UC Riverside; **028:** Savvas Learning Company LLC; **Regents Examination January 2019: 2 (L)** Axel Bueckert/Shutterstock; **2** (R) U.S. Geological Survey (Artist: Susan Trammell); **3** Source: Biology 8th ed., Pearson 2008, p. 859; **4** AlasdairJames/iStock/Getty Images; **5 (L)** Jordan M. Casey; **5 (R)** Petr Kratochvil/publicdomainpictures.net; **18** National Park Service U.S. Department of the Interior; **20** Proceedings of NAS 105(44), 16988–16993. Copyright (2008) National Academy of Sciences, U.S.A.; **24** Image Courtesy of Science Buddies; **30** Source: Adapted from Losos, JB, 2010. Used by permission.; **Regents Examination August 2018: 7** Sylvia Mader and Michael Windelspecht (1997) "Ecosystem pyramid," Human Biology (McGraw-Hill); **21** Alan Rees/Archelon; **Regents Examination June 2021: 003:** Nature Production/Nature Picture Library; **012:** Martini, Frederic H.; Tallitsch, Robert B.; Nath, Judi l., Human Anatomy, 9th Edition, ©2018 Reprinted by permission of Pearson Education, Inc.; **013:** From Biology, 9th Ed. Sylvia Mader, McGraw-Hill, Boston, 2007, p 929; **014:** Chris Gomersall/Royal Society for the Protection of Birds (rspb-images.com); **023:** Chris Bjornberg/Science Source

Text:

Grateful acknowledgment is made to the following for copyrighted material:

164 (May 18, 1999) "Patients to Test Tumor Fighter" by The Associated Press. **Regents Exams: January 2020: 012:** Centers for Disease Control and Prevention (CDC); **018:** NASA Earth Observatory; **Regents Exams: June 2019: 009:** Courtesy of Government of Alberta.; **011:** Michael Pidwirny; **012:** U.S. Food and Drug Administration; **024:** Scripps Institution of Oceanography at UC San Diego; **Regents Examination August 2018: 19** Jason Palmer (February 8, 2013) "Earliest placental mammal ancestor pinpointed," from Science & Environment.; **20** Written by Gordon Orians. Produced by Chris Peterson. © 2015 TuneIntoNature.org. Used by permission.; **24** Gordon Block, (January 19, 2015) "Survey finds invasive snail in Lake Ontario, St. Lawrence River that could threaten waterfowl," Watertown Daily Times"; **Regents Examination June 2021:** 002: Alada Gestió Empresarial, S.L; 016: Charts: "Tree Frogs in the United States" from A Field Guide To Reptiles And Amphibians Of Eastern And Central North America, 3/e by Roger Conant and Joseph T. Collins. Illustrations copyright © 1991 by Roger Conant. Reprinted by permission of Mariner Books, an imprint of HarperCollins Publishers LLC.; 024: Snakes Used to Have Legas and Arms Until These Mutations Happened by Laura Geggel | October 21, 2016, Future US Inc.

New York Regents Examinations

The following examinations are actual Regents Examinations prepared by the New York State Education Department. They are provided here to give teachers and students a clear idea of the format and content of the Regents Examination for The Living Environment. The tests were given to students taking The Living Environment Course. The content of this book is designed to provide specifically what you need to review for The Living Environment Regents Examination.

Using the Regents Examinations

The best way to use these examinations is to take the entire test after you have reviewed the course content. Taking these tests as practice before your review may be both discouraging and of little value. Instead, use the tests to determine if you have reviewed enough to do well on the Regents Examination and to determine where further review will be most helpful.

Do not look up any information or answers while you take the examinations. Answer each question just as you would during a real test. As you take the Examination, use the margin of the paper to note any question where you are just guessing. Leave the more difficult questions for last, but be sure to answer each question. Every point counts so do not skip over a long question that is only worth a point or two. A long question could be easier than it looks and may make the difference between an A or a B or between passing or failing.

When you finish, have your teacher score your Examination and help you determine the areas where you need the most work. Also review the "guesses" you noted in the margin to find out what you need to study to ensure that you will be able to answer similar questions on the next test. Once you have determined your weaknesses, you can focus your review on those topics in this book.

Reviewing the areas where you know the least will give you the best chance of improving your final score. Spending time on areas where you are doing quite well will not produce much improvement in your total score, but it is still important if time permits.

Part A

Answer all questions in this part. [30]

Directions (1–30): For *each* statement or question, record on the separate answer sheet the *number* of the word or expression that, of those given, best completes the statement or answers the question.

1 The respiratory system of an elephant functions in a similar way to which organelle in a single-celled organism?

(1) cell membrane   (3) vacuole
(2) nucleus   (4) chloroplast

2 The carrying capacity of an environment may be *decreased* by

(1) maintaining biodiversity
(2) replacing lost minerals
(3) removing dead organisms
(4) preventing deforestation

3 The offspring of a species of bird known as the European roller possess an effective defense mechanism. When they sense a threat by predators, the young birds vomit and cover themselves with a foul-smelling liquid.

European roller
Source: http:/www.hbw.com/species/

Which two systems work together to alert the young birds of danger and help produce the vomit?

(1) respiratory and excretory
(2) circulatory and immune
(3) nervous and digestive
(4) reproductive and muscular

4 A *decrease* in the biodiversity of an ecosystem usually leads to

(1) an increase in predator and prey populations
(2) the elimination of material cycling
(3) a decrease in stability
(4) an increase in dynamic equilibrium

5 Down syndrome occurs when an individual has an extra copy of chromosome 21. This additional genetic material alters development and results in Down syndrome. This genetic abnormality is an example of

(1) a mutation   (3) a substitution
(2) fertilization   (4) differentiation

6 Most of the reactions by which energy from carbohydrates is released for use by the cell take place within the

(1) mitochondria   (3) ribosomes
(2) nuclei   (4) vacuoles

7 Which human activity best represents a method for recycling nutrients?

(1) mixing lawn clippings with vegetable waste to produce compost used to fertilize gardens
(2) raking and bagging lawn clippings in plastic bags for disposal in landfills
(3) collecting lawn and garden wastes for burning
(4) clearing a forested area to provide open land for cattle

8 Rabbit populations vary in size over time. An increase in which factor would likely prevent the rabbit population from steadily increasing?

(1) food   (3) predators
(2) mates   (4) prey

9 The diagrams below represent two reproductive processes used by different organisms.

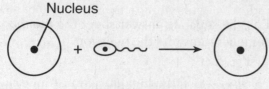

Nucleus

Process A

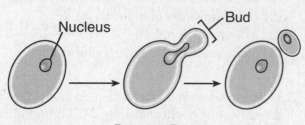

Nucleus   Bud

Process B

(Not drawn to scale)

When compared to organisms that utilize process *A*, organisms that utilize process *B* would most likely produce offspring with

(1) a greater variety of genetic combinations
(2) fewer genetic differences
(3) more genetic combinations
(4) more DNA within each nucleus

10 A weightlifter has spent years building his muscular strength. His newborn daughter has normal strength for a baby. Which statement best explains this situation?

(1) A daughter inherits most of her traits from her mother. The daughter's muscles are unlikely to resemble her father's.
(2) The weightlifter's wife probably did not lift weights. Both parents must have this trait before the baby can inherit it.
(3) Babies do not have strong muscles. The daughter's muscles will be unusually strong in a few more months.
(4) The weightlifter's highly developed muscles resulted from exercise. A characteristic such as this will not be inherited.

11 When it is disturbed, the bombardier beetle is able to produce and release a hot spray of irritating chemicals from the end of its body, as shown in the photo below. As a result, most animals that have experienced this defense avoid the beetles in the future.

Source:http://www.bbc.com/news/uk-england-leeds-11959381

The beetle's defense mechanism has developed as a result of

(1) the need for an effective protection against its enemies
(2) competition with its predators
(3) natural selection over many generations
(4) ecological succession over hundreds of years

12 Rejection of a newly transplanted organ is caused by

(1) the immune system reacting to the presence of the organ
(2) antibiotics that stimulate the immune system to attack the organ
(3) inheritance of genetic disorders from infected individuals
(4) development of cancerous cells in the organ

13 One of the largest and oldest organisms on Earth is located in Fishlake National Forest in Utah. Pando is an 80,000-year-old grove of aspen trees that covers 100 acres. Although it looks like a forest, DNA analysis of several of the "trees" has confirmed it is really just one huge organism. Therefore, the "trees" must have been reproduced

(1) sexually and have genetic variability
(2) asexually and have genetic variability
(3) sexually and are genetically identical
(4) asexually and are genetically identical

14 A female giraffe has 62 chromosomes in each of her skin cells.

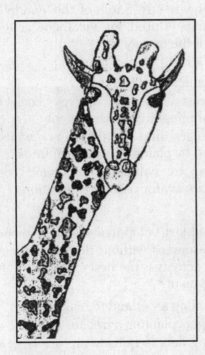

How many chromosomes will be in the skin cells of her offspring?

(1) 124
(3) 31
(2) 62
(4) 30

15 Many female mammals, such as dogs, give birth to litters consisting of multiple offspring. All of the characteristics described below are reproductive adaptations that female dogs have for giving birth and caring for several offspring at once, *except*

(1) a specialized structure for internal development of several young
(2) several pairs of mammary glands that provide milk for their pups
(3) ovaries capable of releasing many gametes at one time for fertilization
(4) a pancreas that produces excess insulin to trigger the release of eggs

16 As blood glucose levels increase, hormones are released to return glucose levels to normal. This is an example of

(1) a nervous system disorder
(2) the synthesis of antibodies
(3) a stimulus and a response
(4) an antigen and antibody reaction

17 BRCA genes are human genes that normally work to help shut down cancer cells before they can harm the body. Scientists have learned that individuals inheriting a damaged form of a BRCA gene are at greater risk of developing breast or ovarian cancer. This discovery is an important first step in

(1) preventing the uncontrolled meiotic division of cells in humans
(2) identifying individuals at risk and recommending preventive treatment
(3) being able to detect all the genes that regulate meiosis
(4) helping to eliminate all BRCA genes

18 In humans, embryonic development during the first two months is more sensitive to environmental factors than during the remaining months. The best explanation for this statement is that

(1) during the first two months, organs are being formed and any unusual change during cell division can interfere with normal development
(2) the genes that control development function only during the first two months of development
(3) no changes occur in a developing fetus after the second month
(4) organ development is not affected by environmental factors after the second month

19 Gene editing can be used to swap out an unwanted gene for a desirable one from the same species. Which statement best explains why the desired gene will be found in all cells that come from the genetically edited cell?

(1) The original cell will reproduce by meiosis and a mutation will occur.
(2) The altered DNA in the edited cell will be replicated and passed on to each new cell during mitosis.
(3) DNA replication in body cells will result in sperm and egg cells with the edited gene.
(4) The desired gene will be inserted into each new cell by using restriction enzymes.

20 Which sequence of events best represents ecological succession?

(1) A squirrel eats acorns, and a hawk eats the squirrel.

(2) Grass grows on a sand dune and is slowly replaced by shrubs.

(3) After many years of planting corn in the same field, minerals present in the soil are used up.

(4) The decomposition of plant material releases nutrients, and other plants use these nutrients.

21 Which human activity has the potential to greatly affect the equilibrium of an ecosystem?

(1) cutting down a few small evergreen trees and using them to make holiday decorations

(2) mowing the playing fields in a city park

(3) washing a car with a detergent-based cleaner

(4) emptying an aquarium containing many nonnative fish of several species into a local lake

22 Which statement describes a failure of homeostasis in humans?

(1) When activity in an individual increases, the body temperature rises and the individual sweats.

(2) As the concentration of carbon dioxide increases in the human body, the lungs begin to expel more carbon dioxide.

(3) A viral infection leads to a decrease in the number of white blood cells being produced in the body.

(4) After an individual gets a cut, certain chemical changes begin the healing process.

23 Some environmental engineering companies have recently designed "manufactured wetlands" to serve as natural sewage treatment plants. Utilizing the ability of wetland organisms to reduce human wastes makes use of naturally occurring

(1) nutrient cycles   (3) limiting factors

(2) energy cycles   (4) finite resources

24 A hummingbird may need to consume up to 50% of its body weight in sugar each day, just to meet its energy needs. Some of this energy is stored and some is used for metabolic activities, but much of the energy is

(1) converted into amino acids needed for the production of starch

(2) released as heat energy back into the hummingbird's environment

(3) changed into radiant energy, which can be used by plants for photosynthesis

(4) used to synthesize inorganic compounds necessary for cellular respiration

25 Sustainable development occurs when people use their resources without depleting them. Which human activity is the best example of sustainable development?

(1) draining a wetland to build houses

(2) loggers planting a tree for each one cut down

(3) using nets to quickly capture large numbers of fish

(4) building coal-burning power plants to provide electricity

26 Ringworm is a skin infection common among school-aged children. Although the name suggests that a worm causes the disease, it is actually caused by a fungus that lives and feeds on the dead outer layer of the skin. The relationship between ringworm and humans can be described as

(1) predator/prey   (3) parasite/prey

(2) predator/host   (4) parasite/host

27 Genetically identical yarrow plants were grown at different altitudes. Even though their genetic makeup was identical, the plants grew to different heights. One likely explanation for the different heights of the plants at each altitude is that

(1) gene expression was influenced by the environment

(2) genes mutated when the plants were grown at higher elevations

(3) chromosomes increased in number with elevation change

(4) the sequence of DNA bases was altered at different altitudes

28 Which biological process is represented in the diagram below?

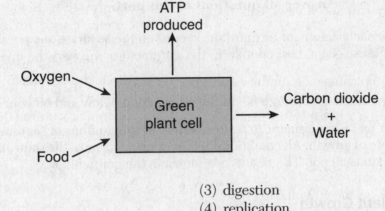

(1) photosynthesis   (3) digestion
(2) respiration   (4) replication

29 The diagram below shows specialized plant cells that control openings called stomates.

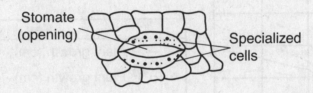

The proper function of these cells is vital to the survival of the plant because they regulate the

(1) rate of glucose use by root cells   (3) products of photosynthesis in the stem
(2) absorption of sunlight by leaf cells   (4) exchange of gases in leaves

30 Substance X directly supplies energy for various life functions, as shown in the diagram below.

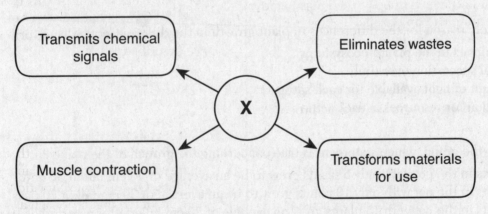

Which substance is represented by X in the diagram?
(1) ATP   (3) starch
(2) DNA   (4) glucose

Part B–1

Answer all questions in this part. [13]

Directions (31–43): For *each* statement or question, record on the separate answer sheet the *number* of the word or expression that, of those given, best completes the statement or answers the question.

Base your answers to questions 31 through 33 on the information below and on your knowledge of biology.

A student set up an experiment to test the effect of the number of seedlings planted in one pot on the rate of growth. All conditions in the experiment were the same, except for the number of plants in each pot. The results are shown in the graph below.

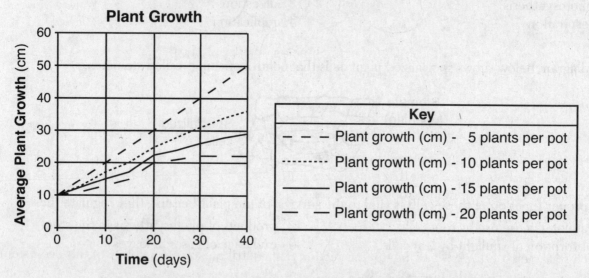

Source: Adapted from http://science.halleyhosting.com/sci/soph/scimethod/q/q1/q9.htmthod

31 The most likely reason for the differences in plant growth in the different pots was

(1) cyclic changes in the plants' ecosystems
(2) ecological succession over time
(3) the amount of light available for each setup
(4) competition for resources in each setup

32 According to the graph, which statement is true concerning the growth of the plants?

(1) The plants in the pot with only 5 plants grew to be an average of 40 cm tall in 30 days.
(2) The plants in the pot with only 10 plants grew to be an average of 30 cm tall in 20 days.
(3) The plants in the pot with 15 plants grew an average of 20 cm taller after a period of 10 days.
(4) The plants in the pot with 20 plants grew an average of 20 cm taller after a period of 40 days.

33 The dependent variable for this experiment was

(1) the number of plants per pot
(2) time in days
(3) average plant growth
(4) the amount of water per pot

June '21 Regents Examination

Base your answers to questions 34 and 35 on the diagram below and on your knowledge of biology. The diagram represents interactions between organisms in an ecosystem.

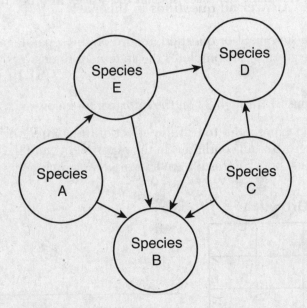

34 Which statement correctly identifies a possible role of *one* organism in this ecosystem?

(1) Species A may carry out autotrophic nutrition.
(2) Species B may be a producer that synthesizes nutrients.
(3) Species C carries out heterotrophic nutrition.
(4) Species D can recycle energy from the Sun.

35 Which statement correctly describes an interaction that contributes to the stability of this ecosystem?

(1) Species E is not affected by the activity of species A.
(2) Species B returns compounds to the environment that may later be used by species C.
(3) Species C recycles nutrients from species B and D to obtain energy.
(4) Species D is directly dependent on the autotrophic activity of species B.

Base your answers to questions 36 and 37 on the information below and on your knowledge of biology.

The Venus flytrap is a plant that uses specialized leaves in order to capture and digest small insects.

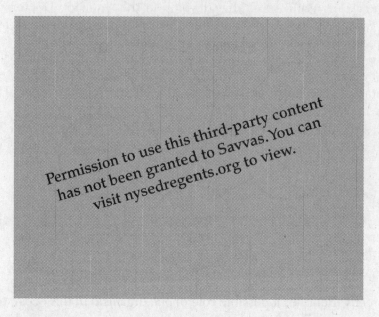

36 Although the Venus flytrap uses its prey to obtain certain molecules that it needs, it is still classified as a producer because it

(1) uses its prey to produce food
(2) consumes the prey to produce energy
(3) synthesizes energy by using oxygen and releasing carbon dioxide
(4) synthesizes glucose by using carbon dioxide and water

37 Enzymes secreted by cells in the leaves of the Venus flytrap can digest

(1) proteins into amino acids
(2) sugars into starches
(3) amino acids into fats
(4) proteins into sugars

Base your answers to questions 38 and 39 on the information below and on your knowledge of biology.

Ulcers: Mystery Solved

Stomach ulcers are painful sores that develop in the stomach. Doctors once thought that ulcers were caused by stress. In the 1980s, a pair of physicians, Barry J. Marshall and J. Robin Warren, questioned the cause of ulcers. They found the bacterium *Helicobacter pylori* in the ulcer tissue of their patients. Even though they repeatedly presented their findings to colleagues, they were ignored until Marshall performed an astonishing experiment: He drank broth containing the bacteria and made himself sick with an ulcer! He then cured himself by taking an antibiotic.

The results were published in 1985, but it took another 10 years for doctors to regularly use antibiotics to treat ulcers. Marshall and Warren received a Nobel Prize in 2005 for this discovery.

38 Which choice represents a possible hypothesis for Marshall's experiment?

(1) Does *Helicobacter pylori* cause stomach ulcers in people?
(2) If a person takes an antibody, then they will not develop an ulcer.
(3) Does exposure to infectious bacterial cells make people sick?
(4) If a patient is infected by *Helicobacter pylori*, then they will get an ulcer.

39 The work of Marshall and Warren shows that

(1) hypotheses made by physicians are always correct
(2) scientific explanations are revised based on new evidence
(3) peer review always leads to the immediate acceptance of results
(4) conclusions must always be consistent with those made by other scientists

40 The structural formulas shown below represent parts of two different complex carbohydrate molecules composed of glucose subunits. Molecules 1 and 2 differ in their overall structure.

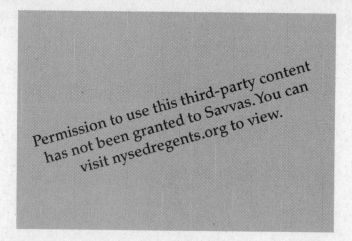

Source: Adapted from http://www.rsc.org/Education/Teachers/
Resources/cfb/carbohydrates.htm

Due to the differences in structure, each of these molecules most likely

(1) is composed of different molecular bases
(2) forms a different protein
(3) contains different elements
(4) performs a different function

41 To capture their prey, spiders have fangs, which pierce the body wall of insects and inject venom. Spider venoms usually contain specific proteins that attack the cell membranes of the prey. The membranes and most of the contents of the insect's body turn into a liquid that the spider then ingests for food.

Permission to use this third-party content has not been granted to Savvas. You can visit nysedregents.org to view.

These specific venom proteins are most likely

(1) ATP molecules
(2) DNA molecules
(3) biological catalysts
(4) regulatory hormones

42 Lymphatic capillaries are found throughout the body. Both the lymphatic and circulatory systems transport substances between the bloodstream and body tissues. These two systems are also involved in fighting infections.

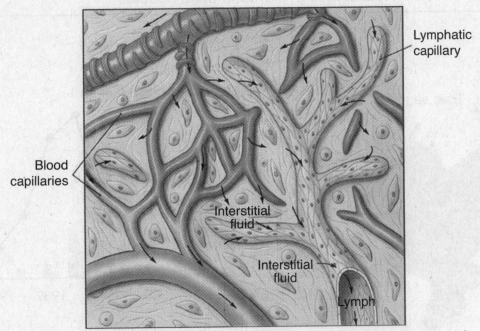

Source: Adapted from http://droualb.faculty.mjc.edu

The arrows shown in the diagram that go from the blood capillaries to the interstitial fluid most likely represent the

(1) release of red blood cells, so that they can diffuse into body cells and fight bacteria
(2) movement of materials from the circulatory system that will eventually enter lymphatic capillaries
(3) transport of digestive enzymes from the blood to help with the digestion of glucose in muscle cells
(4) transport of glucose molecules from the blood to be used by cells to attack proteins and fats

43 The graph below shows how the introduction of the opossum shrimp, as a food source for salmon, affected a lake ecosystem in Montana.

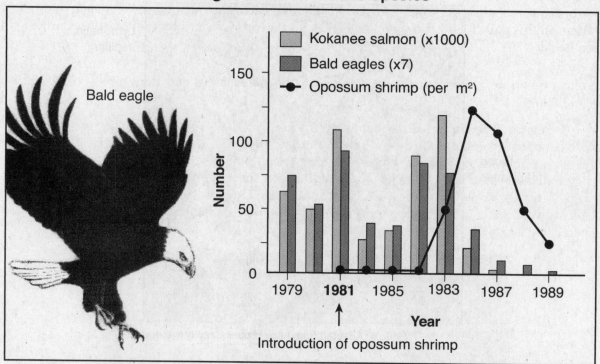

Changes in Montana Lake Species

Legend:
- Kokanee salmon (x1000)
- Bald eagles (x7)
- Opossum shrimp (per m²)

Bald eagle

(Y-axis: Number; X-axis: Year — 1979, 1981, 1985, 1983, 1987, 1989)

↑ Introduction of opossum shrimp

Source: *Biology,* 9th Ed. Sylvia Mader, McGraw-Hill, Boston, 2007, p.929

Based on the data in this graph, one likely conclusion that can be made is that over approximately ten years

(1) the lake ecosystem stabilized after the introduction of the new species

(2) competition between organisms was reduced as more producers were introduced into the lake

(3) more predators moved into the lake ecosystem once the opossum shrimp were added

(4) the introduction of the opossum shrimp into the lake ecosystem disrupted the food webs that were present

Answer all questions in this part. [12]

Directions (44–55): For those questions that are multiple choice, record on the separate answer sheet the *number* of the choice that, of those given, best completes each statement or answers each question. For all other questions in this part, follow the directions given and record your answers in the spaces provided in this examination booklet.

Base your answers to questions 44 through 47 on the information and data table below and on your knowledge of biology.

Peregrine falcons are an endangered species in New York State. This crow-sized predator feeds primarily on birds. Starting in the 1940s, exposure to the pesticide DDT in their prey caused declines in the peregrine falcon population. These pesticides caused eggshell thinning, which drastically lowered breeding success. By the early 1960s, peregrine falcons no longer nested in New York State. After the United States banned DDT in 1972, efforts were made to reintroduce peregrine falcons into the Northeast. Since the 1980s, the peregrine falcons are once again breeding in many areas of New York State.

Source: http://www.dailymail.co.uk/news/article-1018309/Peregrine
-falcons-return-breed-time-200-years.html

The table below shows the number of peregrine falcon offspring produced in New York State over a 20-year period.

Number of Peregrine Falcon Offspring Produced in New York State From 1992 to 2012

Year	Number of Offspring Produced
1992	30
1996	48
2000	75
2004	79
2008	129
2012	148

Directions (44–45): Using the information in the data table, construct a line graph on the grid provided, following the directions below.

44 Mark an appropriate scale, without any breaks in the data, on each labeled axis. [1]

45 Plot the data on the grid. Connect the points and surround each point with a small circle. [1]

Example:

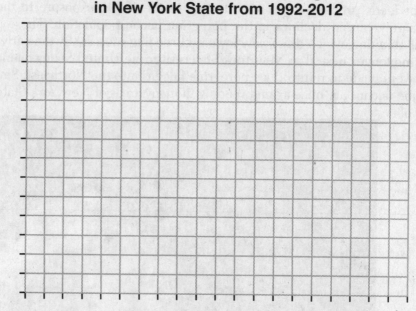

Number of Peregrine Falcon Offspring Produced in New York State from 1992-2012

Number of Young Produced

Years

46 Identify a body system in the falcon that was directly affected by DDT and led to the loss of nesting peregrine falcons from New York State in the early 1960s. Support your answer. [1]

Body system: _____

Support: _____

Note: The answer to question 47 should be recorded on your separate answer sheet.

47 Which conclusion is best supported by the information presented in the graph?
(1) The greatest decrease was during the time period of 1992 and 1996.
(2) The greatest increase was during the time period of 2004 and 2008.
(3) There has been a steady decline since the banning of DDT in 1972.
(4) The population reached carrying capacity in 2004.

Base your answers to questions 48 and 49 on the information below and on your knowledge of biology.

A scientist added an antibiotic to a Petri dish containing bacterial colonies. A day later, the scientist noticed that many colonies had died, but a few remained. The scientist continued to observe the dish and noted that, eventually, the remaining colonies of bacteria increased in size.

48 Explain why the results of this study may indicate *one disadvantage* of using antibiotics to fight infections. [1]

_____

_____

Note: The answer to question 49 should be recorded on your separate answer sheet.

49 The survival of some bacterial colonies was most likely due to

(1) the bacterial cells changing so that they could live
(2) a resistance to the antibiotic
(3) meiotic cell division in the bacteria
(4) a DNA change caused by the antibiotic

Base your answers to questions 50 and 51 on the information below and on your knowledge of biology.

The diagrams below provide information about two separate species of tree frogs found in the United States. The shaded areas represent the habitats of each of the two species.

Tree Frogs of the United States

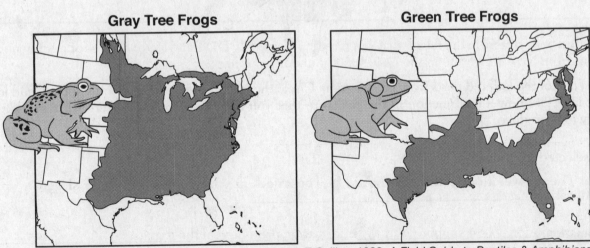

Source: Adapted from Roger Conant and Joseph T Collins. 1998. *A Field Guide to Reptiles & Amphibians of Eastern & Central North America* (Peterson Field Guide Series).

50 One likely reason that the gray tree frog occupies a larger environmental area than the green tree frog is that the gray tree frog species

(1) eats only prey found in central areas in the United States

(2) is adapted to live in any environment in the United States

(3) has adaptations that enable survival in a wider variety of habitats

(4) outcompetes the green tree frogs in Florida and any state where they both live

51 Identify a biological process that led to the presence of 90 different species of frogs throughout the United States. Support your answer. [1]

Biological process: _____

_____

_____

_____

Base your answer to question 52 on the information below and on your knowledge of biology. The diagram below represents the human female reproductive system.

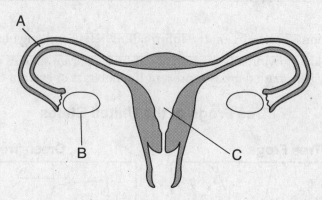

52 Select *one* of the lettered parts from the diagram. Circle the letter of the part that you selected, and identify the part. State how a malfunction in the structure that you identified could interfere with an individual's ability to reproduce. [1]

Part selected (circle one)   A   B   C

Identification: _____

Explanation: _____

_____

_____

53 The diagram below represents a cell nucleus. Complete the diagram so that it shows the arrangement of the genetic material in the two new cells that are produced by mitosis.   [1]

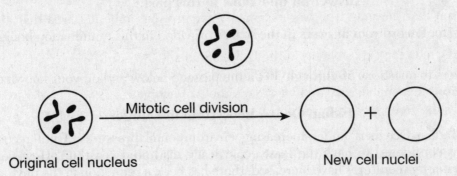

54 Sometimes a hypothesis is not supported. Yet, scientists consider the findings valuable. State *one* reason scientists would value an experiment that does *not* support the initial hypothesis.   [1]

_____

_____

55 The sequence below represents different organizational levels within the human body, from the simplest to more complex. Complete the sequence by correctly filling in the missing levels.   [1]

organelles → _____ → tissues → _____ → organ systems → organism

_____

Part C

Answer all questions in this part. [17]

Directions (56–72): Record your answers in the spaces provided in this examination booklet.

Base your answers to questions 56 through 58 on the passage below and on your knowledge of biology.

Indian Ocean Ecosystem in Danger

The Indian Ocean is under increasing environmental pressures. Until recently, this ocean was considered to have the least ecologically disrupted coastline. However, as the surface water temperatures have increased, there has been a reduction in the phytoplankton population (microscopic producers). This reduction in phytoplankton has been linked to a decline in some fish populations.

Also affecting the fish populations is the urbanization of coastal areas. As the human population grows in this area, more of the coastline region is being developed. In addition, the mining of natural resources has led to oil spills, the destruction of mangrove forests, and an increase in the area's acidity level.

Countries along the coast are trying to encourage development while, at the same time, trying to maintain a healthy coastal ecosystem.

56 Explain how a reduction in phytoplankton can lead to a reduction in fish populations in the Indian Ocean. [1]

_____

_____

57 Describe how *one* specific human activity mentioned in the passage could *negatively* affect the Indian Ocean ecosystem. [1]

Human activity: _____

_____

_____

58 State *one* specific reason why it is important to maintain a healthy ecosystem in the Indian Ocean. [1]

_____

_____

_____

Base your answers to questions 59 through 61 on the photo and reading passage below, and on your knowledge of biology.

Invasive Water Chestnuts Challenge Environmentalists

Environmental scientists are troubled by the rapid spread of the water chestnut plant. This invasive plant is a freshwater species with leaves that blanket the surface of water. The leaves grow so densely, they stop people from swimming and prevent boats from moving.

Invasive water chestnut leaves prevent 95% of the sunlight from reaching the water below. Local animals and insects cannot eat this plant. New York ecosystems infested by the water chestnut are quickly disrupted. Water chestnut seeds can survive more than ten years under water in the sediments.

The most effective way to kill the water chestnut is to pull out each plant by hand. This can be done in a small pond, but for rivers and lakes that are blocked by huge numbers of water chestnut plants, other methods are needed. Chemical herbicides kill the leaves, but, after several weeks, the water chestnut plants grow back. Large machines have been used to clear these plants and seeds from the water and sediments of ecosystems, but the machines remove many other organisms too.

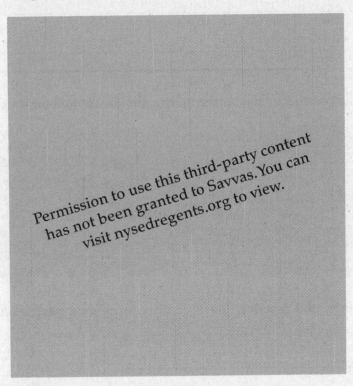

59 State *one* way that the presence of water chestnut plants affects the other organisms in the freshwater ecosystem. [1]

_____

_____

[20]

60 Some scientists recommend bringing in biological controls, such as introducing a new species of insect to eat the water chestnut leaves and stop its growth. State *one* advantage and *one disadvantage* of using biological controls in this situation. [1]

Advantage: _____

_____

Disadvantage: _____

_____

61 Harvesting machines are used to scrape water chestnut plants and seeds from the bottom of lakes and rivers. State *one disadvantage* of this method of controlling water chestnuts. [1]

_____

_____

Base your answers to questions 62 and 63 on the information below and on your knowledge of biology.

Permission to use this third-party content has not been granted to Savvas. You can visit nysedregents.org to view.

62 Identify *one* human activity and describe how it contributes to increasing levels of carbon dioxide in the environment. [1]

Human activity: _____

_____

_____

63 Describe how the inability of sharks to detect their prey could affect an ocean ecosystem. [1]

_____

_____

_____

June '21 Regents Examination

Base your answers to questions 64 through 66 on the information and photo below and on your knowledge of biology. The photo shows an adult female weasel.

Weasels Are Built for the Hunt

Weasels are fierce and quick-witted carnivores that must compete for food with larger predators. Their slender, elongated body plan allows them to pursue prey in tight spaces that other carnivores can't enter, a key factor in controlling rodent and rabbit populations. This body plan is important to the success of weasels. Female weasels have evolved to give birth to fetuses that have not fully completed development. The fetuses complete their development externally. In this way, there is no baby bump to limit the mother's access to tight feeding locations.

A high energy level is key to the weasel's success in capturing prey, but it comes at a price. To survive, weasels need to eat a third of their body weight per day. This need can make them unpopular with poultry farmers, because they can enter through the smallest opening and consume large numbers of chickens.

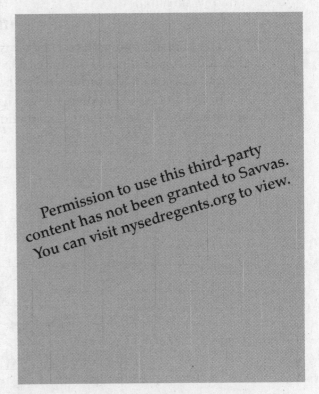

Permission to use this third-party content has not been granted to Savvas. You can visit nysedregents.org to view.

64 State how the body plan of the weasel is effective for successfully competing with other organisms. [1]

_____

_____

65 If the weasels are so successful, explain why they do *not* completely overpopulate the areas where they live. [1]

_____

_____

66 Indicate whether the weasels' relationship with humans is positive or negative by circling the appropriate term below. Support your answer. [1]

Relationship (circle one):   positive   negative

Support: _____

_____

_____

Base your answers to questions 67 and 68 on the information and diagram below and on your knowledge of biology.

HIV Infection

The human immunodeficiency virus (HIV), which can lead to AIDS, is a type of virus that adds its genetic material to the DNA of the host cell. HIV reproduces within the host cell and exits through a process called budding.

In the process of budding, the newly forming virus merges with the host cell membrane and pinches off, taking with it a section of the host-cell membrane. It then enters into circulation.

HIV Budding

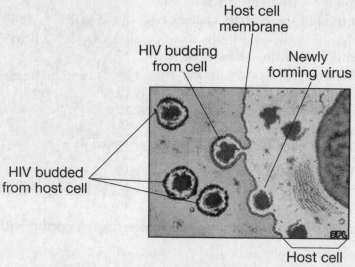

Source: Adapted from http://news.
bbc.co.uk/2/hi/health/5221744.stm

67 Explain how an outer covering composed of a section of a cell membrane from the host would protect HIV from attack by the host's immune system. [1]

_____

_____

68 Describe *one* specific way that HIV makes the body unable to deal with other pathogens and cancer. [1]

_____

_____

Base your answers to questions 69 through 72 on the information below and on your knowledge of biology.

Snakes Used to Have Legs and Arms Until These Mutations Happened

The ancestors of today's slithery snakes once sported full-fledged arms and legs, but genetic mutations caused the reptiles to lose all four of their limbs about 150 million years ago, according to two new studies. ...

Both studies showed that mutations in a stretch of snake DNA called ZRS (the Zone of Polarizing Activity Regulatory Sequence) were responsible for the limb-altering change. But the two research teams used different techniques to arrive at their findings. ...

...According to one study, published online today (Oct. 20, 2016) in the journal *Cell*, the snake's ZRS anomalies [differences] became apparent to researchers after they took several mouse embryos, removed the mice's ZRS DNA, and replaced it with the ZRS section from snakes. ...

...The swap had severe consequences for the mice. Instead of developing regular limbs, the mice barely grew any limbs at all, indicating that ZRS is crucial for the development of limbs, the researchers said. ...

Looking deeper at the snakes' DNA, the researchers found that a deletion of 17 base pairs within the snakes' DNA appeared to be the reason for the loss of limbs.

Source: http://www.livescience.com/56573-mutation-caused-snakes-to-lose-legs.htm

69 State *one* possible advantage for a snake to have no limbs instead of four limbs. [1]

_____

_____

70 Identify the technique that the scientists used to remove the ZRS DNA from mice and replace it with the ZRS section from snakes. [1]

_____

71 Identify the type of mutation responsible for the loss of limbs in snakes. [1]

_____

72 Without having DNA samples from snakes 150 million years ago, state how scientists could know that snakes once actually had legs. [1]

_____

_____

_____

[24]

Part D

Answer all questions in this part. [13]

Directions (73–85): For those questions that are multiple choice, record on the separate answer sheet the *number* of the choice that, of those given, best completes each statement or answers each question. For all other questions in this part, follow the directions given and record your answers in the spaces provided in this examination booklet.

Base your answers to questions 73 and 74 on the information and chart below and on your knowledge of biology.

Finding Relationships Between Organisms

Organisms living in the same environment may have similar body structures, but this does not always indicate a close biological relationship. The chart below provides information about four organisms that live in an Antarctic Ocean ecosystem.

Body Structures of Four Antarctic Marine Organisms				
Organism	Killer whale	Adélie penguin	Leopard seal	Baleen whale
Skin covering	Very little hair	Feathers	Thick hair	Very little hair
Diagram* *Pictures are not drawn to scale.				

Note: The answer to question 73 should be recorded on your separate answer sheet.

73 Two features that would be the most useful in determining which of these organisms are most closely related are

(1) presence of hair and similar proteins
(2) presence of feathers and similar body structures
(3) habitat and diet
(4) body size and color

Note: The answer to question 74 should be recorded on your separate answer sheet.

74 Which lab procedure can be done to find molecular evidence for relationships between these Antarctic marine organisms?

(1) Compare slides of cell organelles.
(2) Examine fossils and ocean sediments.
(3) Set up and perform gel electrophoresis.
(4) Use a dichotomous key and test for pH.

75 As an extension of the lab activity *Making Connections*, a biology teacher asked students to brainstorm variables other than exercise that would affect heart rate. The students hypothesized that eating a lunch high in protein would decrease heart rates. They recorded resting heart rates of 20 students, had them eat high-protein meals, and then recorded their heart rates again. The heart rates of 15 students were lower while the heart rates for 5 students were higher after lunch.

The best explanation for the observation that the heart rates of 5 students were higher after lunch is

(1) the heart rates of female students are not affected by a high-protein meal

(2) the students all participated in physical education class immediately before lunch

(3) the students all had varying physical fitness levels and consumed different amounts of protein

(4) the students were all the same gender and age

Base your answers to questions 76 and 77 on the passage below and on your knowledge of biology.

A recent study of Darwin's finches in the Galapagos Islands identified the gene, HMGA2, that is involved in beak size. It played a role in which finches feeding on smaller seeds survived a severe drought in 2004-2005. Following the drought, the average size of the medium ground finch beak decreased. This change was traced directly to changes in the frequency of the HMGA2 gene. Previous studies have shown that HMGA2 affects body size in animals, including dogs and horses, and even humans.

Note: The answer to question 76 should be recorded on your separate answer sheet.

76 One possible reason that such diverse species could be affected by the HMGA2 gene is that

(1) they all lived on the Galapagos Islands

(2) they share a common ancestor

(3) the drought caused the formation of the gene

(4) the gene allowed all these species to grow larger

77 State *one* possible reason the medium ground finches with a smaller beak were able to survive during the 2004-2005 drought. Support your answer. [1]

_____

_____

_____

Base your answer to question 78 on the information and the Universal Genetic Code Chart below and on your knowledge of biology.

Universal Genetic Code Chart
Messenger RNA Codons and the Amino Acids for Which They Code

		SECOND BASE				
		U	**C**	**A**	**G**	
F I R S T B A S E	**U**	UUU UUC } PHE UUA UUG } LEU	UCU UCC UCA UCG } SER	UAU UAC } TYR UAA UAG } STOP	UGU UGC } CYS UGA } STOP UGG } TRP	U C A G
	C	CUU CUC CUA CUG } LEU	CCU CCC CCA CCG } PRO	CAU CAC } HIS CAA CAG } GLN	CGU CGC CGA CGG } ARG	U C A G
	A	AUU AUC AUA } ILE AUG } MET or START	ACU ACC ACA ACG } THR	AAU AAC } ASN AAA AAG } LYS	AGU AGC } SER AGA AGG } ARG	U C A G
	G	GUU GUC GUA GUG } VAL	GCU GCC GCA GCG } ALA	GAU GAC } ASP GAA GAG } GLU	GGU GGC GGA GGG } GLY	U C A G

(rightmost column labeled: THIRD BASE)

Original DNA for protein *X*:   TAC-GGC-TTA-GCT-CCC-GCG-CTA-AAA

Mutated DNA for protein *X*:   TAC-GGC-TTG-GCT-CCT-GCG-CTA-AAA

78 Would the mutated DNA strand affect the functioning of protein *X*? Support your answer.   [1]

_____

_____

_____

Base your answers to questions 79 and 80 on the diagram below and on your knowledge of biology. The diagram represents a hypothetical result of a technique used in a lab.

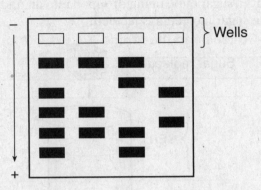

79 State where on the diagram the largest fragments of DNA would be located. [1]

_____

80 Identify the factor that caused the fragments to move through the gel rather than remaining in the wells. [1]

_____

_____

Base your answer to question 81 on the diagram below and on your knowledge of biology.

The diagram represents a sugar cube being dropped into an undisturbed beaker of water at room temperature. One sugar molecule is labeled.

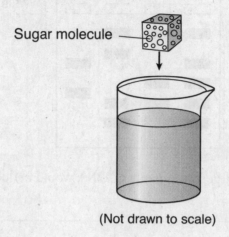

(Not drawn to scale)

Note: The answer to question 81 should be recorded on your separate answer sheet.

81 Which diagram below represents the distribution of sugar molecules in the water a day later?

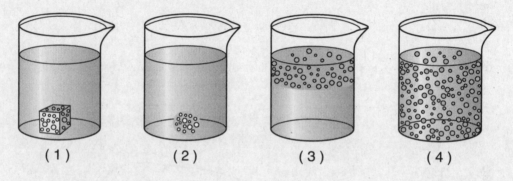

(1)   (2)   (3)   (4)

82 In an effort to determine how closely related several plant species are, a student performed the laboratory test shown below.

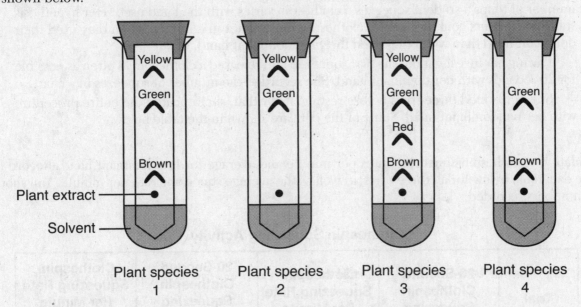

The method used by the student to compare plant extracts from the different species is

(1) gel electrophoresis

(2) DNA banding

(3) a staining technique

(4) paper chromatography

Base your answer to question 83 on the graph below and on your knowledge of biology. The graph shows the average heart rate data for a group of students before, during, and after exercise.

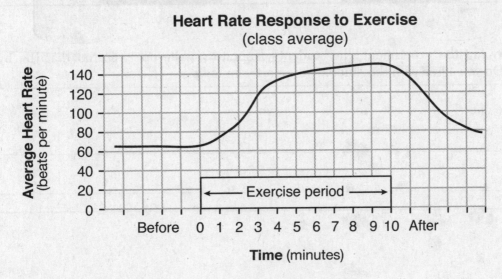

83 State *one* benefit of the increase in average heart rate during exercise. [1]

_____

_____

Base your answers to questions 84 and 85 on the information below and on your knowledge of biology.

A Clothespin Experiment

A student in a Living Environment class designed an experiment to investigate if the number of times a student squeezes a clothespin varies with the hand used. Her hypothesis was that students could squeeze a clothespin more times in a minute when they used their dominant hand than when they used their nondominant hand.

During her investigation, she first squeezed and released a clothespin as often as possible for 20 seconds with her dominant hand. She recorded the number of squeezes in a chart.

She performed three trials before resting. After that, she repeated the entire procedure with her nondominant hand. Some of the data are shown in the table below.

84 Calculate the clothespin-squeezing rates per minute and average for the dominant hand. Record the data in the data table below for all three trials, as well as the average squeezing rate per minute. You should have four numbers recorded. [1]

Clothespin Squeezing Activity

Trial	20-Second Clothespin Squeezing (Dominant Hand)	Clothespin-Squeezing Rate Per Minute (Dominant Hand)	20-Second Clothespin Squeezing (Nondominant Hand)	Clothespin-Squeezing Rate Per Minute (Nondominant Hand)
Trial 1	26	_____	18	54
Trial 2	33	_____	28	84
Trial 3	24	_____	29	87
Average		_____		75

85 After performing the experiment, the student's laboratory write-up indicated that the hypothesis was supported. Do you agree with this student? Support your answer. [1]

Agree (circle one):   Yes   No

Support: _____

_____

_____

Part A

Answer all questions in this part. [30]

Directions (1–30): For *each* statement or question, record on the separate answer sheet the *number* of the word or expression that, of those given, best completes the statement or answers the question.

1 There are over 2000 kinds of edible insects in the world, and they are becoming an increasingly popular source of protein. One cup of cricket flour contains over 28 grams of protein. The building blocks of the protein in cricket flour are

(1) amino acids   (3) simple sugars
(2) water   (4) carbohydrates

2 Which list contains only abiotic conditions that might be found in a pond ecosystem?

(1) temperature of the water, green plant populations, dissolved minerals in the water
(2) temperature of the water, dissolved oxygen in the water, dissolved minerals in the water
(3) bacteria, dissolved minerals in the water, temperature of the water
(4) dissolved oxygen in the water, fish populations, insect populations

3 Protein synthesis is accomplished primarily by the interaction of which two cell structures?

(1) vacuoles and mitochondria
(2) ribosomes and vacuoles
(3) nuclei and ribosomes
(4) nuclei and mitochondria

4 Identical twins were separated at birth and raised by two different families. Years later, one twin was a physically fit member of the cross-country team, and the other twin was overweight with slightly higher-than-normal blood pressure. The differences in these twins could be explained by the fact that

(1) the genes in the two individuals are completely different
(2) in twins, each individual inherits genes from only one parent
(3) the DNA bases in twins combine differently
(4) the environment can influence the expression of genes

5 The diagram below represents various factors in an area.

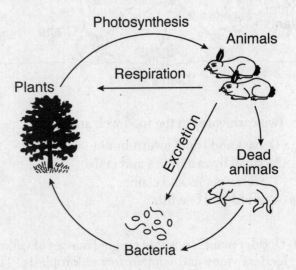

The diagram best represents

(1) the recycling of energy in a forest community
(2) ecological succession after climatic changes
(3) competition for limited resources in a population
(4) the flow of materials in a forest community

6 Traits are passed from parents to offspring. These traits are determined by

(1) chromosomes, located on genes, found in the nucleus
(2) genes, located on chromosomes, found in the nucleus
(3) chromosomes, located on genes, found in the ribosomes
(4) genes, located on chromosomes, found in the ribosomes

7 In which cell structure is energy extracted from nutrients?

(1) chloroplast   (3) mitochondrion
(2) ribosome   (4) vacuole

8 The diagram below represents a food web in a pond ecosystem.

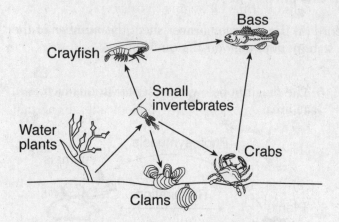

Two carnivores in the food web are

(1) bass and small invertebrates
(2) small invertebrates and crabs
(3) water plants and clams
(4) crabs and crayfish

9 Dodder plants consist of tangled masses of yellow, leafless vines and contain few chloroplasts. The vines twist around and grow into the stems of other plants and absorb water and nutrients from them. Which statement best describes this relationship?

(1) Dodder plants are parasitic, relying on host organisms for resources.
(2) Dodder plants are decomposers, returning organic material back to the environment.
(3) Dodder plants are producers, while the other plants that they attach to are consumers.
(4) Dodder plants are consumers, transferring energy to other plants in the ecosystem.

10 Two kittens in a litter are genetically different from each other and from their parents. These genetic differences are most directly due to

(1) sexual reproduction
(2) asexual reproduction
(3) cloning
(4) evolution

11 A genetic change that occurs in a body cell of a mouse will *not* contribute to the evolution of the species because

(1) body cell mutations will cause the cell to die before it reproduces
(2) the evolution of a species can result from changes in reproductive cells, not body cells
(3) random changes are repaired by enzymes before they are passed on to offspring
(4) the evolution of a species is caused by natural selection, not genetic variation

12 Scientists who have examined the fossil record have noted that some species have changed very little over long periods of geologic time. The lack of change in such organisms is most likely because

(1) all members of their population were genetically identical, and they lived in a rapidly changing environment
(2) there was a large amount of variation in their population, and the environment changed frequently
(3) they could move between different environments when food supplies became scarce
(4) the environment that they lived in remained the same, and they were well-adapted to it

13 Doctors often use certain medications to treat infections. A few people have a reaction to some of these medications, such as itching, swelling, or trouble breathing. This is an example of

(1) using antibodies to cure a medical problem
(2) the body's immune system overreacting to a usually harmless substance
(3) the body creating a mutation to fight unknown pathogens
(4) a vaccine causing the body to produce antigens against the infection

14 Organisms that live on land rarely compete for

(1) food   (3) water
(2) space   (4) oxygen

15 Orcas are endangered whales. Only about 80 individuals remain off the coast of Washington State. Salmon are a source of food for orcas. Some individuals are proposing that four dams in Washington State be removed so that habitat areas for salmon will be increased. Those opposed to the dam removals say that the dams provide low-cost hydroelectric power and positively influence the local economy.

Source: The Times-Tribune 11/3/16

This situation is an example of

(1) direct harvesting of an endangered orca species by humans
(2) orcas overproducing in an ecosystem with no resources
(3) a community relying on nonrenewable energy sources
(4) a decision where benefits and risks have to be weighed

16 A small lizard spends the morning hours lying in the sunlight until its body temperature rises. Later on in the day, the lizard rests in a shady area until its body temperature cools. This type of behavior is important to

(1) maintain homeostasis
(2) detect variations
(3) attract mates
(4) obtain nutrients

17 Sexually reproducing organisms pass on genetic information as a

(1) long chain of amino acids
(2) complex series of inorganic proteins
(3) sequence of complex sugars
(4) sequence of the bases A, T, C, and G

18 Some viruses attack cells by attaching to their outer covering, entering, and taking over their genetic "machinery." Viruses are able to invade cells after first attaching to their

(1) nuclear membrane   (3) genetic machinery
(2) cell membrane   (4) viral proteins

19 Gene mutations can be caused by many things. These mutations are biologically important because they

(1) occur at a regular rate and therefore can be controlled
(2) can be passed to the offspring if they occur in any cell of the body
(3) are always harmful and therefore help to eliminate weak traits
(4) can result in a new variety of gene combinations in the species

20 Maintaining a rich variety of genetic material that may lead to discoveries useful to humans can be ensured by

(1) preserving biodiversity
(2) increasing cloning
(3) asexual reproduction
(4) selective breeding

21 Many bacteria and fungi are important in the environment because they

(1) return energy to the environment, making it available for plants
(2) recycle nutrients, making them available for other organisms
(3) produce glucose through the process of respiration
(4) reverse the flow of energy in the ecosystem

22 Which statement best describes a characteristic of the carrying capacity of an ecosystem?

(1) It can be illustrated with a food web.
(2) It allows organisms to produce populations of unlimited size.
(3) It is determined directly by an organism's reproductive success.
(4) It is limited by the habitat's available energy and nutrients.

23 The Venus flytrap is a plant that has a unique system by which it traps and breaks down its prey. Unsuspecting insects land on the leaf and touch tiny hairs located on the leaf, triggering the leaf to close around the prey.

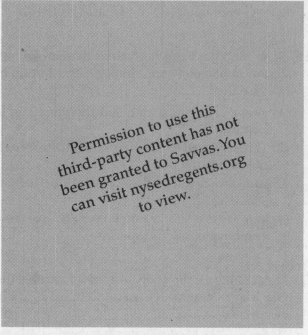

Permission to use this third-party content has not been granted to Savvas. You can visit nysedregents.org to view.

The substance responsible for breaking down the Venus flytrap's prey most likely contains

(1) chlorophyll molecules
(2) glucose molecules
(3) hormone molecules
(4) enzyme molecules

24 It may be harmful when people compete to see who can hold their breath the longest under water. Without oxygen, brain cells

(1) cannot make enough ATP
(2) have too few mitochondria
(3) make too many enzymes
(4) have too much water

25 Students did an experiment comparing the activity of four different enzymes, A, B, C, and D. The results are represented in the graph below.

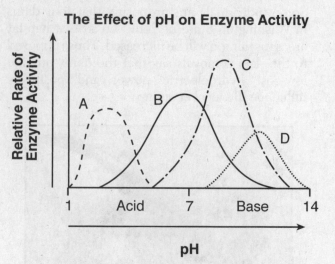

The Effect of pH on Enzyme Activity

A valid conclusion based on the information in the graph is that

(1) the pH of some enzymes changes as the temperature changes
(2) enzymes change color in proportion to the rate of activity
(3) a difference in the pH of an environment changes enzyme activity
(4) enzyme activity causes acids to change into bases over time

26 *Euglena* are unique single-celled organisms. Depending on the physical conditions present in their aquatic environment, *Euglena* can act as either producers or consumers.

Permission to use this third-party content has not been granted to Savvas. You can visit nysedregents.org to view.

Euglena will most likely act as consumers when placed in an environment that has

(1) an acidic pH
(2) a low oxygen level
(3) little or no light present
(4) many predators

27 The diagram below illustrates the movement of glucose across a cell membrane.

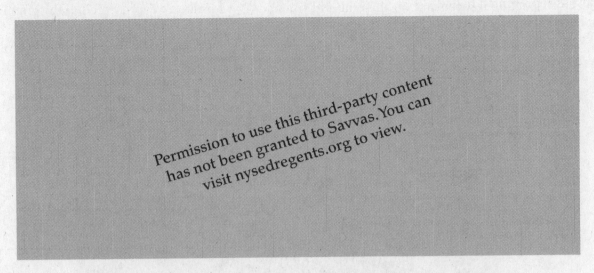

Which two processes are most directly represented in this diagram?

(1) ATP synthesis and the diffusion of water

(2) molecule transport and energy use

(3) homeostasis and ATP synthesis

(4) homeostasis and the diffusion of water

28 The diagram below shows the relationship between the snowshoe hare and the lynx. The snowshoe hare is prey of the lynx.

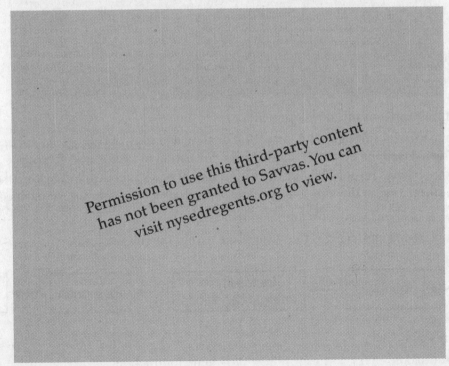

The populations of the two species increase and decrease based on the numbers of each species present. This relationship is an example of

(1) ecological succession

(2) an energy pyramid

(3) interdependency

(4) competition

29 Following fertilization, a zygote divides and soon becomes a multicelled embryo with many different cell types, as represented below.

Which statement best explains this development?

(1) Specialization occurs, resulting in the formation of a great variety of cell types.
(2) Genes are inserted into the zygote to allow for the formation of different cell types.
(3) The expression of genes responsible for the different cell types is controlled by the placenta.
(4) The genetic information in the zygote is divided to produce a complete set for each cell type.

30 The diagram below represents changes that take place within the human body.

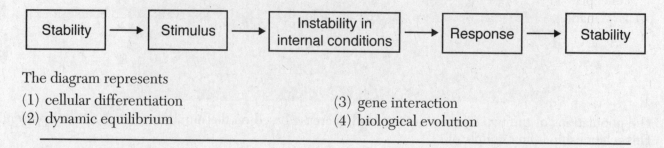

The diagram represents

(1) cellular differentiation
(2) dynamic equilibrium

(3) gene interaction
(4) biological evolution

January '20   Regents Examination

Part B–1

Answer all questions in this part.   [13]

Directions (31–43): For *each* statement or question, record on the separate answer sheet the *number* of the word or expression that, of those given, best completes the statement or answers the question.

31 An experiment is carried out to determine how different pH values of soil will affect the growth of tomato plants. In this experiment, the dependent variable could be the

(1) height of the tomato plants

(3) specific variety of tomato plants used

(2) pH of the soil

(4) pH of enzymes in tomato leaf cells

32 Using microscopes he constructed in the 1600s, Antonie van Leeuwenhoek discovered a new microscopic world. His discoveries paved the way for the development of the microscopes used today and for many important biological breakthroughs.

Source: http://famousbiologists.org/
antonie-van-leeuwenhoek/

Which statement best describes van Leeuwenhoek's work?

(1) His observations alone provided enough information to form modern biological theories.

(2) The microscopes he made were used by all scientists and have remained unchanged over the years.

(3) Knowledge gained by his work has led to the improvement and development of modern scientific concepts.

(4) Explanations of the microscopic world today are solely based on his observations and conclusions.

January '20   Regents Examination

Base your answers to questions 33 and 34 on the information below and on your knowledge of biology.

Anabolic Steroids

Anabolic steroids are hormones that affect muscle growth. Many athletes take synthetic anabolic steroids, in hopes of developing larger muscles so they can perform better at their sport. These hormones can act like the hormone testosterone. When men take an excess of anabolic steroids, they can have an increase in feminine features. This is due to the fact that the excess of these chemicals signals the male body to stop producing testosterone.

33 This signal in the male body to stop producing testosterone is an example of

(1) an underproduction of estrogen
(2) a feedback mechanism
(3) an overproduction of testosterone
(4) a decrease in anabolic steroid use

34 One reason why anabolic steroids can imitate the hormone testosterone is because

(1) anabolic steroids and testosterone both interact with the same cell receptors
(2) testosterone acts only on muscle cells
(3) females produce small amounts of the hormone testosterone
(4) an increase in testosterone in males using anabolic steroids increases male features

Base your answers to questions 35 and 36 on the information in the chart below and on your knowledge of biology.

Leopard Frog Reproduction Facts

Where in New York State do leopard frogs live?	Marshes, ponds, swamps, and slow-moving water
How often do they breed?	Once each year
When is their breeding season?	March until June
How many eggs does one frog produce?	3000 to 6500
How long until the fertilized eggs hatch?	2 to 3 weeks
When do they reach sexual maturity?	Males: 365 days Females: 730 days

35 How does the ability to produce 3000 to 6500 eggs benefit the species?

(1) It decreases the opportunity for more frogs to compete for limited resources.
(2) More offspring are likely to survive and reproduce.
(3) The offspring will be more widely distributed by fast-moving water.
(4) The chances for asexual reproduction in the frogs will increase.

36 One explanation for the timing and length of the leopard frog breeding season is that it occurs

(1) when environmental conditions are most favorable
(2) 365 days after the eggs have hatched the year before
(3) 2 to 3 weeks after female frogs have reached sexual maturity
(4) when there is a greater chance of mutation producing favorable variations

37 Sailors in the past may have heard the greeting from a passing ship, "Avast ye scurvy dogs." This greeting would be a reference to a disease known as scurvy, which is due to inadequate intake of vitamin C. Which row in the chart below correctly identifies the cause of this disease and a possible treatment for it?

Row	Cause	Treatment
(1)	inherited trait	gene manipulation
(2)	organ malfunction	antibiotic injections
(3)	poor nutrition	fresh fruit
(4)	virus	vaccination

38 Male birds of two different species living on the same island have developed different mating behaviors, as shown in the table below.

Species	Mating Behavior of Male Birds
A	rapid chirps while spreading their tail feathers
B	movement in circles while spreading their tail feathers

Which statement is best supported by information in the table?

(1) It is likely that male birds in species A will mate with female birds in species B.
(2) It is likely that birds from species A will only mate with birds from species A.
(3) Male birds from one species will change their mating behavior if the only female birds available are from the other species.
(4) Mating behaviors are important only when these two species live together in the same area.

39 In a DNA molecule, if 38% of the molecular bases are C (cytosine), what percent of the bases are T (thymine)?

(1) 12   (3) 38
(2) 24   (4) 62

40 An increased demand for soybeans has led to an increase in converting native forests and grasslands to fields for growing soybeans. One *negative* consequence of this environmental change has been

(1) an increase in natural resources for the future
(2) an increase in the kinds of foods that can be produced
(3) a decrease in suitable habitats for wildlife
(4) a decrease in the need to set aside land for conservation

41 In the 1660s, Flemish physician Jan van Helmont grew a small willow tree in a pot of soil. He added only water to the pot. At the end of five years, he found that the tree had gained 75 kilograms, but there was very little change in the mass of the soil. Van Helmont concluded that the plant gained weight directly from the water. We now know that this conclusion is only partially correct because, in addition to water, photosynthesis also requires

(1) oxygen from the atmosphere   (3) proteins from animal prey
(2) carbon dioxide from the atmosphere   (4) carbohydrates from the soil

Base your answers to questions 42 and 43 on the illustration below and on your knowledge of biology. The illustration shows two methods of reproduction, method A and method B.

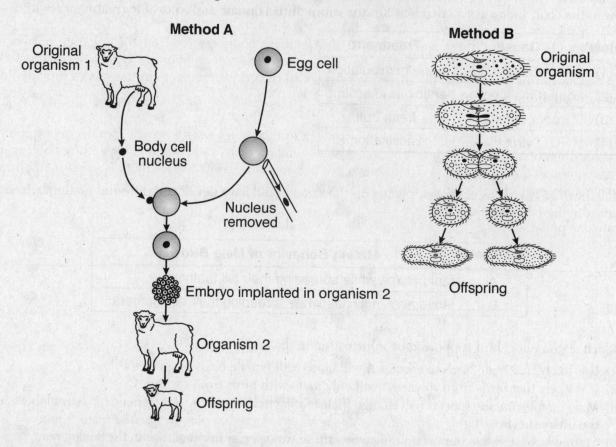

Method A

Original organism 1

Egg cell

Body cell nucleus

Nucleus removed

Embryo implanted in organism 2

Organism 2

Offspring

Method B

Original organism

Offspring

42 Which statement regarding these methods of reproduction is correct?

(1) They are both forms of asexual reproduction.
(2) They are both forms of sexual reproduction.
(3) Method A is a form of asexual reproduction and method B is a form of sexual reproduction.
(4) Method A is a form of sexual reproduction and method B is a form of asexual reproduction.

43 Which process takes place in both method A and method B?

(1) meiosis
(2) mitosis
(3) fertilization
(4) recombination

Part B–2

Answer all questions in this part. [12]

Directions (44–55): For those questions that are multiple choice, record on the separate answer sheet the *number* of the choice that, of those given, best completes each statement or answers each question. For all other questions in this part, follow the directions given and record your answers in the spaces provided in this examination booklet.

44 Corals are a group of organisms that live in shallow, warm areas of the world's oceans. Coral reefs are composed of a hard material that is produced by these small coral animals, and is then colonized by photosynthetic organisms called *Zooxanthellae*. These plant-like organisms generate sugars that are used by their animal partners for food and are needed for the survival of the coral.

State *one* possible reason that coral reefs exist only in shallow waters. [1]

_____

_____

Base your answers to questions 45 through 47 on the information and data table below and on your knowledge of biology.

Measles: Eliminated?

Measles is a highly contagious viral disease. Infected people first experience a fever, cold-like symptoms, and a rash. Several complications can develop, such as ear infections, diarrhea, pneumonia, encephalitis (swelling of the brain), and death. Prior to the widespread use of the measles vaccine in the 1960s, it is estimated that 3–4 million people were infected every year. The Centers for Disease Control and Prevention declared measles eliminated in the United States in 2000. This was accomplished, in part, due to a highly effective vaccination program. However, since 2016 the disease has made a comeback, and there has been an increase in measles cases in recent years.

Number of Measles Cases 2010-2016

Year	Number of Cases
2010	63
2011	220
2012	55
2013	187
2014	667
2015	188
2016	70

Source: www.cdc.gov/measles/
cases-outbreaks.html

Directions (45–46): Using the information in the data table, construct a line graph on the grid below, following the directions below.

45 Mark an appropriate scale, without any breaks in the data, on each labeled axis. [1]

46 Plot the data on the grid. Connect the points and surround each point with a small circle. [1]

Example:

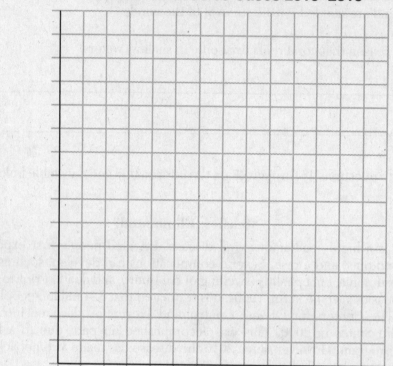

Number of Measles Cases 2010–2016

Number of Cases

Year

Note: The answer to question 47 should be recorded on your separate answer sheet.

47 The reason for the dramatic decline in the number of measles cases from the 1960s to 2010 in the United States was because the vaccine

(1) contained pathogens to fight against this highly contagious virus
(2) prevented the development of serious complications after infection
(3) exposed many people to a weakened form of the measles virus, making them immune
(4) contained an antibiotic that killed the measles virus, preventing its spread

Base your answers to questions 48 and 49 on the information below and on your knowledge of biology.

The line graphs below represent trends in prey fish populations for each of the five Great Lakes.

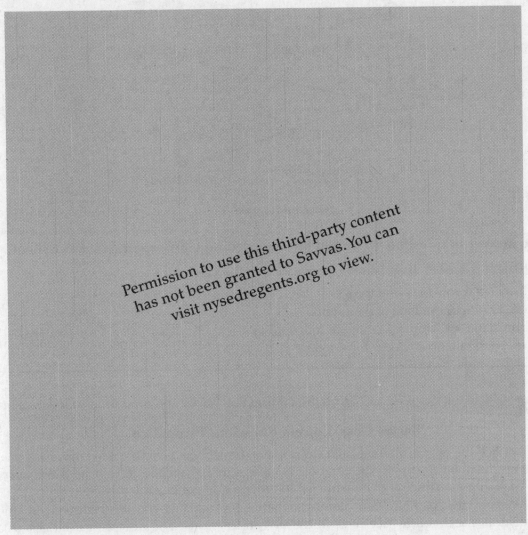

Permission to use this third-party content has not been granted to Savvas. You can visit nysedregents.org to view.

48 Identify in which of the Great Lakes you would expect to see the greatest increase in the number of predatory fish in 2008 and 2009. Support your answer. [1]

_____

_____

Examine the Great Lakes food web represented below.

Food Web in Great Lakes

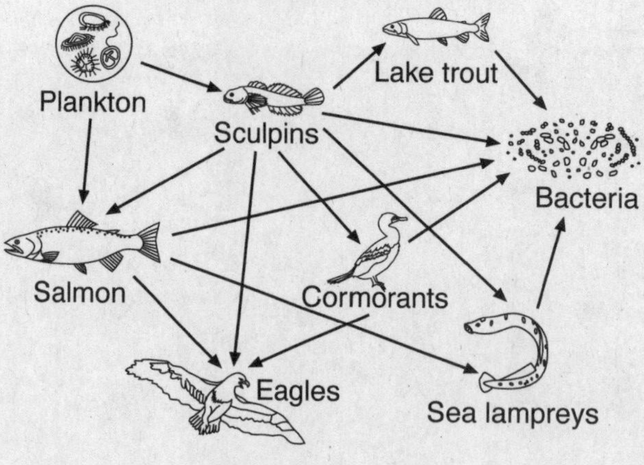

(Not drawn to scale)

Note: The answer to question 49 should be recorded on your separate answer sheet.

49 Which statement is correct, based on the information in the diagram?

(1) Salmon are predators of sea lampreys.
(2) Plankton decompose salmon and sculpins.
(3) Cormorants and sea lampreys compete for bacteria.
(4) Lake trout and salmon compete for sculpins.

Base your answers to questions 50 and 51 on the information below and on your knowledge of biology.

Barley Gene Lowers Emissions From Rice

Over half the people on the planet eat rice as a staple food. Growing rice emits methane, a potent greenhouse gas—to the tune of 25 million to 100 million tons of methane every year, a notable contribution to human-caused greenhouse gas emissions...

...When rice paddies are flooded, methane-producing bacteria thrive on the carbohydrates secreted by rice roots in the oxygen-free soils. The rice plant itself acts as a conduit [pathway], transmitting methane from the soil into the atmosphere...

Source: Times Tribune 7/23/15

Note: The answer to question 50 should be recorded on your separate answer sheet.

50 Scientists have incorporated a barley gene into a type of rice and produced rice plants that have much lower methane emissions. It is most likely that the scientists incorporated the barley gene into the rice, producing a new variety, using the process of

(1) selective breeding
(2) meiosis, followed by recombination
(3) genetic engineering
(4) sexual reproduction, followed by mitosis

51 Now that the scientists have developed this new variety of rice plant, identify *one* method that could be used to produce large quantities of only these beneficial plants. [1]

_____

_____

Base your answer to question 52 on the information and diagram below and on your knowledge of biology. The diagram represents the energy relationships in a forest ecosystem.

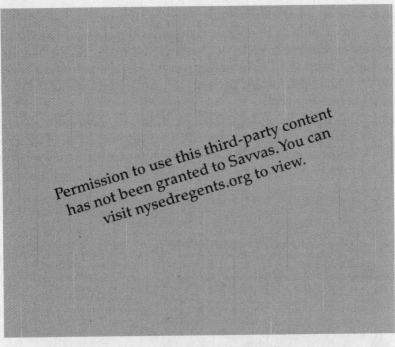

52 Based on the information in the diagram, only some of the available energy is transferred from one energy level to the next. State what happens to the rest of the energy. [1]

_____

_____

_____

Base your answers to questions 53 through 55 on the information below and on your knowledge of biology.

Glow-Worms

The European glow-worm (*Lampyris noctiluca*) is an insect and a member of the firefly family. Males are ordinary-looking beetles with brown wings. Females are much larger, don't have wings, glow, and look like a large larva. Adult glow-worms usually live for less than two weeks. They don't eat, focusing all their energy on finding a mate. The glow-worm has few enemies. Its body contains a poison that protects it from predators and its light warns would-be attackers that it is not safe to eat.

Greenish light glows from the end of a female's abdomen, an organ called the lantern, for up to several hours each night. There are great differences in the size of the female lanterns. In an experiment, scientists found that females with larger lanterns glowed brighter, and the brightest females laid the most eggs. The diagram below shows three different glow-worms.

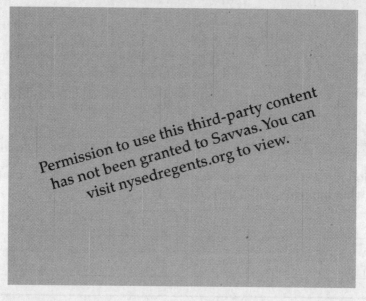

Permission to use this third-party content has not been granted to Savvas. You can visit nysedregents.org to view.

53 Describe *one* way that a glowing abdomen helps the glow-worm increase its reproductive success. [1]

_____

_____

54 Explain why increased light pollution in areas where glow-worms are found could affect glow-worm populations. [1]

_____

_____

55 Although the females glow at night and are easily seen by predators, they have few enemies. State *one* characteristic that protects them from predators. [1]

_____

_____

Part C

Answer all questions in this part. [17]

Directions (56–72): Record your answers in the spaces provided in this examination booklet.

Base your answers to questions 56 through 58 on the information below and on your knowledge of biology.

Global Warming

Throughout its long history, Earth has warmed and cooled time and again. Climate has changed when the planet received more or less sunlight due to subtle shifts in its orbit, as the atmosphere or surface changed, or when the Sun's energy varied. But in the past century, another force has started to influence Earth's climate: humanity. …

…What has scientists concerned now is that over the past 250 years, humans have been artificially raising the concentration of greenhouse gases in the atmosphere at an ever-increasing rate, mostly by burning fossil fuels, but also from cutting down carbon-absorbing forests. Since the Industrial Revolution began in about 1750, carbon dioxide levels have increased nearly 38 percent as of 2009 and methane levels have increased 148 percent. …

Source: http://earthobservatory.nasa.gov

56 Other than the issues mentioned in the passage, state *one* action that humans could take to slow down the rate of global warming. [1]

_____

_____

57 Other than global warming, state *one* specific effect on the environment if the human activities mentioned in the passage continue. [1]

_____

_____

58 On November 4, 2016, the Paris Agreement brought many nations into a common cause to combat climate change and adapt to its effects on a global level. State *one* reason why climate change needs to be addressed globally as well as locally. [1]

_____

_____

Base your answers to questions 59 through 61 on the information and photograph below and on your knowledge of biology. The photograph shows a handful of croton nuts.

The Power of the Croton Nut

The croton nut tree grows in East Africa. It produces a nut that is inedible [to humans], and the tree itself was considered of little use except for firewood. The trees grow over vast areas, and many of these areas have been deforested to get rid of the trees and to make more land available for agriculture.

Recently, scientists and engineers in Kenya have been able to crush the nuts and obtain oil, which can be used as a less expensive substitute for diesel fuel, a nonrenewable fossil fuel. The leftover nut pulp can be processed and sold for fertilizer, compressed into biofuel briquettes for use in cooking stoves, or converted into feed for chickens, making the commercial use of the croton nut a zero-waste process.

Source: http://www.ozy.com/fast-forward/
please-dont-eat-the-diesel-substitute/60533

59 Explain why the use of croton nut oil represents an advantage over the use of conventional diesel fuel.   [1]

_____

_____

60 Describe *one* environmental benefit of maintaining croton forests rather than cutting them down to use the land for farming.   [1]

_____

_____

61 Explain why the commercial use of the croton nut is considered a zero-waste process.   [1]

_____

_____

_____

Base your answers to questions 62 and 63 on the information below and on your knowledge of biology.

DDT: A "Miracle Pesticide"

DDT is a pesticide developed during World War II that successfully killed insects, such as mosquitoes, that were a large problem for our soldiers in the Pacific. DDT was also very effective for preventing insect damage to crops, so it was considered, at the time, to be a "miracle pesticide."

Soon, however, scientists noticed that DDT was negatively affecting other animals and being passed along food chains. For example, some birds accumulated large amounts of DDT in their tissues, which caused them to lay eggs with weakened shells that broke before hatching.

Rachel Carson, a marine biologist and author, became concerned about the use of pesticides and their negative effects on the environment. Carson began to write books and speak about the dangers of pesticides. Her actions eventually led to many changes in our use of pesticides and proved valuable to protecting our environment and people from the negative effects that were being discovered about pesticides.

Rachel Carson

Source: http://www.signature-reads.com/2015/04/
headstrong-52-female-scientists-and-their-earth-shaking-
discoveries/

62 Some scientists began to suspect that DDT was not the "miracle pesticide" that it was originally thought to be. State *one* possible hypothesis that these scientists may have proposed to begin their research to find out more about DDT. [1]

_____

_____

63 All scientific explanations are tentative and subject to change or improvement. Explain how this statement relates to the scientific thinking about DDT. [1]

_____

_____

Base your answers to questions 64 through 67 on the information and graph below and on your knowledge of biology. The graph shows the change in the blood glucose level of one person after eating a cookie.

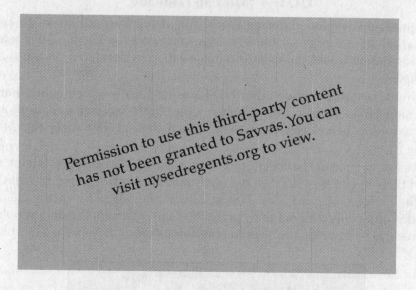

Permission to use this third-party content has not been granted to Savvas. You can visit nysedregents.org to view.

64 Explain why most human cells require a supply of glucose. [1]

_____

_____

65 State *one* specific response of the body to the increase in blood glucose level that would account for the changes that begin about 30 minutes after eating the cookie. [1]

_____

_____

66 Describe how the line representing blood glucose would change if the body could *not* take corrective actions to return this system to normal levels after eating a cookie. [1]

_____

_____

67 Based on the data and information provided, state whether or not it would be valid to conclude that bananas supply more glucose than cookies. Support your answer. [1]

_____

_____

Base your answer to question 68–71 on the information below and on your knowledge of biology.

Artificial Placenta

It is estimated that every year more than 15 million babies are born too early. The lungs of these premature infants are often immature and easily damaged. Premature births happen for a variety of reasons—some known and some unknown. Those that are known include infections and conditions such as diabetes and high blood pressure. Scientists are researching what causes premature births, in an attempt to develop solutions to prevent them.

Scientists are also working on the development of an artificial placenta. At the University of Michigan, five premature lambs were placed in artificial placentas and kept alive for weeks. During this time, each lamb's blood was circulated through its artificial placenta.

68–71 Discuss how the development of an artificial placenta is an important step in the study of premature births. In your answer, be sure to:

- explain why it would be harmful for a human mother's blood to pass across the placenta and into the fetus [1]
- state how an artificial placenta would be of benefit to the lungs of premature infants [1]
- explain why the lambs' blood must be filtered as it circulates through the artificial placenta [1]
- state *one* reason why premature lambs were likely used as model organisms in this study rather than mice [1]

_____

_____

_____

_____

_____

_____

_____

72 As the rate of environmental change has increased over the last 50-100 years, there has been an increase in extinction rates. Lower reproductive rates seem to have also contributed to this increase in extinctions.

Describe *one* possible reason for an increased extinction rate in populations of species with a lower rate of reproduction. [1]

_____

_____

January '20 Regents Examination

Part D

Answer all questions in this part. [13]

Directions (73–85): For those questions that are multiple choice, record on the separate answer sheet the *number* of the choice that, of those given, best completes each statement or answers each question. For all other questions in this part, follow the directions given and record your answers in the spaces provided in this examination booklet.

Base your answers to questions 73 and 74 on the information and Universal Genetic Code Chart below and on your knowledge of biology.

Universal Genetic Code Chart

FIRST BASE	SECOND BASE: U	SECOND BASE: C	SECOND BASE: A	SECOND BASE: G	THIRD BASE
U	UUU, UUC } PHE UUA, UUG } LEU	UCU, UCC, UCA, UCG } SER	UAU, UAC } TYR UAA, UAG } STOP	UGU, UGC } CYS UGA } STOP UGG } TRP	U C A G
C	CUU, CUC, CUA, CUG } LEU	CCU, CCC, CCA, CCG } PRO	CAU, CAC } HIS CAA, CAG } GLN	CGU, CGC, CGA, CGG } ARG	U C A G
A	AUU, AUC, AUA } ILE AUG } MET or START	ACU, ACC, ACA, ACG } THR	AAU, AAC } ASN AAA, AAG } LYS	AGU, AGC } SER AGA, AGG } ARG	U C A G
G	GUU, GUC, GUA, GUG } VAL	GCU, GCC, GCA, GCG } ALA	GAU, GAC } ASP GAA, GAG } GLU	GGU, GGC, GGA, GGG } GLY	U C A G

Note: The answer to question 73 should be recorded on your separate answer sheet.

73 The messenger RNA sequence that codes for the amino acid chain TYR–ARG–GLY–VAL–ALA–LEU is

(1) UAU–CGA–GUU–UUU–UUA–CUC
(2) UAU–CGA–GGA–GUU–GCG–CUC
(3) CUC–GCG–GUU–GGA–CGA–UAU
(4) CUC–UUA–UUU–GUU–CGA–UAU

Note: The answer to question 74 should be recorded on your separate answer sheet.

74 The messenger RNA sequence that is most likely to produce a functional protein is

(1) UGA–UAU–CGA–GGA–GUU–GCG–CUC–UAG
(2) UAG–UAU–CGA–GGA–GUU–GCG–CUC–AUG
(3) AUG–UAU–CGA–GGA–GUU–GCG–CUC–UGA
(4) UAA–CUC–UUA–UUU–GUU–CGA–UAU–UAA

Base your answers to questions 75 and 76 on the information below and on your knowledge of biology.

A forensic scientist is trying to determine if the plant pieces found on a burglary suspect match the plants found outside a home that was robbed. The suspect had plant pieces in the hood of his jacket as well as green stains on the knees of his jeans.

Note: The answer to question 75 should be recorded on your separate answer sheet.

75 In order to compare the composition of the pigments on the suspect's jeans to the pigments of the plants at the home, the forensic scientist should use

(1) restriction enzymes

(2) genetic engineering

(3) paper chromatography

(4) receptor molecules

Note: The answer to question 76 should be recorded on your separate answer sheet.

76 The evidence that would be most convincing in determining that the plant pieces found in the suspect's hood matched the plants outside the home that was robbed would be if they both had the same

(1) color flower petal

(2) gene sequence

(3) kind of pollen grains

(4) type of leaf structure

Base your answers to questions 77 and 78 on the information below and on your knowledge of biology.

The diagram below represents a lab setup. The artificial cell (dialysis tube) contains a starch solution and the beaker contains a solution of starch indicator and water. The setup is left undisturbed for twenty minutes.

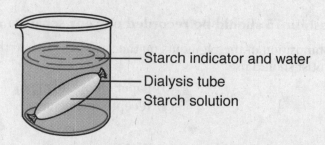

Starch indicator and water
Dialysis tube
Starch solution

77 Identify *one* molecule, present in this setup, that will be able to pass through the dialysis tubing. [1]

_____

78 Describe *one* observation that could be made that would confirm that the molecule you identified in question 77 had passed through the membrane. [1]

_____

_____

_____

Base your answer to question 79 on the diagram below and on your knowledge of biology.

Permission to use this third-party content has not been granted to Savvas. You can visit nysedregents.org to view.

79 A new finch is found to have a diet of worms and caterpillars. Identify *one* finch from the diagram that would have a beak most similar to the new finch. Support your answer. [1]

Finch: _____

_____

_____

_____

80 A student was given forceps (tweezers) as his tool in the *Beaks of Finches* lab. Circle which type of food he would likely pick up most easily – small seeds or large seeds. Support your answer. [1]

Small seeds   Large seeds

Support: _____

_____

Base your answer to question 81 on the information and diagram below and on your knowledge of biology.

A student added equal volumes of water to two different beakers. He then added blue food dye to one and yellow to the other. Next, he placed a white paper towel across the two beakers so that it went down into the liquid and connected the two beakers.

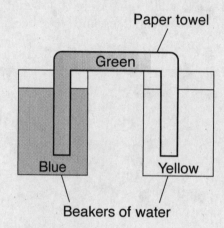

Paper towel

Green

Blue   Yellow

Beakers of water

Note: The answer to question 81 should be recorded on your separate answer sheet.

81 After 20 minutes, the section of paper towel connecting the two beakers had turned color. The towel most likely turned green as a result of the

(1) separation of the dye molecules through the process of chromatography
(2) dyes moving across the towel due to the process of electrophoresis
(3) diffusion of the blue- and yellow-dyed water across the towel
(4) active transport of the blue and yellow food dyes

Base your answers to questions 82 and 83 on the information and photograph below and on your knowledge of biology.

A Close Relative of the Elephant

A hyrax is an animal that has been called a rock rabbit and looks like a guinea pig. Fossil records show that hyraxes first appeared on Earth approximately 37 million years ago. As they evolved, some became mouse-sized, while some were the size of a horse. Some eventually adapted to marine life and are related to manatees, and some became grazers and are related to elephants.

Hyrax and Elephant

Source: https://www.mnn.com/earth-matters/animals/photos/
12-facts-change-way-see-elephants/elephants-closest-relative-rock-hyrax

Note: The answer to question 82 should be recorded on your separate answer sheet.

82 A section of the mammalian evolutionary tree is shown below.

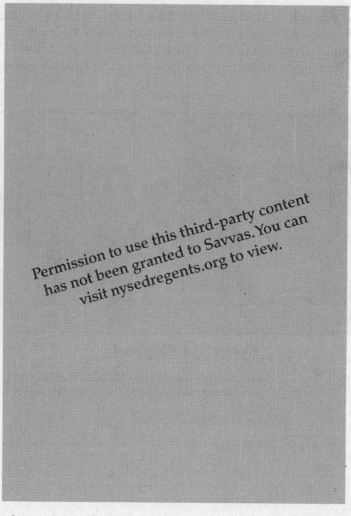

Permission to use this third-party content has not been granted to Savvas. You can visit nysedregents.org to view.

Which number would indicate the most recent common ancestor of the hyrax, elephant, and manatee on the section of this mammalian evolutionary tree?

(1) 1

(2) 2

(3) 3

(4) 4

83 Identify *one* type of molecular evidence that could have been used to develop this mammalian evolutionary tree, and describe one specific way that the evidence could have been used to construct the tree. [1]

Evidence: _____

_____

_____

_____

Base your answers to questions 84 and 85 on the information and graph below and on your knowledge of biology.

During a lab experiment a student took his resting pulse rate, counting 23 beats in 20 seconds. The student then exercised for several minutes. The student's pulse was taken immediately after the exercise, and then every minute for 6 minutes. The graph below shows changes in the pulse rate after the exercise was completed.

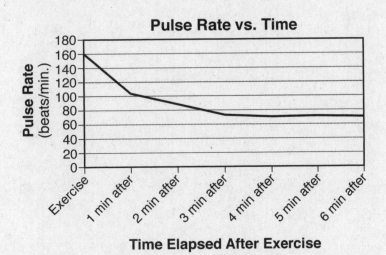

84 What was the student's resting pulse rate in beats per minute? [1]

_____ beats/min.

85 State *one* biological explanation for how the pulse rate increase benefited the student as he exercised. [1]

_____

_____

_____

Part A

Answer all questions in this part. [30]

Directions (1–30): For *each* statement or question, record on the separate answer sheet the *number* of the word or expression that, of those given, best completes the statement or answers the question.

1 The diagram below represents an energy pyramid.

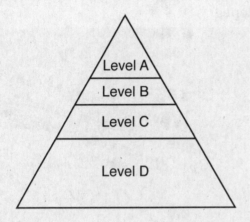

In this pyramid, the greatest amount of stored energy is found at level

(1) *A*   (3) *C*
(2) *B*   (4) *D*

2 A certain species of plant serves as the only food for the young larvae of a particular species of butterfly. In a large field, a disease kills all the members of this plant species. As a result of the plant disease, the butterfly population will most likely

(1) quickly adapt to eat other plants
(2) disappear from the area
(3) evolve to form a new species
(4) enter the adult stage more quickly

3 When handling cat litter, humans can potentially be exposed to a harmful single-celled protozoan. Its primary host is the common domestic cat, but it can also live in humans. This protozoan is an example of a

(1) predator   (3) parasite
(2) producer   (4) scavenger

4 Certain seaweeds contain a greater concentration of iodine inside their cells than there is in the seawater surrounding them. The energy required to maintain this concentration difference is most closely associated with the action of

(1) ribosomes   (3) vacuoles
(2) mitochondria   (4) nuclei

5 Doctors sometimes use a vaccine to prepare the body to defend itself against future infections. These vaccines most often contain

(1) antibodies
(2) antibiotics
(3) white blood cells
(4) weakened pathogens

6 Building large manufacturing facilities can affect ecosystems by increasing the

(1) atmospheric quality
(2) biodiversity in the area
(3) demand for resources such as fossil fuels
(4) availability of space and resources for organisms

7 An ameba is a single-celled organism. It uses its cell membrane to obtain food from its environment, digests the food with the help of organelles called lysosomes, and uses other organelles to process the digested food. From this, we can best infer that

(1) all single-celled organisms have lysosomes to digest food
(2) amebas are capable of digesting any type of food molecule
(3) single-celled organisms are as complex as multicellular organisms
(4) structures in amebas have functions similar to organs in multicellular organisms

8 White blood cells are most closely associated with which two body systems?

(1) circulatory and digestive
(2) immune and circulatory
(3) digestive and excretory
(4) excretory and immune

9 Carnivorous plants, such as pitcher plants and sundews, live in bogs where many other organisms cannot. Due to the high rate of decomposition occurring in bogs, the environment is acidic and contains very little oxygen and nutrients. The bogs only support certain types of organisms because

(1) organisms in an environment are not limited by available energy and resources
(2) the growth and survival of organisms depends upon specific physical conditions
(3) favorable gene mutations only occur when organisms live in harsh environments
(4) photosynthetic organisms can only inhabit environments that have a low acidity

10 Anhidrosis is the inability to sweat normally. If the human body cannot sweat properly, it cannot cool itself, which is potentially harmful. Anhidrosis most directly interferes with

(1) a feedback mechanism that maintains homeostasis
(2) an immune system response to harmless antigens
(3) the synthesis of hormones in the circulatory system
(4) the enzymatic breakdown of water in cells

11 The hair colors of the members of a family are listed below.

mother – brown hair
father – blond hair
older son – brown hair
younger son – blond hair

The hair colors of the sons are most likely a direct result of

(1) natural selection in males
(2) heredity
(3) evolution
(4) environmental influences

12 A sample of DNA from a human skin cell contains 32% cytosine (C) bases. Approximately what percentage of the bases in this sample will be thymine (T)?

(1) 18   (3) 32
(2) 24   (4) 36

13 Carmine, a compound that comes from the cochineal beetle, shown below, is used as a food coloring.

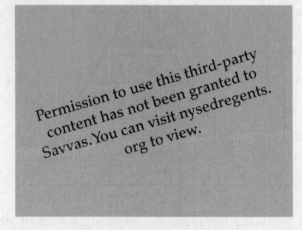

Permission to use this third-party content has not been granted to Savvas. You can visit nysedregents.org to view.

The food coloring is not harmful to most people, but in a small number of individuals, it causes a reaction and affects their ability to breathe. This response to carmine is known as

(1) a stimulus   (3) natural selection
(2) an allergy   (4) an adaptation

14 As a way to reduce the number of cases of malaria, a human tropical disease, a specific DNA sequence is inserted into the reproductive cells of *Anopheles* mosquitoes. Which process was most likely used to alter these mosquitoes?

(1) cloning studies
(2) genetic engineering
(3) natural selection
(4) random mutations

15 Which row in the chart below accurately identifies two causes of mutations and the cells that must be affected in order for the mutations to be passed on to offspring?

Row	Cause of Mutations	Cells Affected
(1)	infections and antigens	body cells
(2)	meiosis and mitosis	body cells
(3)	disease and differentiation	sex cells
(4)	chemicals and radiation	sex cells

16 Many tiny plants can be seen developing asexually along the edge of the mother-of-thousands plant leaf, as shown in the photo below. The tiny plants eventually drop to the ground and grow into new plants of the same species.

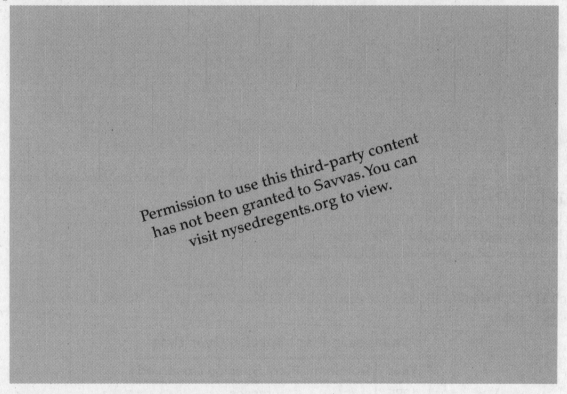

One way this form of reproduction differs from sexual reproduction is

(1) more genetic variations are seen in the offspring
(2) there is a greater chance for mutations to occur
(3) the offspring and the parents are genetically identical
(4) the new plants possess the combined genes of both parents

August '19   Regents Examination

17 A food web is represented in the diagram below.

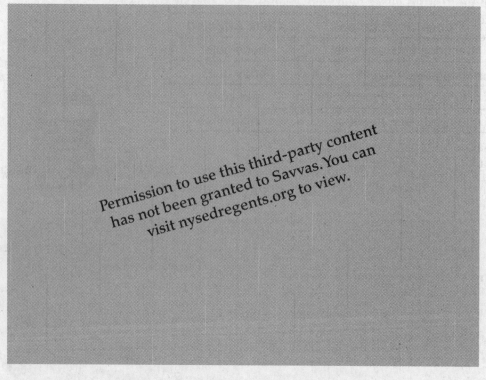

If the fish population *decreases*, what is the most direct effect this will have on the aquatic ecosystem?

(1) The leopard seals will all die from lack of food.
(2) The krill population will only be consumed by seagulls.
(3) The zooplankton population will increase in size.
(4) The phytoplankton population will increase in size.

18 The chart below shows a sequence of events that was observed at an abandoned ski center over a period of years.

Changes in Plant Species Over Time

Year	Dominant Plant Species Observed
1985	grasses
1995	shrubs and bushes
2005	cherry, birch, and poplar trees

This sequence of changes is the result of

(1) ecological succession
(2) decreased biodiversity
(3) biological evolution
(4) environmental trade-offs

19 Some salmon have been genetically modified to grow bigger and mature faster than wild salmon. They are kept in fish-farming facilities. Which statement regarding genetically modified salmon is correct?

(1) Genetically modified salmon produce more of some proteins than wild salmon.
(2) Genetically modified salmon and wild salmon would have identical DNA.
(3) Wild salmon reproduce asexually while genetically modified salmon reproduce sexually.
(4) Wild salmon have an altered protein sequence, but genetically modified salmon do not.

20 Which group of organisms in an ecosystem fills the niche of recycling organic matter back to the environment?

(1) carnivores
(2) decomposers
(3) producers
(4) predators

21 The use of solar panels has increased in the last ten years. A benefit of using solar energy would include

(1) adding more carbon dioxide to the atmosphere
(2) using less fossil fuel to meet energy needs
(3) using a nonrenewable source of energy
(4) releasing more gases for photosynthesis

22 In a sewage treatment facility, an optimal environment is maintained for the survival of naturally occurring species of microorganisms. These organisms can then break the sewage down into relatively harmless wastewater. For these microorganisms, the wastewater facility serves as

(1) its carrying capacity
(2) a food chain
(3) an ecosystem
(4) an energy pyramid

23 The diagram below represents a process taking place in a cell.

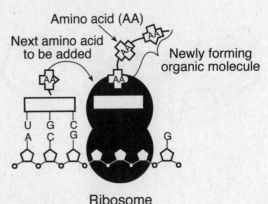

The type of organic molecule that is being synthesized is

(1) DNA
(2) starch
(3) protein
(4) fat

24 The governments of many countries have regulations that are designed to prevent the accidental introduction of nonnative insects into their countries. This is because, in these new habitats, the nonnative insects might

(1) become food for birds
(2) not survive a cold winter
(3) not have natural predators
(4) add to the biodiversity

25 The process of transferring energy during respiration occurs in a series of steps. This prevents too much heat from being released at one time. Maintaining an appropriate temperature is beneficial to an organism because

(1) enzymes need a proper range of temperatures to catalyze vital reactions
(2) cellular waste products can only be excreted in cooler temperatures
(3) hormones can only produce antibodies if temperatures are not excessive
(4) nutrients diffuse faster into cells when temperatures are lower

26 The diagram below represents some structures in the human female reproductive system.

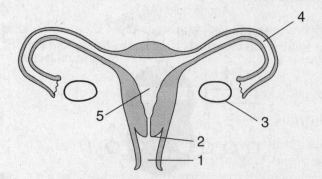

The processes of meiosis and fertilization are essential in human reproduction. Which row in the chart correctly identifies where in the female reproductive system these two processes occur?

Row	Meiosis	Fertilization
(1)	1	3
(2)	2	5
(3)	3	4
(4)	4	5

27 Fruits and vegetables exposed to air begin to brown because of a chemical reaction in their cells. This may result in these foods being thrown out. Some people have found that adding lemon juice (citric acid) to apple slices keeps them from turning brown. The prevention of browning is likely the result of

(1) increasing the concentration of enzymes
(2) increasing the temperature
(3) slowing the rate of enzyme action
(4) maintaining the pH

28 Scientists monitoring frog populations have noticed that the ratio of male frogs to female frogs varies when certain chemicals are present in the environment. The influence of estrogen, for example, has a noticeable effect. In the presence of a higher amount of estrogen, it would be most likely that

(1) fewer males would be found because they are much larger and fewer are produced
(2) fewer females would be found because they are more sensitive to pesticides
(3) more males would be found because estrogen promotes the development of male characteristics
(4) more females would be found because estrogen promotes the development of female characteristics

29 Which action could humans take to slow the rate of global warming?

(1) Cut down trees for more efficient land use.
(2) Increase the consumption of petroleum products.
(3) Use alternate sources of energy such as wind.
(4) Reduce the use of fuel-efficient automobiles.

30 The role of antibodies in the human body is to

(1) stimulate pathogen reproduction to produce additional white blood cells
(2) increase the production of guard cells to defend against pathogens
(3) promote the production of antigens to stimulate an immune response
(4) recognize foreign antigens and mark them for destruction

Part B–1

Answer all questions in this part.   [13]

Directions (31–43): For *each* statement or question, record on the separate answer sheet the *number* of the word or expression that, of those given, best completes the statement or answers the question.

Base your answers to questions 31 and 32 on the information below and on your knowledge of biology.

Fossil Footprints

Scientists examined a trail of fossil footprints left by early humans in soft, volcanic ash in Eastern Africa. A drawing of the trail of footprints is shown below. Each footprint is represented as a series of lines indicating the depth that different parts of the foot sank into the volcanic ash.

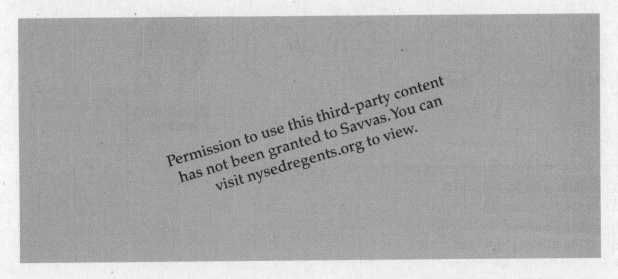

Permission to use this third-party content has not been granted to Savvas. You can visit nysedregents.org to view.

31 Which statement is an accurate observation that can be made based on this trail of footprints?

(1) The individuals were running from a predator.
(2) The volcano was about to erupt again.
(3) One individual was much taller than the other.
(4) One individual had larger feet than the other.

32 The type of information directly provided by these fossil footprints is useful because it

(1) offers details about how these individuals changed during their lifetime
(2) offers data regarding their exposure to ultraviolet (UV) radiation
(3) is a record of information about what these individuals ate during their lifetime
(4) is a record of some similarities and differences they share with present-day species

August '19 Regents Examination

33 Since the early 1990s, proton pump inhibitors (PPIs) have been widely used to treat acid reflux disease. Although clinical tests in the 1980s deemed PPIs to be safe for humans, in 2012 the FDA announced warnings that long-term use of PPIs could increase the risk of bone fractures, kidney disease, and some intestinal infections.

Which statement best explains why the safety of PPIs is now in question when clinical experiments in the 1980s provided evidence that they were safe?

(1) Researchers have been able to collect more data than were available in the 1980s.
(2) Fewer people had acid reflux in the 1980s compared to today.
(3) The medication containing PPIs has changed since the 1980s when tests were done.
(4) The original experiments in the 1980s used only test animals and did not use human subjects.

34 The process of embryonic development is represented in the diagram below.

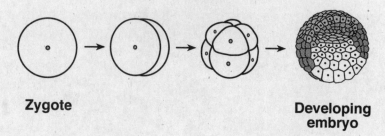

Zygote   **Developing embryo**

The three arrows in the diagram each represent a process known as

(1) mitotic cell division
(2) meiotic cell division
(3) fertilization of gamete cells
(4) differentiation of tissues

35 A cell with receptors for two different hormones is represented below.

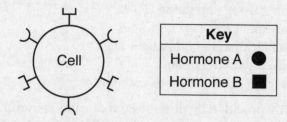

Key	
Hormone A	●
Hormone B	■

Which chemical would most likely interfere with the activity of hormone *A*, but *not* hormone *B*?

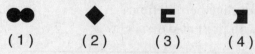

(1)   (2)   (3)   (4)

Base your answers to questions 36 through 39 on the information and photograph below and on your knowledge of biology.

Scientists Investigate Sex Determination in Alligators

The sex of some reptiles, including the American alligator, is determined by the temperature at which the eggs are incubated. For example, incubating them at 33°C produces mostly males, while incubation at 30°C produces mostly females.

Scientists recently discovered a thermosensor protein, TRPV4, that is associated with this process in American alligators. TRPV4 is activated by temperatures near the mid-30s, and increases the movement of calcium ions into certain cells involved with sex determination.

A baby alligator emerges from its egg shell during hatching

Source: http://www.dailymail.
co.uk/news/article-2190839/

36 The results of this scientific investigation will most likely lead other scientists to hypothesize that

(1) human sex cells also contain the TRPV4 protein
(2) other reptiles may have the TRPV4 protein in their eggs
(3) the TRPV4 protein affects the growth of plants
(4) the TRPV4 protein is present in all of the foods eaten by alligators

37 Which information was most essential in preparing to carry out this scientific investigation?

(1) a knowledge of the variety of mutations found in American alligator populations
(2) the arrangement of the DNA bases found in the TRPV4 protein
(3) the effects of temperature on the incubation of alligator eggs
(4) a knowledge of previous cloning experiments conducted on alligators and other reptiles

38 The movement of the calcium ions into certain cells is most likely due to

(1) the destruction of the TRPV4 when it contacts the cell membrane
(2) the action of TRPV4 proteins on the cells involved with sex determination
(3) the sex of the alligator embryo present in that particular egg
(4) the action of receptor proteins attached to the mitochondria in alligator sex cells

39 Environmental changes, such as global warming, could affect species such as the American alligator because even slight increases in environmental temperature could

(1) lead to an overabundance of females and few, if any, males
(2) lead to an overabundance of males and few, if any, females
(3) cause the breakdown of the TRPV4 protein in female alligators
(4) increase the rate at which calcium ions exit the sex cells

40 Which human activity can have a *negative* impact on the stability of a mature ecosystem?

(1) replanting trees in areas where forests have been cut down for lumber
(2) building dams to control the flow of water in rivers, in order to produce electricity
(3) preserving natural wetlands, such as swamps, to reduce flooding after heavy rainfalls
(4) passing laws that limit the dumping of pollutants in forests

Base your answer to question 41 on the diagram below and on your knowledge of biology. The diagram represents a pond ecosystem.

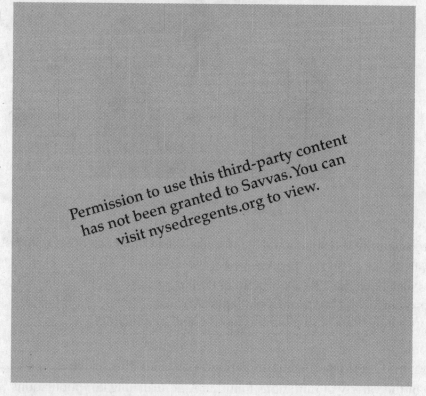

Permission to use this third-party content has not been granted to Savvas. You can visit nysedregents.org to view.

41 Energy in this ecosystem passes directly from the Sun to

(1) herbivores
(2) consumers
(3) heterotrophs
(4) autotrophs

Base your answers to questions 42 and 43 on the information and photograph below and on your knowledge of biology.

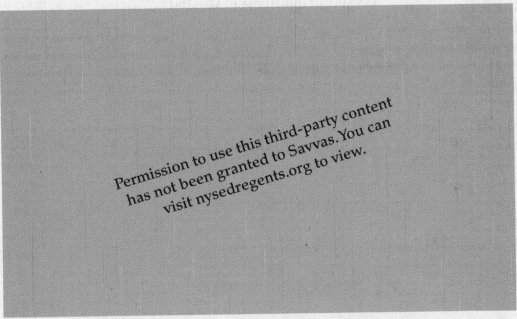

Permission to use this third-party content has not been granted to Savvas. You can visit nysedregents.org to view.

Wild horses called mustangs roam acres of federally owned land in the western United States. These horses have overgrazed the local vegetation to the extent that plants and soils are being lost entirely.

When the number of mustangs that roam the land exceeds the number of horses that the land can sustain, the government organizes helicopter-driven roundups. The horses are guided into a roped-off area and then are sold to the public or brought to pastures in the Midwest. About one percent of the horses captured die from injuries or accidents that occur during roundups.

42 The risk to the horses during the roundups compared to the entire loss of plants and soils is considered

(1) selective breeding
(2) a technological fix
(3) direct harvesting
(4) a trade-off

43 The number of organisms that an area of land can sustain over a long period of time is known as

(1) ecological succession
(2) its finite resources
(3) its carrying capacity
(4) evolutionary change

Part B–2

Answer all questions in this part. [12]

Directions (44–55): For those questions that are multiple choice, record on the separate answer sheet the *number* of the choice that, of those given, best completes each statement or answers each question. For all other questions in this part, follow the directions given and record your answers in the spaces provided in this examination booklet.

GO ON TO THE NEXT PAGE ⇨

Base your answers to questions 44 through 48 on the information and data table below and on your knowledge of biology.

White Nose Syndrome Found in Bats

White nose syndrome (WNS) is a disease found in bats. The disease, first detected in bats during the winter of 2006, is characterized by the appearance of a white fungus on the nose, skin, and wings of some bats, which live in and around caves and mines. It affects the cycle of hibernation and is responsible for the deaths of large numbers of bats of certain species. In some areas, 80-90% of bats have died. Not all bats in an area are affected, and certain bats that are susceptible in one area are not affected in other areas.

The roles of temperature and humidity in the environment of the bats are two of the many factors being investigated to help control the disease. Over the past few years, the Conserve Wildlife Foundation of New Jersey conducted summer bat counts of two bat species at 22 different sites, totaled the number, and reported the results. The approximate numbers of bats counted (to the nearest hundred) are listed in the table below.

Summer Bat Count (Total Number of Bats)

Year	Big Brown Bats (*Eptesicus fuscus*)	Little Brown Bats (*Myotis lucifugus*)
2009	900	6100
2010	1000	1700
2011	1000	500
2012	1000	400
2013	1300	300

Directions (44–46): Using the information in the data table, construct a line graph on the grid on the next page, following the directions below.

44 Mark an appropriate scale, without any breaks in the data, on the axis labeled "Number of Bats." [1]

45 Plot the data for big brown bats on the grid, connect the points, and surround each point with a small circle. [1]

Example:

46 Plot the data for little brown bats on the grid, connect the points, and surround each point with a small triangle. [1]

Example:

August '19 Regents Examination

Summer Brown Bat Count

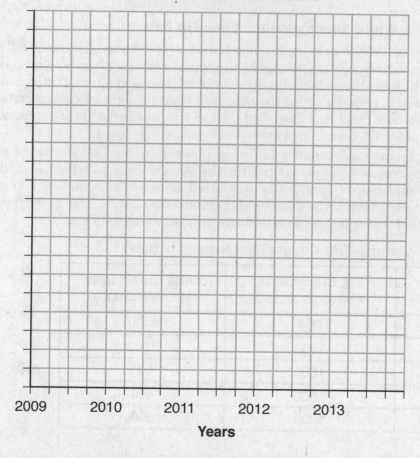

Key
⊙ =Big brown bats
△ =Little brown bats

(graph axes: Number of Bats vs. Years, 2009–2013)

Note: The answer to question 47 should be recorded on your separate answer sheet.

47 Biologists in New York and Vermont have noted that, in recent years, a higher percentage of the little brown bats are now surviving. Which statement best explains this increased survival rate?

(1) A few of the bats possessed an immunity to the WNS disease and produced offspring that were immune.
(2) The bats needed to reproduce in greater numbers, otherwise they would have died out completely.
(3) The people that performed the recent counts did not identify the bats correctly and were counting bats of a different species.
(4) The original decline in the bat population due to WNS was a natural occurrence and is part of a natural cycle.

48 Conservation groups have promoted the building and placing of bat houses in areas thought to be most suitable for bat populations. Explain why this might have a positive effect on the control of WNS in bats. [1]

_____

_____

_____

Note: The answer to question 49 should be recorded on your separate answer sheet.

49 In the coastal waters off western North America, there is a starfish species that feeds primarily on mussels, another marine organism. In an experimental area, the starfish were removed from the waters. The effect of this removal is shown in the graph below.

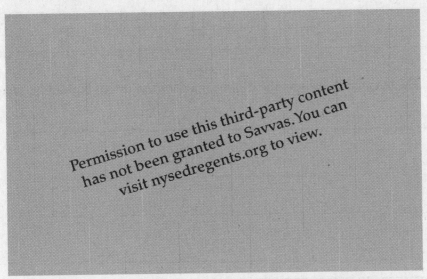

What conclusion can be made regarding the role of the starfish in this ecosystem?

(1) The biodiversity of this ecosystem increased within ten years as organisms adjusted to the loss of the starfish.
(2) The starfish is important in maintaining the biodiversity of this ecosystem.
(3) When the starfish were removed, the ecosystem decreased in stability and increased in biodiversity.
(4) Biodiversity in this ecosystem is not dependent on the presence of starfish.

Base your answers to questions 50 through 52 on the information below and on your knowledge of biology.

Biomass Energy

Biomass is the term for all living, or recently living, materials coming from plants and animals that can be used as a source of energy. Biomass can be burned to produce heat and used to make electricity. The most common materials used for biomass energy are wood, plants, decaying materials, and wastes, including garbage and food waste. Burning the wood and plant matter does produce some air pollutants. Biomass contains energy that originally came from the Sun. Some biomass can be converted into liquid biofuels. These biofuels can be used to power cars and machinery.

Note: The answer to question 50 should be recorded on your separate answer sheet.

50 In a community, before biomass is widely used as an energy source, several experts, including an ecologist, are hired to provide specific information. The ecologist would most likely be asked about

(1) the cost of producing the fuel compared with the profit when the fuel is sold
(2) whether the fuel will be widely accepted by consumers
(3) what effect the production of the fuel will have on the environment
(4) the time it will take to produce large amounts of the fuel

August '19 Regents Examination

51 Explain why biomass is considered a renewable energy source. [1]

_____

_____

_____

52 State *one* specific advantage and *one* specific disadvantage of the use of biofuels as an energy source. [1]

Advantage: _____

_____

Disadvantage: _____

_____

Base your answers to questions 53 and 54 on the information below and on your knowledge of biology.

Photosynthesis is a process that is important to the survival of many organisms on Earth.

53 Identify *two* raw materials necessary for photosynthesis. [1]

_____ and _____

54 State *one* reason why photosynthesis is necessary for animals to survive. [1]

_____

_____

55 The diagram below represents a pond ecosystem.

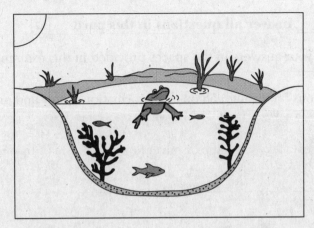

Identify *one* abiotic factor present in the pond ecosystem and explain how this abiotic factor would affect the frogs in the pond. [1]

Abiotic factor: _____

_____

_____

_____

Part C

Answer all questions in this part. [17]

Directions (56–72): Record your answers in the spaces provided in this examination booklet.

Base your answers to questions 56 through 58 on the information below and on your knowledge of biology.

Permission to use this third-party content has not been granted to Savvas. You can visit nysedregents.org to view.

56 State how the TR4 fungus threatens homeostasis within the banana plant. [1]

_____

_____

57 Explain why the entire Cavendish banana crop worldwide is particularly vulnerable to the TR4 fungus. [1]

_____

_____

58 If the fungus cannot be stopped by chemical treatment of the soil, describe *one* other possible way that the growers may be able to combat the disease. [1]

_____

_____

Base your answers to questions 59 through 61 on the passage below and on your knowledge of biology.

Lead Poisoning

Two pathways by which lead can enter the human body are ingestion and inhalation. Once in the bloodstream, lead is distributed to parts of the body including the brain, bones, and teeth.

One reason that lead is toxic is that it interferes with the functioning of a variety of enzymes. It acts like metals such as calcium and iron and replaces them, changing the molecular structure of these enzymes. In the case of calcium, lead is absorbed through the same cell membrane channels that take in calcium.

Lead affects children and adults in different ways. Even low lead levels in children can cause many different problems, including nervous system damage, learning disabilities, decreased intelligence, poor bone growth, and death. In adults, high levels of lead can cause hearing problems, memory and concentration problems, muscle and joint pain, brain damage, and death. It wasn't until 1971 that steps were taken against the use of lead with the passage of the Lead Poisoning Prevention Act. However, lead is still a public health risk today.

59 It is recommended that children eat foods high in calcium and iron as a way to reduce the accumulation of lead in their cells and enzymes. Explain why this is a scientifically valid recommendation. [1]

_____

_____

60 Describe how the presence of lead in body cells could interfere with the ability of enzymes to function. [1]

_____

_____

_____

61 Based on the parts of the body that are most affected by lead intake, identify *one* type of cell that would be expected to have numerous calcium channels. Support your answer. [1]

Type of cell: _____

Support: _____

_____

_____

Base your answers to questions 62 and 63 on the illustration and passage below and on your knowledge of biology.

The Telltale DNA of Manx Cats

Source: http://commons.wikimedia.org/wiki/File:Manx cat (stylizes) 1885.jpg

A few breeds of cat have no tails. Manx cats have extremely short tails and may even appear to have no tail at all. Manx cats were first discovered several hundred years ago.

Scientists have determined that a certain mutation in a group of genes (called T-box genes) interferes with the development of the spine in the cat embryo. Mutations in these T-box genes can cause abnormalities in the number, shape, and/or size of bones in the spines of Manx cats, which results in smaller spines and shorter tails.

If a Manx cat inherits one copy of the mutated T-box gene and one copy of the normal gene, it will have a very short tail or no tail at all.

If the cat embryo inherits two copies of these mutated genes, it will stop developing and die. Therefore, all surviving Manx cats have only one copy of the mutated gene.

62 State *one* reason why the mutation in Manx cat embryos causes them to have such very short tails. [1]

_____

_____

63 Two Manx cats have several litters of offspring. Explain how the genes that the kittens inherit determine whether they will have a normal tail or a short tail. [1]

_____

_____

_____

Base your answer to question 64–66 on the passage below and on your knowledge of biology.

Hummingbirds Are Sugar Junkies

Source: http://bug-bird.com/hummingbirds-large-images/

Most humans enjoy candy, cake, and ice cream. As a result of evolutionary history, we have a wide variety of tastes. This is not true of all animals. Cats do not seek sweets. Over the course of their evolutionary history, the cat family tree lost a gene to detect sweet flavors. Most birds also lack this gene, with a few exceptions. Hummingbirds are sugar junkies.

Hummingbirds evolved from an insect-eating ancestor. The genes that detect the savory flavor of insects underwent changes, making hummingbirds more sensitive to sugars. These new sweet-sensing genes give hummingbirds a preference for high-calorie flower nectar. Hummingbirds actually reject certain flowers whose nectar is not sweet enough!

64–66 Discuss how sweet sensitivity in hummingbirds has developed. In your answer, be sure to:

- identify the initial event responsible for the new sweet-sensing gene [1]
- explain how the presence of the sweet-sensing gene increased in the hummingbird population over time [1]
- describe how the fossil record of hummingbird ancestors might be used to learn more about the evolution of food preferences in hummingbirds [1]

_____

_____

_____

_____

_____

_____

_____

_____

_____

Base your answers to questions 67 through 70 on the information below and on your knowledge of biology.

Folic acid is a type of vitamin that is essential for the normal growth and development of cells in the body. If a woman consumes folic acid in her diet before and during the earliest stages of pregnancy, it can help to reduce her baby's risk for developing a type of birth defect called a neural tube defect. Early in pregnancy, the neural tube forms the brain and spinal cord. If the neural tube does not form properly, serious birth defects may result.

67 Explain why taking folic acid early in pregnancy is important to the prevention of neural tube defects. [1]

_____

_____

_____

68 Describe how a fetus receives folic acid and other essential materials directly from its mother for its development. [1]

_____

_____

69 Identify *one* factor, other than a lack of folic acid, that may interfere with the proper development of essential organs during pregnancy. [1]

_____

_____

70 Many foods, such as breads, cereals, pastas, and rice, are fortified or enriched with folic acid. Explain why adding folic acid to foods is an advantage to people other than pregnant women. [1]

_____

_____

_____

Base your answers to questions 71 and 72 on the diagram below and on your knowledge of biology. The diagram represents an evolutionary tree.

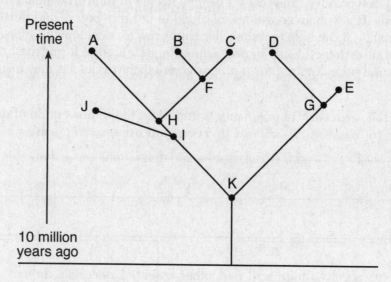

71 Are species *A* and *B* more closely related than *A* and *D*? Circle yes *or* no and support your answer with information from the diagram. [1]

Circle one: Yes   *or*   No

_____

_____

72 State *one* possible cause for the extinction of species *E*. [1]

_____

_____

Part D

Answer all questions in this part. [13]

Directions (73–85): For those questions that are multiple choice, record on the separate answer sheet the *number* of the choice that, of those given, best completes each statement or answers each question. For all other questions in this part, follow the directions given and record your answers in the spaces provided in this examination booklet.

Note: The answer to question 73 should be recorded on your separate answer sheet.

Base your answer to question 73 on the information and diagram below and on your knowledge of biology.

During the *Relationships and Biodiversity* lab, simulated pigments from three plant species were compared to those in *Botana curus*. The results were similar to those represented below.

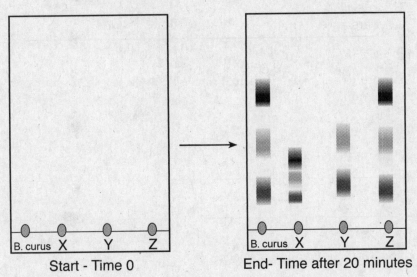

73 Based on the results of this comparison alone, is there enough information to conclude which of the other three species is most closely related to *Botana curus*?

(1) Yes. Only species *X* has the same bands as *Botana curus*.
(2) Yes. Species Z has only two of the bands that *Botana curus* has.
(3) No. Additional tests should be done to test for other chemical similarities.
(4) No. Other rainforest plant species should be tested.

August '19 Regents Examination

Note: The answer to question 74 should be recorded on your separate answer sheet.

Base your answer to question 74 on the diagram below and on your knowledge of biology.

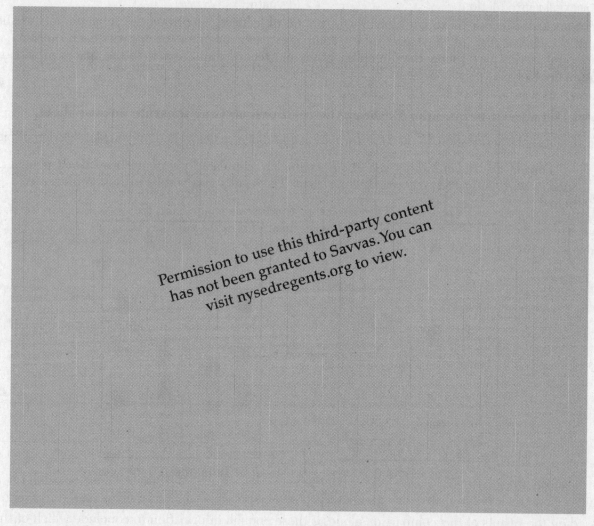

74 Insects can get diseases just like other organisms. A deadly bacteria infected the insects on one Galapagos Island. Among the birds living there, the finches most likely to experience a drastic *decrease* in population size would be the

(1) warbler finches

(2) cactus finches

(3) large ground finches

(4) medium ground finches

Note: The answer to question 75 should be recorded on your separate answer sheet.

75 A variety of species of Galapagos finches evolved from one original species long ago through the process of
(1) asexual reproduction
(2) ecological succession
(3) natural selection
(4) selective breeding

Note: The answer to question 76 should be recorded on your separate answer sheet.

76 If scientists want to determine the similarities in the DNA fragments in several plant species, they should
(1) add salt water to cells from each plant
(2) analyze electrophoresis results
(3) compare seed structures of the plants
(4) examine their chromosomes with a microscope

77 One coach of an Olympic rowing team makes his athletes warm up by doing 30 minutes of stretching and jogging in place before practicing each day. Another coach suggests that resting before practicing will result in better performance by her team. They decide to conduct an experiment to see which practice is correct. One team rests before practice, the other team warms up for thirty minutes, and they then record the time that it takes each team to row a specific distance. Identify the dependent variable in this experiment. [1]

_____

_____

78 A student squeezes a clothespin 82 times in a minute. Then, using the same hand and the same clothespin, he squeezes the clothespin 68 times in a minute. State *one* biological reason for the decrease in the number of squeezes during the second trial. [1]

_____

_____

79 During rest, an adult's heart rate averages 60-100 beats per minute. When exercising, an adult's heart rate may increase to 100-170 beats per minute. State *one* reason why the heart rate increased during exercise. [1]

_____

_____

80 In some single-celled protozoans living in fresh water, such as the paramecium, contractile vacuoles are organelles used to pump excess water out of the cell. Explain why a paramecium would require contractile vacuoles while a similar protozoan living in salt water would *not*. [1]

_____

_____

_____

Base your answers to questions 81 through 83 on the information and diagram below and on your knowledge of biology.

A cube cut from a potato is placed in a beaker of distilled water. The potato cells have a relatively high concentration of starch and a relatively low concentration of water. The diagram represents the water and starch molecules in and around one of the potato cells in contact with the water in the beaker.

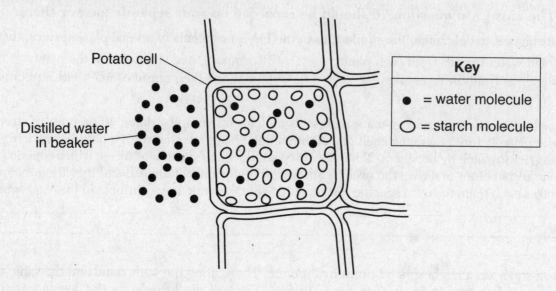

Note: The answer to question 81 should be recorded on your separate answer sheet.

81 Which row in the chart correctly describes what would be expected to occur in the potato cells, with regard to both the starch and water molecules?

Row	Water	Starch
(1)	More water will move into the cell than will leave the cell.	Starch will remain inside the potato cell.
(2)	More water will leave the cell than will enter.	Starch will move out of the cell.
(3)	Water content of the cell will not change.	Starch will move out of the cell.
(4)	More water will leave the cell than will enter.	Starch will remain inside the potato cell.

Note: The answer to question 82 should be recorded on your separate answer sheet.

82 Which statement correctly describes a possible result if starch indicator is added to the water in the beaker one hour after the potato cube was added?

(1) The indicator solution would turn to an amber color in the water if starch molecules were present in the water in the beaker.

(2) The indicator would remain amber in color if starch molecules were not present in the water in the beaker.

(3) The indicator would change to a black color if starch molecules were not present in the water in the beaker.

(4) The indicator solution would remain black in color if starch molecules were present in the water in the beaker.

83 Before placing the potato in the beaker, the student used an electronic balance to determine the mass of the potato cube. The mass of the cube was determined again after it was in the beaker for an hour. Describe how this information could specifically be used to determine if water moved during the investigation. [1]

_____

_____

_____

84 Select *one* row in the chart below and explain how the systems in that row work together during exercise. [1]

	System	System	System
Row 1	Respiratory	Circulatory	Muscular
Row 2	Muscular	Circulatory	Excretory
Row 3	Digestive	Circulatory	Muscular

Row: _____

_____

_____

_____

Base your answer to question 85 on the information below and on your knowledge of biology.

In an experiment, a membrane bag containing 95% water and 5% salt was placed in a beaker containing 80% water and 20% salt, as shown below. The setup was put aside until the next day.

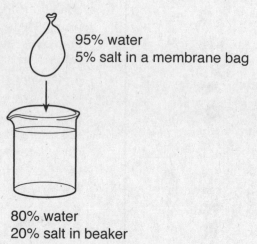

95% water
5% salt in a membrane bag

80% water
20% salt in beaker

85 Based on the information given, state *one* way the bag or its contents will have changed by the next day. Support your answer with an explanation. [1]

_____

_____

_____

August '19   Regents Examination

Part A

Answer all questions in this part. [30]

Directions (1–30): For *each* statement or question, record on the separate answer sheet the *number* of the word or expression that, of those given, best completes the statement or answers the question.

1 Which activity is an example of a decomposer recycling organic compounds back into the environment?
(1) A tree synthesizes starch from simpler molecules.
(2) A bacterial cell performs photosynthesis.
(3) A bird digests proteins from its food.
(4) A fungus breaks down the body of a dead animal.

2 Itching and other skin problems are signs that a cat or dog may have fleas. Fleas are parasites known for their biting and blood-sucking abilities. When they bite, flea saliva enters the pet's circulatory system, sometimes causing an allergic response commonly seen as a "hot spot" on the pet's neck or the base of its tail.

These observations are best explained by the fact that
(1) flea saliva may stimulate an immune response in cats and dogs
(2) fleas are microbes whose bites cause a decreased blood flow
(3) flea saliva is a toxic substance that is released when fleas prey on cats and dogs
(4) fleas are host organisms whose saliva digests cat and dog fur, leaving "hot spots"

3 A German measles (rubella) epidemic during the years 1963 to 1965 resulted in approximately 30,000 babies being born with birth defects. The specific cause of these birth defects was most likely
(1) the development of rubella virus infections in embryos
(2) the failure of zygotes infected with rubella to develop
(3) mutations in the nerve cells of pregnant females at the time of the rubella epidemic
(4) an increase in the amount of time needed for healthy embryonic development

4 Placenta previa is a medical condition that occurs in some pregnant women. Women with this condition are often placed on bed rest, which prohibits them from any strenuous activity that may cause the blood vessels in the placenta to rupture. If not diagnosed, placenta previa can be a very dangerous condition because the placenta is
(1) the primary source of oxygen for the mother
(2) where the fetus obtains milk from the mother
(3) where nutrients and wastes are exchanged
(4) the primary source of estrogen and progesterone in the mother

5 Over time, a tree that once had a total mass of 300 g increased in mass to 3000 kg. This increase in mass comes mostly from
(1) carbon dioxide that enters through the leaf openings
(2) oxygen that enters through the leaf openings
(3) soil that all plants need to grow
(4) chloroplasts that enter the roots and move to the leaves

6 Recently, a type of genetically modified fish has been approved for sale for human consumption. The modified fish contain a growth hormone gene from a different fish species. As a result, the modified fish grow rapidly and are ready to sell in almost half the time it normally would take. The modified fish are able to produce the new growth hormone because

(1) each of their cells contains the new gene to produce growth hormone
(2) each gene contains the code to synthesize carbohydrates
(3) the altered gene directs the mitochondria to synthesize the hormone
(4) the modified body cells are able to reproduce by meiosis

7 Melanoma is a type of skin cancer that can spread to vital organs in the body. Doctors believe that exposure to ultraviolet (UV) radiation from the Sun is a leading cause of melanoma. One practical way governments can help prevent the harmful effects of UV radiation is to

(1) require everyone to remain indoors during daylight hours
(2) regulate the production and release of gases that damage the ozone shield
(3) encourage the building of a greater number of cancer treatment centers
(4) prohibit the use of solar panels on homes and businesses

8 Some birds have recently modified their migratory behavior. Instead of flying to warmer climates during the winter months, the birds are remaining in northern areas where they can consume discarded food that is abundant in landfills. As a result of this change in migratory behavior, many insect populations that the birds normally feed on in the warmer climate areas are now increasing. This is an example of human activity

(1) interfering with ecological succession
(2) increasing competition for infinite resources
(3) disrupting the homeostasis of organisms
(4) altering the equilibrium of ecosystems

9 New York State charges consumers a fee when purchasing beverages sold in aluminum cans and plastic bottles. This money is returned to purchasers when they return these items for recycling. Programs such as these are an attempt to

(1) encourage people to spend more money on their beverages
(2) conserve the resources these containers are made from
(3) reduce the amount of carbon dioxide produced by deforestation
(4) totally eliminate the use of reusable containers

10 Recently, a human trachea (a respiratory organ) was produced by using a patient's own stem cells. The benefit of using the patient's own cells to produce a trachea instead of receiving one from a donor is that

(1) there will be more enzymes produced to help maintain homeostasis in the trachea
(2) there will be an increase in the quantity of antibodies that the patient produces in response to the new trachea
(3) there is less of a chance that the patient's immune system will attack the trachea
(4) there will be a greater response to any infectious agent that may enter the body

11 The diagram below represents the organization of structures within an organism.

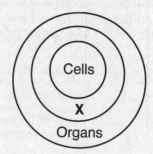

Which term best indicates the structures represented by the circle labeled X?

(1) organelles   (3) organ systems
(2) chromosomes   (4) tissues

12 The chart below shows a comparison of the blood sugar levels for two individuals who took part in a scientific study.

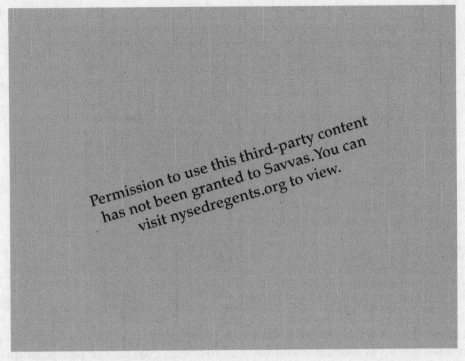

Scientists have observed that blood sugar levels rose by different amounts in the two individuals even though they were given identical portions of bananas and cookies. These results were obtained because

(1) glucose is too large a molecule to be absorbed into the blood, so the researchers were only measuring the amount of glucose already present

(2) participant 445 didn't like bananas, and his body absorbed more of the food that he likes

(3) individuals have genetic differences that alter their responses to environmental factors

(4) two different foods were used; the scientists should have had only one experimental variable

13 Which row in the chart below correctly matches the human activity with its effect?

Row	Human Activity	Effect
(1)	planting 20 acres of one crop	increases biodiversity
(2)	industrialization	decreases fossil fuel use
(3)	habitat destruction	decreases ecosystem stability
(4)	use of finite resources	increases resource renewal

14 Potatoes are an example of a crop that can be reproduced asexually. One potato will produce a number of "eyes," which are sprouts that can grow into new plants. A potato with four eyes can be cut into four pieces, and each piece can be used to produce an individual potato plant.

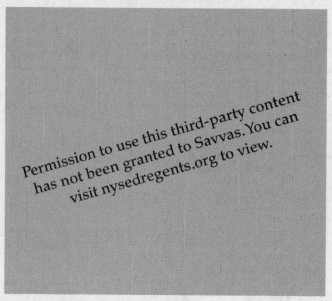

A gardener could produce a small crop of potatoes by planting the eyes from a single potato in her garden. Some of the potatoes grown in this way could be used to obtain eyes for the next season's crop.

One likely *disadvantage* of growing potatoes cloned in this way, year after year, would be that

(1) after a few years, the potatoes would stop producing eyes altogether, so no potatoes could be grown in the garden

(2) the potatoes produced each succeeding year would get larger and larger, eventually being too big for use as food

(3) the cost for growing your own potatoes in the garden would be greatly reduced

(4) a potato plant could become infected with a disease, and it could easily spread to the entire crop, killing all of the plants

June '19 Regents Examination

15 The back of the Namib Desert darkling beetle, shown in the photograph below, is covered in little bumps that collect water from the air. When it tilts forward, the water runs off its back into its mouth.

Source: http://myinforms.com

These specialized structures on the beetle's back allow it to

(1) locate food within the harsh desert environment
(2) obtain a substance that is required for survival
(3) reproduce asexually if mates are not available in the area
(4) increase the chances of survival by producing organic raw materials

16 An increase in human population puts a stress on resources that can be renewed, such as

(1) trees and coal   (3) oil and natural gas
(2) water and gasoline (4) water and trees

17 Mitochondria provide ribosomes with

(1) ATP for protein synthesis
(2) amino acids for protein synthesis
(3) oxygen for respiration
(4) carbon dioxide for the production of sugars

18 Mutations are most directly caused by changes in the

(1) cell organelles of tissues
(2) genes of chromosomes
(3) ribosomes in gametes
(4) receptors on membranes

19 Animals and green plants are similar in that they

(1) both carry out heterotrophic nutrition
(2) all produce offspring by asexual reproduction
(3) both use DNA to transmit hereditary information to offspring
(4) all require oxygen to carry out photosynthesis

20 Two organisms of different species are *not* likely to compete for the same

(1) food   (3) space
(2) mate   (4) water

21 Some salmon have been genetically modified to grow bigger and faster than wild salmon. They are grown in fish-farming facilities. These genetically modified fish should *not* be introduced into a natural habitat because

(1) the salmon would recycle nutrients at a rapid rate
(2) their rapid growth rate could cause them to outcompete native salmon
(3) they would not have enough oxygen for survival
(4) they would reproduce asexually once they were released

22 The diagram below represents a portion of a cell membrane.

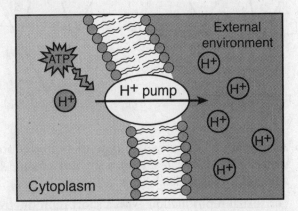

The arrow indicates that the cell membrane is carrying out the process of

(1) respiration   (3) diffusion
(2) cell recognition   (4) active transport

23 The expression of a trait is directly dependent on the

(1) arrangement of amino acids in the protein synthesized
(2) shape of the subunits in the DNA molecule
(3) number of chromosomes present in the nucleus
(4) sequence of bases coded for by the ribosome

24 Global warming is most closely associated with

(1) increased use of solar panels
(2) increased industrialization
(3) reducing the rate of species extinction
(4) removal of environmental wastes

25 Which diagram below indicates that species *D* is more closely related to *C* than it is to either *A* or *B*?

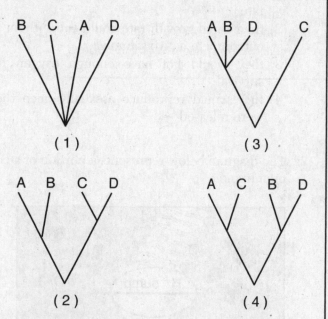

(1)

(3)

(2)

(4)

26 As climate changes, which type of reproduction would most likely result in a greater chance of survival for a species?

(1) sexual reproduction, with a short reproductive cycle
(2) sexual reproduction, with a long reproductive cycle
(3) asexual reproduction, with a short reproductive cycle
(4) asexual reproduction, with a long reproductive cycle

27 Adults of the *Aedes* mosquito genus are responsible for transmitting the viral diseases Zika and Dengue. Scientists have produced a modified form of male *Aedes* mosquitoes. The offspring of these male mosquitoes die before reaching adulthood. This method of reducing the spread of disease is dependent on

(1) vaccines stimulating the immune system of infected people
(2) providing medication to reduce the symptoms of disease
(3) the use of natural selection to modify the viruses so they are no longer pathogenic
(4) the use of genetic engineering to reduce the population of mosquitoes that carry the virus

28 Humans deplete the most resources when

(1) using wind energy as a power source
(2) generating power by using fossil fuels
(3) using water power to generate electricity
(4) recycling glass and plastics

29 The diagram below does *not* represent a sustainable energy pyramid in an ecosystem because

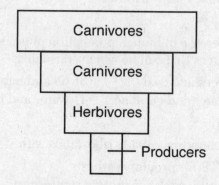

(1) energy is never transferred between levels in ecosystems
(2) ecosystems never have more than three levels of energy transfer
(3) more energy must be available in the producer level than in the consumer levels
(4) producers feed on herbivores in most ecosystems

June '19   Regents Examination

30 The two diagrams below represent a sugar molecule and a fat molecule that are used by living organisms.

Sugar molecule

Fat molecule

Which statement best describes these two molecules?

(1) Sugar molecules are inorganic and fat molecules are organic.
(2) Sugar molecules are organic and fat molecules are inorganic.
(3) Energy for life processes can be stored within the chemical bonds of both molecules.
(4) Energy for life processes can be stored within the chemical bonds of sugar molecules, only.

Part B–1

Answer all questions in this part. [13]

Directions (31–43): For *each* statement or question, record on the separate answer sheet the *number* of the word or expression that, of those given, best completes the statement or answers the question.

31 A scientist analyzed a segment of DNA from a human chromosome and found that the percentage of thymine molecular bases (T) was 35%. Which row in the chart below contains the correct percentages of the other molecular bases in the DNA segment?

Row	Guanine (G)	Cytosine (C)	Adenine (A)
(1)	15%	25%	25%
(2)	25%	25%	15%
(3)	15%	15%	35%
(4)	35%	15%	15%

32 The graph below shows changes in the populations of hares and lynx in a Canadian ecosystem.

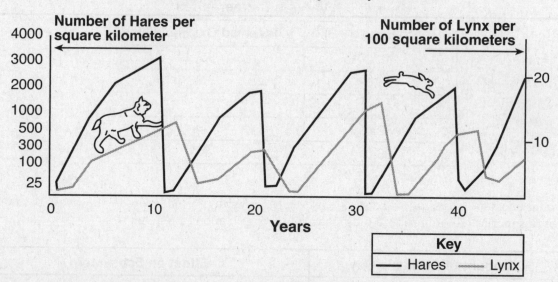

Source: Adapted from http://lbyiene-jardin-wikispaces.com

Which statement about the hares and lynx can be supported with information from the graph?

(1) The hare is the predator of the lynx because it is a larger animal.
(2) The lynx population begins to drop after the hare population drops.
(3) Both populations go through cycles due to the succession of plant species.
(4) Both populations have a carrying capacity of 3000 per square kilometer.

33 The diagram below represents a cell in the human body.

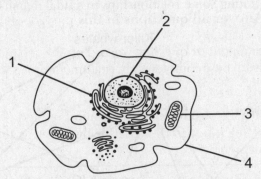

Which statement concerning the structures within this cell is accurate?

(1) Structure 1 is a chloroplast that carries out photosynthesis.
(2) Structure 2 is a vacuole that contains DNA.
(3) Structure 3 is a mitochondrion, where respiration takes place.
(4) Structure 4 is the cell membrane, which provides rigid support for the cell.

Base your answers to questions 34 and 35 on the data table below and on your knowledge of biology. The table below indicates the amount of oxygen present at various water temperatures in a pond.

Amount of Available Oxygen in Water at Various Temperatures

Temperature (°F)	Dissolved Oxygen (ppm)
68.0	9.2
71.6	8.8
78.8	8.2
82.4	7.9
86.0	7.6

34 An aquatic ecosystem experiences an increase in temperature. Which row in the chart below shows the effect of this increased temperature on the available oxygen and ecosystem?

Row	Amount of Available Oxygen	Effect on Ecosystem
(1)	decreases	greater stability of the ecosystem
(2)	increases	lessens competition between predatory organisms
(3)	decreases	reduces carrying capacity for fish
(4)	increases	increases genetic mutations in bacteria

35 Which process performed by organisms produces oxygen for the aquatic ecosystem?

(1) respiration
(2) replication
(3) active transport
(4) autotrophic nutrition

Base your answers to questions 36 and 37 on the diagram below and on your knowledge of biology. The diagram represents a food web illustrating some relationships in a tidal marsh ecosystem.

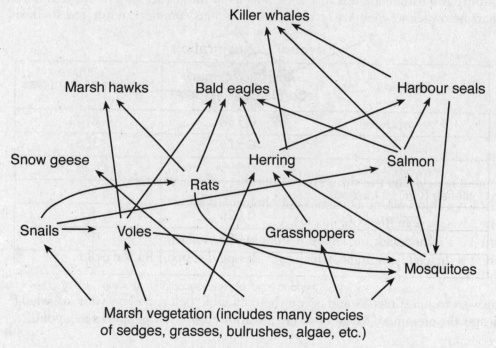

Adapted from: http://www.physicalgeography.net/fundamental/9o.html

36 Examples of autotrophs in this food web are
(1) killer whales and grasses
(2) sedges and bulrushes
(3) mosquitoes and grasshoppers
(4) snails and seals

37 In addition to grasshoppers, herring may also get energy from
(1) algae
(2) bald eagles
(3) snails
(4) voles

Base your answers to questions 38 and 39 on the information below and on your knowledge of biology.

Mercury is a toxic chemical that accumulates in the tissues of animals in a food chain. The chart below shows mercury levels found in various commercial fish and shellfish.

Mercury Concentration

Species	Average Mercury Concentration (ppm)	Number of Samples
king mackerel	0.730	213
shark	0.979	356
swordfish	0.995	636
tilefish (Gulf of Mexico)	1.450	60
catfish	0.025	57
haddock	0.055	50
lobster (spiny)	0.093	13

Source: www.fda.gov/food/foodborneillnesscontaminants/metals/ucm115644.html

38 Each species listed is a predator. If the prey organisms that each predator consumes were tested, they would most likely contain

(1) the same amount of mercury as the predator species
(2) less mercury than the predator species
(3) more mercury than the predator species
(4) no mercury, since the predators probably get it from the polluted water

39 Which statement is best supported by the data in the chart?

(1) Any fish caught in the Gulf of Mexico would have low levels of mercury.
(2) Eating catfish or haddock would be most likely to cause deadly mercury poisoning.
(3) Spiny lobsters may have more or less mercury than indicated because only a few were sampled.
(4) Tilefish are the most nutritious of all the species listed.

---

40 The diagram below represents a laboratory process.

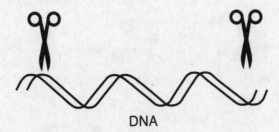

DNA

The substance represented by the scissors shown cutting the DNA is

(1) an enzyme
(2) a starch molecule
(3) a carbohydrate
(4) a fat molecule

41 The human body has many cells that are deep inside the body. For this reason, the human body requires
   (1) a transport system and other organs
   (2) carbon dioxide from the air
   (3) the synthesis of many inorganic compounds
   (4) the breakdown of glucose by the digestive system

Base your answers to questions 42 and 43 on the information below and on your knowledge of biology.

Bird Flu

Researchers are not sure when the H7N9 virus, referred to as bird flu, hit the China poultry markets. In February of 2012, the virus was found to have spread from birds to humans. All cases resulted from direct contact with infected poultry.

The bird flu can cause severe respiratory illness in humans. Since flu viruses constantly mutate, it would be difficult to develop a vaccine ahead of time. Scientists are worried that the virus could spread easily among people, causing a worldwide outbreak of the disease.

42 Based on the information, one danger of the new Bird Flu H7N9 strain is that it
   (1) causes death in over 75% of the individuals who become infected
   (2) is transferred to humans through consuming cooked poultry
   (3) can spread from humans to birds, such as crows and pigeons
   (4) mutates rapidly, making it hard to produce an effective vaccine

43 The fact that the H7N9 virus has only recently infected humans helps explain why
   (1) it is highly transmissible through both the air and water
   (2) it is found only in the U.S.
   (3) humans have little or no immunity to the virus
   (4) the human population has formed antibodies against the virus

Part B–2

Answer all questions in this part. [12]

Directions (44–55): For those questions that are multiple choice, record on the separate answer sheet the *number* of the choice that, of those given, best completes each statement or answers each question. For all other questions in this part, follow the directions given and record your answers in the spaces provided in this examination booklet.

Base your answers to questions 44 through 47 on the information below and on your knowledge of biology.

As part of an experiment, a bacterial culture was grown in a lab for two days. No additional nutrients were added to the culture after the initial set-up. As the bacteria reproduced asexually, the population of the culture was measured every six hours. Some of the data related to the bacterial growth are shown in the data table below.

Bacterial Growth

Time (hrs)	Population (millions)
0	2.0
6	4.5
18	16.0
30	28.0
48	37.0

Directions (44–45): Using the information in the data table, construct a line graph on the grid below, following the directions below.

44 Mark an appropriate scale, without any breaks in the data, on each labeled axis. [1]

45 Plot the data on the grid provided. Connect the points and surround each point with a small circle. [1]

Example: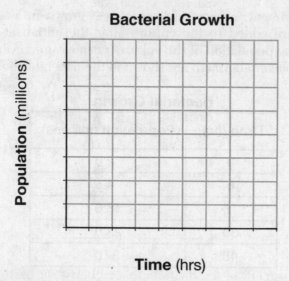

Bacterial Growth

Population (millions)

Time (hrs)

46 If data for the growth of this bacterial population continued to be recorded, would the data point at 60 hours be above or below 37 million? Support your answer. [1]

_____

_____

Note: The answer to question 47 should be recorded on your separate answer sheet.

47 One likely reason bacteria would be grown in laboratory cultures would be to
   (1) increase the number of antibiotics produced by human cells
   (2) eliminate the cloning of cells that can fight disease
   (3) increase the production of specialized proteins by using genetic engineering
   (4) decrease the amount of bacteria naturally present in organisms

Base your answers to questions 48 and 49 on the information and diagram below and on your knowledge of biology. The diagram represents a biological process.

Fossil evidence has demonstrated that birds evolved from a group of small carnivorous dinosaurs. Scientists have hypothesized that some evolved into birds as they filled available niches.

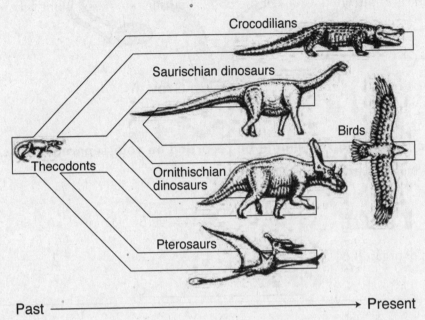

Past ———————————————→ Present

48 Identify *two* groups of organisms from the diagram that still exist on Earth today. Describe how they may have been able to survive to the present. [1]

Organisms: _____ and _____

_____

_____

_____

Note: The answer to question 49 should be recorded on your separate answer sheet.

49 The most recent fossil discoveries have filled in many of the gaps in the evolution of birds from dinosaurs. Before the latest fossils were found, there were some scientists who questioned this idea that birds evolved from dinosaurs. In general, scientists constantly work to

(1) clarify scientific explanations so they can be made into a law that never changes
(2) develop theories based on the data and evidence from a few experiments with inconclusive results
(3) provide enough evidence and accurate predictions to allow for widespread acceptance
(4) develop explanations that are permanent and do not change over time

June '19 Regents Examination

Base your answers to questions 50 through 52 on the diagram below and on your knowledge of biology. The diagram indicates some parts of the human female reproductive system.

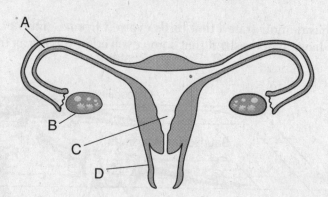

Note: The answer to question 50 should be recorded on your separate answer sheet.

50 The structure in which fertilization normally takes place is

(1) A

(2) B

(3) C

(4) D

51 State *one* function of organ B. [1]

_____

52 State *one* advantage of internal development for the human embryo. [1]

_____

_____

_____

_____

June '19 Regents Examination

Base your answers to questions 53 through 55 on the information below and on your knowledge of biology. The diagram represents an ecological process that occurs in New York State over a long period of time.

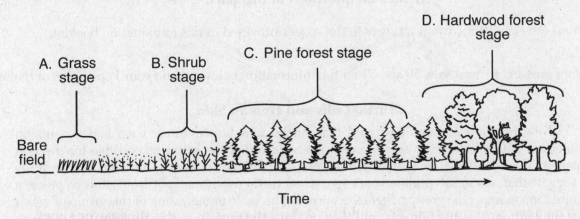

53 Identify the ecological process that is represented from stage A through stage D, and explain why each stage is important to the stage that follows it. [1]

Process: _____

_____

_____

54 Identify *two* abiotic factors that can determine which types of organisms can inhabit an ecosystem. [1]

_____ and _____

55 Identify the short-term effect that a forest fire during stage D would have on the biodiversity of the area. [1]

_____

_____

Part C

Answer all questions in this part. [17]

Directions (56–72): Record your answers in the spaces provided in this examination booklet.

Base your answers to questions 56 and 57 on the information below and on your knowledge of biology.

Turtle Cells and Human Skin

New research has demonstrated that turtles and humans may have had a common ancestor 310 million years ago. A recent study looked at the genes responsible for the skin layers of turtle shells compared to the genes for human skin. The findings of the study suggest that about 250 million years ago, when turtle evolution split from other reptiles, a mutation in a specific group of genes occurred. The basic organization of this group of genes is similar in turtles and humans, and they produce the important skin proteins that produce shells in turtles and protect against infection in the skin of humans.

56 Identify the molecule that contains the hereditary material and the organelle in which it is found in turtle cells. [1]

Molecule: _____

Organelle in turtle cells: _____

57 Describe how the mutation in the genes of a turtle ancestor turned out to be a beneficial evolutionary adaptation. [1]

_____

_____

_____

Base your answers to questions 58 through 60 on the illustration and information below and on your knowledge of biology.

The Little Brown Bat

Source: http://knatolee.blogspot.com/2011/09/not-ducklings.html

The illustration is of a species commonly called the little brown bat. It has 38 teeth and usually lives near bodies of water. The animal is considered beneficial by many people because it eats mosquitoes and many types of garden pests. They feed at night, detecting their prey by echolocation—a form of sonar similar to what is used on ships. They can determine the location and size of their prey by listening to the return echo.

58 The little brown bat eats mainly mosquitoes and night-flying insects. State *one* way in which the animal is adapted to prey on these organisms. [1]

_____

_____

_____

59 If a mutation occurs in some of these bats, it may result in a new inheritable trait that makes them better able to catch insects than other bats in the population. Describe what will most likely happen to the frequency of the *original* trait in the population. Support your answer. [1]

_____

_____

_____

60 Coevolution occurs when the evolution of an adaptation by one species affects the evolution of an adaptation in a second species. Some species of moths have evolved the ability to emit high frequency sounds that can block the little brown bat's echolocation. Based on the information provided, explain how this relationship between moths and bats is an example of coevolution. [1]

_____

_____

_____

_____

Base your answers to questions 61 through 64 on the information below and on your knowledge of biology.

Kaolin as a Spray to Control a Bean Pest

Spraying kaolin, a clay-like material, on the leaves of plants has been effective in reducing insect damage to plants that grow in temperate regions, but has not been tried in tropical areas.

Researchers in the tropical Andean region of South America have recently conducted experiments to see if kaolin can be used there to control the greenhouse whitefly, a significant pest of the region's bean crops.

In the study, four groups of bean plants were used with the following treatments:

Group	Treatment	Whiteflies Killed (%)
1 (control)	No insecticide or other substance applied to the plants	0
2	Synthetic chemical insecticide applied to leaves	90
3	Leaves treated with 2.5% concentration of kaolin spray	80
4*	Leaves treated with 5% concentration of kaolin spray	80

* Note: In group 4 the plants lost 40% less water and showed a 45% increase in chlorophyll content in the leaves.

61 State *one* likely effect of the whiteflies on the bean plants in the control group (group 1) by the end of the study. Support your answer. [1]

_____

_____

62 Should the group 3 kaolin treatments be considered as an acceptable alternative control method to the group 2 insecticide treatment for whiteflies? Support your answer with data from the chart. [1]

_____

_____

63 Based on the results of groups 3 and 4, identify the kaolin treatment that would be best for bean plants grown in areas where low rainfall is a common occurrence. Support your answer. [1]

_____

_____

64 State *one* reason why the scientists are interested in reducing whitefly populations in the Andean region. [1]

_____

_____

_____

June '19 Regents Examination

Base your answers to questions 65 through 68 on the passage below and on your knowledge of biology.

Medical Mystery

Recently, an elderly man went to a hospital. He felt tired and was coughing and dehydrated. At first, the doctor thought he had pneumonia, but an x ray showed a spot on his lung. Because the man was a smoker, the doctor expected to find a tumor.

Instead, the surgeon discovered a pea seed growing inside the man's lung. When the pea seedling was removed, the patient quickly regained his health.

65 When he first arrived at the hospital, the man reported feeling unusually tired. Explain why damage to the man's lung caused fatigue. [1]

_____

_____

66 In this case, the pea seed entered into the man's lung, but the immune system was not able to defend against it. Describe *one* specific way the cells of the immune system usually protect the body against certain molecules or microbes that are breathed into the lungs. [1]

_____

_____

67 Identify *two* environmental factors inside a human lung that would help the pea begin to germinate. [1]

_____

68 State whether the pea seedling could have continued to grow and develop in the lung over a long period of time. Support your answer. [1]

_____

_____

_____

Scientists Reprogram Plants for Drought Tolerance

Source: Lancaster Farming 2/21/15/AAAS

Arabidopsis plants respond to drought conditions by producing a stress hormone called ABA. This hormone slows down plant growth and leads to a decrease in the plant's use of water.

ABA binds to specific receptors in the plant that cause the guard cells on the leaf surfaces to close the stomatal openings through which water vapor can normally pass. This reduces water loss during the drought conditions.

Although it has been suggested that spraying plants with ABA during a drought could be beneficial, it is not practical. The chemical is expensive to produce and quickly loses its ability to bind to cell receptors in the plant cells.

Recently, however, scientists have found a way to modify the ABA receptors in *Arabidopsis* plants so they can be activated by another chemical that is both stable and inexpensive.

69 Describe how the shape of molecules, such as the hormone ABA, is critical to their function in the *Arabidopsis* plant. [1]

_____

_____

_____

70 Explain how the response of the guard cells to a drought is part of a feedback mechanism. [1]

_____

_____

_____

_____

Base your answers to questions 71 and 72 on the passage and graph below and on your knowledge of biology.

Atmospheric Carbon Dioxide

Records from polar ice cores show that the natural range of atmospheric carbon dioxide (CO_2) over the past 800,000 years was 170 to 300 parts per million (ppm) by volume. In the early 20th century, scientists began to suspect that CO_2 in the atmosphere might be increasing beyond this range due to human activities, but there were no clear measurements of this trend. In 1958, Charles David Keeling began measuring atmospheric CO_2 at the Mauna Loa observatory on the big island of Hawaii.

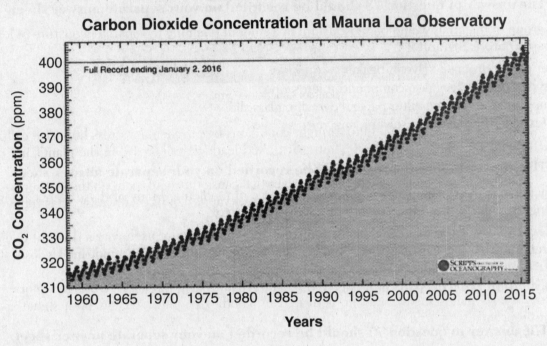

Carbon Dioxide Concentration at Mauna Loa Observatory

71 Record the approximate concentration of carbon dioxide at the start of the study and describe how it compares to the concentration in 2015. [1]

_____ ppm CO_2

Description: _____

_____

72 Identify *one* likely reason for the overall change in CO_2 concentration observed between 1958 and 2015. [1]

_____

_____

_____

Part D

Answer all questions in this part. [13]

Directions (73–85): For those questions that are multiple choice, record on the separate answer sheet the *number* of the choice that, of those given, best completes each statement or answers each question. For all other questions in this part, follow the directions given and record your answers in the spaces provided in this examination booklet.

Note: The answer to question 73 should be recorded on your separate answer sheet.

73 Which group of materials would be most useful to a student planning to separate a mixture of leaf pigments using paper chromatography?

(1) filter paper, dropper, solvent, beaker
(2) enzymes, beaker, goggles, compound microscope
(3) compound microscope, filter paper, coverslip, glass slide
(4) meterstick, thermometer, solvent, enzymes

Note: The answer to question 74 should be recorded on your separate answer sheet.

74 In many parts of the world, plants are used as a source of medicine. Many of these plants are in danger of becoming extinct. It is therefore important for researchers to

(1) collect and dry all the medicinal plants to preserve them for future use
(2) search for other plant species that could be used as a new source of that medicine
(3) use the plants now while we still have them
(4) apply fertilizer to reduce the numbers of the plants that grow in the wild

Note: The answer to question 75 should be recorded on your separate answer sheet.

75 In the lab activity *Making Connections*, an experiment was designed to test the effect of exercise on the ability to squeeze a clothespin. The number of times the clothespin was squeezed served as the

(1) independent variable
(2) dependent variable
(3) hypothesis
(4) control

Base your answer to question 76 on the Universal Genetic Code Chart below and on your knowledge of biology.

Universal Genetic Code Chart

		SECOND BASE			
		U	**C**	**A**	**G**	

FIRST BASE		U	C	A	G	THIRD BASE
U	UUU UUC } PHE / UUA UUG } LEU	UCU UCC UCA UCG } SER	UAU UAC } TYR / UAA UAG } STOP	UGU UGC } CYS / UGA } STOP / UGG } TRP	U C A G
C	CUU CUC CUA CUG } LEU	CCU CCC CCA CCG } PRO	CAU CAC } HIS / CAA CAG } GLN	CGU CGC CGA CGG } ARG	U C A G
A	AUU AUC AUA } ILE / AUG } MET or START	ACU ACC ACA ACG } THR	AAU AAC } ASN / AAA AAG } LYS	AGU AGC } SER / AGA AGG } ARG	U C A G
G	GUU GUC GUA GUG } VAL	GCU GCC GCA GCG } ALA	GAU GAC } ASP / GAA GAG } GLU	GGU GGC GGA GGG } GLY	U C A G

Note: The answer to question 76 should be recorded on your separate answer sheet.

76 When provided with a sequence of bases in one segment of mRNA, the Universal Genetic Code Chart is used to

(1) directly identify the DNA from an animal cell
(2) determine the sequence of amino acids in a protein
(3) change the RNA sequence of a protein into DNA
(4) identify the specific mutations in the genetic material in a cell

---

77 A student was setting up beakers that contained different solutions in order to conduct a laboratory investigation, but the next day he could not tell which beaker contained the starch and water mixture. In order to find out which beaker contained starch, he took a small sample from each of the beakers and conducted a test for starch on each of them.

Describe the test for starch that the student should use and the result that would indicate the presence of starch. [1]

_____

_____

78 In order to survive in its environment, a single-celled organism uses a contractile vacuole to remove excess water that diffuses into its cell. Another species, a hydra, also excretes excess water. Both processes involve the use of energy.

Based on this information, state whether these two organisms live in fresh water or salt water. Support your answer. [1]

_____

_____

79 The diagram below represents two types of carbohydrate molecules, glucose and sucrose.

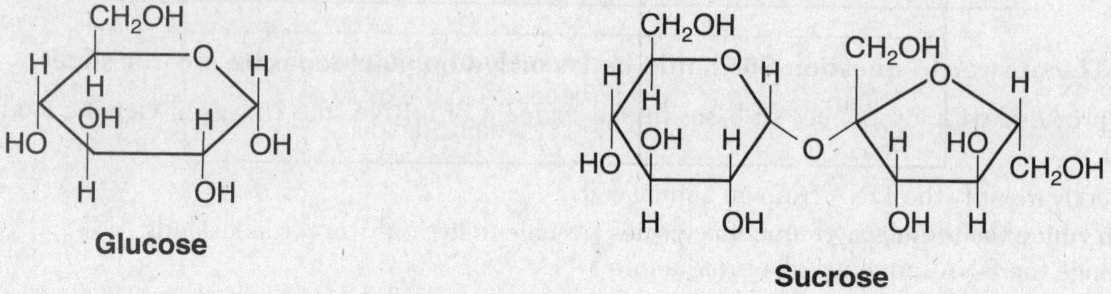

Glucose

Sucrose

State *one* reason why a glucose molecule is more likely than a sucrose molecule to diffuse through an artificial membrane. [1]

_____

Base your answers to questions 80 through 82 on the information below and on your knowledge of biology. The diagram represents some of the various types of giant tortoises that live on the Galapagos Islands. The chart provides information about some individual island environments.

Giant Tortoises of the Galapagos Islands

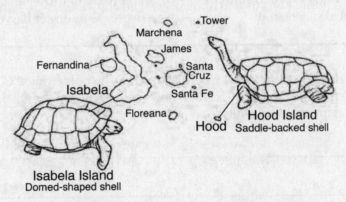

Source: Adapted from http://slideplayer.com/slide/7372273

Environmental Conditions on Certain Galapagos Islands

Galapagos Island	Island Characteristics
Hood Island	sparse vegetation located high off of the ground; hot, dry, arid
Isabela Island	rich variety of vegetation located low to the ground; much rainfall; humid

80 Explain why specific Galapagos tortoise species are able to live only on certain islands. [1]

_____

_____

Note: The answer to question 81 should be recorded on your separate answer sheet.

81 The role that the environment plays in determining which species survive is referred to as

(1) a trade-off

(2) a gene mutation

(3) an ecological niche

(4) a selecting agent

June '19   Regents Examination

Note: The answer to question 82 should be recorded on your separate answer sheet.

82 Over the years, human activity introduced organisms such as goats and other herbivores to the Galapagos Islands. The addition of these invasive organisms caused the tortoise species to be threatened because there was

(1) an increase in competition for food sources

(2) a decrease in ecological succession

(3) an increase in the availability of vegetation

(4) a decrease in direct harvesting

_____

83 As fish are frozen for storage, the water in the cells expands as it cools from 4°C to 0°C and may cause cells to burst. This lowers the quality of the fish. Explain how soaking the fish briefly in salt water before freezing them might prevent this damage to the cells. [1]

_____

_____

_____

Base your answers to questions 84 and 85 on the diagram below and on your knowledge of biology.

Permission to use this third-party content has not been granted to Savvas. You can visit nysedregents.org to view.

84 Identify *one* finch population that would be *negatively* affected if the birth rate of small tree finches increased significantly. Support your answer.   [1]

Finch: _____

Support: _____

_____

_____

85 A student completed two trials of the *Beaks of Finches* lab, each time picking up eleven seeds, as shown in the table below. If the student needs to collect an average of thirteen seeds to survive, how many seeds must he pick up in round 3? Record your answer in the space provided in the table below. [1]

Trial Number	Seeds Picked Up
1	11
2	11
3	_____
Average	13

Part A

Answer all questions in this part. [30]

Directions (1–30): For *each* statement or question, record on the separate answer sheet the *number* of the word or expression that, of those given, best completes the statement or answers the question.

1 In single-celled organisms, materials are stored primarily in
   (1) ribosomes   (3) nuclei
   (2) mitochondria   (4) vacuoles

2 The human female reproductive cycle is regulated primarily by the
   (1) white blood cells of the circulatory system
   (2) muscle cells of the skeletal system
   (3) enzymes of the digestive system
   (4) hormones of the endocrine system

3 A photograph of a Siamese cat is shown below.

Source: www.pinterest.com/explorer/siamese/cats

Siamese cats have dark fur on areas of the body that are cooler and light fur on parts of the body that are warmer. The color differences in this Siamese cat are most likely due to
   (1) a decrease in glucose produced in areas with light fur
   (2) more DNA molecules being produced in areas with light fur
   (3) gene expression being influenced by the environment
   (4) mutations in the genes for eye color

4 When deciding on new environmental policies and laws, which term is used to describe the comparison between benefits and costs of human activities?
   (1) technology   (3) climate change
   (2) trade-off   (4) industrialization

5 If the grass in the front yard of an abandoned house is not cut for several years, the yard may become overgrown with taller grasses, bushes, and shrubs. This is an example of the process of
   (1) evolution
   (2) homeostasis
   (3) ecological succession
   (4) direct harvesting

6 The northern snakehead is a type of Asian fish that eats smaller fish and is adapted to a freshwater habitat.

Source: http://nas.er.usgs.gov/queries/
factsheet.aspx?speciesid=2265

The presence of these fish in American waters is of concern because it might offer too much competition to native
   (1) herbivores   (3) decomposers
   (2) predators   (4) producers

7 In a food web, which type of organism receives energy from the other three types?
   (1) producer   (3) decomposer
   (2) carnivore   (4) herbivore

[2]

8 An ameba is a single-celled, heterotrophic organism. In order to meet its energy needs, it relies directly on the interaction of which cell structures?

(1) chloroplasts and the cell membrane
(2) the cell membrane and mitochondria
(3) nucleus and ribosomes
(4) vacuoles and the nucleus

9 Recently, oil from a wrecked tanker resulted in a disaster in ecosystems containing many unique species. The potential loss of these species could result in

(1) an increase in the variety of genetic material available
(2) a decrease in organisms available for scientific research
(3) an increase in the stability of the affected ecosystems
(4) a decrease in pollution affecting the land and water

10 Which process occurs at each link in a food chain?

(1) All the energy is stored in a newly made structure.
(2) Some energy is released into the environment as heat.
(3) Chemical energy is recycled.
(4) Atoms cycle among living organisms, producing energy.

11 Genetic recombination, production of more offspring than can survive, and struggling with the challenges of the environment are all concepts associated with

(1) natural selection
(2) mitotic division
(3) selective breeding
(4) genetic engineering

12 Mistletoe is a plant that lives on the branches of trees. The mistletoe plant sends its roots in through the bark of trees and takes away water and minerals that the tree needs. In this situation, the mistletoe plant is

(1) a parasite   (3) a decomposer
(2) a predator   (4) an autotroph

13 An example of a population in which evolution could take place in a relatively short period of time could be

(1) pathogenic bacteria exposed to antibiotics
(2) oak trees in a stable ecosystem
(3) elephants living in a wildlife preserve
(4) algae grown under constant conditions

14 Butterflies exposed to radiation leaking from a damaged nuclear power plant in Japan have been observed to have malformed legs, antennae, and wings. For future butterfly generations to have these similar structural abnormalities, gene mutations must be present in the affected butterflies'

(1) wing cells   (3) antenna cells
(2) body cells   (4) sex cells

15 The diagram below illustrates the release of chemical A from a human cell in response to a specific stimulus.

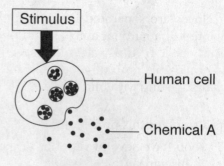

Source: Biology 8th ed., Pearson 2008, p. 859.

Which cell structure plays a direct role in the release of this chemical from the cell?

(1) nucleus   (3) chloroplast
(2) ribosome   (4) cell membrane

16 A rich variety of genetic material in an ecosystem will

(1) reduce the biodiversity of the ecosystem
(2) decrease the carrying capacity of the ecosystem
(3) reduce the likelihood of future medical discoveries
(4) increase the chances that some organisms will survive change

[3]

[OVER]

17 The process of sexual reproduction is an important part of the process of evolution. One reason for this is that meiosis and fertilization directly produce many new

(1) antigens   (3) species
(2) variations   (4) pathogens

18 A garlic bulb consisting of several smaller sections called cloves is shown below.

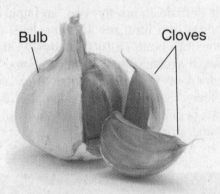

Source: www.sparkpeople.com/resource/
nutrition_articlesasp?id=1791

If cloves are separated from the bulb and later planted in a garden, a new garlic bulb will grow from each. In this way, a home gardener could grow a whole crop of genetically identical garlic plants starting with one bulb.

As a result of this procedure, the gardener would

(1) soon have several varieties of garlic growing in his garden
(2) need to buy new garlic cloves each year in order to keep growing garlic
(3) have to fertilize the female garlic plants each year so the garlic plants could produce their own cloves
(4) need to be aware that if any of his garlic plants became diseased, it could very likely infect the entire crop

19 When humans place grass clippings and other yard waste in landfills, they are most directly interfering with the natural process of

(1) recycling energy
(2) the production of energy
(3) recycling organic compounds
(4) the production of organic compounds

20 Which statement is an example of a feedback mechanism in humans?

(1) An increase in the level of blood sugar results in the pancreas increasing the amount of insulin it secretes.
(2) Increased exposure to pathogenic bacteria results in an increase in the number of red blood cells produced.
(3) An increase in exercise results in a decrease in the rate of respiration.
(4) Increased muscle activity results in a decrease in heart rate.

21 Many disorders are due to the inability of an individual to break down a particular chemical. Sometimes these disorders can be treated by giving the affected individual the appropriate

(1) enzymes   (3) chromosomes
(2) antigens   (4) organelles

22 The removal of the predator populations from an ecosystem would most likely result in

(1) a decrease in all the prey populations
(2) an increase in all the producer populations
(3) an increase in ecosystem diversity
(4) a decrease in ecosystem diversity

23 Two new wind turbines have recently been built within the Eiffel Tower in Paris. The power that these turbines generate will be enough to power the entire first floor of the tower, including the restaurants, shops, and exhibits. A benefit of using wind power as an alternative source of energy is that it

(1) is nonrenewable, so additional resources will be depleted by tower businesses
(2) is renewable, so it will decrease the environmental impact of the tower businesses
(3) increases the use of resources that cannot be renewed in the future
(4) decreases the amount of fossil fuels available for future generations

[4]

24 In the photograph below, two fish are displaying a behavior commonly observed among pairs of rabbitfish. While one has its head down feeding on coral, the other remains upright, alert for predators.

Source: NY Times 9/28/15

This behavior continues to be present in the rabbitfish population because

(1) this behavior was learned by observing other fish species
(2) both fish could not fit into the small spaces in the coral
(3) this behavior increases their chance of survival
(4) the fish species needed to become alert to survive

25 The fast food industry in the United States buys many russet potatoes from farmers. Therefore, most potato farmers grow russet potatoes. If farmers continue to plant the same crop in the same fields year after year without putting additives into the soil, the end result could be

(1) smaller yields in future years due to the loss of nutrients
(2) larger potatoes because they will adapt to the soil
(3) new varieties of potatoes because they will reproduce sexually
(4) genetically engineered potatoes that are resistant to disease

26 A corn field includes corn plants, mice, hawks, and various insects, fungi, and bacteria. Which nutritional role is correctly paired with organisms that carry out that role?

(1) heterotrophs – corn and bacteria
(2) producers – insects and fungi
(3) consumers – mice and insects
(4) decomposers – hawks and bacteria

27 Each female housefly can lay approximately 500 eggs in a lifetime. She does this in several batches of about 75 to 150 eggs. Within a day, larvae (maggots) hatch from the eggs. They live and feed on organic material, such as garbage and feces. Scientists have calculated that a pair of flies beginning reproduction in April could be the ancestors of 191,010,000,000,000,000,000 flies by August.

Source: http://www.publicdomainpictures.net/download-picture.php?adresar=10000&soubor+1-1220978631q1uO.jpg&id+1137

Which statement best explains why this does *not* happen?

(1) Mutations develop in the young flies.
(2) Environmental factors keep the population in check.
(3) Flies continue to reproduce in large numbers.
(4) More female flies survive than male flies.

[5]

[OVER]

28 Which sequence best represents the levels of organization in a paramecium, a single-celled organism?

    (1) cells $\longrightarrow$ tissues $\longrightarrow$ organs $\longrightarrow$ organ systems $\longrightarrow$ organism
    (2) organelles $\longrightarrow$ organ systems $\longrightarrow$ organism
    (3) cells $\longrightarrow$ organs $\longrightarrow$ organ systems $\longrightarrow$ organism
    (4) organelles $\longrightarrow$ organism

29 More than 100 years ago, Earth's atmosphere contained about 280 parts per million (ppm) of carbon dioxide. It is predicted that by the year 2050, the level of carbon dioxide in the atmosphere could reach 700 ppm, greatly increasing Earth's temperature. It has been suggested that growing more green plants would help to slow this increase. The best explanation for why increased numbers of plants would help is that plants

    (1) serve as food for herbivores
    (2) serve as a nonrenewable energy resource
    (3) remove carbon dioxide from the atmosphere during respiration
    (4) remove carbon dioxide from the atmosphere during photosynthesis

30 The brown tree snake was accidentally introduced to the island of Guam during World War II. Since then, this snake has caused the extinction of twelve native bird species by eating their eggs and young.

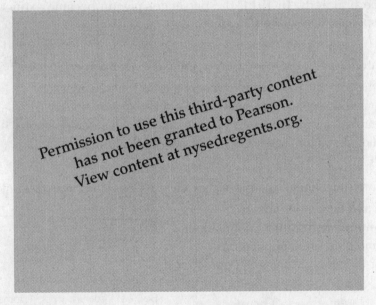

Permission to use this third-party content has not been granted to Pearson. View content at nysedregents.org.

One *negative* result of this snake's introduction was most likely

    (1) an increase in diversity as new species evolved to replace extinct species
    (2) an increase in mosquitoes due to an increase in bird species in the environment
    (3) a disruption of food chains and food webs in Guam's ecosystems
    (4) an abundance of brown tree snakes as a food source for humans

Part B–1

Answer all questions in this part.   [13]

Directions (31–43): For *each* statement or question, record on the separate answer sheet the *number* of the word or expression that, of those given, best completes the statement or answers the question.

Base your answers to questions 31 through 33 on the information below and on your knowledge of biology.

The Extinction of the Passenger Pigeon

In the early 1800s, the passenger pigeon was the most abundant bird species in North America. These pigeons traveled in flocks sometimes larger than a billion birds. The enormous flock sizes helped protect them from predation by foxes, lynx, owls, and falcons. It also helped them outcompete other animals (squirrels, chipmunks) for chestnuts and acorns, their main food source.

Unfortunately, this flocking behavior made the passenger pigeons easy targets for the people who killed them for food. The invention of the telegraph to broadcast flock locations to hunters and the expansion of the railroads to ship the pigeons to new food markets had devastating results. By the 1890s, their numbers had dwindled dramatically, with flocks only numbering in the hundreds. In 1914, the passenger pigeon became extinct when the last member of the species died at the Cincinnati Zoo.

31 Which factor contributed *least* to the extinction of the passenger pigeon species?

(1) laws that banned the hunting of passenger pigeons to sell in new markets
(2) improved communication technology, which tracked the pigeon flocks
(3) expansion of the railroads, which opened up new markets for selling pigeons
(4) increased use of the passenger pigeons as a food source for humans

32 A direct result of the rapid decline of the passenger pigeon population was most likely

(1) an increase in owl and falcon populations
(2) an increase in chipmunk and squirrel populations
(3) a decrease in fox and chipmunk populations
(4) a decrease in squirrel and chestnut tree populations

33 The extinction of the passenger pigeon illustrates that

(1) humans are the only cause of species extinctions
(2) it takes hundreds of years for a species extinction
(3) the benefits of technology always outweigh the ecological risks
(4) human activities can irreversibly affect ecosystems

Base your answers to questions 34 and 35 on the information and diagram below and on your knowledge of biology.

To study how bacteria respond to antibiotics, four paper discs, three treated with different antibiotics and one treated with water, were placed on a nutrient source with bacteria and left for 24 hours. The water and the antibiotics on the discs diffused into the nutrient source. If the antibiotic stopped the bacteria from growing, a circular area of no bacterial growth around the discs could be seen.

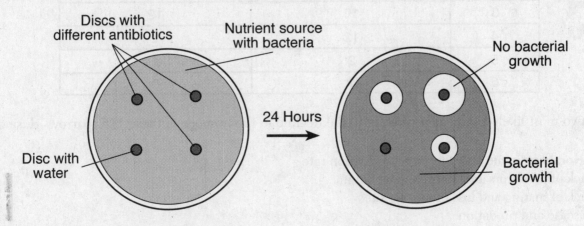

34 After 24 hours, the results represented by the diagram demonstrate
   (1) which of these antibiotics most effectively stopped bacterial growth
   (2) the nutrient source that resulted in the most bacterial growth
   (3) whether the bacteria were resistant to most antibiotics or not
   (4) that these bacteria were harmful to antibiotics

35 In this experiment, the purpose of using a disc treated with water is that it
   (1) serves as the conclusion for the experiment
   (2) is needed to provide additional moisture
   (3) serves as a control for the experiment
   (4) is needed as a standard safety procedure

36 The diagram below represents some stages in the process of development.

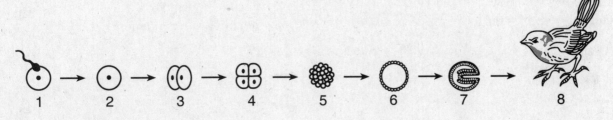

Stage 2 represents a cell that
   (1) contains half the genetic material of an adult cell
   (2) shows clear evidence of tissue differentiation
   (3) has the complete genetic information to form an adult
   (4) is genetically identical to one of the parents that produced it

[8]

37 The table below shows the results of a study on the lifespan of 115 individual song sparrows.

Song Sparrow Lifespan

Year	Number at Start of Year	Number at End of Year
1	115	25
2	25	19
3	19	12
4	12	2
5	2	1
6	1	0

The two most likely factors contributing to the decline in the number of these 115 sparrows during year 1 were

(1) favorable climate and a rapid reproduction rate
(2) lack of predators and an expanding habitat
(3) lack of mating and loss of nesting sites
(4) disease and predation

38 The diagnostic test for HIV, the virus that causes AIDS, involves testing the blood for antibodies associated with this pathogen. Antibodies are produced when the body

(1) stimulates enzyme production
(2) secretes specific hormones
(3) detects foreign antigens
(4) synthesizes microbes

39 Body cells include nerve cells and muscle cells. Each makes a number of different proteins. For example, nerve cells make cholinesterase and muscle cells make myosin. Which statement best compares the DNA normally found in these two types of cells in an individual?

(1) The two cells have identical DNA sequences and use the same section of the DNA to make these two proteins.
(2) The two cells have identical DNA sequences, but use different sections of the DNA to make these two proteins.
(3) The two cells have different DNA sequences, but use the same section of the DNA to make these two proteins.
(4) The two cells have different DNA sequences and use different sections of the DNA to make these two proteins.

40 The chart below compares the greenhouse gas emissions of several fuel sources.

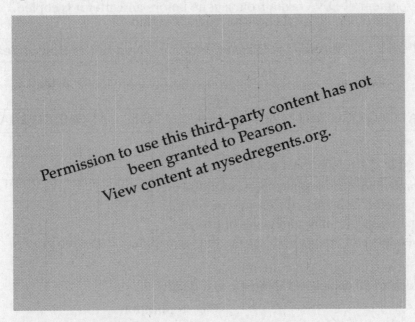

An accurate prediction that could be made regarding the information shown in the chart is that

(1) a total change from gasoline to ethanol as a fuel would have no effect on greenhouse gas emissions

(2) fossil fuels emit the least amount of greenhouse gases

(3) the use of any one of the ethanol sources for fuel will each produce less greenhouse gases than the use of gasoline for fuel

(4) the use of biomass-based fuels instead of fossil fuels will greatly increase the production of greenhouse gases

41 Studies have shown that children are especially vulnerable to the effects of ultraviolet (UV) radiation. Tanning beds expose the skin to nearly ten times as much UV radiation as natural sunlight. With that knowledge, a law was passed in New York State to prevent individuals under the age of 18 from using tanning beds. Which statement best explains why UV radiation is so harmful?

(1) Certain environmental factors can increase the occurrence of harmful gene mutations.

(2) Diseases are all caused by exposure to environmental factors.

(3) Homeostasis in an organism is increased by the presence of radiation.

(4) Radiation decreases the likelihood that infectious agents cause mutations.

Base your answers to questions 42 and 43 on the diagram below and on your knowledge of biology. The diagram shows a small segment of DNA taken from a gene before and after it is copied.

Changes made during the copying process are represented by * in the diagram.

Before   **After**

GTC CAT CAC CGG TAG TCG   ⟶   GTC CAT G*AC CGG TAG TC*C

42 The errors indicated by * could affect a cell by
   (1) altering the number of chromosomes present in the cytoplasm
   (2) converting the original cell into a different type of cell
   (3) converting sugar molecules into molecules of protein
   (4) changing the sequence of amino acids during the formation of a specific protein

43 The process by which a cell copies its DNA before it divides is
   (1) mutation   (3) replication
   (2) diffusion   (4) respiration

[11]   [OVER]

Part B–2

Answer all questions in this part. [12]

Directions (44–55): For those questions that are multiple choice, record on the separate answer sheet the *number* of the choice that, of those given, best completes each statement or answers each question. For all other questions in this part, follow the directions given and record your answers in the spaces provided in this examination booklet.

Base your answers to questions 44 through 47 on the information and data table below and on your knowledge of biology.

Invasive species have damaged agricultural crops all over the world. One study, completed in Japan, calculated the number of invasive insect species present in Japan from 1880 to 1990. Some of the data are recorded in the table below.

Permission to use this third-party content has not been granted to Pearson. View content at nysedregents.org.

January '19   Regents Examination

Directions (44–46): Using the information in the data table, construct a line graph on the grid provided, following the directions below.

44 Mark an appropriate scale, without any breaks in the data, on each labeled axis. [1]

45 Plot the data on the grid. Connect the points and surround each point with a small circle. [1]

Example: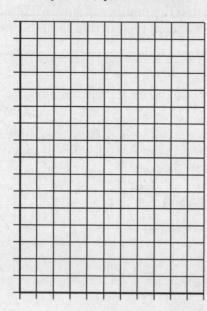

**Number of Invasive Insect
Species per Decade**

(y-axis) **Number of Invasive Insect Species**

(x-axis) **Years**

46 State *one* reason why invasive insect species are a major problem for agriculture. [1]

_____

_____

Note: The answer to question 47 should be recorded on your separate answer sheet.

47 In the last decade of this study, there was a decrease in the number of invasive insects that entered Japan. One likely reason for this decrease is that people have

  (1) produced insecticides that are strong enough to kill every insect that is present in crops going from one country to another
  (2) improved inspections of crops that are transported from one area of the world to another area of the world
  (3) genetically altered all insects so they don't feed on crops that humans use
  (4) stopped the transportation of all food crops from other countries, requiring each area to use only locally grown crops

48 A double-stranded DNA sample was analyzed to establish the percentage of different molecular bases present. The data table below shows the percentage of adenine bases found. Calculate the percentage of each of the three remaining molecular bases, and write the percentages of each in the chart.   [1]

Base	Percent Found (%)
A (Adenine)	20
T (Thymine)	_____
G (Guanine)	_____
C (Cytosine)	_____

Base your answers to questions 49 and 50 on the information and diagram below and on your knowledge of biology.

An investigation was conducted to compare two different types of plants. A student used a microscope to observe the cells in a cross section of a lilac leaf (diagram A) and a cell from the leaf of a freshwater plant (diagram B).

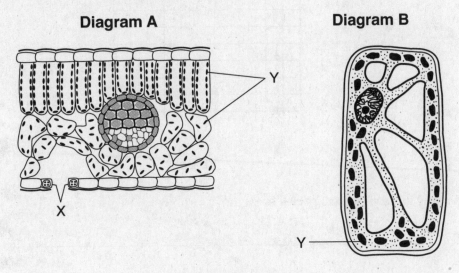

Diagram A

Y

X

Diagram B

Y

Y

(Not drawn to scale)

Note: The answer to question 49 should be recorded on your separate answer sheet.

49 Which row in the chart below correctly identifies the structure labeled *Y* in both diagrams and the process it performs?

Row	Structure	Process
(1)	mitochondrion	excretion
(2)	nucleus	regulation
(3)	chloroplast	photosynthesis
(4)	ribosome	protein synthesis

Note: The answer to question 50 should be recorded on your separate answer sheet.

50 Which technique could be used to make the structures in the cells more visible when using a compound light microscope?

(1) paper chromatography   (3) electrophoresis

(2) staining   (4) gene manipulation

Base your answers to questions 51 through 54 on the information and photograph below and on your knowledge of biology.

Transgenic (GMO) Tomatoes

The use of pesticides to control insects costs billions of dollars every year. Genetically modified organisms (GMOs) are an attempt to reduce this cost. Tomato plants that are genetically modified can make proteins that are poisonous to the insects that feed on them. Using these GMO tomatoes would reduce the need for the chemical control of insects.

51 Identify a specific technique used to produce the GMO tomatoes. [1]

_____

52 State *one* possible advantage of having tomato plants that make proteins that are poisonous to insects. [1]

_____

_____

53 Identify the type of chemical substance a scientist would need to use to cut and paste the genes to produce genetically modified tomato plants. [1]

_____

54 Identify the process responsible for passing the gene for insect resistance in a leaf cell of a genetically modified tomato plant on to the cells that develop from it. [1]

_____

55 The diagram below represents the human female reproductive system.

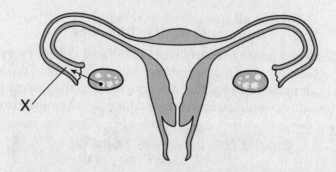

State *one* way a complete blockage at location X would affect the reproductive process.   [1]

_____

_____

_____

Part C

Answer all questions in this part. [17]

Directions (56–72): Record your answers in the spaces provided in this examination booklet.

Base your answers to questions 56 through 58 on the food web represented below and on your knowledge of biology. The food web contains some of the organisms found in Glacier National Park.

Glacier National Park Food Web

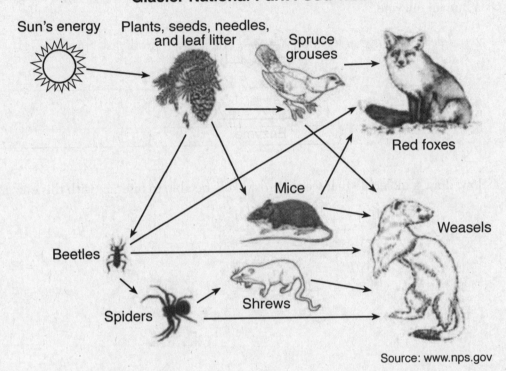

Source: www.nps.gov

56 Identify which group of organisms in this food web would contain the greatest amount of stored energy. Support your answer. [1]

Organisms: _____

Support: _____

_____

57 Explain why a major increase in the number of cloudy days that extends over a period of years would be expected to affect the populations of both plants and animals in this ecosystem. [1]

_____

_____

[18]

58 Describe how the niche of the mouse population differs from the niche of the shrew population in this ecosystem. Support your answer with information from the food web. [1]

_____

_____

Base your answers to questions 59 through 61 on the diagram below and on your knowledge of biology. The diagram represents a human enzyme.

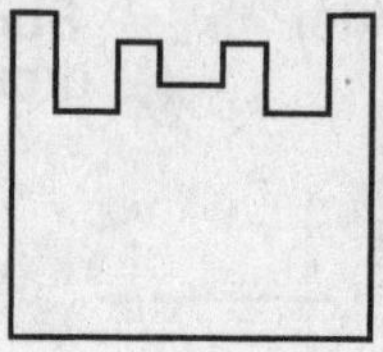

Enzyme

59 In the space below, draw a molecule that would most likely be able to interact with this enzyme. [1]

60 Describe *one* role of enzymes in the human body. [1]

_____

_____

61 A person has a high fever of 105°F. State *one* effect that this high fever would likely have on enzyme activity. [1]

_____

_____

_____

Base your answers to questions 62 through 64 on the information and graph below and on your knowledge of biology.

Dr. Liz Hadly studied the ecology of Yellowstone National Park for 30 years, specifically the amphibians inhabiting the park for 20 of those years. Dr. Hadly studied 46 ponds in 1992-1993. Of these, 43 supported amphibians. From 2006-2008, only 38 of the original 46 ponds contained water. The graph below represents population data for four amphibian species collected by Dr. Hadly during 1992-1993 and 2006-2008.

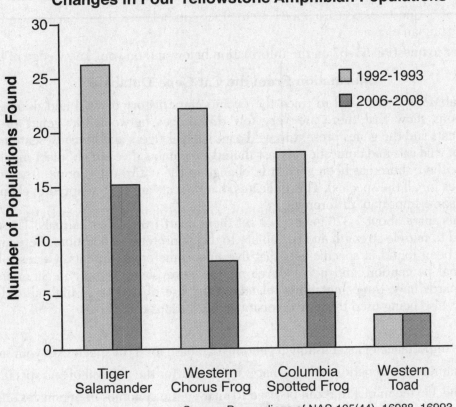

Changes in Four Yellowstone Amphibian Populations

Source: Proceedings of NAS 105(44), 16988 -16993

62 Explain why such a long-term study is more likely to be accepted by Dr. Hadly's peers than one that took place over a shorter period of time. [1]

_____

_____

63 Describe the trend in the amphibian populations over the course of the study. Support your answer with information from the graph. [1]

_____

_____

64 Explain how global warming could have affected Yellowstone frog and salamander habitats, resulting in changes in the populations of these species. [1]

_____

_____

_____

Base your answer to question 65–67 on the information below and on your knowledge of biology.

Information From the Cat Gene Database

A database is being used to trace the evolutionary history of wild and domestic cats. Comparisons show that there are very few differences between the genes present in domestic cats and the genes present in wild cats, such as tigers and lions. Research has also shown that wild cats and domestic cats last shared a common ancestor about 11 million years ago. Since then, there has been very little change in the entire cat genome (the complete set of genes for all the species). This indicates that the cats are well-adapted to change. Yet, there are some important differences.

Big cats share about 1,376 genes that set them apart from other animals. These genes are related to muscle strength and the ability to digest protein. In addition, there are genes that have been found in specific cats that live in specific environments. Genes related to smell, visual perception, and nerve development are evolving rapidly in Siberian tigers. Snow leopards have three mutations related to the use of oxygen at high altitudes. The database is also being used to study diversity within various cat species.

65–67 Discuss the importance of establishing a genome database for a cat species. In your answer, be sure to:

- state *one* example of a genetic variation that is important for the survival of *one* specific cat species [1]
- identify a specific technique that can be used to analyze the genomes of organisms and explain how the results are used [1]
- explain how genes for a trait, such as a specific fur color, can increase in frequency in a population over time [1]

_____

_____

_____

_____

_____

_____

Base your answers to questions 68 through 70 on the passage below and on your knowledge of biology.

68 Describe *one* way the immune system could respond when it is exposed to the genetically altered *Bacillus subtilis*. [1]

_____

_____

69 Will individuals who have taken the vaccine be protected against future tetanus infections? Support your answer. [1]

_____

_____

70 State *one* advantage of using edible modified spores as vaccines. [1]

_____

_____

[22]

Base your answers to questions 71 and 72 on the information below and on your knowledge of biology.

Reproductive Adaptations of Mammals

Mammals have unique reproductive adaptations that have contributed to their evolutionary success. One of the distinguishing characteristics of mammals is their mammary glands, which allow for the production of milk. Even the more primitive mammals, such as the duck-billed platypus and the kangaroo, have some type of mammary glands. However, only the placental mammals (e.g. humans, horses, dogs) have a placenta, which supports the internal development of the embryo. The most primitive mammals have no placenta and can't support the internal development of the embryo.

71 Explain how the mammary glands contribute to the reproductive success of mammals.   [1]

_____

_____

72 Describe *one* function of the placenta found in mammals such as humans, horses, and dogs.   [1]

_____

_____

Part D

Answer all questions in this part. [13]

Directions (73–85): For those questions that are multiple choice, record on the separate answer sheet the *number* of the choice that, of those given, best completes each statement or answers each question. For all other questions in this part, follow the directions given and record your answers in the spaces provided in this examination booklet.

Note: The answer to question 73 should be recorded on your separate answer sheet.

73 A procedure used in paper chromatography is represented below:

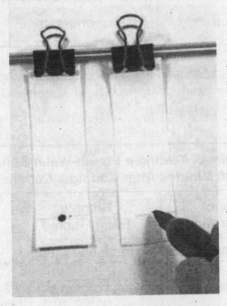

Source: www.sciencebuddies.org/
sciencefair

The student is preparing two strips of paper for a chromatography activity. After adding a dot of the ink from the marker pen to the line on the paper on the right, the next step should be to place the strips in a beaker of solvent with the solvent level

(1) between the bottom of the paper and the dot of ink
(2) even with the dot of ink on the paper
(3) just below the bottom edge of the paper
(4) slightly above the dot of ink on the paper

[24]

Note: The answer to question 74 should be recorded on your separate answer sheet.

Base your answer to question 74 on the information below and on your knowledge of biology.

Some students tested two samples of a mixture of starch and water with two different indicators. The results of these tests are shown in Table 1 below.

Table 1: Results of Testing a Starch-Water Solution with Indicators.			
Indicator Used	Color of Indicator Alone	Sample Being Tested	Color of Sample After Indicator Was Added
starch indicator	amber	starch and water	black
glucose indicator + heat	blue	starch and water	blue

Next, a specific protein was added to two new samples of the starch and water mixture. After waiting 30 minutes, the students tested these samples with the same two indicator solutions. The results are shown in Table 2 below.

Table 2: Results of Testing a Starch-Water Solution with Indicators 30 Minutes After Adding a Certain Protein			
Indicator Used	Color of Indicator Alone	Sample Being Tested	Color of Sample After Indicator Was Added
starch indicator	amber	starch and water	amber
glucose indicator + heat	blue	starch and water	brick red

74 Based on these results, it can be concluded that the specific protein that was added to the samples was

(1) a salt solution

(2) a new indicator

(3) a pancreatic hormone

(4) a biological catalyst

Base your answers to questions 75 and 76 on the information and diagram below and on your knowledge of biology. The diagram represents red blood cells placed in three test tubes, each containing a different salt solution.

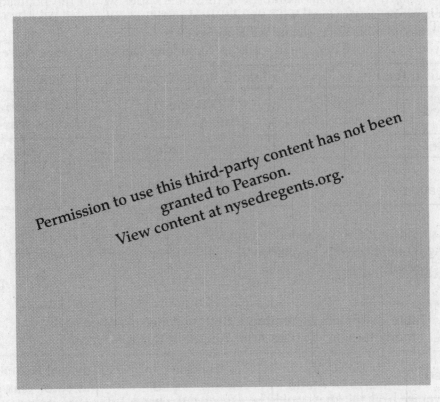

Permission to use this third-party content has not been granted to Pearson. View content at nysedregents.org.

Note: The answer to question 75 should be recorded on your separate answer sheet.

75 Which statement best describes solution *C*?

(1) The concentration of dissolved salt in the solution is greater than the concentration in the cells.
(2) The concentration of dissolved salt in the solution is less than the concentration in the cells.
(3) The concentration of water in the solution is greater than the concentration in the cells.
(4) The concentration of water in the solution is equal to the concentration in the cells.

Note: The answer to question 76 should be recorded on your separate answer sheet.

76 Which solution would be most similar in concentration to the normal internal environment of the human circulatory system?

(1) solution *A*, only
(2) solution *B*, only
(3) solutions *A* and *B*
(4) solutions *A* and *C*

Base your answers to questions 77 and 78 on the information and graph below and on your knowledge of biology.

A species of bird lives on an island. Beak thickness varies within the population. The birds feed mainly on seeds. Birds with smaller beaks can eat only small seeds. Only birds with larger beaks are able to crush and eat large seeds.

During years with more rain, small seeds are abundant. During dry years, there are very few small seeds, but there are many large seeds.

77 Predict how the average beak thickness would be expected to change after 1985 if there were eight very dry years in a row. Support your answer. [1]

_____

_____

78 State *one* specific advantage for this bird species to have members of this population with beaks that range from approximately 9.4 mm to 9.9 mm in thickness. [1]

_____

_____

[OVER]

January '19 Regents Examination

79 Identify *one* biotic factor that can affect the survival of a finch population in the Galapagos Islands. [1]

_____

_____

80 During a laboratory activity, students ran in place for three minutes. Students then complained of muscle fatigue in their legs. State *one* biological reason why the students experienced muscle fatigue after exercising. [1]

_____

_____

Note: The answer to question 81 should be recorded on your separate answer sheet.

81 A student is viewing a plant stem cross section using a compound light microscope.

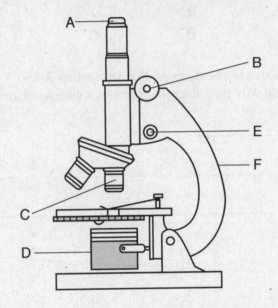

What parts of the microscope should the student use to bring the image into focus?

(1) A and F

(2) B and E

(3) C and D

(4) D and F

Note: The answer to question 82 should be recorded on your separate answer sheet.

82 A rare tropical plant was found to have medicinal properties. A search was conducted to find other plants that are closely related to the rare plant. Which combination of characteristics would best identify the plant most closely related to the original one?

(1) shape of seeds, number of flower petals, leaf pigments

(2) number of flower petals, positive reaction to a specific enzyme

(3) leaf pigments, sequence of DNA bases, positive reaction to a specific enzyme

(4) presence of DNA bases, internal stem structure, shape of seeds

83 The diagram below represents three branching diagrams that show relationships between three different species, X, Y, and Z.

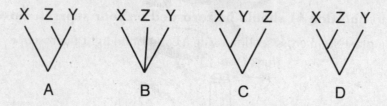

On the line below, write the letter of the diagram that shows that X and Y are more closely related to each other than to species Z. Explain why that diagram indicates a close relationship. [1]

Diagram: _____

Explanation: _____

_____

Base your answer to question 84 on the information below and on your knowledge of biology.

Anoles are a diverse group of lizards that live on several islands including Cuba, Hispaniola, Jamaica, and Puerto Rico. Large populations of several species exist on these islands. The preferred region of the tree inhabited by the six species of anole lizards is represented in the diagram below.

Island Anoles

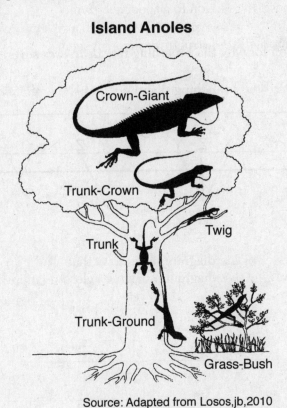

Source: Adapted from Losos,jb,2010

84 Would you expect the crown-giant and trunk-ground anoles to compete for resources if they lived on the same tree? Circle yes *or* no and support your answer with an explanation. [1]

Circle one: Yes   *or*   No

Explanation: _____

_____

_____

Base your answer to question 85 on the information below and on your knowledge of biology.

A class carried out an experiment to test the effect of rest time after exercise on the breathing rate. Each member of the class ran up and down stairs for 60 seconds. After exercising, they rested. The students then measured their rate of respiration by counting the number of inhales and exhales per minute for 7 minutes. The class then averaged their data.

85 Provide a biological explanation for why the breathing rate *decreases* several minutes after physical activity has stopped. [1]

_____

_____

_____

Part A

Answer all questions in this part. [30]

Directions (1–30): For *each* statement or question, record on the separate answer sheet the *number* of the word or expression that, of those given, best completes the statement or answers the question.

1 Which human activity most directly causes a significant increase in the amount of carbon dioxide in the atmosphere?

(1) growing corn for food
(2) not using products containing plastics
(3) driving cars long distances
(4) planting large numbers of trees

2 An immune response is primarily due to the body's white blood cells recognizing

(1) a hormone imbalance
(2) abiotic organisms
(3) foreign antigens
(4) known antibiotics

3 In an effort to reduce the number of deaths due to malaria, scientists have successfully introduced a gene into mosquitoes. The gene makes the mosquitoes unable to support the development of the parasite that causes malaria. The technique used to produce this new variety of mosquito is most likely

(1) chromatography
(2) genetic engineering
(3) electrophoresis of genes
(4) selective breeding

4 The organic compounds that scientists use to cut, copy, and move segments of DNA are

(1) carbohydrates   (3) hormones
(2) enzymes   (4) starches

Base your answers to questions 5 and 6 on the diagram below and on your knowledge of biology.

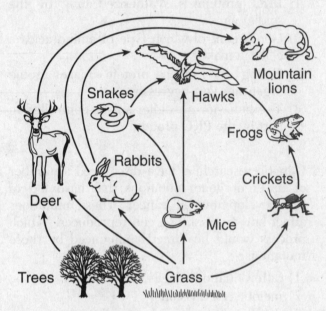

5 Which statement most accurately predicts the result of interfering with populations in the web?

(1) Removing the cricket population will have little effect on the balance of the food web.
(2) Removing all the mountain lions from the food web will benefit the ecosystem.
(3) Removing the cricket and rabbit populations would cause the number of trees to decrease.
(4) Removing deer from the food web will affect the rabbit and grass populations.

6 A factor *not* shown in the diagram that provides energy for living organisms is

(1) carbon dioxide   (3) the Sun
(2) water   (4) oxygen

[2]

7 Scientists have found a gene that makes a protein called PKG that controls certain behaviors in many types of ants. The soldier ant will help collect food when it has a low level of PKG. When it has a high level of PKG, the soldier ant will protect and defend its colony. Soldier ants that are given PKG are more likely to ignore food sources and attack intruders. Which conclusion can best be made from this information?

(1) PKG protein is synthesized only by the soldier ants.
(2) Genes control which type of amino acids a cell can make.
(3) Eating too much protein makes some organisms very aggressive.
(4) The behavior of soldier ants is controlled in part by the PKG protein.

8 Genetic researchers have discovered a number of different gene mutations that have led to the development of cancer. These mutations affect how frequently a cell reproduces. Which process would be directly influenced by these mutations?

(1) differentiation of cells in an embryo
(2) meiotic cell division
(3) division of sperm and egg cells
(4) mitotic cell division

9 Lobsters are crustaceans related to crayfish, crabs, and shrimp. Most lobsters are a reddish-brown color, but on rare occasions, they can be orange, blue, or even multicolored. These color differences can be caused by

(1) genetic variations
(2) different numbers of offspring
(3) overpopulation and excessive resources
(4) the instability of the ecosystem

10 Which two factors could lead to the evolution of a species over time?

(1) overproduction of offspring and no variation
(2) changes in the genes of body cells and extinction
(3) struggle for survival and fossilization
(4) changes in the genes of sex cells and survival of the fittest

11 As human red blood cells mature, they lose their nuclei. As a result of this loss, which process would be impossible for mature red blood cells to carry out?

(1) excretion
(2) respiration
(3) reproduction
(4) transport

12 To clone a mammal, a cloned embryo is often put into an adult female of the same species to continue internal development. The structure in which the embryo will develop is the

(1) ovary
(2) placenta
(3) uterus
(4) egg

13 Nuclear power plants, which produce electrical energy, use large quantities of water for cooling. Often, small fish, larvae, and fish eggs are sucked in along with the cooling water and destroyed. This example illustrates how

(1) industrialization can have positive and negative effects
(2) removal of these organisms has no effect on an ecosystem
(3) direct harvesting increases the natural fish population
(4) energy is generated without producing wastes

14 Acid rain is a major problem in the Adirondack Mountains. Evidence that acid rain *negatively* affected the Adirondack ecosystem is that

(1) this rain has increased the amount of water in Adirondack lakes
(2) there has been a decrease in the variety of fish found in Adirondack lakes
(3) the amount of carbon dioxide in the air over the Adirondack Mountains has drastically decreased in recent years
(4) the number of heterotrophic organisms in Adirondack lakes has increased

15 Which system in a multicellular organism functions most like the cytoplasm in a single-celled organism?

(1) immune
(2) reproductive
(3) nervous
(4) circulatory

[3]

[OVER]

16 A common cycle in biology is represented below.

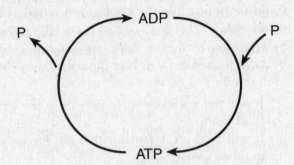

The ATP molecule above is commonly used to

(1) actively transport molecules in an organism
(2) diffuse water across a membrane
(3) move molecules from a high to a low concentration
(4) balance the nutrients in an ecosystem

17 Fat molecules typically contain long chains of carbon atoms. Animals tend to store fats for use when food resources are scarce. This is an advantage to the animal because

(1) much energy can be gained by breaking the bonds between atoms in the fats
(2) fats give off carbon dioxide that can be used by the muscles
(3) amino acids from fat synthesis are more easily digested than carbohydrates
(4) energy can only be created by digesting fats

18 While looking at the bottom surface of a leaf with a compound light microscope, a student notices pairs of cells with openings between them on the surface of the leaf. The main purpose of these openings and the cells that surround them is

(1) removing excess sugars
(2) synthesis of carbon dioxide
(3) regulating gas exchange
(4) purification of water

19 An immune response to a usually harmless environmental substance is known as

(1) an antigen   (3) an allergy
(2) a vaccination   (4) a mutation

20 Scientists at Penn State have sequenced the DNA of the extinct woolly mammoth. The data suggested that the woolly mammoth was more closely related to present-day elephants than previously believed.

Elephant   Woolly mammoth

Which statement could account for the similarities between the woolly mammoth and present-day elephants?

(1) Common gene mutations were caused by agents such as industrial chemicals and radiation.
(2) Present-day species developed from earlier, different species.
(3) Selective breeding results in offspring better able to survive.
(4) Both animals have identical genetic information.

21 Single-celled organisms are able to maintain homeostasis, even though they lack higher levels of organization such as organs and organ systems, because

(1) single-celled organisms do not carry out the same life processes as multicellular organisms
(2) multicellular organisms do not rely on tissues or organs to carry out life processes
(3) cell structures work together to maintain homeostasis in single-celled organisms
(4) single-celled organisms are able to coordinate organ functions to maintain homeostasis

22 Sharks are often followed by smaller fish that eat some of the scraps from the organisms eaten by the shark. These smaller fish are acting as

(1) decomposers   (3) producers
(2) scavengers   (4) herbivores

[4]

23 The photographs below are side-by-side images of twins A and B with identical genetic information. Twin A is a nonsmoker, while twin B is a longtime smoker.

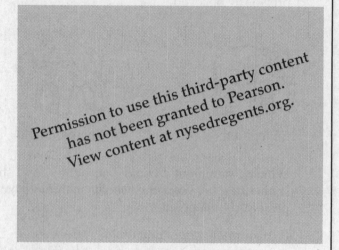

Permission to use this third-party content has not been granted to Pearson. View content at nysedregents.org.

The best explanation for the differences in the appearance of the twins is that

(1) twin B is older than twin A
(2) they each inherited half of their DNA from each parent
(3) the expression of genes is influenced by the environment
(4) one twin resembles the mother and the other resembles the father

24 Under the supervision of experts, certain areas in a nature preserve are regularly exposed to frequent, low-intensity fires. These controlled fires maintain specific populations of plants by directly

(1) increasing the consumption of finite resources
(2) decreasing the carbon dioxide level in the atmosphere
(3) stopping the process of evolution
(4) interfering with the process of ecological succession

25 An invasive species, the spiny water flea, was recently found in a New York lake. These water fleas eat zooplankton, a food also consumed by native fishes. The fleas spread from lake to lake by attaching to fishing lines, anchor ropes, and boats. Which statement best describes the effect of the water flea on the lake?

(1) It will not compete with animals in the local food chain.
(2) It will feed on organisms that are important to other species.
(3) The number of water fleas will decrease due to a lack of food.
(4) There will be no effect on native species in the lake.

26 A stable ecosystem can have high biodiversity because each species in that ecosystem

(1) occupies a different niche
(2) inhabits a different environment
(3) is part of a different community
(4) lives in a different biosphere

27 Stability within an ecosystem is achieved partially by the presence of organisms that break down important molecules and make them available for other organisms to use. These organisms are

(1) plants   (3) scavengers
(2) herbivores   (4) decomposers

[5]   [OVER]

28 The diagram below represents a feedback mechanism.

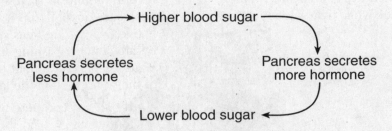

The hormone referred to in this feedback mechanism is

(1) estrogen   (3) progesterone

(2) insulin   (4) testosterone

29 After a lake dried up during a severe drought, a section of undisturbed rock layers was exposed. The layers are represented below.

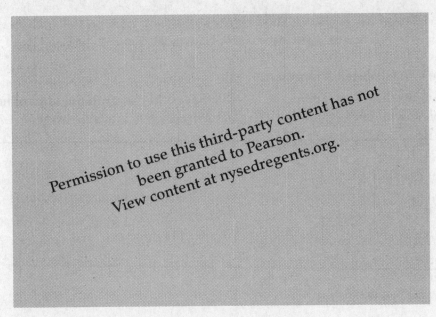

Permission to use this third-party content has not been granted to Pearson. View content at nysedregents.org.

This sequence of rock layers best illustrates the concept that

(1) the living and nonliving environment both change over time

(2) it is important to preserve the diversity of species and habitats

(3) new inheritable characteristics can result from the recombining of genes

(4) living organisms have the capacity to produce populations of unlimited size

30 Some organisms in an ecosystem are represented in the pyramid below.

Source: Sylvia Mader, *Human Biology* (McGraw-Hill, 1998), p.476.

In the pyramid, the arrows labeled *X* represent

(1) the loss of organisms due to predation

(2) a decrease in photosynthetic organisms

(3) the loss of energy in the form of heat

(4) a decrease in available oxygen

Part B–1

Answer all questions in this part. [13]

Directions (31–43): For *each* statement or question, record on the separate answer sheet the *number* of the word or expression that, of those given, best completes the statement or answers the question.

Base your answers to questions 31 and 32 on the information below and on your knowledge of biology.

A student designed an experiment to determine if air temperature had an effect on the rate of photosynthesis in corn plants.

31 Which tool is correctly paired with a procedure that could be used during this experiment?

(1) an electronic balance to measure the volume of soil in which each corn plant is grown
(2) a graduated cylinder to measure 30 mL of water for each plant daily
(3) a metric ruler to determine the mass of each plant each week
(4) a Celsius thermometer to determine the pH of the soil

32 The independent variable in this experiment is the

(1) air temperature at which the corn plants were grown
(2) amount of carbon dioxide used by the corn plants
(3) volume of oxygen produced by the corn plants
(4) number of corn plants used

Base your answers to questions 33 and 34 on the information and graph below and on your knowledge of biology. The graph shows the number of animals in a population throughout the course of a year. The population migrated into the area at the beginning of 2011.

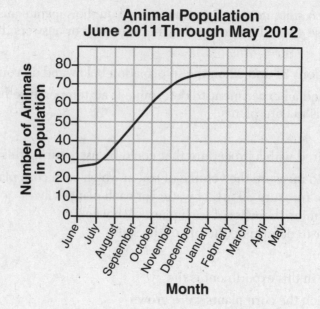

Animal Population June 2011 Through May 2012

33 The graph can best be used to illustrate
(1) a food chain
(2) ecological succession
(3) natural selection
(4) carrying capacity

34 The approximate number of animals that were found in June 2012 was most likely
(1) 16
(2) 26
(3) 76
(4) 86

35 To prepare for an experiment, ten different sources of food were sterilized and kept in a sterile container. Bacteria of the same species were placed on each of the ten different food sources and kept at 26°C for two days. During this time, bacteria grew in nine of the containers. Based on this observation, the scientist could conclude that
(1) all ten food sources used in the experiment are capable of supporting this species of bacteria
(2) the temperature varied greatly in nine of the containers during this experiment
(3) only the container that failed to grow any bacteria was prepared correctly
(4) this species of bacteria synthesizes enzymes needed to digest the food in nine of the ten containers

36 The graph below shows three projections for future carbon dioxide (CO_2) levels.

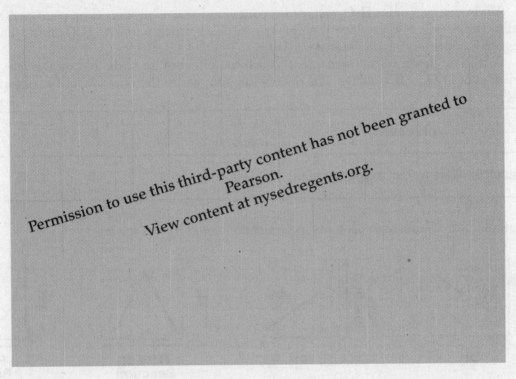

Permission to use this third-party content has not been granted to Pearson.
View content at nysedregents.org.

— The "Business as usual" line shows CO_2 levels if emissions remain at current levels.
— The "Constant 1990 emissions" line shows CO_2 levels if emissions are cut to the same level that they were in 1990.
— The "Half 1990 emissions" line shows CO_2 levels if emissions are cut to half of the level that they were in 1990.

Which statement is supported by the graph?

(1) Climate change will result in the melting of polar ice caps.
(2) The increase in carbon dioxide levels will cause a decrease in global average temperature.
(3) Human activities have no effect on atmospheric carbon dioxide levels.
(4) Future generations can be affected by the choices of current generations.

Base your answers to questions 37 through 39 on the information below and on your knowledge of biology.

Hydrogen peroxide (H_2O_2) is a toxic compound that is produced by plant and animal cells. These cells also produce the enzyme catalase, which converts H_2O_2 into water and oxygen gas, preventing the buildup of H_2O_2.

A student designed an experiment to test the effect of an acidic pH on the rate of the reaction of H_2O_2 with catalase. The data below summarize the outcome of the experiment.

pH Level	7 (neutral)	6	5	3
Reaction Rate (mL of oxygen/minute)	1.5	1.3	1.0	.55

37 Which graph most accurately represents the results obtained by this student?

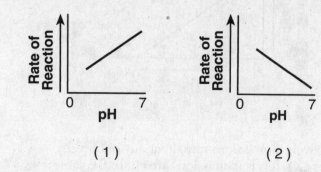

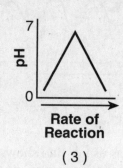

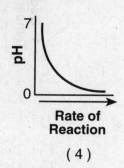

(1)   (2)   (3)   (4)

38 Which conclusion is valid based upon the data collected by the student?

(1) The change in pH prevents catalase from breaking down water.
(2) Catalase has the greatest activity at a pH of 7.
(3) Oxygen production will increase if more water is added to the reaction.
(4) Catalase caused the greatest production of oxygen at a pH of 3.

39 The best explanation for the change in catalase activity as the pH changed from 7 to 3 is that

(1) strong acid digests the catalase, causing the reaction rate to increase
(2) the student most likely cooled the H_2O_2 solution, causing the reaction rate to increase
(3) in acidic solutions, the shape of catalase changes, causing the reaction rate to decrease
(4) decreased oxygen production causes catalase to increase the rate of reaction

[11]   [OVER]

40 Which graph best illustrates the body temperature in an individual maintaining dynamic equilibrium?

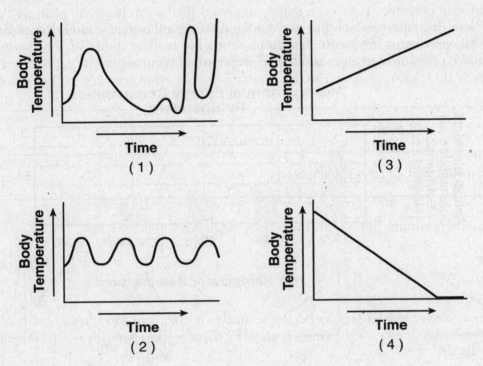

Base your answers to questions 41 and 42 on the information and graph below and on your knowledge of biology.

Federal legislation establishes and updates energy-efficiency standards for consumer products, including refrigerators. The graph shows the average annual energy consumption of similar types of refrigerators and the year they were manufactured.

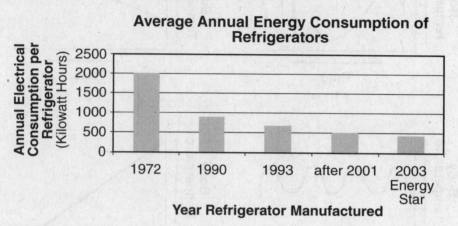

Average Annual Energy Consumption of Refrigerators

41 The 2003 Energy Star models of refrigerators use an average of about 450 kilowatt hours of electrical energy annually. Approximately how much energy is saved by these models annually when compared to the models produced in 1972?

(1) 500 kilowatt hours

(2) 550 kilowatt hours

(3) 1500 kilowatt hours

(4) 1550 kilowatt hours

42 Which statement best represents an outcome of federal standards that require increasing the energy efficiency of appliances, such as refrigerators?

(1) More technological improvements in appliances can help conserve finite resources.

(2) Increased efficiency of appliances requires greater use of our energy resources.

(3) Newer appliances are manufactured from a greater number of finite resources.

(4) Manufacturing more efficient appliances will reduce the biodiversity of ecosystems.

43 A student placed a test tube containing elodea (an aquatic plant) and pond water 10 cm from a light source. He observed that the plant gave off bubbles of a gas and counted how many bubbles were released in one minute. He moved the plant farther away from the light source to see if distance from the source made a difference. The data table below shows his results.

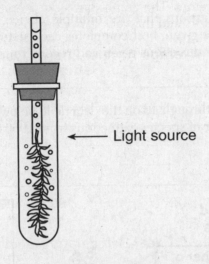

← Light source

Gas Production

Distance from Light (cm)	Bubbles Produced per Minute
10	40
20	30
30	7
40	4

The gas that was being produced was most likely

(1) carbon dioxide as a product of the process of respiration
(2) carbon dioxide as a product of the process of photosynthesis
(3) oxygen as a product of the process of respiration
(4) oxygen as a product of the process of photosynthesis

Part B–2

Answer all questions in this part. [12]

Directions (44–55): For those questions that are multiple choice, record on the separate answer sheet the *number* of the choice that, of those given, best completes each statement or answers each question. For all other questions in this part, follow the directions given and record your answers in the spaces provided in this examination booklet.

Base your answers to questions 44 through 46 on the data table below and on your knowledge of biology. The data table shows the estimated number of species extinctions from 1960 to 2010.

**Number of Estimated
Species Extinctions**

Year	Estimated Number of Species Extinctions
1960	5000
1970	10,000
1980	15,000
1990	25,000
2000	35,000
2010	50,000

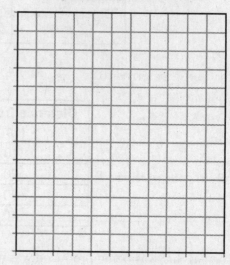

**Number of Estimated
Species Extinctions**

Estimated Number of Species Extinctions

Year

Directions (44–45): Using the information in the data table, construct a line graph on the grid above, following the directions below.

44 Mark an appropriate scale, without any breaks in the data, on each labeled axis. [1]

45 Plot the data on the grid, connect the points and surround each point with a small circle. [1]

Example:

46 State *one* possible cause for the increase in the number of species extinctions from 1960-2010. [1]

_____

_____

[15]   [OVER]

Base your answers to questions 47 through 49 on the information and diagram below and on your knowledge of biology.

Icefish Evolution

Over the last 50 million years, icefish evolved many adaptations that contributed to their success in surviving the decreasing water temperatures of the ocean surrounding Antarctica. For example, they have the ability to produce an antifreeze protein that prevents their blood from freezing in waters that are now below the normal freezing point of fresh water.

Note: The answer to question 47 should be recorded on your separate answer sheet.

47 Scientists have analyzed the icefish DNA and documented genetic changes that gave rise to the antifreeze gene. Their findings are represented in the diagram below.

```
┌────────────────────┐                    ┌────────────────────┐
│  Digestive enzyme  │   Process X        │  Antifreeze protein │
│       gene         │ ─────────────────► │       gene          │
└────────────────────┘                    └────────────────────┘
```

Process X is referred to as

(1) mitosis
(2) mutation

(3) differentiation
(4) meiosis

48 Explain how the process of natural selection can account for the increase in frequency of the antifreeze protein gene in the icefish population. [1]

_____

_____

Note: The answer to question 49 should be recorded on your separate answer sheet.

49 In addition to the appearance of the antifreeze gene, icefish have also been found to have DNA sequences similar to the DNA sequences in hemoglobin genes of other fish species. However, these DNA sequences are not complete and therefore not functional in icefish. This evidence makes it likely that

(1) icefish ancestors had hemoglobin
(2) icefish will soon produce offspring with hemoglobin
(3) hemoglobin is a molecule made by some fish that do not have genes for it
(4) soon all fish will stop producing hemoglobin

[16]

Base your answers to questions 50 and 51 on the passage below and on your knowledge of biology.

Green sea slugs are animals that live in water and have developed the ability to produce their own chlorophyll. These creatures can also pass this ability to make chlorophyll to their offspring. Once the offspring have one meal of algae, they are able to make food using sunlight. This one meal provides the baby slugs with the chloroplasts needed to make use of the chlorophyll, and they are able to produce their own food in the future.

Note: The answer to question 50 should be recorded on your separate answer sheet.

50 The best explanation for why sea slugs are able to pass on this ability to make food to their offspring is that

(1) the gene for making algae is in all their body cells
(2) making food is beneficial, so the slugs needed to mutate
(3) the environment causes the slugs to become green
(4) the gene for chlorophyll production is part of their DNA

51 Explain how green sea slugs can be considered both a producer and a consumer. [1]

_____

_____

_____

52 State why fossil fuels are considered a finite resource. [1]

_____

_____

_____

53 The diagram below represents an organelle.

Identify the process that occurs in this organelle, and explain the importance of this process to the survival of organisms. [1]

Process: _____

Importance: _____

_____

Base your answers to questions 54 and 55 on the information below and on your knowledge of biology.

The testes of a human male produce gametes. The process that produces these gametes differs from the process that produces new skin cells in the same individual.

54 Identify the type of cell division involved in each process. [1]

Skin cells: _____

Gametes: _____

55 How does the genetic makeup of the skin cells differ from the genetic makeup of the gametes? [1]

_____

_____

_____

Part C

Answer all questions in this part. [17]

Directions (56–72): Record your answers in the spaces provided in this examination booklet.

Base your answers to questions 56 through 58 on the information below and on your knowledge of biology.

Placental mammals – as opposed to the kind that lay eggs, such as the platypus, or carry young in pouches, such as the kangaroo – are an extraordinarily diverse group of animals with more than 5000 species today. They [placental mammals] include examples that fly, swim, and run, and range in weight from a couple of grams to hundreds of tons. …

Source: "Earliest Placental Mammal Ancestor Pinpointed," BBC News, February 7, 2013.

56 Describe *one* function of the placenta during the internal development of an offspring. [1]

_____

_____

57 Describe *one* advantage for an offspring to develop internally as opposed to developing externally. [1]

_____

_____

58 Identify *one* factor, besides genetics, that could influence the development of human offspring. [1]

_____

_____

Base your answers to questions 59 through 61 on the information below and on your knowledge of biology.

Birds Are Evolving Rapidly–Today

Many people think that evolutionary change occurs so slowly, we cannot observe it directly. Not so!

For example today in the U.S., house finches are evolving rapidly and visibly. In 1941, some captive house finches from California escaped near New York City. They spread rapidly and are now found across most of the United States and in southern Canada. Many of these areas have cold, snowy winters, during which many birds die. The finches have evolved, because those that survive differ from their parents. Size is one example.

Male house finches in recently established populations in Michigan and Montana are larger than the males that escaped. Large males outcompete small males for food, so are more likely to survive the winter. They also pair more successfully with females early in the spring.

Smaller females survive better than larger females as nestlings. Also, because they need less food to maintain their own bodies, they can breed earlier in spring. Females that breed earlier raise more young than those that start breeding later.

Rapid evolution of house finches reminds us that evolutionary changes are occurring visibly all around us.

Source: birdnote.org/show/birds-are-evolving-rapidly-today

59 Explain why it is an advantage for female finches to be small.   [1]

_____

_____

60 Explain why the population of large male house finches in Michigan and Montana continues to increase.   [1]

_____

_____

61 Predict what both the male and female finch populations might be like 10 years in the future, based on what is currently happening with the finch populations.   [1]

Male: _____

Female: _____

Base your answers to questions 62 through 64 on the information below and on your knowledge of biology.

New Threat to Endangered Sea Turtles

Endangered sea turtles in tropical areas are facing a new threat in the form of changing beach temperatures caused by climate change. The sex of sea turtle hatchlings is determined by the temperature inside the nest. Embryos develop into males when the temperature is approximately 28°C (82°F), whereas female embryos develop at approximately 31°C (88°F). If the temperature inside the nest is between these values, then both male and female turtles are produced.

If these endangered sea turtles are going to survive in the long term, we need to protect their nesting habitat, ensure that the potential nest sites have adequate amounts of shade-producing vegetation (such as palm trees) nearby, and ensure that they are not affected by tourist activities in the area.

62 Temperatures at beaches where these turtles nest are expected to slowly increase with global climate change. State *one* specific effect that a continuous rise in temperature could have on the sex ratio of the hatchling populations of these sea turtles. [1]

_____

_____

63 Explain how having adequate amounts of shade-producing vegetation nearby, such as palm trees, can affect the nesting success of endangered sea turtles. [1]

_____

_____

64 State *one* way that tourist activities in areas where turtles make their nests could have a *negative* impact on the nesting success of the turtles. [1]

_____

_____

_____

Base your answers to questions 65 through 68 on the information and photograph below and on your knowledge of biology. The photograph shows a grasshopper mouse howling after eating a scorpion.

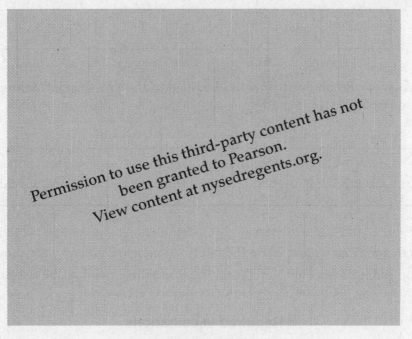

Grasshopper Mice

In the Sonoran Desert in the southwestern United States, the grasshopper mouse is active at night, searching for crickets, rodents, tarantulas, and even scorpions. The mouse ignores the venom of the scorpion, kills it, and consumes its flesh. The ability of the mouse to ignore the pain normally associated with the venom of the scorpion is due to the presence of a mutated protein. This protein prevents the pain signal from reaching the brain.

These mice are born killers, capable of taking down prey that are much larger than themselves. They are also aggressive neighbors and take over nests by displacing other desert inhabitants rather than making their own. Under difficult environmental conditions, they may even eat members of their own species.

65 State the role of the population of grasshopper mice in the Sonoran Desert food web.   [1]

_____

_____

66 State *one* advantage grasshopper mice have over the other local populations when competing for resources.   [1]

_____

_____

[22]

67 Identify *one* advantage to grasshopper mice of being active during the night rather than daylight.   [1]

_____

_____

68 Explain how research on the mutated protein identified in the grasshopper mouse could benefit humans suffering from chronic pain.   [1]

_____

_____

Base your answers to questions 69 and 70 on the information below and on your knowledge of biology.

To attend public school in New York State, children need to be vaccinated against various diseases. The list below shows some required vaccinations.

Required Vaccinations

Polio

Tetanus

Pertussis

Measles

Mumps

Rubella

Diptheria

69 Explain how vaccinations protect against diseases.   [1]

_____

_____

70 The flu is a disease caused by a virus that can undergo frequent genetic changes. A different flu vaccination is needed each year. Explain why a single vaccination is *not* effective against all flu viruses.   [1]

_____

_____

[23]   [OVER]

Base your answers to question 71–72 on the information below and on your knowledge of biology.

Survey Finds Invasive Snail in St. Lawrence River That Could Threaten Waterfowl

New research has found a larger presence of faucet snails in the Great Lakes than previously recognized, including the northern parts of Lake Ontario and the St. Lawrence River. The invasive species can carry three types of intestinal parasites that can injure and kill waterfowl such as ducks. ...

...When the waterfowl eat the snails, the parasites attack internal organs, causing lesions [sores] and hemorrhage [uncontrolled bleeding]. Birds affected by the snail will fly and dive erratically before their eventual death. The university said that the snails are about 12 to 15 millimeters in height at full size, brown to black with a distinctive whorl of concentric circles on the shell opening cover that looks like tree rings. ...

...Mr. Kosnicki [an ecologist] said the spread of snails, along with other invasive species, shows the need for increased awareness of possible contaminants coming from boats and in runoff from land. ...

Source: Watertown Daily Times, Monday, January 19, 2015, by Gordon Block

71–72 Discuss how invasive species can harm an ecosystem. In your answer, be sure to:
- explain *one* negative effect that faucet snails have on the lake ecosystem   [1]
- describe *one* human activity that can slow the spread of the faucet snail   [1]

_____

_____

_____

_____

Part D

Answer all questions in this part. [13]

Directions (73–85): For those questions that are multiple choice, record on the separate answer sheet the *number* of the choice that, of those given, best completes each statement or answers each question. For all other questions in this part, follow the directions given and record your answers in the spaces provided in this examination booklet.

Note: The answer to question 73 should be recorded on your separate answer sheet.

73 The diagram below represents one of many microscopic air sacs in a human lung. The alveolus (air sac) is the place where oxygen (O_2) and carbon dioxide (CO_2) move into or out of the blood, as represented in the diagram.

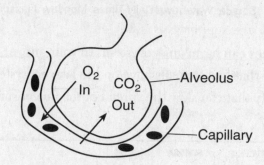

Which statement best explains why these gases are able to move in the directions shown in the diagram?

(1) The CO_2 moves out of the capillary and into the alveolus to make more room for the blood to carry O_2.
(2) The O_2 is needed by the cells, so it is actively transported into the blood. The CO_2, which is not needed, is actively transported out of the blood.
(3) The blood coming to the lungs is low in CO_2 and high in O_2, so the gases each diffuse from a lower to a higher concentration in this area.
(4) The blood coming to the lungs is high in CO_2 and low in O_2, so the gases each diffuse from a higher to a lower concentration in this area.

Note: The answer to question 74 should be recorded on your separate answer sheet.

74 During the process of chromosome replication, a genetic error occurs. As a result, a sequence of events occurs as described below.

        Event *A*: a protein with a new sequence of amino acids is produced
        Event *B*: a DNA strand with an altered base sequence is formed
        Event *C*: a new inheritable trait is expressed in an organism
        Event *D*: an mRNA strand with a new sequence of bases is synthesized

The usual order in which these events would occur is

(1) *B — D — A — C*
(2) *B — D — C — A*

(3) *D — A — B — C*
(4) *D — C — B — A*

[25]

[OVER]

Base your answers to questions 75 through 77 on the information below and on your knowledge of biology. The evolutionary tree below represents possible relationships between several species of plants.

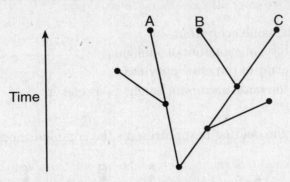

Time

Note: The answer to question 75 should be recorded on your separate answer sheet.

75 According to the tree, species *B* and *C* are more closely related to each other than to species *A*. Which gel electrophoresis diagram would best support this statement?

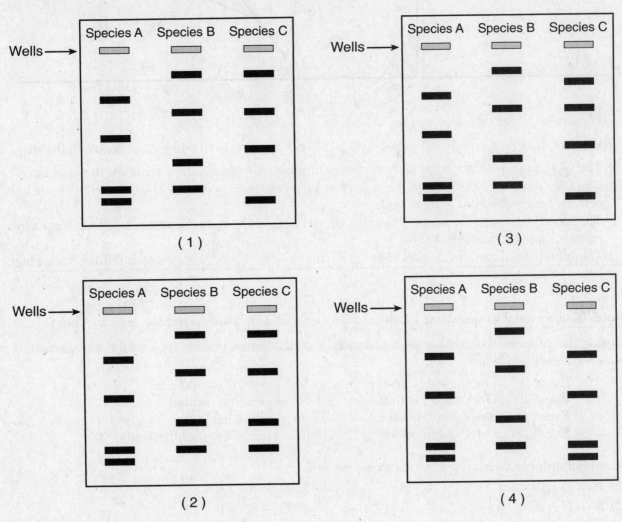

76 In addition to analyzing DNA, what other evidence could be used to best support the evolutionary relationship between species *B* and *C*?

(1) Species *B* and *C* live in the same ecosystem.
(2) Species *B* and *C* require the same amount of sunlight.
(3) Species *B* and *C* possess many of the same enzymes.
(4) Species *B* and *C* grow to the same maximum height as species *A*.

77 On the diagram below, circle the dot that best represents the common ancestor of species *A*, *B*, and *C*. [1]

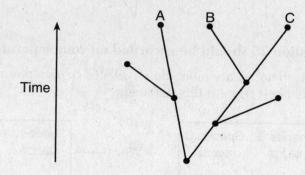

Base your answers to questions 78 and 79 on the information and chart below and on your knowledge of biology. The chart below shows variations in the beaks of finches in the Galapagos Islands.

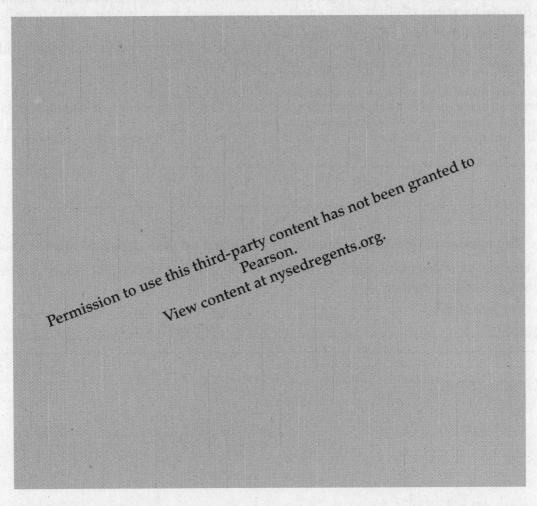

78 Explain *one* way that sharp-billed ground finches and small tree finches could possibly compete with each other if they lived on the same island. [1]

_____

_____

79 A small tree finch and a large tree finch inhabit the same island. Describe a situation that would allow both populations to live on the same island even though they both feed on animal food. [1]

_____

_____

[28]

Base your answers to questions 80 and 81 on the information below and on your knowledge of biology.

In his journey to the Galapagos Islands, Charles Darwin was amazed by the variation in the characteristics of plants and animals he encountered. In any habitat, food can be limited and the types of foods available may vary.

One year, there was no rain on these islands. Many plants failed to bloom and produced no new seeds. This left mostly large, tough seeds for the finches to eat.

80 Describe *one* change in beak characteristics that would most likely occur in the finch population after many generations if this change in seed size became permanent.   [1]

_____

_____

Note: The answer to question 81 should be recorded on your separate answer sheet.

81 The different tools (such as spoons, chopsticks, or pliers) used during *The Beaks of Finches* laboratory activity represented variations in

(1) feeding adaptations
(2) seed size

(3) finch migration
(4) island ecosystems

[OVER]

Base your answers to questions 82 through 84 on the information below and on your knowledge of biology.

Respiratory Rates

A student completed a lab activity that demonstrated the connection between pulse rate, heart rate, and flow of blood during exercise. She left her class wondering if there is a connection between breathing rate and exercise. With the help of her track coach, she conducted an investigation to try and find an answer to her question.

In the investigation, the respiratory rates of thirty athletes were measured before any exercise. To measure their rates, they counted the number of times they took a breath in one minute. Then, they ran one lap around the track, and their respiratory rates were determined again. Finally, they ran two laps around the track and checked their respiratory rates one last time. All of their data were recorded, and the averages were calculated. The data table shows the information obtained in this investigation.

The Effect of Exercise on the Respiratory Rates of Thirty Athletes

Type of Activity	Average Respiratory Rates (breaths per minute)
At rest	13
After one lap	30
After two laps	38

Note: The answer to question 82 should be recorded on your separate answer sheet.

82 During this activity, what was the purpose of finding the respiratory rates of the students at rest?

(1) to determine if the students were healthy   (3) to use as a comparison

(2) to practice using the timer   (4) to use as the variable

83 State *one* likely hypothesis that the student was testing in this investigation. [1]

_____

_____

84 When determining the respiratory rates of the students at rest, the student found that the rates ranged from 10 to 20 breaths per minute. State *one* reason why students would have a range of respiratory rates. [1]

_____

_____

_____

[30]

85 The diagram below represents a container of water divided by a dialysis membrane into two areas, X and Y.

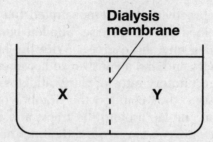

Dialysis membrane

X   Y

Starch solution was added to the water on side X. One hour later, amber-colored starch indicator solution was added to both sides. Identify the colors that could be observed at X and at Y after the addition of the starch indicator. [1]

Final color of X: _____

Final color of Y: _____